THIS AND THAT
GENEALOGY TIPS

BY

SHIRLEY HORNBECK

23340 Bunker Ct.
Tehachapi, CA 93561
E-mail - hornbeck@s-hornbeck.com
This and That Web page at: http://homepages.rootsweb.com/~hornbeck/

CLEARFIELD

Printed for
Clearfield Company, Inc. by
Genealogical Publishing Co., Inc.
Baltimore, Maryland
2000

International Standard Book Number: 0-8063-5027-X

Made in the United States of America

INTRODUCTION

My interest in genealogy was born about 25 years ago by a desire to know more about my ancestors. THIS AND THAT GENEALOGY TIPS came about by accident more than by purpose or planning. In the beginning, I collected every tip I found that I thought would be useful to me in my research. After a while, I was publishing several surname genealogy newsletters and using my collection of tips as "fillers" in the newsletters. They were great to fill up those empty white spaces and were received with great enthusiasm. Soon my subscribers were writing letters of thanks, asking for more, and I started hearing from genealogy societies asking permission to reprint my tips in THEIR newsletters.

It wasn't long before personal computers became the thing, and I purchased my first computer with no idea how I was going to use it. In no time I owned a genealogy application and started entering my family information all the while collecting more and more genealogy tips. With the help of my computer, I soon published my first family genealogy book and then there were others. In 1994 I published a 750-page book on the surname HORNBECK, entitled HORNBECK HUNTING (THE BOOK) & DESCENDANTS OF WARNAAR HORNBECK BORN 1645. This book was a 25-year accumulation of information on every Hornbeck I had ever come across while searching for my husband's roots. In 1994 that was about 8000 Hornbecks....and now I have over 20,000 Hornbecks, and a new book is in the works. All the while, I was still collecting and saving genealogy tips.

Along came the Internet, and before you knew it I was online and had my own web page devoted to my family genealogy. I started contributing tips to online genealogy newsletters and had so many favorable comments, requests for more of them, and for permission to use, that the idea came to me to put these tips on my web page. At first, This and That Genealogy Tips were just a few pages of miscellaneous tips in no particular order, but soon I felt the need to put them together by subject and topic in order to make them easier to use.

Requests to publish started coming in, and the idea for this book was conceived. My web page has now grown so that it includes all of what you see here in this book and continues to grow. If you are online, visit my This and That Genealogy Tips page at: http://homepages.rootsweb.com/~hornbeck/

I feel that the tips you will find here in this book and on my web page are some of the best tips I have come across in my 25 years of doing genealogy. They pertain to just about every genealogy topic you may come across and are put in an easy-to-use format.

When the tip came from others, permission to use has been given with acknowledgments.

I hope that you enjoy this book and that it helps you in your search for your roots. Good look and happy hunting.

Shirley Hornbeck

THIS AND THAT GENEALOGY TIPS ON AFRICAN-AMERICAN GENEALOGY

African-Americans, regardless of whether their ancestors were free or slave, are usually able to trace their ancestry back to the end of the Civil War without too much difficulty, Pre-Emancipation slaves were considered the personal property of their owners and are identified by the plantation records. You must research all public and historical records of the slave-owning family.

The census records of 1870 are the first to list blacks by name. In 1850 and 1860 slave statistics were gathered but did not list slaves by name. Free blacks and their families names were included in the 1850 and 1860 census. Military records from the Revolutionary War are available for searching. Birth records are available as the slave owner needed to protect his personal property by officially recording it. If you know the birth date, you can search the birth records for a male or female slave born on that date and an owner/plantation name will be given. Bills of sale will be found among land records, estate records or miscellaneous county records. Slave trade manifests are available at the National Archives, Washington, DC. Also write to the Registry of American Black Ancestry, Box 417, Salt Lake City, UT 84110.

The following article (First Africans to Virginia) appeared in the Roanoke, VA Times - Sunday, January 24, 1999
    TAG: 9901250202   SECTION: VIRGINIA   PAGE: B1 EDITION: METRO

RESEARCHERS DISCOVER WHO FIRST AFRICANS IN VIRGINIA WERE - WHAT WE'RE FINDING OUT IS REVOLUTIONARY:

Evidence suggests that these unwilling immigrants were likely to have been Christians and spoke a common language.

In the scant history of forgotten persons, many people are faceless. But few have been swallowed by the dark shadows that obscure the first blacks known to have lived in Virginia. Except for a few passing references from Capt. John Smith and members of the Virginia Company, these "20-odd Negroes" left virtually no trace after disembarking from a Dutch ship in late summer 1619.

And for nearly 400 years that lack of evidence made it hard for anyone, including many determined scholars, to talk about one of early America's most historic moments. A recent survey of Portuguese colonial shipping records, however, may have turned up the very vessel in which these unwilling immigrants came to the New World. New studies of the Portuguese African colony of Angola have shed unexpected light on the subject.

"When I gave a talk on the arrival of the first Africans in 1994, I really had very little to say," said Jamestown Settlement curator Tom Davidson. "But in five years the whole story has changed - almost completely. Gradually, we're taking what was the poorest known segment of 17th-century Virginia's population and moving into a realm where we can talk about them as people."

Davidson gave a lecture that focused on several studies, including two pioneering works that appeared in the scholarly journal William & Mary Quarterly. The first revolutionized the field by pinpointing the name, nationality and port of origin of the ship that carried the blacks from Africa to the New World. Sifting through Colonial shipping records, California historian Engel Sluiter came across a Portuguese merchant-slaver that lost its human cargo to English and Dutch privateers in the West Indies. The timing and description of the attack almost certainly tie that ship, known as the San Juan Bautista, to the Dutch adventurers who brought the first blacks to Virginia. They also link that human cargo to the Angolan port town of Luanda.

"Before this, we knew nothing about the Africans themselves. We didn't know if they were slaves. We didn't even know if they were Africans or Creoles from the West Indies," Davidson said. "Now we have not only a probable origin - the Portuguese ship sailed from Angola - but a specific locale in Angola. And that's enabled us to discover what kind of people these first Africans were." Other scholars, including William & Mary Quarterly editor Philip

Morgan, an award-winning author in the field, believe Sluiter's careful work leaves little doubt about the identity of the Portuguese vessel. And that crucial missing link has led to a fast-growing chain of information about the first blacks who landed in Virginia, he says.

In 1998, the journal published a study by Pennsylvania historian John Thornton that examined the Portuguese colony of Angola during the early 17th century. Thornton's search through the records of the period turned up not only the region in Angola from which the blacks came, but also the military campaign in which they were probably captured. He also turned up evidence suggesting that these Africans were likely to have been Christians, that they had years of experience in trading and dealing with Europeans and that they spoke a common language.

Such traits would have made them better able to adapt to their lot in Virginia than the ethnically and linguistically diverse groups of blacks that began to arrive from West Africa later in the 1600s. Continued trading with Portuguese Angola may help explain why the first generations of Africans were so much more successful in working their way out of servitude than those that followed. It may also help scholars understand why attitudes about race hardened in the late 1600s, when the concept of limited-term indenture began to mutate into the institution of lifelong slavery.

To post information or find information about former slaves on the Internet: http://www.afrigeneas.com

An article on the Internet "Enjoying the Challenge of African-American Research" appeared in Ancestry Magazine Sep 10, 1997, Vol 15, #5. Go to: http://www.ancestry.com/magazine/articles/enjafam.htm - BLACK GENEALOGY LINKS, RESOURCES AND GENEALOGY ARTICLES ONLINE.

"The Source: A Guidebook of American Genealogy," Revised, Edited by Loretto D. Szucs & Sandra H. Luebking -- Chapter 15, "Tracking African American Family History," by David Thackery: http://www.ancestry.com/home/source/src488.htm

"African-American Case Studies" by Roseanne Hogan, Ph.D. (Ancestry Magazine, Nov/Dec 1996, Vol. 14, No. 6): http://www.ancestry.com/magazine/articles/afamcase.htm

"African-American Family Research" Part 1 by Roseanne Hogan, Ph.D. (Ancestry Magazine, Mar/Apr 1996, Vol. 14, No. 2): http://www.ancestry.com/magazine/articles/afamres1.htm

"African-American Family Research" Part 2 by Roseanne Hogan, Ph.D. (Ancestry Magazine, Jul/Aug 1996, Vol. 14, No. 4): http://www.ancestry.com/magazine/articles/afamres2.htm

"The Challenge of African American Research" (above) by Curt B. Witcher, FUGA (Ancestry Magazine, Sep/Oct 1997, Vol. 15, No. 5): http://www.ancestry.com/magazine/articles/enjafam.htm

"The Freedman's Savings and Trust Company and African American Genealogical Research" By Reginald Washington (Prologue: Quarterly of the National Archives and Records Administration Summer 1997, vol. 29, no. 2): http://www.nara.gov/publications/prologue/freedman.html

"Institutions of Memory and the Documentation of African Americans in Federal Records" By Walter B. Hill, Jr. (Prologue: Quarterly of the National Archives and Records Administration Summer 1997, vol. 29, no. 2): http://www.nara.gov/publications/prologue/hill.html

"Preserving the Legacy of the United States Colored Troops" by Budge Weidman (Prologue: Quarterly of the National Archives and Records Administration, Summer 1997, vol. 29, no. 2): http://www.nara.gov/education/teaching/usct/usctart.html

Christine's Genealogy Web site: http://ccharity.com/

Africa World GenWeb Page: http://www.rootsweb.com/~africagw/

The African - Native Genealogy Homepage: http://members.aol.com/angelaw859/index.html

Civil War Soldiers & Sailors System - U.S. Colored Troops: http://www.itd.nps.gov/cwss/

Black Studies - A Select Catalog of NARA Microfilm Publications:
http://www.nara.gov/publications/microfilm/blackstudies/blackstd.html

Everything Black - History & Culture: http://www.everythingblack.com/

Black History - Exploring African American Issues on the Web:
http://www.kn.pacbell.com/wired/BHM/AfroAm.html

African Heritage Month: http://www.dal.ca/~acswww/dalbh.html

Smithsonian - African American History and Culture: http://www.si.edu/resource/faq/nmah/afroam.htm

African American Perspectives - Daniel A. P. Murray Pamphlet Collection, 1818-1907, From the Library of Congress' American Memory Project: http://memory.loc.gov/ammem/aap/aaphome.html

Lest We Forget, The Untold History of America: http://www.coax.net/people/LWF/default.htm

The Riverside, California, Sons of the American Revolution have a page devoted to the black soldiers who served on both sides in the American War of Independence 1775 - 1783: http://americanrevolution.org/

African American Odyssey - A Quest for Full Citizenship from the Library of Congress American Memory Project: http://memory.loc.gov/ammem/aaohtml/aohome.html

THIS AND THAT GENEALOGY TIPS ON BLACK DUTCH, BLACK IRISH, MELUNGEONS, MORAVIANS, AND PENNSYLVANIA DUTCH

PENNSYLVANIA DUTCH:

The people known to the tourist business as the Pennsylvania Dutch, often falsely depicted in the travel advertisements with images of a little Holland Dutch girl with wooden shoes, are not Dutch. Do not look for Pennsylvania Dutch in Dutch records. By far, most were Germans and were Lutherans. But if not specifically German, they were more likely to be German speaking Swiss or refugee French Huguenots, rather than Dutch. They are more correctly described as Pennsylvania Germans. The Germans and Swiss, even then, spoke different dialects of German. They were not only Lutherans, but also German Reformed, and pietists such as Moravians, Mennonites, Amish, and the various Brethren groups, including the ones known as Dunkers. From the Oxford English Dictionary the phrase Pennsylvania Dutch is defined as follows: "The descendants of the original German settlers in Pennsylvania."

How did the misnomer of Pennsylvania Dutch come about? Here are a few theories.

In the 15th and 16th centuries, the English referred to all people of Germanic heritage as Dutch or Dutchmen regardless of whether they came from the Netherlands or from lands now known as Germany. They were referred to by the English as the Low Dutch for the Netherlanders and the High Dutch for the Germans and German speaking Swiss, referring to the elevation of their native lands. However, after the United Provinces (the Netherlands) became an independent state, and competition and even wars developed between England and the Netherlands, the English language terms for these two people began to diverge such that by the 17th century the Netherlanders were referred to as the Dutch and the people from areas now in Germany where referred to as Germans. Thus, some theorize that the phrase Pennsylvania Dutch is a linguistic carry over from the earlier, broader usage of the word Dutch.

Another theory - The German word for German is "Deutsche". Thus, if a person described themselves as a Pennsylvania "Deutschman", he meant Pennsylvania German. Thus, recent generations of English speaking people in the United States, corrupted the pronunciation and spelling to Pennsylvania "Dutchman".

And another theory - The Dutch predominantly settled in New Amsterdam (now New York). The Germans predominantly settled in Southeastern Pennsylvania, in the inland counties of Berks, Bucks, Lancaster, Lehigh, Northampton, Montgomery, and other counties. Some very early Palatine German refugees were settled in New York by the British. However, most of these eventually migrated overland to Pennsylvania where William Penn offered religious freedom and better treatment. The languages sound similar to the untrained ear. Because of similarities in the sound of the language, some people theorize that the Pennsylvania Germans were called Pennsylvania Dutch by the English to differentiate them geographically from the similar sounding New York Dutch.

Most of the German immigrants sailed to Pennsylvania from Dutch ports, such as Rotterdam and Amsterdam in Holland, after coming down the Rhine River from Germany. Thus, English speaking people may have confused them as being Dutch because the ship lists reported they embarked for the new world from Dutch ports. Thus, some people may have incorrectly thought these Palatine Germans and other German speaking people were Dutch.

Dutch Reformed congregations in New York and Holland provided financial and spiritual assistance to the early German Reformed congregations in Pennsylvania due to their shared spiritual beliefs. Dutch ministers, who were also fluent in German, preached to the early Pennsylvania German settlers in order to insure the Reformed faith was nurtured and grew in the early settlements until such time as the German Reformed Church was solidly established. With the Dutch church heavily involved with the early settlers, this could have further confused the true heritage of these early German speaking settlers as viewed by the English speaking settlers. Whatever the exact reason for the improper identification of their true heritage, it took root, even among the descendants of the Pennsylvania Germans themselves. This was aided by the decline of the use of the German language by these people. It also gained more acceptance during the two world wars with Germany, when many Pennsylvania Germans did not discourage the

4

confusion of their true nationality because of the large public backlash against people of German sympathy and nationality, which occurred in this country during the wars.

Today the tourist industry promotes the Pennsylvania Dutch & Pennsylvania Dutch Country as a tourist attraction because of the quaintness of the people, their architecture, their culture, and their crafts.

BLACK IRISH, BLACK DUTCH, ETC:
One theory is that in 1688 the Spanish armada having being defeated by the British or by a bad storm, depending on your interpretation, went east and then north. They made landfall in Ireland and did the usual things conquistadors were supposed to do: looted, pillaged and raped the local women. The offspring of their activities in Ireland who have dark hair are referred to by some as Black Irish.

Black Irish can also indicate those who came as immigrants from other places (generally England) and sometimes their names were noted as such: "Fitz" as in Fitzwilliam - the English king 'gave' land to those who could hold it, take it and keep it. The black part was not referring to skin or hair or even eye color; it was indication of 'blaggard' = black = a negative connotation

Some say that the term Black Dutch refers to Sephardie Jews who married Dutch Protestants to escape the Inquisition, many of their descendants later moving to the Americas, the "black" referring to their dark hair and complexions; perhaps rarely, German immigrants from the Black Forest. Others disagree and say it is doubtful that the Black Dutch were of Jewish or (Holland) Dutch heritage.

Others say that no authoritative definition exists for this intriguing term. There are strong indications that the original Black Dutch were swarthy complexioned Germans but Anglo-Americans loosely applied the term to any dark-complexioned American of European descent. Some say the term was adopted as an attempt to disguise Indian or tri-racial descent. Some Cherokee & Chickasaw Indians are called Black Dutch.

Black Dutch may be synonymous with Pennsylvania Germans who settled in the area of Pennsylvania in groups together. When asked where they were from, they said "Deutsche" sounding to us like "Dutch", but actually meaning "German" in their own language. Because they weren't blonde and blue eyed but darker, they were called Black Dutch.

Some genealogists have suggested that the Black Dutch were either an offshoot of the Melungeons or one of the tri-racial isolate groups in Appalachia.

Another fanciful and widely circulated explanation about the Black Dutch is that they were Netherlanders of dark complexion who were descendants of the Spanish who occupied The Netherlands in the late 16th century and early 17th centuries, and intermarried with the blonde natives. However, the Dutch government's Central Bureau for Genealogy, established as a state archive and genealogical organization, is unable to offer an explanation for the term.

Some say that Black Dutch, Black Irish, and other terms, were applied to those persons who were the offspring of local women and shipwrecked sailors from Spain or other countries where the people have darker skins. Others will say that the term pertains to a person of a very mean disposition.

According to the web page at: http://new-jerusalem.com/genealogy/part23.html - a Dutch revolt against the Spanish monarch began in 1555 and continued until 1609. The nation could not find enough soldiers to defend its empire and Spain subjected neighboring Portugal and impressed Portuguese men into Spanish regiments throughout the empire. A new race was created in he southern part of Holland during the six decades that Spanish and Portuguese soldiers were stationed there. It produced dark-skinned children that were the beginning of the Black Dutch.

By the mid-1800s the term had become an American colloquialism; a derogative term for anything denoting one's small stature, dark coloring, working-class status, political sentiments, or anyone of foreign extraction. It has been used as a derogatory expression labeling German Union troops in the Civil War. has come down through history with the designation of the Great Moravian Empire. It included not only the Czech Lands of Moravia, Bohemia and Silesia, but Slovakia and parts of Austria, Hungary, Poland and Germany as well.

Interesting websites concerning Black Dutch and Black Irish:

http://www.hypertext.com/blackirish/

http://new-jerusalem.com/genealogy/part11.html

MORAVIANS:
Moravia is part of the Czech Republic and persons living there will speak either Czech or German. Brno is the capital of Moravia. Moravia was one of the small eastern European "kingdoms" that ended up being a part of a "larger" nation. Bohemia is another locality in the same region that was once an independent nation... for a short while.

Northern Moravia and Silesia is the second largest region of the Czech Republic. It has about 2 million inhabitants. Poland and Slovakia are its neighboring countries. Northern Moravia has large mountain areas and fertile lowlands, beautiful countryside, caves and a number of castles, museums and galleries. It is a region of woods, lakes and water basins, good Moravian cuisine with special dishes and excellent beer. Haná is a region of flatland, one of the most fertile regions in the country.

In the 9th century the Slavic inhabitants of Moravia established a political state in the heart of Europe. Their creation has come down through history with the designation of the Great Moravian Empire. It included not only the Czech Lands of Moravia, Bohemia and Silesia, but Slovakia and parts of Austria, Hungary, Poland and Germany as well.

The Slavic princes of Great Moravia, Mojmir I (830-846) and Rastislav I (846-870) had to deal with the two-headed problem of converting their people to the Christian faith and maintaining their political and cultural independence.

The term Moravian can be used in several contexts to refer to diverse people over the past dozen centuries. The ancient Slav who accepted Christianity from Saints Cyril and Methodius were Moravians. The Anabaptists of Swiss origin who found their promised land in the 16th century may have been Moravians. The German and Czech speaking Protestants who sought refuge in Herrnhut and evangelized the far corners of the earth were Moravians. The Czech speaking inhabitants of what we know today as Moravia, who stayed in their native land and preserved the language and carried on the traditions and culture of their forefathers were Moravians. The 19th Century Czech immigrants who left their native villages in the foothills of the Carpathians (mountains) and the fertile plains of Hana were Moravians. All of these diverse and varied people were Moravians, and where ever their descendants are today, be it in the Czech lands or off in the far corners of the earth, all are the rich beneficiaries of the two great Moravian moments in history.

There are Moravian settlements in Bethlehem, PA and Winston Salem, NC which remain a tremendous source of history as to the Moravian culture. These are German Moravians and they have basis in their religious beliefs which are a direct link to the Czech Moravians.

The Moravian Church, based on the principles of John Hus, was formed in Bohemia in 1457, and at that time was called Unitas Fratrum, or Unity of the Brethren. They were known as Brethren for many years, but that is not the same as the United Brethren Church, which was, and still is, a different animal altogether. The Pietist movement of the early 1700's mostly reform minded Lutherans - revived the Brethren Church. They were joined by refugees from Moravia after 1722, and the church was reorganized then as the Moravian Church.

The Evangelical United Brethren Church was an independent church, begun in the American colonies in the early 19th (1800-1807) century. It had three founders, Philip Otterbein, a German Reformed; Martin Boehm, a Mennonite bishop; Jacob Albright, a new flavor of Methodist. The Moravian Church itself still exists. The United Brethren movement (not to be confused with the several Brethren churches) was a German speaking equivalent of the Methodist movement. Years later, the two denominations (Methodist and Evangelical United Brethren - not Moravians) acknowledged their common heritage, and merged to become today's United Methodist Church. Some EUB's did not agree, and so there is still a Evangelical United Brethren Church today. It might be called the Evangelical UB Church, or something like that.

To subscribe to the Moravian Heritage Society, go their website at: http://www.czechusa.com or contact Tom Hrncirik at THrncirik@aol.com.

Check out: http://www.iarelative.com - scroll down until you find the link regarding the history of Brno or Moravian history - both give a wealth of information.

Susan Schlack at smschlack@enter.net has a website called Moravian Church Genealogy Links at: http://www.enter.net/~smschlack. She also runs the Rootsweb Discussion Group which you can subscribe to by sending the word   subscribe   to: MORAVIANCHURCH-L-REQUEST@rootsweb.com

Sue says it's easy to mix up MORAVIAN. Definition 1. People who come from the geographical region of Moravia. Definition 2. Members of the Unitas Fratrum / Unity of the Brethren / Evangelische Brudergemein. It is officially known in the USA as the "Moravian Church," hence the "Moravian Church Official Homepage" at: http://www.moravian.org

MELUNGEONS:
If you have been researching your family in the Cumberland Plateau of Virginia, Kentucky, North Carolina, West Virginia, and Tennessee, during the early migration years, you may be able find them through a connection to this newly re-discovered group of people. The Melungeons are a people of apparent Mediterranean descent, typically dark complexioned, who may have settled in the Appalachian wilderness as early or possibly earlier than 1567.

Dr. N. Brent Kennedy author of, 'The Melungeons: The Resurrection of a Proud People,' started the recent research into this group of people. His book is a must read for anyone who is connected to this group. Most bookstores can order this book in paperback for you. Dr. Kennedy documents his own family tree in the book and gives some startling theories which are being confirmed by current researchers. He mentions the need to hide the family connection to the Melungeon community as the main reason our Melungeon ancestors are so hard to find. Dr. Kennedy believes the Melungeons were a people who almost certainly intermarried with Powhatans, Pamunkeys, Creeks, Catawbas, Yuchis, and Cherokees to form what some have called, perhaps a bit fancifully, 'a new race'.

They appear to have been in the southern Appalachias with mining as a common occupation before the English settlers explored the area. One theory is they are descended from people of mixed ancestry in Spanish settlements in the South East who kept moving into the interior to avoid English colonists. This is supported by genetic evidence. Genetic diseases appear in Melungeon populations which only seem to appear elsewhere in populations from the Iberian peninsula and north Africa.

The Melungeons were 'discovered' in the Appalachian Mountains in 1654 by English explorers and were described as being dark-skinned with fine European features, (meaning they were not black) and as being a hairy people, who lived in log cabins with peculiar arched windows, (meaning they were not Indians). They practiced the Christian religion, and told the explorers in broken Elizabethan English, that they were 'Portyghee,' but were described as being 'not white,' that is, not of Northern European stock, even though some of them had red hair and others had VERY striking blue or blue/green eyes. Where did these people come from? Recent research is answering that question. And it appears that they may be a combination of Turks, Spaniards, Portugese, Moor, Berber, Jew and Arab.

Some cultural traits include the practice of putting tiny houses over graves, putting a pattern of nails over doors for good luck or protection, and working with metals, gems, or mining.

The Melungeon descendants have some rather unique physiological characteristics. There is a bump on the back of the head of some descendants, that is located at mid-line, just above the juncture with the neck. It is about the size of half a golf ball or smaller. If you cannot find the bump, check to see if you like some descendants, have a ridge, located at the base of the head where it joins the neck, rather than the Anatolian bump. To find a ridge, place your hand at the base of your neck where it joins your shoulders, and on the center line of your spine. Run your fingers straight up your neck toward your head. If you have a ridge, it will stop your fingers from going on up and across your head.

There is also a ridge on the back of the first four teeth (upper and lower) of some descendants. If you place your fingernail at the gum line and gently draw (up or down) you can feel it and it makes a slight clicking sound. The back of the teeth also curve outward rather than straight as the descendants of Anglo-Saxon parentage do. Teeth like these are called Asian Shovel Teeth or just Shovel Teeth which are typical of Native Americans.

Some descendants have what is called an Asian eye fold. This is rather difficult to describe. At the inner corner of the eye, the upper lid attaches slightly lower than the lower lid. That is to say that it overlaps the bottom lid. If you place your finger just under the inner corner of the eye and gently pull down, a wrinkle will form which makes the fold more visible. Some people call these eyes, sleepy eyes, dreamy eyes, bedroom eyes.

Some other characteristics are, extremely high arches, an extra bone in the foot, and the foot may be wider than normal and double-jointedness. There is also a kind of squat that some Melungeon descendants seem to be able to do which may be connected to being double jointed. Squat down with your feet and knees TOGETHER, keeping your feet flat on the floor, and your buttocks almost touching the ground. You may put your arms around your legs, but do not lean back on your hands. If you can do this without falling over backwards, you have performed the squat! Some families may have members with fairly dark skin who suffer with vitiligo, a loss of pigmentation, leaving the skin blotched with white patches. Some descendants have had six fingers or toes. There is a family of people in Turkey whose surname translated into English is Six Fingered Ones.

There are some Mediterranean diseases which show up in some of the descendants of the Melungeons. Some of these diseases can be quite severe, even life threatening, and if you or a family member have suffered from a mysterious illness, I can give you the names of these, but there is ongoing research into some areas that are less severe, but which pose problems for some descendants who seem to suffer with them. Sleep problems, including periodic limb movement, shaky (restless/active) leg syndrome, and sleep apnea are one such area. Allergies, including lactose intolerance, are another.

If your family has an Indian grandmother/father myth which you have been unable to prove, and they have been hard to trace and they lived in NC, TN, KY, VA, WV areas in the early migration years or if they seem to have moved back and forth in these areas and if they share any of the certain surnames and characteristics, you may find a connection here. Some descendants do not show the physical characteristics and of course, there are many people with the surnames who are not connected to this group.

Melungeon people were discriminated against by their Scots-Irish and English neighbors as they moved into the areas where the Melungeons lived. They wanted the rich valley lands occupied by the Melungeons they found residing there. They discriminated against the Melungeons because they were darker skinned than their own Anglo-Saxon ancestors and because this helped them obtain the lands they coveted. This discrimination carried into the 1940's-50's and perhaps even longer because of the work of a man called Plecker who was the state of Virginia's Director of Vital Statistics and an avowed racist. He labeled the Melungeons, calling them mongrels and other worse terms - some were labeled FPC - Free Person of Color in Virginia. This in turn led to their children being labeled as Mulatto (M) and both of those terms came to mean BLACK. If you find such a term for any of your ancestors, it does not necessarily mean that they actually were black. Some Melungeon families married white, some black, some Indian, some a combination. But for all of them the terms led to rulings in which they couldn't own property, they couldn't vote, and they couldn't school their children. As a result, they hid their backgrounds with the Indian myth, with the orphan myth (my family are all dead), and the adopted myth, and they changed either the spelling of their surnames or they picked an entirely new name, moving many times, anything to distance themselves from their Melungeon heritage. They sometimes became "Black Dutch" or "Black Irish", or some other combination.

The following article entitled, The Mysterious Melungeons by Mr. Arlee Gowen, appeared in the September 1992 issue of Stripes, the Texas State Genealogical Society Quarterly: A Dutch revolt against the Spanish monarch began in 1555 and continued to its successful conclusion in 1609. The nation could not field enough soldiers to defend the empire, and as a consequence, Spain subjected neighboring Portugal and impressed Portuguese men into Spanish regiments throughout the empire. [Some regiments were in Tennessee on a Spanish expedition which explored eastern Tennessee in 1567]. It is more than credible that Portuguese soldiers would desert or defect in Tennessee if the opportunity presented itself. As a sidelight, a genealogical anomaly resulted from this war. A new race was created in the southern part of Holland during the six decades that Spanish and Portuguese soldiers were stationed there. Their fraternization with the Dutch girls produced dark-skinned children which were the beginning of the Black Dutch. Mr. Gowen notes that these Melungeons were a dark skinned people who wore beards and had straight black hair. Many had dark blue eyes. They were found by John Seiver when his expedition crossed the Appalachians in 1774.

ARE YOU OF MELUNGEON HERITAGE? - Specific things to consider:
CENSUS & OTHER OFFICIAL DATA -- was your ancestor listed as non-white for any years? Try to review each census that was taken during your ancestors lifetime. In my family, I have found some ancestors listed as mulatto in some years and white in others. Review birth, death, marriage records, etc.

FAMILY TRADITION -- Is there an oral history of Cherokee or other Native American ancestry that cannot be verified? Is there a tradition of being Black Dutch, Black Irish, Black Italian, etc.? Did your family change surnames for no apparent reason?

GEOGRAPHIC LOCATION -- Did your ancestors live in any of the areas traditionally associated with Melungeons during the time periods that the Melungeons occupied the area? Remember the Melungeons and other mixed ethnic groups were forced out of areas as Scots-Irish and English settlers moved in and forced them out.

SURNAMES -- Brent Kennedy and others have identified common surnames associated with Melungeons, Lumbees, etc. Having a surname on these lists should be considered only as an indicator and not hard evidence of Melungeon heritage, for example, Mullins is a common Melungeon name but not everyone named Mullins is of Melungeon heritage.

PHYSICAL TRAITS -- There are lists of physical characteristics associated with some Melungeon descendants i.e. ridge or bump on the back of the head, shovel teeth, etc. Again, the presence of these traits should be used only as indicators of possible Melungeon heritage not as proof and conversely, an absence of these traits doesn't disprove Melungeon heritage.

DISEASES/ILLNESSES -- Many descendants of Melungeons are susceptible to diseases with Mediterrean and other exotic origins, for example, Bechet's Syndrome, Joseph's Disease, Mediterrean Familial Fever, Sarcoidosis, Thallasemia, etc. so the presence of a genetically inherited disease in your family which normally affects persons of genetic backgrounds that don't agree with your believed background can provide clues to your true genetic makeup.

PHYSICAL APPEARANCE OF ANCESTORS -- Look at photos and descriptions of early ancestors and evaluate their appearance against Melungeon characteristics i.e. skin tone and eye color, however, don't put a lot of faith in this test since the appearance of Melungeons can vary widely even within the same immediate family group.

HOW WERE YOUR ANCESTORS REGARDED BY OTHERS -- Look at personal recollections, court appearances or depositions, and nicknames your ancestors were given by their contemporaries. Were your ancestors regarded as strange or different for no apparent reason? Did later generations refuse to talk about certain ancestors while gushing over others?

MELUNGEON WEB PAGES:
SO, WHAT IS A MELUNGEON ANYWAY? - By Bill Fields: http://www.bright.net/~kat/sowhatis.htm

THE MELUNGEON OUTPOST: http://www.bright.net/~kat/melung.htm

http://www.syix.com/bevans/barbara/news4.htm

TO JOIN THE MELUNGEON ROOTSWEB Mailing List, send the word .... subscribe .... to:
MELUNGEON-L-REQUEST@ROOTSWEB.COM

SEPHARDIC GENEALOGY SOURCES:
Sephardic Jews are those from the Iberian Peninsula and along with other ethnic groups of that often overlooked part of Europe, they took part in the spread of European culture to the rest of the world, most especially America, vast portions of which were colonized by Spanish and Portuguese speaking people. An excellent website is at: http://www.orthohelp.com/geneal/sefardim.htm - and it is a treasure-house of information helpful to Jews with Sephardic heritage and includes many links to other informative sites on this subject

THIS AND THAT GENEALOGY TIPS ON CANADA

Prior to the War of 1812 there were few requirements for restriction of travel between what is now Canada and what is now the U.S. Especially before the Revolutionary War there were few legal restrictions to travel between the two countries and borders were not strictly defined except where settlements or forts were set up. Usually then if you dared to enter and were not ambushed, you were usually allowed to stay as long as you did not run afoul of the community. Seven of the original colonies did have some degree of "denization" or laws of naturalizing citizens before the Revolutionary War. Most of these are apparently indexed and source of original given in Filby's Passenger and Immigration Lists Index.

In 1790 the first U.S. federal law required a two years residency in the U.S. and one year in the state of application but the states also could provide naturalization under their own terms until 1906 when federal law superceded the state laws in this matter.

In Canada any British subject after 1763 was considered a citizen of the colony and any non-French speaking person was welcomed in Canada especially during the Revolutionary War (1783-84) British loyalists were welcomed from the US. Meanwhile the U.S. accepted many of the deported Acadians during the period of British occupation starting in 1755.

The next major change occurred in the years following the onset of the War of 1812. Canada restricted immigration from the U.S. and vice versa. Loyalists were arrested as traitors if they tried to cross back to the U.S.

The period after 1812 saw a change in the immigration and thus naturalization laws in both countries. Loyalty oaths were required on both sides. On the Canadian side the Loyalists oaths were often filed with the land grant papers as it was a condition of being given the land title.

However, this did not stop many Canadian citizens from streaming into the U.S. in the 1830s-1850s. It started with "Michigan Fever" in the 1830s as Canadians and immigrants to Canada looked for greener pastures across the border. After 1849 it was the California "Gold Rush Fever" that caused as many as 80% of the expansion of population through immigration to be lost by emigration to the US. That is for every 100 people arriving in Canada, 80 people left Canada (including new immigrants and those born in Canada) for the U.S. I don't know what the U.S. emigration to Canada was during the same period but some of those returning were the former loyalists who hoped for a moratorium.

Some of records of the Canadian immigration to the U.S. after the 1820s are also found indexed in Filby's or in the Soundex of ship's passenger lists.

It was not until 1895 that the U.S. decided to record immigrants in border-crossing lists. After that emigrants from Canada were required to state names, origin, destination and purpose of travel at the border. These records are documented as St. Albans Manifest Records of Aliens Arriving from Foreign Contiguous Territory (i.e. Canada as the Mexican crossings are not in the St. Albans lists).

There are various lists through various ports starting with the main lists from January 1895 to 1915. These are on 937 rolls of microfilm at the FHL of the LDS church. Besides the Soundex index, these rolls include the original manifests which gives all the information recorded by the U.S. officials, such as name, traveling companions, birth date, latest residence, address of person they are traveling to see, next of kin, weight, height, color of eyes. etc.

Prior to 1915 the crossings are for all crossings from Maine to Washington State. These are found on the following rolls of microfilm including the Soundex index: #1472801-#1473200.

After 1915 the St. Albans lists are only for those passing through Vermont-New York Districts.

The 1924-1952 period is found on films #1570714-#1570811.

Another set is the set called The Manifests of Passengers (M1461) - Arriving in the St. Albans District through Canadian Pacific & Atlantic ports. There are both passenger lists and monthly lists of the names of aliens crossing by train. They are found arranged by year, month and then by name of port and railroad.

These are as follows: Jan. 11, 1895 - Jan. 1921 films #1561087-#1561499 and June 1949 #1549387-#1549411. I am missing some film numbers from the FHLC as there are other film numbers for the periods from 1915-1954.

Some of the St. Albans lists films after 1915 do not include the original manifest. The film acts as a Soundex index and the originals can be obtained then from the National Archives (U.S.) .

In addition to the St. Albans lists after 1915 some additional records exist for border crossings from Michigan ports of entry. These are called Detroit District Manifest Records of Aliens Arriving from Foreign Contiguous Territory. These record the years from 1906 to 1954 and are on films 1490449-1490565. These 117 films include the original manifest and are arranged alphabetically so no Soundex is included.

For those who are interested in border crossing from the U.S. to Canada - there apparently are Canadian records (also on microfilm), but the records are in order by border crossing area (nearest town) and by year. I don't know if these are at the FHL but the Canadian National Archives has them.

Something to keep in mind when using the microfilms from the LDS church and those from the National Archives is that the same film for the same record will have different film numbers - i.e. the LDS has their own sets of numbers and so does the National Archives. The numbers I gave above (except for the M.. may be a Canadian National Archive number) are from the LDS catalog (FHLC).

This does not cover the rules from either country as it applies to other immigrants (i.e. from noncontiguous North American countries). Canada did not restrict entry from any British colony from the time of 1763 to 1947. The U.S. became an exception when it no longer considered itself a British colony and in fact declared war on Britain and, therefore, British territory. However, the modern restrictions of length and type of entry appears to have started in 1895.

An interesting note on the differences between the two countries is that Canada will allow dual citizenship - i.e. you can be or become a Canadian citizen without revoking your citizenship in another country. Even now if you do not want to take the oath of allegiance to the Queen you do not have to as long as you declare you will swear allegiance (even if not sole loyalty) to the country of Canada. However, the U.S. requires you to revoke all loyalty to any sovereign or rule of any other country and swear allegiance only to the U.S. Does this mean the U.S. is more restrictive in whom it allows in the country and for how long? I don't know as I have never tried to cross into Canada from the U.S. as a non-citizen. Other than that simply crossing to visit or shop has not been a problem and can be done by showing a driver's license and birth certificate at the border. No passport required if you are a Canadian citizen and wish to travel to the U.S. and back again.

Until 1763, Canada was known as New France and was first used by the French as a source of raw materials...fur, mostly. This economic base was not in favor of settlement as it would cause settlement and competition for the fur traders. New France was conquered by the English in 1763 and present day English Canada evolved from here.

In 1800, the main raw material changed to timber due to Napoleon blocking off England's trade route to the Scandinavian countries. By 1800 Canada's population was still only about 5 000 compared to the 13 colony's one million. The timber trade needed population.

The English were in favor of settlement so offered land grants to anyone who would accept them. These concessions were planned in accordance with the English Township system. In return they were required to clear the land, raise stock and/or begin planting to become self sufficient. Some assistance was given the first year until they were getting established.

Most of Ontario was initially occupied by the Loyalists and poor immigrants from the British Isles who arrived after the American's got their independence from England. In 1840 Canada West (Ontario) had 450, 000 inhabitants, by 1860 the population had exploded to 1,400, 000.

Ontario has been called Upper Canada and Canada West at different points in our history.

Ontario, Government of Canada: http://www.calder.net./canada/canada.htm

CANADIAN GENEALOGY MAGAZINE - Each week's issue of The Global Gazette, Canada's Genealogy & Heritage On-line Magazine is posted and available to all who are interested at: http://globalgenealogy.com/Gazette/ and if you like what you see, you can subscribe to the e-mail version free by sending an e-mail with the word "subscribe" in the body of your message to: rroberts@globalgenealogy.com.

Information about the National Archives of Canada can be found at: http://www.archives.ca/

THIS AND THAT GENEALOGY TIPS ON CEMETERIES

OLD TOMBSTONE CARVINGS:
The term "Relict" on a tombstone means that the woman was a widow at time of death, consort means that her husband survived her.

"Cenotaph" engraved on a tombstone indicates an empty grave, with the stone erected in honor or memory of a person buried elsewhere - often erected in honor of a person lost at sea.

The words G.A.R. (with a flying flag) on a tombstone means Grand Army of the Republic. It was a political organization of Civil War Union Army Soldiers. They held annual encampments and had various decorations to wear.

V.D.M. on Tombstone - verbi Dei minister - Minister of the Word of God

W.O.W stands for "Woodmen of the World" the upright tree stump markers are typical of the type of grave stone used by the fraternity.

MEANINGS OF CARVINGS:

Anchors and Ships	Hope or Seafaring profession
Arches	Victory in Death
Arrows	Mortality
Bouquets/flowers	Condolences, grief, sorrow
Broken Column	Loss of head of family
Broken Ring	Family circle severed
Buds/Rosebud	Morning of life or renewal of life
Bugles	Resurrection and the military
Butterfly	Short-lived; early death
Candle being Snuffed	Time, mortality
Cherub	Angelic
Corn	Ripe old age
Cross	Emblem of faith
Crossed Swords	High-ranking military person
Dart	Mortality
Doves	The Soul, purity, innocence, affection, gentleness
Father Time	Mortality, The Grim Reaper
Flowers	Brevity of early existence, sorrow
Flying Bird	Flight of the soul
Fruits	Eternal plenty
Full-Blown Rose	Prime of life
Garlands	Victory in death
Hands of God Chopping	Sudden Death
Handshakes	Farewell to earthly existence
Harp	Praise to the Maker
Hearts	Soul in bliss or love of Christ
Horns	The Resurrection
Hourglass	Swiftness of time
Hourglass w/Wings of Time	Time flying; short life
Imps	Mortality
Ivy	Friendship and immortality
Lamb	Innocence
Laurel	Fame or victory

Lily or Lily of Valley	Emblem of innocence and purity
Morning Glory	Beginning of life
Oak Leaves & Acorn	Maturity, ripe old age
Open Book/Bible	Deceased teacher, minister, etc.
Palm Branch	Signifies victory and rejoicing
Picks and Shovels	Mortality
Poppy	Sleep
Portals	Passageway to eternal journey
Roses	Brevity of earthly existence
Sheaf of Wheat	Ripe for harvest, divine harvest time
Shells	Pilgrimage of life
Stars & Stripes Around Eagle	Eternal vigilance, liberty
Suns	The Resurrection
Thistles	Remembrance
Tomb	Mortality
Torch Inverted	Life extinct
Trees	Life
Tree Stump w/Ivy	Head of family; immortality
Trumpeters	Heralds of the resurrection
Urn with Blaze	Undying friendship
Urn with /wreath or crepe	Mourning
Weeping Willow	Emblem of sorrow
Willows	Eternal sorrow
Winged Effigies	Flight of the soul

ODD FELLOWS:
Many times the letters FLT will be found on a flag holder or on a tombstone with each letter in a link of a chain. This is actually the described logo for the Independent Order of Odd Fellows (I.O.O.F.). The letters stand for: Friendship, Love and Truth. The symbol of the three link chain goes hand-in-hand with the three words. Other branches (sub-organizations to the Odd Fellows) also go by a three word motto & logo. There is no special, additional meaning as it is placed on a headstone. It can also be found engraved in foundation cornerstones.

The Independent Order of Odd Fellows is (probably) the only fraternal organization that offers a death benefit to its members, and actually has developed, supported and maintained their own cemeteries and Homes (for the aged). Although in these times, there are far fewer of these on record.

The only requirement for becoming an Odd Fellow is that the applicant believe in a Supreme Being. The Order is nondenominational.

A VISIT TO THE CEMETERY:
Here are a few tips to make your visit to that old cemetery a pleasant experience.

You will be lucky if the cemetery is in a well-kept, suburban area, and is well documented by a local church, funeral director, or county courthouse. Unfortunately this is usually not the case. A good county map may show locations of cemeteries.

Marriage, birth and death certificates should be consulted first. These will pinpoint your ancestors in time, as well as provide you with the proper names. The locations listed on these records may assist you in finding the place that they lived and possibly where they died. Church records and obituaries may be your best bet for finding burial sites for your ancestors. Sometimes funeral directors may also be able to provide you with burial information.

Deeds and Grants should be checked. The GRANTEE index at the local County Courthouse will be invaluable for determining places of residence as well as Probate records.

You may also find a plat map of the cemetery at the County Courthouse or a local historical society. These plats are drawings of the cemetery, much like a floor plan of a house, that indicates not only who is buried in the cemetery, but the exact grave site within the cemetery. When searching for the cemetery that contains the remains of your relatives, remember that most people were buried within 5 miles of their homes. Prior to 1850, particularly in rural areas, many people were buried in small, privately maintained cemeteries, located on the family property or in cemeteries associated with the church of their particular faith. If the cemetery is still maintained, you should contact the caretaker, church secretary or pastor, or other official before you disturb any plantings, dig away dirt or grass from around a head or footstone or attempt to lift fallen stones.

Before you go trekking into the woods, you need to be properly prepared for the excursion. Build yourself a "Cemetery Kit" and consider first protecting yourself. You need to wear clothing appropriate for the terrain and weather that you will be facing. Wear protective clothing (jeans or work pants, and a flannel shirt are advisable). It may be hot out, but don't be tempted to try to make your way through heavy overgrowth wearing shorts and a "T" shirt. A wide-brim hat can be a lifesaver on a hot sunny day. Be sure you have good walking shoes or boots and thick socks. Don't wear thongs, sandals or canvas.

Make sure you have plenty of drinking water and perhaps some snack foods. You would also be well advised to take enough water to enable you to wash off your arms, legs and face once you return to your car. Use plenty of insect repellant on your shoes, socks, and pants legs and consider treating your skin with repellant. Be sure to bring a small First Aid Kit and possibly a Snake Bite Kit. First Aid Kits for campers will be light and compact and probably available at most department stores or sporting goods stores.

Don't forget the sun screen blocker cream or lotion. Beware of poison ivy or poison oak. The other caution is yellow jackets and bees. They are attracted to the sugar in open cans of soda and half eaten fruit. It is especially painful to take a swallow of soda pop and find that a yellow jacket was drinking in the can and is now in your mouth.

A few tools will also come in handy. In areas that are particularly wild or overgrown, a machete will just about be a necessity. You will need something to break a trail through dense brush. You also need to take a small set of hand garden tools including a small garden shovel and hand held hoe. The two tools will be needed to clear grass and dirt away from headstones and footstones that may have sunk. And lastly you should take some kind of wooden pry bar. You will find that some headstones may have fallen over and if lying face down will have to be turned. A pry bar will help you do this. I suggest wood, such as oak, as metal instruments may scar or fracture the stone. Include a pair of heavy canvas gardening gloves in your kit. Another good idea for the tool kit is a four-foot rod of reinforcing bar (rebar) used for probing for sunken headstones.

Assuming that no plat map was available to lead you to the exact site, you will have to walk up and down the row of graves, examining each stone. At cemeteries where woods closely bound the cemetery, be sure to go a bit into the trees in each direction to be sure that you have found all of the grave sites. Look for fences, stone walls, or corner stones that may mark the boundaries of the cemetery. You may want to bring some graph paper along to diagram the layout of the area where your ancestors are buried. This will help to remember where the graves were. Be sure to write down any fixed objects that will help locate the grave and the drives and also include compass directions (N, S, E, W).

CLEANING GRAVESTONES:
First - check the condition of the stone on all surfaces. No stone should be cleaned if its condition is questionable or there is some sign that the stone is delicate, brittle, or otherwise vulnerable. If there is any question as to the stone's condition, do not attempt to clean it as the surface could be damaged in the process.

Mix a solution of one heaping tablespoon of ORVUS to one gallon of clean water. ORVUS is a detergent that comes in either liquid or paste form and can be found in feed stores.

Wet the stone thoroughly with clear water to make sure the detergent solution will not be absorbed directly into the dry stone. Do not let it dry. Use natural, bristled, wooden handled brushes of various sizes and rinse thoroughly with lots of clean water. Never use abrasives, acids, solvents, household cleaners or wire brushes to clean the stone.

When cleaning marble or limestone, one tablespoon of household ammonia can be added to the above mixture. This will help remove some greases and oils. Do not use ammonia on or near any bronze or other metal elements. Do not clean marble, limestone, or sandstone more than once every 18 months. These types of stone may occasionally be rinsed with clean water. Granite can be cleaned as needed.

Lichens and algae can be removed by first thoroughly soaking the stone and then using a wooden scrapper to gently remove the growth. This process may need to be repeated several times.

A great way to save your memories of that visit is with a video camera. Take extra batteries and extra video tapes with you. Video taping creates a record of the condition of the tombstones at the time you visited. Some tombstones may not be readable in five or ten years but the video tape will always be there. Why not do a test taping at a local cemetery to develop a technique before you embark on your trip to that distant cemetery. If you don't have a video camera, take along your tape recorder and a couple of cameras instead. A tip for photographers is to bring a roll of aluminum foil with you and set it up to reflect the sunlight onto or away from a poorly lit stone - or better yet - use a large mirror. Take along lots of film and have one of the cameras loaded with black and white film. Take pictures with both cameras in case one doesn't come out. Hopefully one of them will have a long cable release or take along a friend to help you. A tripod would be most helpful. Once you set up your camera and focus as best you can, use the mirror to reflect light onto the stone and take your pictures from different angles with the mirror placed in different locations. You should definitely make a written record of what is inscribed on the headstone and the footstone if there is one as photographs will often fail to pickup all of the inscriptions on the stone.

Whether you take photographs, rubbings, or both, you may need to clean the stone first. You can try a block of Styrofoam to clean off lichen and moss which damage stone. When cleaning a stone, remember that you must not cause any more damage than is already there. Most accumulated dirt and debris can be removed with a brush. Select a brush that is soft enough to not damage the stone but strong enough to remove clods of dirt. Or use your garden tools to remove grass and dirt from the base of the stone until all of the inscription is revealed. Don't dig farther than necessary as you don't want to cause the stone to topple over. You may need to use a little water to get dirt out of the inscriptions. Plain water and gentle scrubbing from the bottom up does wonders for removing soil and most lichens. Soap is not recommended for cleaning gravestones.

In order to read the inscriptions, some have recommended using shaving cream. Shaving cream is damaging to gravestones and is not recommended. One method you might try - place a soaking wet lightweight piece of white cloth flat on the stone - "ironing" it with the fingers. The words will show up, especially if incised. It is also safe to use chalk, however it is hard to remove. You might consider mud instead or even ordinary baking flour dusted on with a small paint brush.

Rubbings are perhaps the most popular way to record headstones. There are many techniques for making rubbings and many materials that can be used. Make some trips to a local cemetery and practice making rubbings using different materials and techniques until you are happy with your results before you make a potentially expensive trip to a remote cemetery. Take something to sit on, especially if there are chiggers around, or use a small stool if your knees are stiff.

Many types of paper can be used to take the rubbing on, including newsprint, tracing paper, architects paper, shelf paper, or pellon. You can purchase pellon at just about any fabric or craft shop and other papers will be available at most art supply stores. You are going to need some medium to transfer the rubbing. There are many things you can use; crayon, graphite, charcoal and boot wax are a few of the choices. Bootwax on the pellon makes an attractive rubbing, and graphite or charcoal on newsprint is another good selection. You can get boot wax at most shoe repair shops and sticks of charcoal and graphite are available at art supply stores. Graphite sticks are often available in several colors and other drawing sticks are also available. You will need some tape to hold the paper in place on the stone while you make the rubbing. Freezer or masking tape doesn't leave a lot of residue when you remove it from the stone and it will also stick to a damp stone. Cut a piece of your material (paper or pellon, etc.) approximately the same size as the stone and secure it tightly across the surface of the stone using the tape. Begin rubbing at the upper left corner of the stone and work across and down. Rub in a diagonal direction as rubbing straight up and down or side to side will tend to stretch the paper and cause it to tear or make a distorted image. Whatever you have chosen to make the rubbing with, use a broad side or edge (several inches long) to rub with. You do not need to rub hard but rubbing too gently will cause you to lose the detail. Be sure that you are happy with your results before you remove the paper and that all lettering is legible. Once you remove the paper don't try to replace it in the same location. When you are done with the rubbing remove it carefully from the stone, and lay it flat. Remove all tape and residue from the stone. You should now "fix" the rubbing. If you are using charcoal, or graphite the image can be easily fixed with either hair spray or a commercial fixative available at the art supply store. Other mediums may need the commercial fixative or some other special treatment. When spraying the fixative do not spray it on the stone. Use a gentle side to side sweeping motion, and do not apply it too heavily. The fixative will usually cause your rubbing to darken. Follow the instructions on the bottle or can. I store my rubbings in tubes such as from wrapping paper. They are particularly good for this but you can buy mailing tubes commercially if you like. Cemetery rubbings are fun to do. They can be mounted or framed and make an interesting conversation piece. The rubbings can be stapled to a couple of dowels or matted and framed. They are particularly interesting if you use more than one color in your rubbing.

A novel way to do a rubbing - make a "cake" in a margarine tub. Fill tub with plaster of paris and mix with water and allow to dry. When you find a stone that is difficult to read, gently wipe the "cake" across the stone. This will not harm the stone and letters and numbers will be easier to read. You can brush off what's left or the next rain will take care of it.

The Oldstone Enterprises, 77 Summer Street, Boston, Mass. 01110 sells a kit with directions for making rubbings of grave stones. Their materials may also be purchased from the Hearthstone Bookshop, 8405-H Richmond Highway, Alexandria, Va. 22309. The paper you want to use is sometimes referred to as "synthetic rice paper" or "print makers paper". Anything that does not tear easily will probably do. You may also use the non-woven interfacing or pattern materials that are sold at dress fabric stores, such as PELLON (non-fusible variety). Oldstone sells a crayon that is about the size and shape of a bar of hand soap. Carpenter's crayon or Lumberman's crayon may also be used, or a crayon from the thick box of crayolas would do. If you find the right kind of paper, no spray or protective materials need be used.

A "leave-behind" might be several miniature pedigree charts in a small glass jar with a tight-fitting lid. I use a copy machine that reduces a 4 generation pedigree chart to index card size. Be sure your name and address are on each one either with a stamp or a sticker or type it on the back. Put a few of these in a jar and leave it by the headstone.

Be sure to clean up the site before you leave. Once you get back to your car rinse off your arms and legs using either water or a gentle antiseptic. If you have ever had chigger bites you will understand why this is advisable. Once back to the hotel or your home, be sure to wash thoroughly and apply astringent all over. Be careful of tics that you may pick up in the woods.

GLOBAL POSITIONING SYSTEM:
Add a GPS in his cemetery kit - a hand held device about the size of a cell phone. It receives signals from a series of satellites circling the globe. If you go to the center of the cemetery and take a reading, and record the latitude and longitude those cemetery locations will be known, forever. even if the stones are totally obliterated with time. Generations of the future will always know the location, even hundreds of years from now, of that site. As the ravages of acid rain, vandalism, development continue, there will be a record of the location of tour ancestors final "home". I know everyone can't afford to go out to buy a GPS receiver, but maybe your local societies can - or maybe you could borrow one from a mountain climber or hiker, when you do your excursions. The price has been dropping on these units, as well as better features have been added. this technology can also be used for marking ancestral

homesteads and lands, so even if the land gets developed into suburban sub-divisions, you'll know where the home originally stood. There are probably dozen of other uses that haven't been thought of yet, but I'm sure will be. It's just nice to be able to put a location down that will never change, even centuries from now. You can compute the exact position of the grave and store this information as a "waypoint".

FINDING GRAVES IN NATIONAL CEMETERIES:
To find out what National Cemetery an ancestor was buried in during the Civil War, write: Veterans Administration, 810 Vermont Ave., N.W., Washington DC 20420.

INTERMENTS IN NATIONAL CEMETERIES:

Alexandria (Pineville), LA -	4,723
Alexander, VA -	3,584
Andersonville, GA -	13,738
Andrew Jackson (Greenville), TN -	63
Annapolis, MD -	2,523
Antietam (Sharpsburg), MD -	4,828
Arlington, (Ft. Myer), VA -	40,313
Balls Bluff (Leesburg), VA -	54
Barrancas, FL -	2,360
Baton Rouge, LA -	3,375
Battle Grounds (Tacoma Park Sts) , WA) -	44
Beaufort, SC -	9,751
Beverly, NJ -	272
Camp Butler (Springfield), IL	1,640
Camp Nelson KY -	3,673
Cave Hill (Louisville), KY -	5,445
Chalmette (Arabi), LA -	13,662
Chattanooga, TN -	14,542
City Point (Hopewell), VA -	5,213
Cold Harbor (Richmond), VA -	1,974
Corinth, MS -	5,758
Crown Hill (Indianapolis), IN -	1,100
Culpeper, VA -	1,380
Custer Battlefield MT -	1,667
Cypress Hills (Brooklyn), NY -	13,699
Danville, KY -	363
Danville, VA -	1,331
Fayeville, AR -	1,402
Finns Point (Salem), NJ -	2,654
Florence SC -	3,019
Fort Donelson (Dover), TN -	682
Fort Gibson, OK -	2,606
Fort Harrison (Richmond), VA -	819
Fort Leavenworth, KS -	4,487
Fort McPherson (Brady), NE -	1,120
Fort Scott, KS -	1,105
Fort Smith, AR -	2,641
Fredericksburg, VA -	15,238
Gettysburg, PA -	3,770
Glendale, VA -	1,205
Grafton, WV -	1,351

Hampton VA -	13,863
Jefferson Barracks, MO -	14,603
Jefferson City, MO -	924
Keokuk, LA -	1,073
Knoxville, TN -	3,961
Lebanon, KY -	880
Lexington, KY -	1,266
Little Rock AR -	7,467
Louden Park (Baltimore), MD -	5,302
Mariette GA -	10,639
Memphis, TN -	15,125
Mexico City, Mexico -	1,563
Mill Springs (Somerset), KY -	750
Mobile, AL -	2,479
Mound City, IL -	5,578
Nashville (Madison), TN -	16,907
Natchez, MS -	3,701
New Albany, IN -	3,382
Newbern, NC -	3,484
Philadelphia (Pittsville Sta.), PA -	4,954
Popular Grove (Petersburg), VA -	6,263
Port Hudson, LA -	3,861
Quincy, IL -	320
Raleigh, NC -	1,259
Richmond, VA -	6,675
Rock Island, IL -	651
Salisbury, NC -	12,193
San Antonio, TX -	3,829
San Francisco (Presidio Sta.) CA -	12,821
Santa Fe, NM -	1,571
Seven Pines (Richmond), VA -	1,407
Shiloh (Pittsburg Landing), TN -	3,639
Soldiers Home, (Washington), DC -	9,107
Springfield, MO -	2,785
St. Augustine, FL -	1,886
Staunton, VA -	774
Stone River (Murfreesboro), TN -	6,170
Vicksburg, MS -	17,404
Wilmington, NC -	2,425
Winchester, VA -	4,563
Woodlawn (Elmira), NY -	3,320
Yorktown, VA -	2,204
Zachary Taylor (Louisville), KY -	2
Alaska -	121
Total as of 1933	422,365

Tombstones, carvers, symbolism, locations, preservation, etc. - Association for Gravestone Studies, 278 Main St., Suite 207, Greenfield, MA 01301 - e-mail: ags@javanet.com, web site: http://www.gravestonestudies.org/

THIS AND THAT GENEALOGY TIPS ON THE CENSUS

THE MISSING 1890 FEDERAL CENSUS:

The Eleventh Census of the United States taken in June 1890 would have provided a wonderful study of our country if available today. Over 47,000 enumerators usually chosen by political appointment, distributed the schedules in advance to give the residents time to complete the forms. Once completed the population of the US topped over 62 million individuals.

Shortly before publication in 1896, the original 1890 special schedules for mortality, crime, pauperism and benevolence, special classes, and portions of the transportation and insurance schedules were damaged and finally destroyed by the Department of the Interior. According to a 1903 census clerk the general population schedules seemed to be in good shape at that time. However, disaster struck in the afternoon of January 10, 1921, when a building fireman reported seeing smoke in the Commerce Building where the schedules were located in the basement. The fire department was called and the fire was contained to the basement level of the building. However, water flooded most of the area. After the fire was extinguished, no immediate surveys were done of the damage. The records were allowed to remain soaking in water overnight and the next morning when the damage was assessed, the census director, Sam Rogers sent a note to the Secretary of Commerce reporting:

......"A cursory examination show that the census schedules from 1790 to and including 1870, with the exception of those for 1830 and 1840, are on the fifth floor of the Commerce Building and have not been damaged. The schedules of the censuses of 1830, 1840, 1880, 1900 and 1910 have been damaged by water, and it is estimated that ten percent of these schedules will have to be opened and dried and some of them recopied. These schedules were located in the basement in a vault considered at the time to be fire and waterproof, but the archivist discovered a small broken pane of glass, which allowed water to seep in damaging the schedules located in low shelves."

The 1890 schedule did not fair as well as it was located outside the vault. Approximately 25 percent of these schedules have been destroyed and it is estimated the 50 per cent of the remainder have been damaged by water, smoke and fire.

The cause of the 1921 fire was never determined. Although some speculate that a worker in the basement was smoking and set off the blaze, others believe that bundles of papers spontaneously combusted causing the blaze.

The remaining schedules of the 1890 census abandoned by the government, survived for many years. Rumors speculated that Census Director Sam Rogers had recommended that the schedules be destroyed. The public and historians were outraged and began a letter writing campaign which resulted in everyone being told that the records were NOT going to be destroyed and plans were being made to provide a suitable archive. In May of 1921, the census remained in temporary storage and the new census director William Steuart reported that they would gradually deteriorate, so they were returned to the census building for storage at his order.

Ten years would pass and finally in December of 1932, the Chief clerk of the Bureau of Census sent the Librarian of Congress a list of papers to destroy. Included in the list was Item 22, "Schedules, Population-1890, Original." The librarian gave the OK to destroy these records including the 1890 Census Schedule. Congress authorized the destruction. Sadly, just one day before Congress authorized the destruction of the census, President Herbert Hoover laid the cornerstone of the permanent National Archives building.

Many researchers fail to realize that some of the original schedules still exists. In 1942 during the move to the new building, a bundle of the Illinois schedules appeared during a shipment. In 1953, more fragments were discovered including those from Alabama, Georgia, Illinois, Minnesota, New Jersey, New York, North Carolina, Ohio, South Dakota, Texas and the District of Columbia. The remnants of the 1890 census have been filmed and are available through many sources. There are only three rolls of microfilm containing the records. Only about 6,000 names are listed on these precious pieces of our past.

According to the National Archives, the ONLY surviving U.S. census records for 1890 are as follows:
ALABAMA-Perry County; two precincts only.
DISTRICT OF COLUMBIA-two precincts only.
GEORGIA-part of Muscogee County- town of Columbus only.
ILLINOIS-only one precinct in McDonough Co.
MINNESOTA-Rockford precinct in Wright Co.
NEW JERSEY-Jersey City in Hudson Co.
NEW YORK-two townships in two counties: Westchester and Suffolk.
NORTH CAROLINA-two townships in Gaston Co, and one in Cleveland Co.
OHIO-Cincinnati in Ellis Co, and Wayne township in Clinton Co.
SO DAKOTA-one township in Union Co.
TEXAS-three precinct is Ellis Co, one in Hood Co, parts of two precincts in Rusk, two in Trinty Co, and one in
                     Kaufman.

I would recommend that anyone wanting the real story of the 1890 census go read Kellee Blake's well-researched and documented article, "'First in the Path of the Firemen:' The Fate of the 1890 Population Census," published in the Spring 1996 issue (vol 28, no. 1) of "Prologue: Quarterly of the National Archives and Records Administration." The article is available online at: http://www.nara.gov/publications/prologue/1890cen1.html

THE MORTALITY SCHEDULES:
In 1850, 1860, 1870, and 1880, census enumerators were directed to secure in addition to the usually required census data, information as to all persons dying within the 12 months preceding the census taking. These lists became known as the "Mortality Schedules".

SOUNDEX FOR 1880, 1900, 1910, & 1920:
These 4 sets of records were turned over to the States in 1918-19 and those few states that did not want them had theirs sent to the National DAR Library who in 1980 turned them back over to the National Archives. These are not on the same roll of film as the regular census records and must be consulted on either microfilm or in the location at the state level where they were deposited. NYS Mortality Schedules are at the State Library. The type of information typically found in Mortality Schedules is the name of the person, his age, sex, state of birth, month of death and cause of death.

The 1880 schedules also included the state of birth of each parent of the deceased, but not their names. To find an individual name among the millions listed in the 1880, 1900, 1910 (Only 21 States were indexed in 1910, New York not included) or 1920 Census records you must use the Soundex. The 1880 Soundex was limited and only indexed families that contained children under the age of ten. If the child was not a child of head of house hold, he and the family were indexed on separate cards.

A Soundex code is a four character representation based on the way a name sounds rather than the way it is spelled. Theoretically, using this system, you should be able to index a name so that it can be found no matter how it was spelled. The WPA used the Soundex coding system in the 1930s to do a partial indexing on 3x5 cards of the 1880 (all households with a child age 10 or younger) and 1900 censuses and a nearly full indexing of the 1910 (not all states completed) and 1920 (not yet released to the public) censuses. The Soundex indexes of the 1880, 1900 and 1910 census records are available on microfilm at the National Archives (and its branches) and many libraries or other archives these microfilms also can be purchased from the National Archives. The names are arranged on the Soundex indexes by first letter, then numerically within that letter, then alphabetically by the first name of the head of household within each different Soundex code. There is usually a separate card for each individual within the household whose surname is different from that of the head of household. Besides telling where the original record can be found, the microfilmed Soundex cards give basic information about each person in the household, such as place of residence, age, sex, relationship to head of household, state born, state where parents were born, etc. However, all of the information that is contained in the original census records is not included.

The Soundex Code consists of the first letter of the surname followed by 3 numbers. These numbers are figured according to the Soundex coding guide listed below.

SOUNDEX CODING GUIDE - The number represents the letters.

    1 - B P F V
    2 - C S K G J Q X Z
    3 - D T
    4 - L
    5 - M N
    6 - R
    Disregard the letters A E I O U W Y H.

Most surnames can be coded using the following 4 steps. See the three special easy rules below that apply for surnames with double letters, letters side by side that have the same number on the Soundex Coding Guide, or surnames that have prefixes:

Step 1 - On line 1, write the surname you are coding.

Step 2 - On line 2, write just the first letter of the surname.

Step 3 - On line 1, disregard the first letter and slash through the remaining letters A, E, I, O, U, W, Y, and H.

Step 4 - On line 2, write the numbers found on the Soundex Coding Guide for the first three remaining un-slashed letters Note: Since there must be three numbers, use only the first three code numbers in long names.

Names that have less than 3 code numbers, simply add "Zeros" to the end to obtain your three numbers.

If your surname has double letters, they should be treated as one letter. Slash out the second "r" in the name "Burrows" and the second "l" in Lloyd.

If your surname has letters side by side that happen to have the same number from the Soundex Coding Guide, keep only the first letter and slash out the remaining side by side letters that have the same code.

Slash out the "K" and the "S" in the name "Jackson" It does not matter where the side by side letters are located. Even if the first two letters of the name such as "Pfister", the f would be slashed out.

If your surname has a prefix such as Van, Von, De, Di, or Le the Soundex Code should be figured both with and without the prefix because it might be listed under either code. (Mc and Mac are not considered prefixes).

Thus, variations in spellings or misspellings should produce the same code number:
SMITH = S530
SMYTH = S530
SMITHE = S530
SMYTHE = S530

Note, however, that some names which are pronounced essentially the same produce different codes. An example is the "tz" sound in German names, which is normally pronounced the same as "ce" or "se." Also, the German "B" is often pronounced as the English "P." Thus the German name Bentz could be spelled that way or as Benz, Bens, Bents, Bennss, Bense, Bennss, Bants and Banz, or as Penz, Pentz, Pence, Pens, Pense, Penz, Pents, Penns, Pense, Penze, Pentze, etc. It has been found in census record indexes under all of these - and more. Remember: Those making the index have as hard a time reading the handwriting of census takers as we do. They will sometimes mistake an script "z" as a "y" and record Penty instead of Pentz, or mistake a "c" for an "e" and record Penee, for examples.

Therefore, to make sure you don't miss finding your ancestor, you may have to look under a half dozen or more different Soundex codes:

BENTZ (and equivalents) = B532
PENTZ (and equivalents) = P532
PENZ (and equivalents) = P520
BENTY (and equivalents) = B530
PENTY (and equivalents) = P530
PENEE = P500

Think through the possible variant spellings (and misspellings and misreadings) of the surname you are searching before concluding that it can't be found in the Soundex listings. Use your imagination. No mistake is beyond possibility! For instance, the name Pence has been indexed as Peirce (the reader mistook the written letter "n" for an "I-r" combination) and vice versa.

NOTE: A researcher found that some names of men who were Sr. (as in John Jones, Sr.) have been filed under the Soundex code of S600 for Sr. instead of the codes for their actual last names. So if any of you have trouble finding your Sr.'s, try S600.

An unknown Soundex rule that may effect about 1% of population. It is: "that if two or more equivalent key letters appear separated by an h or w, the two or more letters are encoded as one letter, i.e., by a single number." Example: Ashcroft correctly encoded is A261, NOT A226 produced "by Soundex rules which omit the unknown rule."

Another example given was for the surname SCHKLAR...Correct Soundex code is S460, not S246....last example: ACHZEHNER is A256 not A225. According to a recent article, even the NARA Soundex machine does not use this rule.

GETTING MORE THAN MEETS THE EYE OUT OF THE CENSUS:
In the census returns that show the birthplace of an individual and the birth place of the individual's parents, much circumstantial evidence is present to the family structure. If it shows the mother of the household's place of birth as New York but the place of the birth of some or all of the children's mother as Massachusetts, one can start making other assumptions as to how many wives the husband had and which children if not all might be from another marriage.

The presence of an elderly person in the household of the same surname might indicate a parent, aunt or uncle of the husband. If the surname is different, it might be a mother or father-in-law and watch out for the remarriages of this newly found grandma before jumping to the conclusions that you have discovered a maiden name for the wife.

Always take note of the families nearby (census takers usually took the houses in order that they were situated) and also take note of any families that are housing one person of your surname of interest. The data you transcribe in doing this will very often reap rewards of family connections later down the line. Take note of the places of birth of your family and the other families in the area with the same origins whether it be the same state or the same country. You will often find people moved in groups or invited friends and relatives from their former home to join them.

Taking note of the places of birth of all the children can tell a story of family movement and judging from the length of time they lived in a particular area (perhaps 3 children were born in Vermont over a 10 year period) one can determine whether or not a search for a deed or other documents in that area would be worthwhile.

The education of a family can be determined from the number in the family who can read and write and if the children did or did not attend school.

The value of property and other monetary facts might give you a clue as to whether a will or other estate papers might be found. It could also help you determine whether they might be mentioned in a local history.

LIMITATIONS AND PITFALLS OF CENSUS RESEARCH:
Due to the fact that federal census enumeration was not done until 1790, a large gap is open in American History and other records must be used for the colonial period. Ear census records give far less information than those taken in 1850 and later. Many families were missed completely and some were listed twice during enumeration because of the length of time needed to take a complete census combined with the mobility of American families.

Early censuses took 9 months to complete. In 1850 the time was reduced to 6 months and in 1870 it was further reduced to one month.

Many families that lived in multiple dwelling units were missed because the census taker did not know that a large house had more than one family.

Schedules for certain census years are completely missing for some counties or even entire states.

Many enumerators were not well qualified and did not follow instructions. Unfamiliar abbreviations and ditto marks (I. e. Conn., Ct., Cn., Cnct. were all used for Connecticut and I've seen IA for Indiana.

Poor quality paper and ink were used and difficulty in reading microfilm copies (due to poor photography, double papers or pages filmed, making writing too small, etc.). Filmers accidentally missed pages by accidentally turning two pages.

Incorrect data was given to enumerators by family members. Anyone who has researched multiple census schedules for a particular family can tell you of the inconsistencies in ages, places of birth and other important data. It is often hard to tell whether the errors were intentional or not and who made the errors..

Even though the census page you are researching was taken on a certain date, only the information for the census year was to be included. If a child was born on Aug. 2nd, the just before the census taker took the information, he would not be listed in the enumeration if the census date was June 1st. The census dates for various years are as follows: 1790 - 1820 First Monday in August; 1830 - 1900 June 1st; 1910 April 15th; 1920 January 1st; 1930 - present April 1st.

SOME DO'S AND DON'TS WITH CENSUS RECORDS:
Do not stop with Soundex finds -- do look at the original record.
Do copy the information at the top of the page in the header.
Do not assume census indexes are correct or complete.
Do not assume spellings are as you think.
Do not assume relationships are exactly as stated.
Do not assume a wife is the mother of all or any of the listed children.
Do not assume ages listed are correct.
Don't forget to copy all of the entries for the surname in the county. And better look over the neighbors too! Four
Smiths in a row with a Jones in between could mean Jones is married to a daughter.
Don't think the records before 1850 can't help. They may only have one name listed, but at least you'll know how
many to look for in a family.
Do believe that all census records are important -- even the earlier ones.
Do make use of the Veteran's column in the 1840 census.
Do use the 1890 Veterans (and widows of Veterans) Schedules.
Do use the state census records.
Do not believe all census data to be true and correct.
Do study the enumerator's handwriting so you can make comparisons.

Do watch for families split onto two pages with the surname not repeated at the top of the next page.

Do try to find your ancestors in every census taken in their life time.

Do check family histories and other sources of neighbors who might have come from the same state to locate a town of residence if you can not determine that information on your ancestor.

Do remember that when searching an entire town for ancestor, the town enumeration may be split and not be kept together on the film --- cities are often listed separately from the town they are connected with.

Do take note of real estate and personal property values to determine if a deed or will search is appropriate.

Do use maps in conjunction with your census searching.

Do search across state, county, and town lines if your ancestors lived near a border.

Do go back and look again at census records to see what you might have missed -- especially if you have learned of new surnames (maiden names) or other family connections.

Do consider typographical errors when using indexes -- know the keyboard and what letters could have been punched in by mistake.

Don't think census information gives all the answers.

Don't forget the 1900 veterans census if your ancestor was in the military. Widows are also listed.

Don't forget about state census records.

Be careful - "IA" on some census means Indiana and not Iowa.

CENSUS DAY is that day set aside by law for each census enumeration to begin (i.e. who lived in the household of the said date). Although the Assistant Census Marshall may have quizzed the head of the family in September on the make-up of his family, the return was to show " all persons in the family June 1st." No baby born between June 1st and the enumerator's visit was to be included. But anyone who died between June 1st and the enumerator's visit was to be included as well as anyone who was a member of the family June 1st but was absent from the home when the enumerator came by. All forts, Navy yards, prisons, asylums, colleges schools, etc., the superintendent, commanding officer, keeper or headmaster was considered to be the "Head of Household" and was instructed to furnish information of the number of people in his charge.

OFFICIAL CENSUS DATES:
Enumerators of the census were instructed to take the census as of a certain date regardless of when they visited. If the visit was made after that date, babies born after that date were not included, but deaths were. Census dates were:
1790-1820---1st Monday in August
1830-1900---June 1
1910---April 15
1920---January 20
1930-1980---April 1

INTERESTING FACTS ABOUT THE CENSUS:
The Constitution called for a census of all "Persons . . . excluding Indians not taxed" for the purpose of apportioning seats in the House of Representatives and assessing direct federal taxes. The "Indians not taxed" were those not living in the settled areas. In later years, Native Americans everywhere were considered part of the total population, but not all were included in the apportionment figures until 1940.

Before we can really do justice to documented ancestors in the area west of the Ohio and Mississippi Rivers, we need to sort through the older states and counties, so that we don't keep repeating the same mistakes that were published by others. At one time (as early as 1728 or as late as 1863) a person shown as being born in VA might have actually been born in IL (1781-1818); IN (1787-1819); KY (1775-1792); MO (1755-1792); NC (1728-1803); OH (1728-1803); PA (1752-1786); TN (1760-1803); WV (1769-1863).

The government did not provide printed forms or even paper until 1830. If was up to each assistant to copy his census return on whatever paper he could find and post it in two public places in his assigned area. Those who saw and could read them were supposed to check for discrepancies or omissions. The highest pay rate, two cents per person, barely covered expenses, especially where settlers were scattered and living in places that were difficult to find or access.

OBTAINING CENSUS RECORDS 1930-1990:
A branch of the Census Bureau will assist you in obtaining census information from the 1930-1990 Federal returns. If you provide proof of death, Age Search will, for $25.00, search any two census records. The search is limited to the person for whom you are requesting information, but you may ask for other family members to be included for a $2.00 per person fee. The full line of information from the census return will be provided with payment of a $6.00 fee. The basic fee includes an official document stating the person's name, age, place of birth, citizenship and relationship to the head of the household. Form BC-600 which is required may be obtained by writing: Bureau of The Census, "Age Search", P.O. Box 1545, Jeffersonville, IN 47131.

AFRICAN-AMERICANS AND THE CENSUS:
African-Americans, regardless of whether their ancestors were free or slave, are usually able to trace their ancestry back to the end of the Civil War without too much difficulty using the same sources white Americans use. Pre-Emancipation slaves were considered the personal property of their owners and are identified by the plantation records. Research then focuses upon the owner's family and the records it produced as slave owners, as well as on the slave family itself. Searching for slave ancestors always requires a thorough investigation of the white slave-owning family in all public and historical records. The census records of 1870 are the first to list blacks by name. In 1850 & 1860 slave statistics were gathered, but did not list slaves by name, just tallied, and are useful as circumstantial evidence that a slave of a certain age and sex was the property of a particular owner. Free blacks and their families names were included in 1850 & 1860. Military records from Revolutionary War are available. Birth records are available as the slave owners need to protect his personal property by officially recording it. If you know the birth date, you can search the birth records for a male or female slave born on that date and an owner/plantation name will be given. Bills of sale will be found among land records, estate records or miscellaneous county records. Slave trade manifests are available at the National Archives, Washington, DC. Also write to the Registry of American Black Ancestry, Box 417, Salt Lake City, UT 84110.

VIEW ORIGINAL CENSUS RECORDS:
Did you know that the National Archives allows you to read the original census records when it is impossible to read the microfilm? They also have a list of professional researchers who, for a fee, will read the original census lists for you. This is permitted under rigidly controlled conditions and you can carry into the room only a pencil and pad of paper. You must deposit all other items in lockers outside the room. Some of the original census sheets did not microfilm well because a very pale blue ink was used, which is perfectly legible on the original document but almost impossible to read on the microfilm.

FINDING LIVING RELATIVES:
To contact a living person whom you have lost, write a letter to the person, be sure to include your address and telephone number in the letter. Send the letter in an unsealed stamped envelope, along with a cover letter to the Social Security Administration, Letter Forwarding Unit, 6401 Security Blvd., Baltimore, MD 21235. Include in your cover letter as much as you know about the person: Name, Social Security number, birthplace, birth date, name of the person's parents. You do not have to know all of the information, but the process will be quicker if you give more identifying information. If the person you are seeking is listed in the SSA files, the letter will be forwarded to them and it's up to that person to contact you.

WHAT HAPPENED TO THE ORIGINAL CENSUSES AND HOW MANY COPIES WERE MADE?
1880+ and 1840 back=1 original
1850-1870=1 original and 2 copies, 1 to the National Archives, 1 to the State Archives, 1 to the County (most of the State and County have been destroyed)
1900-1920=no original available

When you can't read the film, and there is an original available, write to the National Archives for a better copy. On the census years where there is more than one, write to other places for a copy. Also, there is no telling who got the actual original. There are probably many differences from each of the copies, since it was common knowledge for everyone to sit at the table and make the extra copies.

MARSHALS AND THE U. S. CENSUS:

The marshals were given the task of executing the orders of the federal courts. Congress gave the marshals other duties that were outside their normal duties and one of these was the enumeration for the first census of 1790. They were chosen because of their positions in the country.

Each Marshall received a fee at the rate of one dollar for every 150 persons in the country, and one dollar for every 300 persons in cities or towns with a population of 5000 or more. If the population was sparse, as in Maine, the fee was one dollar for every 50 people.

President Washington gave the responsibility of coordination to Secretary of State Jefferson. But since Jefferson was still in France, his secretary Tobias Lear, issued the instructions by letter to the marshals on 5 March 1790. They were given nine months to make the count. Because of difficulties, the completed census was not sent to Congress until 27 Oct. 1791. The total was 3,929,214 free people in the U. S.

One man noted that the census was supposed by many to be inaccurate and "the assumed error was imputed, I know not on what evidence, to the popular notion that the people were counted for the purpose of being taxed, and that not a few had, on this account, understated to the deputy marshals the number of persons in their families".

Secretary Jefferson, when he distributed copies of the results, added a note that the number was far too low, and added in red ink his own estimation. Later censuses proved Jefferson was incorrect and that the marshals numbers were more accurate.

The marshals continued taking the census until 1870 when the Bureau of the Census was created.

CENSUS INFORMATION FOR SOCIAL SECURITY:

Social Security was inaugurated in 1935. Since births were not generally required to be recorded prior to the early 1900's (almost everywhere in the US), it was determined that the 1880 census could be used as proof of age. Since persons born before 1870 were over 65 in 1935 and thus not eligible to sign up for Social Security. The Soundex created for the 1880 census was deliberately limited to those families who had children age 10 or under. Thus persons born after 1870 and before 1880 could use the census record as proof of their age.

SOME TIPS WHEN USING CENSUS RECORDS:

Just because two families are next to each other on the census page doesn't mean they lived near each other. More often than not those listed next to each other are neighbors but no guaranties. The assumption is that the census taker visited every household in his assigned district in a systematic manner. Not only will getting their names help you sort out land records but you'll find that they witnessed each other legal documents and that they married each other. District boundaries had to be drawn somewhere. There are always going to be relatively close households that wound up in different districts and were enumerated by different people on different days.

Just because two families are at opposite ends of the census doesn't mean they were NOT neighbors. If the census taker started out on a county, beginning with his neighbor on the south, and went all over the county until he ended up back at his house with his neighbor on the east, the first and last census entries could be neighbors and were certainly living close together even if they weren't officially next door to each other. The "neighbor" problem is twofold. First, you don't know what path the census taker followed. Second, and even worse, it's impossible to draw out a path through a town for a census taker to follow that puts everybody on that path next to each of their neighbors on the census. Try it if you don't believe it. In trying it, you will gain some additional insight into the "neighbor problem" on census returns. It's a problem even in a small town with only four blocks. There are some assumptions, however, that seem relatively safe.

If you find two families you know were related and they were listed next to each other on the census, then they probably were neighbors. This assumption is warranted only because it seems improbable that two specific related families living across town from each other would end up next to each other on the census by chance. It could happen but it's not likely.

If you find two families listed next to each other in different censuses (for instance, 1840 and 1850), then they probably were neighbors. The reasoning is obvious.

ILLEGIBLE FILM:
The LDS Census films are copies of the National Archives films. Those early censuses were filmed back in the 30s, and the films used were very insensitive to blues, hence did a very poor job of picking up faded blue ink. There is one hope: the first filming of the 1860 census was so bad that it was re filmed later. If you were reading the roll from the first filming, you might try looking at the second filming. The LDS census film catalog lists the two filmings in two separate series. So check. If you had the first series, the second may well be better. If you had the second, though, that's all there is. You might, in that case, find the appropriate city directory of use.

OBTAINING CURRENT U.S. FEDERAL CENSUS DATA - AGE SEARCH SERVICE:
The Census Bureau provides an "age search" service to the public. They will search the confidential records from the Federal population censuses of 1910 to 1990 and issue an official transcript of the results (for a congressionally mandated fee). NOTE: Information can be released only to the named person, his/her heirs, or legal representatives.

Individuals can use these transcripts, which may contain information on a person's age, sex, race, State or country of birth, and relationship to the householder, as evidence to qualify for social security and other retirement benefits, in making passport applications, to prove relationship in settling estates, in genealogy research, etc., or to satisfy other situations where a birth or other certificate may be needed but is not available.

FEE REQUIRED: $40. for a search of one census (1997) for one person only. Personal checks and money orders accepted. No credit cards.

ACCESS: Census records with individual names are not on computer. They are on microfilm, arranged according to the address at the time of the census. Most agencies require the earliest census after the date of birth.

REQUIRED: A completed BC-600 Application for Search of Census Records, signed by the person for whom the search is to be conducted. This person may authorize the results to be sent to another person/agency by also completing item 3 of the application.

Minor children - Information regarding a child who has not yet reached the legal age of 18 may be obtained by written request of either parent or guardian. A guardian must provide a copy of the court order naming them as such.

Mentally incompetent persons - Information regarding these persons may be obtained upon the written request of the legal representative, supported by a copy of the court order naming such legal representation.

Deceased persons - the application must be signed by (1) a blood relative in the immediate family (parent, child, brother, sister, grandparent), (2) the surviving wife or husband, (3) the administrator or executor of the estate, or (4) a beneficiary by will or insurance.

In all cases involving deceased persons, a copy of the death certificate must be provided and the relationship to the deceased must be stated on the application. Legal representatives must also furnish a copy of the court order naming such legal representatives, and beneficiaries must furnish legal evidence of such beneficiary evidence.

An official census transcript will list the person's name, relationship to household head, age at the time of the census, and state of birth. Citizenship will be provided if the person was foreign born. Single items of data such as occupation for Black Lung cases can be provided upon request. If a person is not found, a form will be sent with that information.

Additional data on the same person (Full Schedule) - The full schedule is the complete one line entry of personal data recorded for that individual ONLY. This will be furnished in addition to the regular transcript. There is an additional charge of $10.00 for each full schedule. They are not available for 1970, 1980, and 1990.

The normal processing time is 3 to 4 weeks. Cases are processed on a first in, first out basis. Passport and other priority cases can be processed in a week or less. To expedite, send by Next-Day Air via the Post Office or private carrier and enclose a prepaid Express return envelope. Applications can be faxed to you.

CENSUS AND SOUNDEX RELATIONSHIP ABBREVIATIONS:
A-Aunt
GGM-Great Grandmother
R-Roomer
AdD-Adopted Daughter
GGGF-Great Great Grandfather
S-Son
AdS-Adopted Son
GGGM-Great Great Grandmother
SB-Stepbrother
At-Attendant
GM-Grandmother
SBL-Stepbrother-in-law
B-Brother
GNi-Grandniece
Se-Servant
BL-Brother-in-law
GS-Grandson
SF-Stepfather
Bo-Boarder
GU-Great uncle
SFL-Stepfather-in-law
C-Cousin
Hh-Hired hand
Si-Sister
D-Daughter
I-Inmate
SiL-Sister-in-law
DL-Daughter-in-law
L-Lodger
SL-Son-in-law
F-Father
M-Mother
SM-Stepmother
FB-Foster brother
ML-Mother-in-law
SML-Stepmother-in-law
FF-Foster father
N-Nephew
SS-Stepson
FL-Father-in-law

Ni-Niece
SSi-Stepsister
FM-Foster mother
Nu-Nurse
SSiL-Stepsister-in-law
FSi-Foster sister
O-Officer
SSL-Stepson-in-law
GA-Great aunt
P-Patient
Su-Superintendent
GD-Granddaughter
Pr-Prisoner
U-Uncle
GF-Grandfather
Pri-Principal
W-Wife
GGF-Great grandfather
Pu-Pupil
Wa-Warden

200 YEARS OF CENSUS TAKING 1790-1990:

A nationwide population census on a regular basis dates from the establishment of the United States. Article I, Section 2, of the United States Constitution required in 1787 that Representatives and direct Taxes shall be apportioned among the several States which may be included within this Union, according to their respective Numbers, which shall be determined by adding to the whole Number of free Persons, including those bound to Service for a Term of Years, and excluding Indians not taxed, three-fifths of all other Persons. The actual Enumeration shall be made within three Years after the first Meeting of the Congress of the United States, and within every subsequent Term of ten Years, in such Manner as they shall by Law direct.

In subsequent decades, the practice of "Service for a Term of Years" died out. "Indians not taxed" were those not living in settled areas and paying taxes; by the 1940's, all American Indians were considered to be taxed. The Civil War of 1861-65 ended slavery (abolished legally through the 13th Amendment in 1865), and the 14th Amendment to the Constitution, ratified in 1868, officially ended Article I's three-fifths rule. Thus, the original census requirements were modified Direct taxation based on the census never became practical.

The 1790 Census:

The first enumeration began on the first Monday in August 1790, little more than a year after the inauguration of President Washington and shortly before the second session of the first Congress ended. The Members assigned responsibility for the 1790 census to the marshals of the U.S. judicial districts under an act that, with minor modifications and extensions, governed census-taking through 1840. The law required that every household be visited and that completed census schedules be posted in "two of the most public places within [each jurisdiction], there to remain for the inspection of all concerned.." and that "the aggregate amount of each description of persons" for every district be transmitted to the President.

The six inquiries in 1790 called for the name of the head of the family and the number of persons in each household of the following descriptions: Free White males of 16 years and upward (to assess the country's industrial and military potential), free White males under 16 years, free White females, all other free persons (by sex and color), and slaves. Marshals took the census in the original 13 States, plus the districts of Kentucky, Maine, and Vermont, and the Southwest Territory (Tennessee). There is no evidence of a 1790 census in the Northwest Territory.

A twenty-dollar fine, to be split between the marshals' assistants and the government, would be levied against anyone who refused to answer the numerator's questions.

The marshals were expected to finish the census within nine months of the Census Day -- by 1 May 1791. Although most of the returns were in long before the deadline, Congress had to extend the count until 1 March 1792. By that time some people probably were counted who had not been born or present in 1790.

The jurisdictions of the thirteen original states stretched over an area of seventeen present-day states. Census schedules survive for only two-thirds of those states. The surviving schedules were indexed by state and published by the Bureau of the Census in the early 1900s. Bureau of the Census, Heads of Families at the First Census of the United States Taken in the Year 1790, 12 vols. (Washington, D.C.: Government Printing Office, 1908), can be found in most research libraries; it has been reprinted by various publishers over the years.

The first census comprised an enumeration of the inhabitants of the present states of Connecticut, Delaware, Georgia, Kentucky, Maine, Maryland, Massachusetts, New Hampshire, New Jersey, New York, North Carolina, Pennsylvania, Rhode Island, South Carolina, Tennessee, Vermont and Virginia. The 1790 census today, however, is not complete. The schedules were filed in the State Department, but some were burned when the British burned the Capitol at Washington in the War of 1812 -- the returns for the states of Delaware, Georgia, Kentucky, New Jersey, Tennessee and Virginia having been destroyed then.

For Virginia, every effort was made to secure duplicates and some records were secured from manuscript lists of state enumerations made in the years 1782, 1783, 1784 and 1785.

Through the courtesy of the State Librarian and members of the Library, an Act was passed by the Legislature allowing the Census Office to withdraw the lists for purposes of making copies and publishing names in lieu of the Federal Census returns.

In response to requests from genealogists, etc. a bill was passed authorizing publication of the names of heads of families in the 1790 census. As the Federal census schedules of the state of Virginia are missing, the lists of the state enumerations made in 1782, 1783, 1784 and 1785 while not complete, have been substituted.

The schedules for 1790 form a unique inheritance for the Nation, since they represent for each of the States concerned, a complete list of the heads of families in the United States at the time of the adoption of the Constitution. The framers were the statesmen and leaders of thought, but those whose names appear upon the schedules of the First Census were in general the plain citizens who by their conduct in war and peace, made the Constitution possible and by their intelligence and self-restraint put it into successful operation.

In Mar 1790, the Union consisted of twelve states -- Rhode Island the last of the original thirteen to enter the Union, being admitted May 29 of the same year. Vermont, the first addition, was admitted in the following year before the results of the first census were announced. Maine was a part of Massachusetts, Kentucky was a part of Virginia and the present states of Alabama and Mississippi were parts of Georgia. The present states of Ohio, Indiana, Illinois, Michigan and Wisconsin, with part of Minnesota, were known as the Northwest Territory, and the present state of Tennessee, then a part of North Carolina, was soon to be organized as the Southwest Territory.

The territory west of the Allegheny Mountains, with the exception of a portion of Kentucky, was unsettled and scarcely penetrated.

The boundaries of towns and other minor divisions and even those of counties, were in many cases unknown or not defined at all.

Both the original and printed 1790 census schedules are available on microfilm for Connecticut, Maine (then part of Massachusetts), Maryland Massachusetts, New Hampshire, New York, North Carolina, Pennsylvania, Rhode Island, South Carolina, and Vermont. The schedules for Delaware, Georgia, Kentucky, New Jersey, Tennessee, and Virginia were burned during the War of 1812 (there are substitutes for most of these). Published and microfilmed 1790 schedules for Virginia were reconstructed from state enumerations and tax lists.

Because of the availability of the printed 1790 census schedules, researchers tend to overlook the importance of consulting the original schedules, which are readily available on microfilm. As in most cases, the researcher who relies on printed transcripts may miss important information and clues found only in the original version. The 1790 census records are useful for identifying the locality to be searched for other types of records for a named individual. The 1790 census will, in most cases, help distinguish the target family from others of the same name; identify immediate neighbors who may be related; identify slave holders; and spot spelling variations of surnames. Free men "of color" are listed as heads of household by name. Slaves appear in age groupings by name of owner. By combining those age groupings with probate inventories and tax list data, it is sometimes possible to determine names of other family members and the birth order of those individuals.

Into the 19th Century:
Starting with the 1800 census, the Secretary of State directed the enumeration and, from 1800 to 1840, the marshals reported the results to him. From 1850 through 1900, the Interior Department, established in 1849, had jurisdiction.

The 1800 and 1810 population censuses were similar in scope and method to the 1790 census. However, Members of Congress, as well as statisticians and other scholars both within and outside the Federal Government, urged that while the populace was being canvassed, other information the new Government needed should be collected The first inquiries on manufacturing were made in 1810 and, in later decades, censuses of agriculture, mining, governments, religious bodies (discontinued after 1936, business, housing, and transportation were added to the decennial census. (Legislation enacted in 1948 and later years specified that the various economic, agriculture, and government censuses would be taken at times that did not conflict with those in which the population and housing censuses occurred) The census of 1820 covered the subject of population in somewhat greater detail than the preceding one. This census is notable for having obtained, for the first time, the numbers of inhabitants engaged in agriculture, commerce, and manufacturing.

The 1830 census related solely to population, but its scope concerning this subject was extended substantially. The marshals and their assistants began using uniform printed schedules; before that, they had to use whatever paper was available, rule it, write in the headings, and bind the sheets together.

The census act for 1840 authorized the establishment of a centralized census office during each enumeration and provided for the collection of statistics pertaining to "the pursuits, industry, education, and resources of the country." The new population inquiries included school attendance, illiteracy, and type of occupation.

Through the census of 1840, the household, rather than the individual, was the unit of enumeration in the population census, and only the names of the household heads appeared on the schedules. There was no tabulation beyond the simple addition of the entries the marshals had submitted, and there was no attempt to publish details uniformly by cities or towns, or to summarize returns for each State, other than by county, unless the marshals had done so.

Census Expansion:
The act which governed the taking of the Seventh, Eighth, and Ninth Decennial Censuses (1850-1870) made several changes in census procedures:

Each marshal was responsible for subdividing his district into "known civil divisions," such as counties, townships, or wards, and for checking to ensure that his assistants' returns were completed properly. The number of population inquiries grew; every free person's name was to be listed, as were the items relating to each individual enumerated For the first time, in 1850, the marshals collected additional "social statistics" (information about taxes, schools, crime, wages, value of estate, etc.) and data on mortality. Decennial mortality schedules for some States and territories exist for 1850-1880 and for a few places in 1885; (you are referred to see page 12 for text and location of records)

1860 population breakdown:
NORTHERN FREE STATES & TERRITORIES
WHITE = 18,810,123
FREE NEGRO = 225,973
SLAVE = 64
TOTAL = 19,034,434

BORDER STATES
(Delaware, District of Columbia, Kentucky, Maryland, Missouri & New Mexico Territory)
WHITE = 2,743,728
FREE NEGRO = 129,243
SLAVE = 432,586
TOTAL = 3,305,557

SOUTHERN SECEDED STATES
WHITE = 5,449,462
FREE NEGRO = 132,760
SLAVE = 3,521,110
TOTAL = 9,103,332

Noteworthy features of the 1870 census were the introduction of a rudimentary tallying device to help the clerks in their work, and the publication of maps, charts, and diagrams to illustrate the most significant census results.

The general scope of the 1880 census was expanded only slightly over that of 1870, but much greater detail was obtained for many of the items -- such detail, in fact, that beyond the basic counts, which were made and released promptly, it took almost until the 1890 census (because of budget constraints) to tabulate and publish some of the 1880 data The census act for 1880 replaced the marshals and their assistants with specially appointed agents (experts assigned to collect technical data, such as on manufacturing processes), supervisors, and enumerators, every one of whom was forbidden to disclose census information. Ever since the first census in 1790, some people had regarded many of the questions as an invasion of privacy, but before the 1880 census, there was no law limiting the extent to which the public could use or see the information on any schedule. (Subsequent demographic and economic censuses, as well as most surveys, have been carried out according to statutes that make compliance mandatory, with penalties for refusal; and responses confidential, with penalties for disclosure. Congress codified these laws in 1954 as Title 13, U.S. Code.) For the first time, enumerators were given detailed maps to follow so they could account for every street or road and not stray beyond their assigned boundaries. The National Archives' Cartographic and Architectural Branch has a collection of these maps.

Again, in 1890, there was a slight extension of the decennial census's scope, and some subjects were covered in even greater detail than in 1880. Data were collected in supplemental surveys on farm and home mortgages and private corporations' and individuals' indebtedness. The 1890 census also used, for the first time in history, a separate schedule for each family. Herman Hollerith, who had been a special agent for the 1880 census, developed punch cards and electric tabulating machines in time to process the census returns, reducing considerably the time needed to complete the clerical work. Hollerith's venture became part of what is now the IBM Corporation. Both the cards and the machines were improved progressively over the next 50 years.

The 1890 census was historic in another way. In the first volume of the results, the Superintendent of the Census wrote these significant words:

Up to and including 1880 the country had a frontier of settlement, but at present the unsettled area has been so broken into by isolated bodies of settlement that there can hardly be said to be a frontier line. In the discussion of its extent, its westward movement, etc., it can not, therefore, any longer have a place in the census reports.

Commenting on this statement in a classic paper delivered in 1893, one of America's great historians, Frederick Jackson Turner, wrote, "Up to our own day American history has been in a large degree the history of the colonization of the Great West. The existence of am area of free land, its continuous recession, and the advance of American settlement westward, explain American development. The censuses that followed 1890 reflected the filling in rather than the expansion of the colonized areas, and this meant a turning point in American life.

An act of March 1, 1889, provided that the Superintendent of Census in taking the Eleventh Census (1890) should "cause to be taken on a special schedule of inquiry, according to such form as he may prescribe, the names, organizations, and length of service of those who had served in the Army, Navy, or Marine Corps of the United States in the war of the rebellion, and who are survivors at the time of said inquiry, and the widows of soldiers, sailors, or marines." Each schedule calls for the following information: name of the veteran (or if he did not survive, the names of both the widow and her deceased husband); the veteran's rank, company, regiment or vessel, date of enlistment, date of discharge, and length of service in years, months, and days; post office and address of each person listed; disability incurred by the veteran; and remarks necessary to a complete statement of his term of service.

Practically all of the schedules for the States Alabama through Kansas and approximately half of those for Kentucky appear to have been destroyed, possibly by fire, before the transfer of the remaining schedules to the National Archives in 1943.

The censuses that followed 1890 reflected the filling in rather than the expansion of the colonized areas, and this meant a turning point in American life.

Moving into the 20th Century:
The 1900 census was limited to those questions asked for all the population in 1890, with only minor changes in content. The period, however, featured the first U.S. censuses outside the continental States and territories.

Following its annexation in 1898, Hawaii (where the local government took a census every 6 years from 1866 through 1896) was included in the 1900 census, which also had the first count of the U.S. population abroad (Armed Forces and Government civilian employees, and their households).

The War Department carried out an enumeration in Puerto Rico in 1899 following that island's acquisition from Spain in 1898 (there were periodic censuses from 1765 to 1887 under Spanish rule), and there have been decennial censuses in the Commonwealth (its status since 1952) from 1910 onward.

The Census Bureau compiled and published one census of the Philippine Islands following their accession by the United States in 1898; this census was taken under the direction of the Philippine Commission in 1903. (Under Spanish rule, there had been censuses in 1818 and 1876. The Philippine legislature directed a census in 1918, and the Commonwealth's statistical office began periodic enumeration's in 1939. The Philippines became an independent republic in 1946.)

The Isthmian Canal Commission ordered a general census of the Panama Canal Zone when the United States took control of the area in 1904; there was another general census in 1912 and several special censuses at various times, but the Canal Zone was included in the U.S. censuses from 1920 to 1970. (Sovereignty over the Zone was transferred to the Republic of Panama in 1979.)

The United States occupied Guam in 1899, and the local governor conducted a census there in 1901 and later years; the island was included in U.S. censuses from 1920 on.

The governors of American Samoa took censuses at various times after U.S. acquisition in 1900, and the population there was enumerated in U.S. censuses from 1920 onward.

In what have been the Virgin Islands of the United States since 1917, the Danish Government took periodic censuses between 1835 and 1911; there was a Federal census in 1917, and the islands appeared in the 1930 and subsequent U.S. censuses.

The Census Bureau took a census of Cuba under a provisional U.S. administration there in 1907; there were earlier censuses under Spanish rule (which ended m 1898), then a U.S. War Department enumeration in 1899, and subsequent ones under the Republic (established in 1901) beginning in 1919.

Later in the 20th century, the decennial census reports included figures for the Trust Territory of the Pacific Islands. There had been quinquennial Japanese censuses in these islands from 1920 to 1940; the U.S. Navy enumerated in 1950, and the U.S. High Commissioner carried out the 1958 census (the results of which appeared in the 1960 U.S. census). The Census Bureau conducted the 1970 and 1980 censuses; in 1980 and 1990, there was a separate census of the Commonwealth of the Northern Mariana Islands, which had been part of the Trust Territory.

A number of the censuses noted above collected data on agriculture, housing, and economic subjects and included enumerations on isolated islands, such as Truk and Yap, mainly in the Pacific.

In some censuses, there were supplemental questionnaires for American Indians; in 1980, enumerators used these forms only on reservations to collected additional information about households with one or more American Indian, Eskimo, or Aleut residents.

From the 1840 through the 1900 censuses, a temporary census office had been established before each decennial enumeration and disbanded as soon as the results were compiled and published. Congress established a permanent Bureau of the Census in 1902 in the Department of the Interior, so there would be an ongoing organization capable of taking frequent censuses throughout the decades instead of concentrating all the work in the years ending in "0." The Bureau moved to the new Department of Commerce and Labor in 1903 and continued with the Commerce Department when the Labor Department was split off in 1913.

The 1910 census had several notable features. First, prospective census employees took open competitive examinations administered throughout the country (since 1880, appointees had been given noncompetitive tests). Second, the way in which results were published was changed. Those statistics that were ready first -- and especially those in greatest demand (such as the total population of individual cities and States, and of the United States as a whole) -- were issued first as press releases, then in greater detail as bulletins and abstracts, the latter appearing 6 months to a year before the final reports were issued.

In 1920 and also in 1930, there were minor changes in scope. A census of unemployment accompanied the 1930 census; data were collected for each person reported to have a gainful occupation but who was not at work on the working day preceding the enumerator's visit.

IN A NUTSHELL - WHAT'S ON EACH CENSUS:
1790
Name of the head of family; profession or occupation; number of free white males in the household of 16 years and up (to assess the country's industrial and military potential); number of free white males under 16; number of free white females; number of all other free persons (by sex and color); number of slaves and sometimes town or district of residence.

1800 & 1810
Name of head of family; number of free white males (followed by females) under 10 years, 10 and under 16, 16 and under 26, 26 and under 45, 45 and up; all other free white persons except Indians not taxed; number of slaves.

1820
Name of head of family; number of free white males (followed by females), same age categories as 1800, plus free white males between 16 and 18 years (which can result in a double-count); number of foreigners not naturalized;

number of persons engaged in Agriculture, Commerce, and Manufactures; male and female slaves and free colored persons under 14 years, 14 and under 26, 26 and under 45, and 45 and up; all other free persons, except Indians not taxed.

1830
Name of head of family; number of free white males (followed by females) in 5-year age groups to 20, 10-year age groups from 20 to 100, and 100 years old and over. For each household: number of slaves and free colored persons in six broad age groups (males and females, under 10, 10 and under 24, 24 and under 36, 36 and under 55, 55 and under 100, over 100); number of deaf and dumb (under 14, 14 to 24, and 25 years and up); number of blind; number of foreigners not naturalized.

1840
Name of head of family; number of free white males (followed by females) in same age groups as 1830. For each household: number of slaves and free colored persons in same groups as 1830; number of persons in each family employed in each of seven classes of occupations (mining, agriculture, commerce, manufactures and trades, navigation of the ocean, and navigation of canals, lakes and rivers); number of pensioners for Revolutionary or military service and their ages; number of white persons deaf and dumb (same groups as 1830), blind, the insane and idiots (at public charge and at private charge); number of colored persons deaf and dumb, blind, the insane and idiots (at public charge and at private charge); type of schools and number of scholars; number of white persons over 20 who could not read and write.

1850
Names; age; sex; color (white, black or mulatto) for each person; profession, occupation, or trade for each male person over 15; all free persons required to give value of real estate owned; place of birth of each person; whether married within the year; whether attended school within the year; whether unable to read and write for persons over 20; whether deaf and dumb, blind, insane or idiotic, pauper or convict. Supplemental schedules for slaves. For each owner: slave's age; sex; color (B, M); fugitive from the state; number manumitted; deaf, dumb or idiotic.

1860
Name; age; sex; color; occupation as for 1850; value of real estate; value of personal estate (personal property); place of birth; whether married within the year; whether attended school within the year; for persons 20 years old and over whether able to read and write; whether deaf and dumb, blind, insane or idiotic, pauper, or convict. Supplemental schedules for slaves. For each owner: slave's age; sex; color (B, M); fugitive from the state; number manumitted; deaf, dumb or idiotic; number of slave houses.

1870
Name; age last birthday; sex; color; occupation; value of real estate; value of personal estate; place of birth; whether father was foreign born; whether mother was foreign born; month of birth if born within the year; month of marriage if married within the year; whether attended school within the year; literacy; whether deaf and dumb, blind, insane or idiotic; male citizens 21 and over; number of males over 21 with right to vote.

1880
Address; name; color, sex, age prior to June 1st; month of birth if born in census year; relationship to head of family; marital status; whether married within the year; profession, occupation or trade; number of months unemployed; whether person is sick or temporarily disabled so as to be unable to attend to ordinary business or duties; if so, what is the sickness or disability; whether blind, deaf and dumb, idiotic, insane, maimed, crippled or bedridden; whether attended school within the year; ability to read and write; place of birth of person, father, and mother. Soundex indexing available for all states but it is very limited in that it only indexed families that contained children under the age of ten. If the child was not a child of head of house hold, he and the family were indexed on separate cards.

1890
Nearly all of the general schedules were destroyed by fire in the Commerce Department Building in Jan 1921.

Schedules for small parts of Alabama, District of Columbia, Georgia, Illinois, Minnesota, New Jersey, New York, North Carolina, Ohio, South Dakota, and Texas remain. Content was similar to that of the 1900 census. Supplemental schedules for Union veterans of the Civil War and their widows survive for part of Kentucky and the states alphabetically after Kentucky. Soundex not available.

1900

Address (street and house no. in large cities); name; relationship to head of family; color or race (White, Black, CHinese, JaPanese, and INdian); sex; month and year of birth; age at last birthday; marital status (single, married, divorced, widowed); number of years married to present spouse; number of children of wife; number of her children living; place of birth of person and parents (state or country only); citizenship (if foreign born, year of immigration, and number of years in U.S.); citizenship status if over 21 (ALien, PA=declaration of intent filed, NAturalized); occupation for persons age 10 and over; number of months unemployed; whether attended school within the year; education (whether can read, write, and speak English); ownership of home (Owned, Rented); whether a Home or a Farm; and whether Free or mortgaged. Separate schedules were prepared for institutions, military establishments, and Indian reservations. Soundex available for all states.

1910

Address; name of person whose place of abode on April 15, 1910 was in the family; relationship to head of family; sex; color or race; age last birthday; marital status (single, widowed, married, divorced); number of years of present marriage; for women, number of children born and number now living; birthplace of person and parents; if foreign born, year of immigration, whether naturalized, and whether able to speak English, or if not, language spoken; occupation, industry, and class of worker (employer, employee or self-employed); if an employee, whether out of work during year; literacy; school attendance; home owned or rented; if owned whether free or mortgaged; whether farm or house; whether a survivor of Union or Confederate Army or Navy; whether blind in both eyes or deaf and dumb. Soundex available for 21 states: AL, AR, CA, FL, GA, IL, KS, KY, LA, MI, MS, MO, NC, OH, OK, PA, SC, TN, TX, VA, WV.

1920

Address; name of each person whose place of abode on January 1, 1920 was in the family including every person living on January 1 and excluding children born since January 1; relationship to head of family; whether home is owned or rented; if owned, whether free or mortgaged; sex; color or race; age at last birthday; marital status; if foreign born, year of immigration to the U.S., whether naturalized, and year of naturalization; whether attended school since September 1, 1919; whether able to read and write; birthplace and mother tongue of person and parents; ability to speak English; occupation; industry, and whether employer or employee. Soundex available for all states.

State wide indexes are available for every federal census from 1790 through 1850 and for many of the 1860 and 1870 federal censuses. Soundex indexes are available for the 1880 and 1900 census and for eleven states for the 1910 census. There are Mortality Schedules for 1850 through 1880 which list those who died in the 12 months preceding the census. There are state wide indexes available for these Mortality Schedules.

1930

All census records are regarded as "private" for 72 years from the census date. In other words, there could still be living persons on that census. Since the 1930 Census was taken on April 1st, it will not be released until April 1, 2002 72 tear lapse required) with partial indexing (only for select states and some counties in a couple more states). There is no Soundex for the 1930 Census. According to the National Archives website, the indexed states are Alabama, Arkansas, Florida, Georgia, Kentucky (part), Louisiana, Mississippi, North Carolina, South Carolina, Tennessee, Virginia, and West Virginia (part). You can read more, including the list of indexes, at: http://www.nara.gov/genealogy/1930cen.html

Questions added to the 1930 Census were - a person's age at their first marriage, amount of rent or mortgage payment (monthly), if the household had a radio. They did not ask the number of children or number of marriages.

If you need a census record for proof of age , the Census Bureau provides an "age search" service to the public and will search the confidential records from the Federal population censuses of 1910 to 1990 and issue an official transcript of the results for a fee of $40.00 (personal check or money order). NOTE: Information can be released only to the named person, his/her heirs, or legal representatives. Individuals can use these transcripts, which may contain information on a person's age, sex, race, State or country of birth, and relationship to the householder, as evidence to qualify for social security and other retirement benefits, in making passport applications, to prove relationship in settling estates, in genealogy research, etc., or to satisfy other situations where a birth or other certificate may be needed but is not available. The census records are on microfilm and you have to submit a completed BC-600 Application for Search of Census Records, signed by the person for whom the search is to be conducted. Information regarding a child who has not yet reached the legal age of 18 may be obtained by written request of either parent or guardian. A guardian must provide a copy of the court order naming them as such.

Information regarding mentally incompetent persons may be obtained upon these persons may be obtained upon the written request of the legal representative, supported by a copy of the court order naming such legal representation.

Deceased persons - the application must be signed by (1) a blood relative in the immediate family (parent, child, brother, sister, grandparent), (2) the surviving wife or husband, (3) the administrator or executor of the estate, or (4) a beneficiary by will or insurance. IN ALL CASES INVOLVING DECEASED PERSONS, you must provide the death certificate as well as state the relationship to the deceased in the application. Legal representatives MUST also furnish a copy of the court order naming such legal representatives, and beneficiaries MUST furnish legal evidence of such beneficiary evidence.

An official census transcript will list the person's name, relationship to household head, age at the time of the census, and state of birth.

Citizenship will be provided if the person was foreign born. Single items of data such as occupation for Black Lung cases can be provided upon request. If a person is not found, a form will be sent with that information.

Additional data on the same person (Full Schedule) The full schedule is the complete one line entry of personal data recorded for that individual ONLY. This will be furnished in addition to the regular transcript. There is an additional charge of $10.00 for each full schedule. They are not available for 1970, 1980, and 1990. It usually takes 3-4 weeks to receive the information.

INSTITUTIONS:
In 1920, there is one roll of Soundex film (roll M1605) which covers "various institutions." In addition, almost every state has institutions soundexed on the last Soundex roll, following the "Z" surnames. A research hint in the microfilm catalog states, "Many institutions, even if enumerated at their street addresses, are found at the end of the enumeration district." In 1900, the institutions are on eight rolls of film designated T-1083. In 1880 and 1910, institutions seem to be indexed state by state, following the "Z" surnames.

THIS AND THAT GENEALOGY TIPS ON THE CIVIL WAR

CHRONOLOGY OF THE CIVIL WAR:

1861

November 6: Slave states call conventions to consider secession, following Abraham Lincoln's election as the first antislavery president

December 20: South Carolina is the first of seven states to secede in the next six weeks

February 4: Convention of seceded states in Montgomery, Alabama

February 8: Constitution of Confederate States of America (CSA) adopted

February 9: CSA elects Jefferson Davis provisional president

February 18: Inauguration of Jefferson Davis

March 4: Inauguration of Abraham Lincoln as President of the United States

April 8: U.S. fleet departs new York to resupply Fort Sumter, South Carolina

April 12: Confederates attack Fort Sumter

April 13: Fort Sumter surrenders

April 15: Lincoln calls out militia to suppress insurrection

April 17: Virginia is the first of four more slave states to secede

July 21: First Battle of Bull Run (Manassas)

1862

February 6: Union capture of Fort Henry, Tennessee

February 16: Union Capture of Fort Donelson, Tennessee

February 22: Jefferson Davis inaugurated President of the Confederacy for six-year term

February 25: Nashville is first Confederate state capital to fall to Union forces

April 6-7: Battle of Shiloh

April 16: Confederates enact conscription

April 25: New Orleans falls to Union navy

June 1: Robert E. Lee takes command of the army of northern Virginia after Joseph E. Johnston is wounded in Battle of Seven Pines

June 25-July 1: Seven Days Battles drive the Union forces away from Richmond

August 29-30: Second Battle of Bull Run (Manassas)

September 4: Army of northern Virginia crosses Potomac river to invade Maryland

September 17: Battle of Antietam

September 22: Lincoln issues preliminary Emancipation Proclamation

December 13: Battle of Fredericksburg

1863
January 1: Lincoln issues final Emancipation Proclamation

March 3: Union government enacts conscription

May 1-6: Battle of Chancellorsville

May 10: Stonewall Jackson dies of pneumonia following amputation of his arm at Chancellorsville

May 15: Confederate government approves Lee's plan to invade Pennsylvania

June 6: Lee's army begins to move north

June 16: First Confederate units cross the Potomac

June 25: Jeb Stuart's cavalry begins raid in rear of Union army

June 28: George G. Meade replaces Joseph Hooker as commander of the Army of the Potomac

June 30: John Buford's union cavalry enters Gettysburg

July 1, early morning: Advance units of Henry Heth's infantry division of the Army of Northern Virginia clash with Buford's cavalry

July 1, midmorning: John Reynolds' 1st corps of the Army of the Potomac arrives; stops Confederate advance; Reynolds killed

July 1, early afternoon: Confederates renew attack; Ewell's corps arrives and attacks Union 11th corps; Lee arrives on battlefield

July 1, late afternoon: Union line breaks; survivors retreat through town to Cemetery Hill; Lee gives Ewell discretionary orders to attack Cemetery Hill; Ewell does not attack

July 1, midnight: Meade arrives on battlefield; decides to stay and fight

July 2, morning: Longstreet recommends maneuver to south; Lee disagrees and orders Longstreet to attack Union left on Cemetery Ridge

July 2, 4:00 p.m. to dark: Longstreet's attack; heavy fighting in peach orchard, wheat field, Devil's Den, Little Round Top, Cemetery Ridge

July 2, dusk: Units of Ewell's corps attack Cemetery and Culp's Hills with limited success; Stuart's cavalry and George Pickett's infantry division arrive on battlefield

July 2, midnight: After counsel with subordinates, Meade decides to stay and fight

July 3, morning: Union 12th corps attacks and retakes trenches on Culp's Hill

July 3, afternoon: Cavalry Battle three miles east of Gettysburg blocks Stuart's advance toward Union rear

July 3, 1:07 p.m.: Confederate artillery barrage begins, preceding Pickett's assault

July 3, 3:00-4:00 p.m.: Attack on Union center, spearheaded by Pickett's division; repulsed, with heavy Confederate loss

July 4: Confederates begin retreat to Virginia; Vicksburg surrenders to Ulysses S. Grant's Army

July 13-16: New York City draft riots

July 14: Confederates recross Potomac to Virginia

July 18: Union assault on Fort Wagner, South Carolina, spearheaded by 54th Massachusetts infantry; repulsed, with heavy loss; black soldiers praised

September 19-20: Battle of Chickamauga

November 19: Lincoln's Gettysburg Address

November 23-25: Battles of Chattanooga open Union gateway to Georgia

1864
May 5-June 18: Campaign from Wilderness to Petersburg, Virginia; siege of Petersburg begins

May 7-September 2: Sherman's Atlanta campaign, culminating in surrender of Atlanta

November 15-December 20: Sherman's march from Atlanta to the sea

November 30: Battle of Franklin

December 15-16: Battle of Nashville destroys Confederate army of Tennessee

1865
February 1-March 23: Sherman's march through the Carolinas

April 2: Fall of Richmond and Petersburg

April 9: Lee surrenders at Appomattox

April 14: Assassination of Lincoln

June 23: Last Confederate army surrenders

December 18: Thirteenth Amendment to Constitution ratified, abolishing slavery

CIVIL WAR RECORDS AT THE NATIONAL ARCHIVES IN WASHINGTON, DC:
This subject is very complex and covers a large amount of records. There are several kinds of records of interest to the genealogist and family historian. I will divide these into two basic groups; they are (1) Union Records and (2) Confederate records. Many, but certainly not all, of these records are on film. Most of the useful records are also indexed but sometimes not very well.

(I) Union Records

    (A) Regular Army
        (1) Registers of Enlistments
        (2) Muster Rolls
        (3) various returns from Posts and Regiments
    (B) Records of Volunteer Union Soldiers
        (1) Compiled Service Records (Military Record)
        (2) Movements and histories of Volunteer Union Organizations (no genealogical info to speak of, but interesting if you would like to know what your soldier did during the war)
    (C) Records that pertain to both Regular and Volunteer soldiers
        (1) Pension Application Files (best for family history Information)
        (2) Index to General Correspondence of the Record and Pension Office
        (3) Records of the Adjutant General's Office

(II) Confederate Records, record pertaining to service only (pension records are held by the various states)
    (A) Compiled service records (many records where lost)
    (B) Records relating to Confederate and Marine Personnel
    (C) Selected Records of the War Department Relating to Confederate Prisoners of War.
    (D) Confederate States Army Casualties: Lists and Narrative Reports.
    (E) Records of Confederate Movements and Activities

There are many more records that could be added here but few that could provide the genealogical information of the ones mentioned above. Other web pages about the Civil War:

The Civil War in Mississippi: http://www.researchonline.net/mscw

The Civil War in Georgia: http://www.reseearchonline.net/gacw

The Civil War in South Carolina: http://www.researchonline.net/sccw

Civil War Records: http://www.nara.gov/genealogy/civilwar.html

Confederate Pension Records: http://www.nara.gov/genealogy/confed.html

Military Service records on Microfilm: http://www.nara.gov/publications/microfilm/military/service.html

American Civil War Homepage: http://sunsite.utk.edu/civil-war/warweb.html

The Civil War in South Carolina: http://members.aol.com/superstore/sccd.htm

The Civil War in Georgia: http://members.aol.com/superstore/gacd.htm

Links to Other Civil War. Sites: http://www.kiva.net/~bjohnson/links.html and

1st KY Cav. (Union) Col. Frank Wolford's Regiment "The Wild Riders", 1861-5 - busykngt@airmail.net (Larry Farris).

1st KY Cav., USA, 1861-5, dparker@kih.net (Dennis Parker): http://www.users.kih.net/~dparker/index.html

2nd KY Cav., Co. H, 1861-5 - Lyon@tiac.net (Doug Lyon): http://www.tiac.net/users/lyon/civilwar

4th KY Vol. Cav. (USA) - rbtc@flash.net (Bob Crouch)

5th KY Inf., 1861-4 - sixthky@ntr.net (Joe Reinhart): http://www.rootsweb.com/~jadmire/kyhenry/6kyhist.htm

6th KY Inf. (US), 1861-4 - sixthky@ntr.net (Joe Reinhart)

6th KY Vol. Cav., 1861-5 - chesnut@kgs.mm.uky.edu (Don Chesnut): http://www.users.mis.net/~chesnut/gendef.htm

7th KY Vol. Inf. (USA) - miles@usmo.com (Margy Miles): http://www.rootsweb.com/~kycrrsek/military.com

7th KY Inf., Co E - ralphinla@earthlink.net (Ralph Clark): http://ralphinla.rootsweb.com/civilwar.htm

7th KY Cav. (USA), 1862-5 - DutchR@Sprintmail.com (J. Dutch Revenboer): http://members.tripod.com/~DutchR/7cav/index.html

8th KY Inf. (USA), Co. A & E, 1861-4 - spiff@atlantic.net, (JohnCarter)

8th KY Cav Company B - spiff@atlantic.net, (JohnCarter)

9th KY Vol. Inf. Regt - wcross@okway.okstate.edu

9th KY Vol. Cav., Co. H - jadmire@myfamily.org or jadmire@bighorn.dr.lucent.com (Jim Admire): http://www.rootsweb.com/~jadmire/kyhenry/9thky.htm - This is part of Henry County, KY website for the USGenWeb project which is located at: http://www.rootsweb.com/~jadmire/kyhenry/henry.htm
Other Military Units listed at: http://www.rootsweb.com/~jadmire/kyhenry/hmil.htm
Crawford Co., IL military units webpage at: http://www.rootsweb.com/~jadmire/ilcrawf/cmil.htm

9th KY Cav. Cos. I, K, L, M - http://www.rootsweb.com/~kymercer/CivilWar/Union/

10th KY Inf., 1861-4 - sixthky@ntr.net (Joe Reinhart)

11th KY (US) - mercury@pop.uky.edu (Wayne Fields) - Will do Civil War Veteran lookups for any soldier who fought in the war but MUST have fullnames...no surname only searches please: http://home.okstate.edu/homepages.nsf/toc/11th.htm

11th KY Cav. (USA), 1862-5 - jaj23@juno.com (Jerry Johnson)

12th KY Vol. Inf. (USA) - miles@usmo.com (Margy Miles): http://www.rootsweb.com/~kycrrsek/military.com

12th KY Vol. Inf. (US), 1861-5 - jsewell@edm.net (Jim Sewell): http://www.edm.net/~Pjsewell/12th.htm

12th KY Inf., Co A - ralphinla@earthlink.net (Ralph Clark): http://ralphinla.rootsweb.com/civilwar.htm

13th KY Inf. Regt (USA) - gene_perkins@juno.com or: http://www.flash.net/~geneperk/13thKyInf.html

13th KY Cav. (USA) - kncundiff@aol.com

14th KY INF, USA - wildcat89@hotmail.com, (Marlitta H. Perkins): http://www.geocities.com/Pentagon/Quarters/1365

14th KY Vol. Cav., 1862-4 - chesnut@kgs.mm.uky.edu

18th Inf., KY Volunteers, 1862-5 - dennis.heltemes@newways.com

20th KY Vol. Inf., USA - reb4life@tennessee-scv.org (AllenSullivant)

20th Reg. KY Cav., Co. D - stumpf@merle.acns.nwu.edu

21st KY Vol. Inf., 1861-5 - rbblack@ni.net

23rd KY Inf. (US), 1861-5 - gwjchris@rust.net (Bill Christen):   http://www.rust.net/~gwjchris/

23rd KY Inf., 1861-4 - sixthky@ntr.net (Joe Reinhart)

23rd Reg't KY Inf. (US), Co. C 1861-5 - hardwic2@ix.netcom.com

24th KY Inf., Co. H, 1861-2 - ralphinla@earthlink.net (Ralph Clark): http://ralphinla.rootsweb.com/civilwar.htm

39th KY (Union) - jburton@itctel.com.

John Rigdon at GaLinaHist@aol.com maintains 3 primary sites for Civil War Research:
The Civil War in Georgia: http://www.researchonline.net/gacw
The Civil War in South Carolina: http://www.researchonline.net/sccw
Search Engine to the Official Records of the Union and Confederate Armies: http://www.researchonline.net/or
He will do lookups in his index of approx. 200,000 names of primarily Georgia and South Carolina Soldiers.

SCV Camp #1575 provides a list of 1100+ Confederate Graves in Aiken County, SC in their Memorial Section at:
http://www.battleofaiken.org

Civil War in SE KY - hollyft@bright.net (Holly Timm):
http://www.rootsweb.com/~seky/civilwar/homefire/index.html

Mercer Co. KY CW Units: http://www.rootsweb.com/~kymercer/

IL 48th Inf. CW Unit (Pharoah's Army) - stumpf@merle.acns.nwu.edu: http://stumpf.org/Ill48Inf/index.html

A book entitled *"The Union Regiments of Kentucky"* published by the Union Soldiers and Sailors Monument Association in 1897, and sometimes attributed to Capt. Thomas Speed as author, contains brief histories (3 to 8 pages) of all of Kentucky's Union regiments and artillery batteries, and rosters for each. It contains over 700 pages. Many large Kentucky libraries have this book. It has recently been reprinted by McDowell Publications, 11129 Pleasant Ridge Road, Utica, KY 42376. Cost is $80 plus shipping of $4 plus sales tax, if applicable. Ask them if they are still offering a half-price special at $40 plus shipping and tax.

THIS AND THAT GENEALOGY TIPS ON COLONIAL AMERICA

COMPREHENSIVE HISTORY OF EASTHAM, WELLFLEET AND ORLEANS by Rev. Enoch Pratt pub 1844 Describing 17th Century Massachusetts and the Customs of our Forefathers - Manner of Dress; Manner of Living; Voting; Housing; Beards; Addressing Others; Walking and Riding:

MANNER OF DRESS. In general, men old or young had a decent coat, vest, and some small clothes as well as some kind of fur hat. Old men had a great coat, and a pair of boots; the boots were substantially made of good leather and lasted for life; they were long and reached to the knee. For every day they had a jacket reaching about half way down the thigh, striped vest, and the small clothes, like the jacket; made of home spun flannel cloth, fulled at the mill, but not sheared; flannel shirts, and knit woolen stockings, with leather shoes, and a silk handkerchief for holidays. In the summer they wore a pair of wide petticoat trowsers, reaching half way from the knee to the ankle. Shoes and stockings were not worn in summer when at work on the farm. Boys, as soon as they left their petticoats, were put into small clothes, summer or winter. These were made of home manufactured cloth for common, and everlasting for meeting dress. The oldest son had a pair of the latter cloth, and when he had outgrown them, the next took them, and so down to the tenth son, if there were so many of the family. This manner of dress continued till long trowsers were introduced which were called tongs, and did not differ much in shape from those now in use. They were made of tow cloth, linen and cotton, in the summer, and in the winter of flannel, and were soon worn by old men, as well as by young men and boys. Young men never wore great coats. I recollect, says a writer of those past times, a neighbor of my fathers, who had four sons between nineteen and thirty years of age; the oldest got a pair of boots, the second a surtout, the third a watch, and the fourth a pair of silver shoe buckles. This made a neighborhood talk, and the family was supposed to be on the high road to insolvency.

The women, old and young, wore home made flannel gowns in the winter, and in the summer, wrappers, or shepherdess; it was without a waist, and gathered round the neck. They were usually contented with one calico gown; but generally had a calimanco or camlet, and some had them made of poplin. The sleeves were short, and came only to the elbow; on holidays, they wore one, two, or three ruffles on each arm, sometimes ten inches wide. They wore long gloves, coming up to the elbow secured by what was called tightens, made of black horse hair; round gowns had not come in fashion, so they wore aprons, made of checked linen, cotton, and for Sunday, white cotton, long lawn, or cambric. They seldom wore caps, only when they appeared in full dress; they had two kinds; one, was called strap cap, which was tied under the chin, and the other, round cord cap, which did not come over the ears. They wore thick and thin leather and broadcloth shoes, with wooden heels covered with cloth or leather, an inch and a half high, with peaked toes which turned up. They generally had very small muffs, and some wore masks.

The manner of living, and the mode of dress, was much more favourable to health than at the present time. Acute fevers were frequent, the principal of which were called the long or slow fever, which ran thirty-five, forty, and sometimes fifty days before it formed a crisis; and the slow nervous fever, which ran generally longer than the former. Pulmonary complaints, or consumptions were much less frequent than now; indeed a young person was rarely visited with this disease. The duty of the sexton of the church, was not only to ring the bell, and sweep the house, but keep the hour-glass, and turn it at the commencement of the minister's sermon, who was expected to close at the end of the hour; if he went on, or fell short of the time, it was sufficient cause of complaint.

Their dinners in the winter season were generally the same. First they had a dish of broth, called porridge, with a few beans in it, and a little summer savory; then an Indian pudding with sauce; and then a dish of boiled pork and beef, with round turnips, and a few potatoes. Potatoes were then a scarce article; three of four bushels were considered a large crop, and these not larger than a hen's egg. Their suppers and breakfast were generally the same; those who had milk ate it with toasted bread; if not, sweetened cider, with bread and cheese. Sabbath mornings, they generally had chocolate, or bohea tea; the first sweetened with molasses, and the last with brown sugar, and with them, pancakes, dough-nuts, brown toast, or some sort of pie. They had no dinners till after meeting; when they had a roast goose, or turkey, or spare rib, or a stew pie; in the spring and summer, they generally ate bread and milk for supper and breakfast.

At that time, no family had a barrel of flour; the farmers broke up a piece of new ground and planted with wheat, and turnips; this wheat, by the help of the sieve, was their flour. A writer of years gone by, says "the chiefest corn they planted, was Indian grain, before they had ploughs; and let no man make a jest at pumpkins, for with this food the Lord was pleased to feed his people, to their good content, till corn and cattle were increased." Their corn before they had built mills to grind it, was pounded with a wooden or stone pestle in a mortar made of a large log hollowed out at one end. They cultivated barley, much of which was made into malt for beer, which they drank instead of ardent spirit. They raised flax, which they rotted in the water, and then manufactured it in their families into thread and cloth.

By an order of the Massachusetts General Court, corn and beans were required to be used in voting for counsellors; the corn to manifest elections, the beans the contrary, on the choice or refusal of a candidate; the law imposed a heavy penalty, if more than one corn or bean was used by one person.

The first houses which they built were very coarse rude structures. They had steep roofs covered with thatch, or small bundles of sedge or straw, laid one over another. The fireplaces were made of rough stones, and the chimneys of boards, or short sticks, crossing each other, and plastered inside with clay. In a few years houses of a better construction began to appear. They were built with two stories in front, and sloped down to a low one in the rear; the windows opened outward on hinges, and were small. The glass was small, and in the shape of a diamond, and set in sashes of lead. The fireplaces were hugely large, and could receive a four foot log besides seating the family of children in the corners, where they could look up and count the stars. They were uniformly placed, so as to front to the south, on whatever side of the road they might be, and the object was that, when the sun shone on it, the house might serve as a sundial

It is said to have been the custom of the first settlers to wear their beards so long, that in the winter, it would sometimes freeze together so that it was difficult to get their vessels to their mouths, from which they took their drink.

The common address of men and women was Goodman and Goodwife; none but those who sustained some office of dignity, or belonged to some respectable family were complimented with the title of Master or Mistress; in writing they did not use the capital F, but two small ones as ff.

In those days the young women did not consider it a hardship, nor a disgrace, to walk five or six miles to meeting on the Sabbath, or on lecture days; in the country towns, scarcely a chaise, or any other vehicle was used. The common conveyance was by horses fitted out with saddles and pillions. A man and woman rode together on the same horse, and sometimes a little boy rode before the man, and an infant in the lap of the woman: no inconsiderable journeys were made in this way. Horses then were made to pace, that they might carry their riders more gently. It was not until a little before the revolutionary war, that they were learned to trot. A horse that would sell for forty dollars was considered as of the first quality, and one more than nine years old, was considered of little value.

In those days every body went to meeting on the Sabbath and lecture days, however distant they lived. Those who owned horses, did not consider them any more their own, than their neighbors, on that day. It was the custom in many, if not all country towns, for the owner, with his wife, to ride half way to a horse block made for that purpose, and there hitch his horse, and walk on, for his neighbor to ride who set out on foot, and so when they returned.

INDENTURED SERVITUDE:
Soon after the settling of Jamestown, there was a tremendous demand for labor, skilled and unskilled, in the American colonies. Many early Virginians were English convicts who arrived in this country as "transported " felons. In England a system was introduced in 1655 which enabled death sentences to be reduced to transportation overseas, and two years later justices of the peace were empowered to transport vagrants. Many crimes carried the death penalty, but today many of those crimes would be considered misdemeanors.

After 1655 and before the Transportation Act of 1718 some prisoners of each circuit court were selected to be reprieved from the gallows on condition of their accepting a term of transportation to the Colonies. Each formal pardon, signed by the king, was enrolled in the great series of patent rolls that are preserved in the Public Record Office in London as Class C 66.

Nearly 400 convict ships carrying 50,000 men, women and children left England bound for the American colonies where their human cargoes were sold and/or indentured as servants to work off their passage for a term of years. Facilities were developed for the reception and sale of convicted prisoners. The tidal wave of involuntary laborers became known as ``His Majesty's Seven-Year Passengers." Of the more than 400 convict ships identified as having crossed the Atlantic from the ports of London, Bristol, Liverpool and Bideford between 1716 and 1776, a dozen or so were destined for the West Indies or the Carolinas before 1730. Thereafter Maryland or Virginia were the invariable destinations. English prisons were cleared on a regular basis two or three times a year at times to suit demands of tobacco exporters in the colonies.

Cromwell sent an estimated 50,000-80,000 Irish woman and children into slavery in the West Indies. The men were slaughtered in a battle. But most Irish history books only give this event one or two sentences. There were 100,000 or so orphaned boys and girls, ages 14-16, shipped to the islands by Cromwell and his son Henry in an organized slave trade. The number sent into slavery are variously estimated at between thirty and eighty thousand. In addition to those sent into slavery, large numbers were sent into the military service of foreign kings in Europe. In 1640, 200 Frenchmen were kidnaped, concealed and sold in Barbados for 900 pounds of cotton each. Englishmen taken in the course of Monmouth's rebellion against James II (1685-86 or thereabouts) were sold off as slaves for use in the colonies. A large number of those transported died on the journey.

Many ordinary individuals, who for numerous varying reasons wished to emigrate to the colonies, were quite unable to pay for their passage, and so a scheme gradually evolved whereby the emigrant could received a free passage to the colonies provided that he were willing to be sold into bondage for a few years upon arrival. The agent received an acreage of land for each servant he brought into the colony and the servant, at the end of his time, received a reward in the shape of land, tools, etc.

Like all schemes dealing with humanity, this one suffered many abuses, and many of the indentured servants, as they were called, suffered from great hardships. Unscrupulous dealers occasionally kidnaped persons and sold them abroad, while conditions of servitude in the colonies often left much to be desired. It is the opinion of various scholars, however, that without some such scheme, the 17th and 18th century settlement of the American colonies could not have taken place. It has been estimated that one half to two third of all white immigrants were indentured servants, redemptioners (a similar scheme) or convicts.

When the prospective servant offered his services, he was issued an indenture, which he carried away with him as proof of his terms, and was supposed to register himself as soon as he arrived in the colony. A copy of the indenture was supposed to be kept in the office where he registered in England but it seems that in the majority of cases, this was not done. Very few copies of the hundreds of thousands of indentures issued were kept, and those which are extant are in several different forms. In Bristol, an entry book was used. Middlesex kept an actual copy of the agreement. London used a special printed form whereon the details of the indenture were copies. Certain details were copied into a register book also.

GENERAL NOTES ON THE RECORDS:
The British treasury, which became responsible after 1718 for payments to contractors regarding transportation of felons from the London, Middlesex, Home Circuit and Buckinghamshire prisons, maintained meticulous records of the numbers and names of those transported and often the name of the ship. The records of Quarter Session and Borough Courts, which exercised the power in every county to transport convicted offenders, are all preserved in London and in some 50 county or borough record offices in England. However few of the surviving county Quarter Sessions have been calendared, transcribed or indexed.

The details transcribed in this volume are taken from the records in the Guildhall in London labeled Agreements To

Serve in America. They have been arranged in chronological order by the archivists and carefully numbered. From their location in the Guildhall and the fact that most of them were witnessed by the mayor of London or an Alderman of the City, it is presumed that they were issued at the Guildhall, possibly under a special arrangement of the City of London, for they are mostly copied by the same hand and in the same style and signed by successive mayors, while all the participants are young and unmarried. Why they exist for this period only is not known; perhaps they were kept only during the lifetime of a certain official. From a study of other records at the Guildhall, it is clear that the present series are survivals and certainly do not represent the origin of the system.

The printed forms are of two kinds, one intended for persons over 21 and the other intended for persons under 21. In the spaces were written in by hand the date of issue, name of servant, parish and county of origin, agent, destination, but not the name of the ship on which the servant was to sail. The forms were signed or marked by the servant and also by the mayor or alderman, usually on the same date on which the indenture was issued but occasionally several days later. Specimens of the forms are shown at the end of the introduction.

In 1733 Latin was suddenly discarded. "Memorandum" and "Jurat coram me" were crossed out and "be it remembered" and "sworn before me" written in by hand. Later the forms were printed that way.

Occasionally an indenture was copied twice, probably through an error, but on several occasions the same person crops up again, days, months or even years later. One can only conjecture the circumstances which delayed his departure the first time.

The old-fashioned handwriting is often difficult to read. The spelling of personal names varies considerably even on the same form, and towns are frequently spelled phonetically. Occasionally there are outright lapses of memory on the part of the scribe, when he has written such things as "vinter" for destination, when he presumably meant Virginia. One wonders how many undetectable lapses occurred and whether these lapses are also responsible for some of the untraceable places which the servants are said to have come from.

The register book which accompanies the Agreements to Serve does not tally completely with the separate forms. Many of the forms were not entered in the register and there are a number of entries for which there is no form.

You may want to read Roger Ekrich's book "BOUND FOR AMERICA: THE TRANSPORTATION OF BRITISH CONVICTS TO THE COLONIES, 1718-1775" Oxford, England 1987. It is a general interpretive history and contains a very limited number of case studies and examples and specific names.

Advertisements for many "runaways" who were sought by their masters can be found in the VIRGINIA GAZETTE. My husband's ancestor, indentured for a term of years as a blacksmith, was a "runaway" and his master advertised in the VIRGINIA GAZETTE. Microfilm of the Williamsburg VIRGINIA GAZETTEs are available in or through just about any Virginia library, good reference or research library, or public library with interlibrary loan connections.

There is a personal name index for the pre-1781 VIRGINIA GAZETTEs that sometimes names individual convicts who have run away from their masters or escaped from their jailers. See Lester J. Capon and Stella F. Duff's VIRGINIA GAZETTE INDEX, 1736-1780 (Williamsburg, Virginia 1950) . For more on this index visit http://leo.vsla.edu:80/vanotes/ - Library of Virginia's home page, Number 9 in the Library of Virginia's VA-Notes series, which is available through the Library of Virginia Home Page.

The FHL has the index to the VIRGINIA GAZETTE. It is on about 19 microfiche which cost about 10 or 15 cents apiece. The microfiche would remain in the FHL from which you order them. You could try a University library for the actual papers. Stanford University has the Gazette on film.

The surviving files of the Williamsburg newspapers are filled with gaps and you may also want to look for Virginia news in the ANNAPOLIS MARYLAND GAZETTE or in some of the Philadelphia newspapers, especially the PENNSYLVANIA GAZETTE.

The College of William and Mary in Williamsburg, VA may have copies of all issues of the VIRGINIA GAZETTE.

The books published on Botetourt, Montgomery, and Augusta Co, VA have printed the lists of transported people and their buyers, with home of buyer. I do not know if that has been done for other counties.

The Public Records Office in Knew, London SW, has the original ship's manifest of prisoners and also the court records and trial transcripts. The PRO has recently started a program of public access by e-mail and the World Wide Web (WWW) and they will do some limited searches at that end. Find them at: http://www.pro.gov.uk/

The latest work of Peter Wilson Coldham, author of several books pertaining to English emigrants in bondage, is called "The King's Passengers to Maryland and Virginia," The 433-page work contains names of some 25,000 passengers. They are shown alphabetically by surname and in the order of the English cities or counties where they were condemned. Additionally a comprehensive list of convict "runaways" has been compiled from contemporary Maryland, Virginia and Pennsylvania newspapers and cross-referenced to the passenger lists. "The King's Passengers to Maryland & Virginia," is from Family Line Publications, Rear 63 E. Main St., Westminster, MD 21157, (800) 876-6103.

From THE COMPLETE BOOK OF EMIGRANTS IN BONDAGE 1614-1775 by Peter Wilson Coldham, Genealogical Publishing Co. 1988: "Between 1614 and 1775, some 50,000 Englishmen were sentenced by legal process to be transported to the American colonies. With notably few exceptions their names and the record of their trial have survived in public records together with much other information which enables us to plot the story of their unhappy and unwilling passage to America. These records are now combined and condensed in this volume to form the largest single collection of transatlantic passenger lists to be found during the earliest period of migration."

"The idea of swelling the numbers of colonial laborers by employing the gaols of England was almost as old as the founding of the colonies themselves and, indeed, Virginia was first recommended in 1606 as a "place where idle vagrants might be sent"."

"The forcible emigration system appears to have fallen into decline by the 1630's and was soon put out of mind with the onset of the English Civil War. The reforming Parliament, which took control of the nation's affairs in 1649, quickly found a use for the old methods, however. Having first disposed of several thousand defeated Royalists by sending them to New England, Virginia and the sugar colonies, Parliament revived and reinforced the earlier provisions for disposing of unwanted felons. In 1655 a formal system was introduced for pardoning convicted felons on condition of their transportation; and in 1657 an Act was passed enabling Justices of the Peace to transport idle vagrants. These arrangements, in turn, were taken over and further developed after the restoration of the monarchy in 1660. Between then and 1717 pardons on condition of transportation were issued regularly each year".

"Such modest measures were perceived as inadequate by 1717. In the aftermath of the Scottish uprising of 1715, many of the 'rebels" were crowded into inadequate prisons before being shipped off to the colonies, and this served only to throw into high relief the problem of increasing gaol populations at a time when over 200 offences were on the statue books which merited the death penalty. Early in 1718, a new Act was introduced which, for the first time, gave the Assize Courts the power to impose a sentence of transportation for a vast range of crimes ranging from petty larceny to bigamy. This measure, and the continuation of pre-existing arrangement for the issue of Royal pardons, at least achieved one humanitarian result for, in proportion to the large number of death sentences handed down in the English courts, relatively few were ever carried out."

"Thus arrangements were made for the shipment to Virginia and Maryland of convicted felons. London and Middlesex provided more than half of all transported felons, all of them housed in Newgate Prison before being embarked in one or other of ships which also plied black slave trade to the southern colonies."

The outbreak of the Revolutionary War in 1775 bought to an end this trade in human cargo which had been plied successfully and profitably for well over 150 years. In 1787 the transportation of convicts from English gaols was restarted, this time to Australian colonies.

Some abbreviations which were used are:
CAPS - indicates the ship name when known.
R - reprieved for transportation
M - Middlesex
SW - Sentenced for transportation at Westminster Session
T - transported
S - sentenced to transportation
s - stealing
NT - Nottingham
TB - transportation bond
G - Gloucestershire
Wa - Warwickshire
So - Somerset
Ca - Cambridgeshire

Original ship's manifest of prisoners and court records and trial transcripts can be found in Knew, London SW Public Records Office.

http://www.linkline.com/personal/xymox/ - Ancestor Roll of Honor on America's First Families Web site. When you enter the site, scroll down to near the bottom of the page where the Ancestor Roll of Honor is located. On the same page you will also find a link to the 1600's Ancestor Data Base that contains over 14,000 names of proven ancestors from that era.

THIS AND THAT GENEALOGY TIPS ON COPYRIGHT

COPYRIGHT LAWS:

The original copyright law was enacted in 1790. Books were usually protected for 28 years, and the copyright could be renewed for an additional 47 years. After Jan 1, 1978 copyrights are good for the life of the author plus fifty years. Books for hire, anonymous, and pseudonymous works are currently protected for 100 years from creation or 75 years from publication, whichever is shorter. Another amendment on Mar 1, 1989 eliminated the requirement for a copyright notice in a book: original works are automatically copyrighted. So, anything published 75 years before 1978 is probably safe to use, although it would be courteous to include a citation. On the other hand, someone else may have already reprinted some or all of this material and obtained a new copyright on their work, making the use of what is apparently in the public domain, illegal. If you copy pages from books with the intent of using them in your genealogy book, you may have violated copyright law, unless you obtain written permission to do so, or the material has passed into the public domain. When you reprint a work that's in the public domain, you can copyright any new material that you add such as an introduction, notes, explanatory text, etc.

There may be a way for you to include at least some of the material, however. Fair use comes into play here -- you are permitted to quote brief passages from another work. The conservative estimate of "brief" is one paragraph. Now that doesn't mean one total paragraph from the family history -- that means one paragraph for each quote. So, you can quote from the same source numerous times without worrying about having quoted more than a paragraph. (That isn't license to do tons of quotes, each a paragraph long -- just a way to quote pertinent material without going too gray worrying over it.) So, if the material you have has some particularly pithy paragraphs, quote away, but save your quoting for those.

The burden is on anyone who wants to reprint a work to determine if it is still covered by copyright. In the case of named authors, the Copyright Office maintains a list you can search for known dates of death. For anonymous works, if the 75 year or 100 year test is met, the Copyright Office presumes the author has been dead for 50 years.

Unless you know the copyright has expired or your use clearly comes within one of the "fair-use" exemptions of the Copyright Act, you're very likely violating the copyright owner's rights if you don't have permission---preferably in writing---to use it. The fair-use exemption (other than single copies for personal reference or a reasonable number for classroom use) that most often applies would be the use of brief excerpts for the purpose of review or critical comment. Just using it for the information of other people wouldn't seem to qualify.

Data in family histories is not copyrighted. That means that you can use the data all you want to, as long as you don't quote reams of stuff. Data means facts and not conclusions or the way Great Aunt Maude expressed herself when she said that Uncle Albert was such a scoundrel that his own vest pockets kept checking themselves to see if they'd been robbed. Quote that stuff. And if you do use the raw facts, it's good to cite your source anyway. "According to a family history written in 1832 by the Queen of Prussia, Tobias the First was born in 1597 on a snowy December Saturday in Bavaria." That way people will know that your sources are secondary.

This is general information and isn't intended as legal advice. A copyright attorney would be a good idea if you are planning to reproduce blocks of text, especially considering all of the genealogy CD's which are being published these days. For more on copyright laws, information, pamphlets are available from the United States Copyright Office.

WELDING LINKS - DARK SIDE OF THE INTERNET - by Myra Vanderpool Gormley, CG, rwr-editors@rootsweb.com

Disguised as the nicest people on earth, many genealogists are nevertheless thieves, plagiarists, and copyright infringers. Some are high-tech robbers using computers, mice, and Internet Service Providers to steal intellectual property. Some try to hide their crimes under mantles of excuses such as:

o I thought everything on the Internet was FREE.
o I'm just looking up information for FREE. I don't charge people anything.
o You can't copyright facts and that's what genealogy is.
o Genealogy was meant to be shared.
o This is information about my family and I'm entitled to it.
o Reproduction of copyrighted materials was intended to keep people from distributing information for profit.
o Authors are too greedy and should be grateful they are getting free advertising on the Web.

No matter how easy it is to copy from the Web, a book, or a CD, taking another's work is wrong. Access to a great deal of genealogical material may be free, but that does not give you a right to copy and use someone's intellectual property -- without his or her permission. If you offer to do lookups for others (whether you charge or not) in books or CDS that you own, you may be guilty of copyright infringement. Obtain the author's permission first -- you might be surprised at how gracious most authors are. Broderbund, one of the largest producers of genealogical CDS, clearly notes in all of its CD booklets that it considers the following wholesale sharing a copyright violation:

o Systematically making a CD freely available to more than one person at a time.
o Systematically make large parts of a CD's contents freely available to others.
o Uploading all or part of a CD's contents onto an electronic bulletin board.
o Circulating a printout taken straight off the CD.

The USGenWeb Project offers four "golden rules of copyright" at:
http://www.usgenweb.org/volunteers/copyright.html:

o Materials older than 1923 are absolutely safe. (They are in the public domain.)
o Relaying FACTS is OK. (This does not mean copying.)
o If the use of material created by someone else diminishes the market value of that person's work, then the copyright
              has been violated.
o Getting written (not e-mail) permission from the author/publisher is the surest way to ensure that you are not
              violating copyright law.

So what is copyrightable? Some like to argue that genealogy is just facts, and facts can not be copyrighted or that the information came from public records and therefore can not be copyrighted. It is true that original public records in the U.S. cannot be copyrighted, but a compilation of them can be. The law recognizes the right of transcribers and compilers to be compensated and have their work protected. If you don't think this is work, transcribe some 17th-century Virginia court records or decipher some 19th-century ship passenger lists. Accumulated genealogical information, to the extent that it is an expression, can be protected by copyright, but the actual facts in the information cannot be protected.

If authors quit compiling records and writing books because of copyright infringements, what will happen to genealogy? It is true that the basic facts about your ancestors -- name, birth date and place, spouse, date and place of the marriage, death date and place, are not copyrightable. However, adding any kind of narration to the basic genealogical facts gives rise to a copyright in the creative portion of the work. See Gary B. Hoffman's article "Who Owns Genealogy? Cousins and Copyrights" at: http://www.genealogy.com/14_cpyrt.html

Does living far from genealogical repositories, having a physical limitation, being a certain age, or being in reduced circumstances entitle us to any special privileges of copying or using someone's material? Is it ever right to take anything that belongs to someone else? Would your ancestors be proud of your answers and your actions?

For more information about copyright issues see 10 Big Myths About Copyright Explained by Brad Templeton at:
http://www.templetons.com/brad//copymyths.html

The United States Copyright Office: http://lcweb.loc.gov/copyright/

Written by Myra Vanderpool Gormley.   Previously published by Julia M. Case and Myra Vanderpool Gormley, CG, Missing Links: Rootsweb's Genealogy Journal, Vol. 4, No. 39, 22 September 1999. Rootsweb: http://www.rootsweb.com/

OTHER COPYRIGHT QUESTIONS?
http://www.benedict.com/basic/basic.htm
http://www4.law.cornell.edu/uscode/17/ch5.html

THIS AND THAT GENEALOGY TIPS ON DEATH RECORDS

DEATH RECORDS:
Together with birth and marriage records, death records make up the category known as "vital records".
Genealogists should keep in mind that many types of records should be consulted when researching information about an individual's death, including cemetery, census, church, military, probate, Railroad Retirement Board, and Social Security.

In the United States prior to 1850, few states had laws requiring that deaths be registered, and the year in which such laws were enacted varied from state to state. The earliest records generally record only the name of the deceased, the date of death, and the place of death.

Records from the 19th century tend to include more information, such as the cause of death, the age of the deceased, the date and place of birth, the name of the parents, the occupation of the deceased, the name of the spouse, the name of the person who provided the information and that person's relationship to the deceased. Race and slave-status may be included as well.

Death records from the 20th century may be even more elaborate than those of the 19th century. They may include sex, marital status, Social Security number, residence, place of burial, and birthplace of parents.

One valuable use of death records is to provide a date and location that can be used to locate an obituary, which may then provide a wealth of information about the deceased. Another valuable use of death records is to provide cause of death, critical information when you are attempting to document genetic predispositions to illnesses in a family.

CURTESY:
Prior to the enactment of the Succession Law Reform Act in 1978, a surviving husband was entitled to elect to take curtesy, that is, a life estate in his deceased wife's real property not disposed of by deed or will, in lieu of his statutory right to a preferential and distributive share. [Curtesy] was abolished by the Act.

Similarly, a surviving wife was entitled, as her primary right, to take dower, that is, a life estate in one-third of the real property of which her husband died solely seized ["entitled to"] or to which he was beneficially entitled [like in a trust]. She could, however, elect to give up dower and take her statutory rights of inheritance instead. The life estate was abolished by the Family Law Reform Act. However, the old law remains important for titles to land, for...the Act only abolished the right prospectively."

Dower and curtesy still exist in some provinces and states.

Wives could "bar their dower" on any or all of their husband's property by signing a contract which should have been registered prior to any transaction conveying the land (sometimes it is contained as a term of the deed itself). It is important to remember that dower and curtesy only give life estates, i.e. the right dies with the surviving spouse and can't be passed on. The big difference between dower and curtesy is that dower is the wife's primary right in the estate of the husband, who can elect to take the preferential and distributive share [preferential share is an amount set by law which the spouse gets before all other claims; distributive share is split with the children], but the preferential and distributive share was the primary right of the husband who can elect to take curtesy instead. I suppose that is why you don't see husbands "barring their curtesy" as a matter of course.

MOURNING RINGS:
In Colonial days gifts (rings, scarves, gloves, etc.) were given to those invited to the funeral as a way of paying tribute to the dead. The custom came from England and was so strongly ingrained that even pauper funerals required a minimum of gifts. Prominent persons' funerals could require the distribution in excess of, for example 2,000 pairs of gloves. The cost of the gifts was deducted from the estate of the deceased, which eventually led to laws prohibiting

the custom, which frequently had left a widow and her children virtually paupers.

DOWER RIGHTS refers to a married woman's 1/3 interest in her husband's estate, at his death. This was to protect her from an unscrupulous husband leaving her out of his will, or in the case of no will, she had protection. When a married man sold property, or took a mortgage, the wife had to sign for herself relinquishing her 1/3 interest to the buyer or the mortgagee otherwise she still had a 1/3 interest in someone else's property. The word is "Dower" rather than dowager; several of the original colony states continued this practice of dower rights for many years.

THIS AND THAT GENEALOGY TIPS ON DEFINITIONS & ABBREVIATIONS

DEFINITIONS:
ABSTRACT - Summary of important points of a given text, especially deeds and wills.

ACRE - See measurements.

ADMINISTRATION (of estate) - The collection, management and distribution of an estate by proper legal process.

ADMINISTRATOR (of estate) - Person appointed to manage or divide the estate of a deceased person.

ADMINISTRATRIX - A female administrator.

AFFIDAVIT - A statement in writing, sworn to before proper authority.

ALIEN - Foreigner.

AMERICAN REVOLUTION - U.S. war for independence from Great Britain 1775 - 1783.

ANCESTOR - A person from whom you are descended; a forefather.

ANTE - Latin prefix meaning before, such as in antebellum South, "The South before the war"

APPRENTICE - One who is bound by indentures or by legal agreement or by any means to serve another person for a certain time, with a view of learning an art or trade.

APPURTENANCE - That which belongs to something else such as a building, orchard, right of way, etc.

ARCHIVES - Records of a government, organization, institution; the place where records are stored.

ATTEST - To affirm; to certify by signature or oath.

BANNS - Public announcement of intended marriage.

BENEFICIARY - One who receives benefit of trust or property.

BEQUEATH - To give personal property to a person in a will. Noun -- bequest.

BOND - Written, signed, witnessed agreement requiring payment of a specified amount of money on or before a given date.

BOUNTY LAND WARRANT - A right to obtain land, specific number of acres of unallocated public land, granted for military service.

CENSUS - Official enumeration, listing or counting of citizens.

CERTIFIED COPY - A copy made and attested to by officers having charge of the original and authorized to give copies.

CHAIN - See measurements.

CHATTEL - Personal property which can include animate as well as inanimate properties.

CHRISTEN - To receive or initiate into the visible church by baptism; to name at baptism; to give a name to.

CIRCA - About, near, or approximate -- usually referring to a date.

CIVIL WAR - War between the States; war between North and South, 1861 - 65.

CODICIL - Addition to a will.

COLLATERAL ANCESTOR - Belong to the same ancestral stock but not in direct line of descent; opposed to lineal such as aunts, uncles & cousins.

COMMON ANCESTOR - Ancestor shared by any two people.

CONFEDERATE - Pertaining to the Southern states which seceded from the U.S. in 1860-1861, their government and their citizens.

CONSANGUINITY - Blood relationship.

CONSORT - Usually, a wife whose husband is living.

CONVEYANCE - See deed.

COUSIN - Relative descended from a common ancestor, but not a brother or sister.

DECEDENT - A deceased person.

DECLARATION OF INTENTION - First paper, sworn to and filed in court, by an alien stating that he wants to become a citizen.

DEED - A document by which title in real property is transferred from one party to another.

DEPOSITION - A testifying or testimony taken down in writing under oath of affirmation in reply to interrogatories, before a competent officer to replace to oral testimony of a witness.

DEVISE - Gift of real property by will.

DEVISEE - One to whom real property (land) is given in a will.

DEVISOR - One who gives real property in a will.

DISSENTER - One who did not belong to the established church, especially the Church of England in the American colonies.

DISTRICT LAND OFFICE PLAT BOOK - Books or rather maps which show the location of the land patentee.

DISTRICT LAND OFFICE TRACT BOOK - Books which list individual entries by range and township.

DOUBLE DATING - A system of double dating used in England and America from 1582-1752 because it was not clear as to whether the year commenced January 1 or March 25

DOWER - Legal right or share which a wife acquired by marriage in the real estate of her husband, allotted to her after his death for her lifetime.

EMIGRANT - One leaving a country and moving to another.

ENUMERATION - Listing or counting , such as a census.

EPITAPH - An inscription on or at a tomb or grave in memory of the one buried there.

ESCHEAT - The reversion of property to the state when there are no qualified heirs.

ESTATE - All property and debts belonging to a person.

ET AL - Latin for "and others".

ET UX - Latin for "and wife".

ET UXOR - And his wife. Sometimes written simply Et Ux.

EXECUTOR - One appointed in a will to carry out its provisions. Female = Executrix.

FEE - An estate of inheritance in land, being either fee simple or fee tail. An estate in land held of a feudal lord on condition of the performing of certain services.

FEE SIMPLE - An absolute ownership without restriction.

FEE TAIL - An estate of inheritance limited to lineal descendant heirs of a person to whom it was granted.

FRANKLIN, STATE OF - An area once known but never officially recognized and was under consideration from 1784 - 1788 from the western part of North Carolina.

FRATERNITY - Group of men (or women) sharing a common purpose or interest.

FREE HOLD - An estate in fee simple, in fee tail, or for life.

FRIEND - Member of the Religious Society of Friends; a Quaker.

FURLONG - See measurements.

GAZETTEER - A geographical dictionary; a book giving names and descriptions of places usually in alphabetical order.

GENEALOGY - Study of family history and descent.

GENTLEMAN - A man well born.

GIVEN NAME - Name given to a person at birth or baptism, one's first and middle names.

GLEBE - Land belonging to a parish church.

GRANTEE - One who buys property or receives a grant.

GRANTOR - One who sells property or makes a grant.

· GREAT-AUNT - Sister of one's grandparent.

GREAT-UNCLE - Brother of one's grandparent.

GUARDIAN - Person appointed to care for and manage property of a minor orphan or an adult incompetent of managing his own affairs.

HALF BROTHER/HALF SISTER - Child by another marriage of one's mother or father; the relationship of two people who have only one parent in common.

HEIRS - Those entitled by law or by the terms of a will to inherit property from another.

HOLOGRAPHIC WILL - One written entirely in the testator's own handwriting.

HOMESTEAD ACT - Law passed by Congress in 1862 allowing a head of a family to obtain title to 160 acres of public land after clearing and improving it for 5 years.

HUGUENOT - A French Protestant in the 16th and 17th centuries. One of the reformed or Calvinistic communion who were driven by the thousands into exile in England, Holland, Germany and America.

ILLEGITIMATE - Born to a mother who was not married to the child's father.

IMMIGRANT - One moving into a country from another.

INDENTURE - Today it means a contract in 2 or more copies. Originally made in 2 parts by cutting or tearing a single sheet across the middle in a jagged line so the two parts may later be matched.

INDENTURED SERVANT - One who bound himself into service of another person for a specified number of years, often in return for transportation to this country.

INFANT - Any person not of full age; a minor. "Infant of Tender Years" would refer to a minor under the age of 14. Guardians were appointed for them by the Court. Children 14-21 had the legal right to choose their own guardian. So if you find a court record showing an orphan "came to court and chose as (his/her) guardian" as the legal phrasing read, you know the child was a minor over 14 and under 21 (if male) or 18 (if female and unmarried); girls reached legal majority when they turned 18 or married, as when they married their rights passed automatically to their husband.

INSTANT - Of or pertaining to the current month. (Abbreviated inst.).

INTESTATE - One who dies without a will or dying without a will.

INVENTORY - An account, catalog or schedule, made by an executor or administrator of all the goods and chattels and sometimes of the real estate of a deceased person.

ISSUE - Offspring; children; lineal descendants of a common ancestor.

LATE - Recently deceased.

LEASE - An agreement which creates a landlord - tenant situation.

LEGACY - Property or money left to someone in a will.

LEGISLATURE - Lawmaking branch of state or national government; elected group of lawmakers.

LIEN - A claim against property as security for payment of a debt.

LINEAGE - Ancestry; direct descent from a specific ancestor.

LINEAL - Consisting of or being in as direct line of ancestry or descendants; descended in a direct line.

LINK - See measurements.

LIS PENDENS - Pending court action; usually applies to land title claims.

LODGE - A chapter or meeting hall of a fraternal organization.

LOYALIST - Tory, an American colonist who supported the British side during the American Revolution.

MADSTONE - A stone taken from the stomach of a deer (aided in digestion), preferably a white deer, which was applied to the body of a person who was bitten by a rabid animal. If the stone stuck to the wound, it was supposedly drawing out the poison and the person would hopefully live. If the stone fell off, the bite was not rabid. These stones were much cherished, bragged out, hidden from people who would want to steal them, and passed from generation to generation.

MAIDEN NAME - A girl's last name or surname before she marries.

MANUSCRIPT - A composition written with the hand as an ancient book or an un-printed modern book or music.

MARRIAGE BOND - A financial guarantee that no impediment to the marriage existed, furnished by the intended bridegroom or by his friends.

MATERNAL - Related through one's mother, such as a Maternal grandmother being the mother's mother.

MEASUREMENTS - Link - 7.92 inches;   Chain - 100 Links or 66 feet;   Furlong - 1000 Links or 660 feet;   Rod - 5 ½ yds or 16 ½ ft (also called a perch or pole); Rood - From 5 ½ yards to 8 yards, depending on locality; Acre - 43,560 square ft or 160 square rods.

MESSUAGE - A dwelling house.

METES & BOUNDS - Property described by natural boundaries, such as 3 notches in a white oak tree, etc.

MICROFICHE - Sheet of microfilm with greatly reduced images of pages of documents.

MICROFILM - Reproduction of documents on film at reduced size.

MIGRANT - Person who moves from place to place, usually in search of work.

MIGRATE - To move from one country or state or region to another. (Noun : migration).

MILITIA - Citizens of a state who are not part of the national military forces but who can be called into military service in an emergency; a citizen army, apart from the regular military forces.

MINOR - One who is under legal age; not yet a legal adult.

MISTER - In early times, a title of respect given only to those who held important civil officer or who were of gentle blood.

MOIETY - A half; an indefinite portion.

MORTALITY - Death; death rate.

MORTALITY SCHEDULES - Enumeration of persons who died during the year prior to June 1 of 1850, 1860, 1870, and 1880 in each state of the United States, conducted by the bureau of census.

MORTGAGE - A conditional transfer of title to real property as security for payment of a debt.

NAMESAKE - Person named after another person.

NECROLOGY - Listing or record of persons who have died recently.

NEE - Used to identify a woman's maiden name; born with the surname of.

NEPHEW - Son of one's brother or sister.

NIECE - Daughter of one's brother or sister.

NUNCUPATIVE WILL - One declared or dictated by the testator, usually for persons in last sickness, sudden illness, or military.

ORPHAN - Child whose parents are dead; sometimes, a child who has lost one parent by death.

ORPHAN'S COURT - Orphans being recognized as wards of the states, provisions were made for them in special courts.

PASSENGER LIST - A ships list of passengers, usually referring to those ships arriving in the US from Europe.

PATENT - Grant of land from a government to an individual.

PATERNAL - Related to one's father. Paternal grandmother is the father's mother.

PATRIOT - One who loves his country and supports its interests.

PEDIGREE - Family tree; ancestry.

PENSION - Money paid regularly to an individual, especially by a government as reward for military service during wartime or upon retirement from government service.

PENSIONER - One who receives a pension.

PERCH - See measurements.

POLE - See measurements.

POLL - List or record of persons, especially for taxing or voting.

POST - Latin prefix meaning after, as in postwar economy.

POSTERITY - Descendants; those who come after.

POWER OF ATTORNEY - When a person in unable to act for himself, he appoints another to act in his behalf.

PRE - Latin prefix meaning before, as in prewar military buildup.

PRE-EMOTION RIGHTS - Right given by the federal government to citizens to buy a quarter section of land or less.

PROBATE - Having to do with wills and the administration of estates.

PROGENITOR - A direct ancestor.

PROGENY - Descendants of a common ancestor; issue.

PROVED WILL - A will established as genuine by probate court.

PROVOST - A person appointed to superintend, or preside over something.

PROXIMO - In the following month, in the month after the present one.

PUBLIC DOMAIN - Land owned by the government.

QUAKER - Member of the Religious Society of Friends.

QUIT CLAIM - A deed conveying the interest of the party at that time.

RECTOR - A clergyman; the ruler or governor of a country.

RELICT - Widow; surviving spouse when one has died, husband or wife.

REPUBLIC - Government in which supreme authority lies with the people or their elected representatives.

REVOLUTIONARY WAR - U.S. war for independence from Great Britain 1775 - 1783.

ROD - See measurements.

SHAKER - Member of a religious group formed in 1747 which practiced communal living and celibacy.

SIBLING - Person having one or both parents in common with another; a brother or sister.

SIC - Latin meaning thus; copied exactly as the original reads. Often suggests a mistake or surprise in the original.

SPINSTER - A woman still unmarried; or one who spins.

SPONSOR - A bondsman; surety.

STATUTE - Law.

STEPBROTHER / STEPSISTER - Child of one's stepfather or stepmother.

STEPCHILD - Child of one's husband or wife from a previous marriage.

STEPFATHER - Husband of one's mother by a later marriage.

STEPMOTHER - Wife of one's father by a later marriage.

SURNAME - Family name or last name.

TERRITORY - Area of land owned by the united States, not a state, but having its own legislature and governor.

TESTAMENTARY - Pertaining to a will.

TESTATE - A person who dies leaving a valid will.

TESTATOR - A person who makes a valid will before his death.

TITHABLE - Taxable.

TITHE - Formerly, money due as a tax for support of the clergy or church.

TORY - Loyalist; one who supported the British side in the American Revolution.

TOWNSHIP - A division of U.S. public land that contained 36 sections, or 36 square miles. Also a subdivision of the county in many Northeastern and Midwestern states of the U.S.

TRADITION - The handing down of statements, beliefs, legends, customs, genealogies, etc. from generation to generation, especially by word of mouth.

TRANSCRIBE - To make a copy in writing.

ULTIMO - In the month before this one.

UNION - The United States; also the North during the Civil War, the states which did not secede.

VERBATIM - Word for word; in the same words, verbally.

VITAL RECORDS - Records of birth, death, marriage or divorce.

VITAL STATISTICS - Data dealing with birth, death, marriage or divorce.

WAR BETWEEN THE STATES - U.S. Civil War, 1861 - 1865.

WARD - Chiefly the division of a city for election purposes.

WILL - Document declaring how a person wants his property divided after his death.

WITNESS - One who is present at a transaction, such as a sale of land or signing of a will, who can testify or affirm that it actually took place.

WPA HISTORICAL RECORDS SURVEY - A program undertaken by the US Government 1935 - 1936 in which inventories were compiled of historical material.

YEOMAN - A servant, an attendant or subordinate official in a royal household; a subordinate of a sheriff; an independent farmer.

CONFUSING DEFINITIONS:
Mistress - Not necessarily a married woman. A term of respect for any married woman.

Gentleman - Might be used to describe a retired man of wealth or education.

Housekeeper - Once meant property owner and could be used for male or female.

Domestic - Once meant a housewife and not necessarily a servant.

Inmate - As used in the Pennsylvania Archives, refers to a man living in the home of another person - not necessarily a person in an institution. It may also mean someone who did not own the real estate on which he resided.

Freeman - As used in Pennsylvania Archives, meant a young man not yet married.

Alias - Usually meant illegitimacy. The surname of the father and mother were jointed. It did not have a criminal meaning.

Senior or Junior - These terms did not necessarily refer to father and son. If two men in the same town had the same name, the older was "Senior" and the younger "Junior" even if they weren't related. In earlier times, a Father might have done the same in naming his sons.

Niece - This could refer to any female relative but usually a granddaughter.

Nephew - This could refer to an illegitimate son but usually a grandson.

Cousin - A cousin might be a nephew or uncle.

Brother - This term could refer to an adopted brother but could also mean an in-law or lodge or Church brother.

Domestic - A wife could be called a domestic because she was "at home".

Crazy - Usually meant a person who was ill or in generally poor health, not necessarily mentally ill.

ABBREVIATIONS:
1C - first cousin (2c, second cousin, etc.)
1R - once removed (2r, twice removed, etc.)
ACW - American Civil War
AFRA - American Family Records Association
AGLL- American Genealogical Lending Library
AGRA - Association of Genealogists and Record Agents (Professional)
APG - Association of Professional Genealogists, headquartered in Salt Lake City, Utah.
ASCII - American Standard Code for Information Interchange - type of file on a computer that is usually readable / writeable by most word processors
AIS - Accelerated Indexing System
b - born
bap or bapt - baptized
BBS - Bulletin Board System Phone dial up connection for PC's.
BK - Brother's Keeper, a genealogy program
BMD - Births, Marriages and Deaths

BMP - Bit Mapped Picture - file format of a computer disk file
Bp - Bishop
bur - buried
C18 - Eighteenth century (etc.)
ca - circa, about, (as in ca. 1840.)
CANINDEX - Index of emigrants from British Isles to Canada and Newfoundland
CC - County Court (USA)
CD - Compact Disk - An optical disk used with some PC's to store lots of data.
CFI - Computer File Index (precursor of IGI)
chr - Christened.
CW - Civil War
d - died.
DAR - Daughters of the American Revolution
DC - District Court
DOCS - Documents / Documentations
div - divorced.
d.s.p. - died without issue (from Latin: decessit sine prole)
FAQ - Frequently Asked Questions
FFV - First Families of Virginia
FGRA - Family Group Record Archives
FGS - ancestral charts or "Family Group Sheets"
FHC - Family History Center (LDS satellite centers)
FHL - Family History Library (LDS main library in Utah)
FHLC - Family History Library Catalog
FOIA - Freedom of Information Act
FTM - Family Tree Maker, a genealogy program from Banner Blue Software
FTP - File Transfer Protocol (networking, technical)
GEDCOM - GEnealogical Data COMmunications
GIF - A format to hold images on a computer disk file
GIM - Genealogical Information Manager
GOONS - Guild Of One Name Studies
IGI - International Genealogical Index
IOOF - Independent Order of Odd Fellows
ISO - In Search Of
LDS - Latter Day Saints (Mormons)
LOCIS - Library of Congress Information System
NARA - National Archives and Records Administration
NATF - National Archives Trust Fund
NEHGS - New England Historical Genealogy Society
NGC - National Genealogical Conference
NGS - National Geographical Society
PAF - Personal Ancestry File, genealogy program of the Mormon Church (LDS)
ROOTS-L - a mailing list of subscribers who are interested in genealogy
RW - Revolutionary War
SAR - Sons of the American Revolution
SASE - Self Addressed, Stamped Envelope
SOUNDEX - A method of translating a name to a one letter code followed by three numerical digits. The aim of the translation is to render all names which sound alike (or sufficiently similar) to the same code.
TMS - Tiny Tafels Software genealogy program also Tafel Matching System
WW1 - World War One
WW2 - World War Two

SOME MILITARY DEFINITIONS:
"Associators" were volunteers who had sworn to protect their homes by any means.

"Rangers" were scouts who guarded the frontier and were usually formed from the militia who were the "home guard", along with the "State Line," these were similar to the National Guard.

THIS AND THAT GENEALOGY TIPS ON DISEASES, MEDICAL TERMS, EPIDEMICS

MEDICAL TERMS AND DISEASES:
Ablepsy: Blindness

Abscess: A localized collection of pus buried in tissues, organs, or confined spaces of the body, often accompanied by swelling and inflammation and frequently caused by bacteria. See boil.

Addison's disease: A disease characterized by severe weakness, low blood pressure, and a bronzed coloration of the skin, due to decreased secretion of cortisol from the adrenal gland. Synonyms: Morbus addisonii, bronzed skin disease.

Ague: Malarial or intermittent fever characterized by paroxysms (stages of chills, fever, and sweating at regularly recurring times) and followed by an interval or intermission of varying duration. Popularly, the disease was known as "fever and ague," "chill fever," "the shakes," and by names expressive of the locality in which it was prevalent, such as, "swamp fever" (in Louisiana), "Panama fever," and "Chagres fever."

Ague-cake: A form of enlargement of the spleen, resulting from the action of malaria on the system.

American Plague: Yellow fever.

Anasarca: Generalized massive dropsy/edema. See Dropsy.

Anchylosis: Stiff joint.

Anidrosis: Too little perspiration.

Anthrax: Carbuncle or large painful boil.

Aphonia: Laryngitis.

Aphtha: The infant disease "thrush"

Apoplexy: Paralysis due to stroke.

Aphthae: See thrush.

Aphthous stomatitis: See canker.

Arachnitis: Inflammation of membranes in the brain.

Ascites: Water in the stomach. See dropsy.

Asphycsia/Asphicsia: Cyanotic and lack of oxygen.

Asthenia: See debility.

Atrophy: Wasting away or diminishing in size.

Bad Blood: Syphilis.

Barbers Itch: Ringworm of the beard.

Bilious Colic or Fever: A term loosely applied to certain intestinal and malarial fevers. Typhoid. Hepatitis. Elevated temperature and bile emesis. See typhus.

Biliousness: A complex of symptoms comprising nausea, abdominal discomfort, headache, and constipation, formerly attributed to excessive secretion of bile from the liver.

Black Plague or Death: Bubonic Plague.

Black Fever: Acute infection with high temperature and dark red skin lesions and high mortality rate.

Black Small Pox/Black Vomit: Vomiting old black blood due to ulcers or yellow fever.

Blackwater Fever: Dark urine associated with high temperature.

Bladder in Throat: Diphtheria.

Blood Poisoning: Bacterial infection, Septicemia.

Bloody Flux: Inflammation of the large bowels aka colitis. Bloody stools.

Bloody Sweat: Sweating sickness.

Boil: An abscess of skin or painful inflammation of the skin or a hair follicle usually caused by a staphylococcal infection. Synonym: furuncle.

Bone Shave: Sciatica.

Brain fever: Intense headache, fever, vertigo. See meningitis, typhus.

Breakbone: Dengue fever.

Bright's Disease: Chronic inflammatory disease of kidneys. Glomerulonephritis (kidney inflammation).

Bronchial asthma: A disorder of breathing, characterized by spasm of the bronchial tubes of the lungs, wheezing, and difficulty in breathing air outward, often accompanied by coughing and a feeling of tightness in the chest.

Bronze John: Yellow fever.

Bule: Boil, tumor or swelling.

Cachexy: Malnutrition.

Cacospysy: Irregular pulse.

Cacogastric: Upset stomach.

Caduceus: Subject to falling sickness or epilepsy.

Camp fever, Camp diarrhea: Typhus.

Cancer: A malignant and invasive growth or tumor. In the nineteenth century, cancerous tumors tended to ulcerate, grew constantly, and progressed to a fatal end and that there was scarcely a tissue they would not invade. Synonyms: malignant growth, carcinoma.

Canine Madness: Rabies, hydrophobia.

Cancrum otis: A severe, destructive, eroding ulcer of the cheek and lip. In the last century it was seen in delicate, ill-fed, ill-tended children between the ages of two and five. The disease was the result of poor hygiene. It was often fatal. The disease could, in a few days, lead to gangrene of the lips, cheeks, tonsils, palate, tongue, and even half the face; teeth would fall from their sockets. Synonyms: canker, water canker, noma, gangrenous stomatitis, gangrenous ulceration of the mouth.

Canker: An ulcerous sore of the mouth and lips, not considered fatal today. Herpes simplex. Synonym: Aphthous stomatitis. See Cancrum otis.

Catalepsy: seizures/trances

Catarrhal: Inflammation of a mucous membrane, especially of the air passages of the head and throat, with a free discharge. Bronchial catarrh was bronchitis; suffocative catarrh was croup; urethral catarrh was gleet; vaginal catarrh was leukorrhea; epidemic catarrh was the same as influenza. Synonyms: cold, coryza.

Cerebritis: Inflammation of cerebrum or lead poisoning.

Chilblains: Painful sore or swelling of the foot or hand caused by exposure to the cold.

Child Bed Fever: Infection following birth of a child.

Chin cough: Whooping cough.

Chlorosis: iron deficiency anemia.

Cholera: An acute, infectious disease characterized by profuse diarrhea, vomiting, and cramps. Cholera is spread by feces-contaminated water and food. Major epidemics struck the United States in the years 1832, 1849, and 1866.

Cholera infantum: A common, noncontagious diarrhea of young children, occurring in summer or autumn. It was common among the poor and in hand-fed babies. Death frequently occurred in three to five days. Synonyms: summer complaint, weaning brash, water gripes, choleric fever of children, cholera morbus.

Cholecystitus: Inflammation of the gall bladder.

Cholelithiasis: Gall stones.

Chorea: Any of several diseases of the nervous system, characterized by jerky movements that appear to be well coordinated but are performed involuntarily, chiefly of the face and extremities. Synonym: Saint Vitus' dance.

Clap: Gonorrhea.

Cold plague: Ague which is characterized by chills.

Colic: Paroxysmal pain in the abdomen or bowels. Infantile colic is benign paroxysmal abdominal pain during the first three months of life. Colic rarely caused death. Renal colic can occur from disease in the kidney, gallstone colic from a stone in the bile duct.

Congestion: An excessive or abnormal accumulation of blood or other fluid in a body part or blood vessel. In congestive fever the internal organs become gorged with blood.

Congestive Fever/Chills: Malaria.

Consumption: A wasting away of the body; formerly applied especially to pulmonary tuberculosis. Synonyms: marasmus (in the mid-nineteenth century), phthisis.

Convulsions: Severe contortion of the body caused by violent, involuntary muscular contractions of the extremities, trunk, and head. See epilepsy.

Corruption: Infection.

Coryza: A cold. See catarrh.

Costiveness: Constipation.

Cramp colic: Appendicitis.

Croup: Any obstructive condition of the larynx (voice box) or trachea (windpipe), characterized by a hoarse, barking cough and difficult breathing occurring chiefly in infants and children. In the early nineteenth century it was called cynanche trachealis. The crouping noise was similar to the sound emitted by a chicken affected with the pip, which in some parts of was called roup; hence, probably, the term croup. Synonyms: roup, hives, choak, stuffing, rising of the lights.

Crusted Tetter: Impetigo.

Cyanosis: Dark skin color from lack of oxygen in blood.

Cynanche: Diseases of throat.

Cystitis: Inflammation of the bladder.

Day Fever: Fever lasting one day; sweating sickness.

Debility: Abnormal bodily weakness or feebleness; decay of strength. This was a term descriptive of a patient's condition and of no help in making a diagnosis. Synonym: Asthenia.

Decrepitude: Feebleness due to old age.

Delirium tremens: Hallucinations due to alcoholism.

Dengue: Infectious fever endemic to East Africa.

Dentition: Cutting of teeth.

Deplumation: Tumor of the eyelids which causes hair loss.

Diary fever: A fever that lasts one day.

Diphtheria: An acute infectious disease acquired by contact with an infected person or a carrier of the disease. It was usually confined to the upper respiratory tract (throat) and characterized by the formation of a tough membrane (false membrane) attached firmly to the underlying tissue that would bleed if forcibly removed. In the nineteenth century the disease was occasionally confused with scarlet fever and croup.

Distemper: Usually animal disease with malaise, discharge from nose and throat, anorexia.

Dock fever: Yellow fever.

Dropsy: A contraction for hydropsy. The presence of abnormally large amounts of fluid. Congestive heart failure.

Dropsy of the Brain: Encephalitis.

Dry bellyache: Lead poisoning.

Dyscrasy: An abnormal body condition.

Dysentery: A term given to a number of disorders marked by inflammation of the intestines (especially of the colon). There are two specific varieties: (1) amebic dysentery (2) bacillary dysentery. Synonyms: flux, bloody flux, contagious pyrexia (fever), frequent griping stools.

Dysorexy: Reduced appetite.

Dyspepsia: Indigestion and heartburn. Heart attack symptoms.

Dysury: Difficulty in urination.

Eclampsia: A form of toxemia (toxins, or poisons, in the blood) accompanying pregnancy. See dropsy.

Eclampsy: Symptoms of epilepsy, convulsions during labor. <br.

Ecstasy: A form of Catalepsy characterized by loss of reason.

Edema: Nephrosis; swelling of tissues.

Edema of lungs: Congestive heart failure, a form of dropsy.

Eel thing: Erysipelas.

Effluvia: Exhalations. In the mid-nineteenth century, they were called "vapours" and distinguished into the contagious effluvia, such as rubeolar (measles); marsh effluvia, such as miasmata.

Elephantiasis: a form of leprosy.

Emphysema, pulmonary: A chronic, irreversible disease of the lungs.

Encephalitis: Swelling of brain; aka sleeping sickness.

Enteric fever: Typhoid fever.

Enterocolitis: Inflammation of the intestines.

Enteritis: Inflammation of the bowels.

Epilepsy: A disorder of the nervous system, characterized either by mild, episodic loss of attention or sleepiness (petittnal) or by severe convulsions with loss of consciousness (grand mal). Synonyms: falling sickness, fits.

Epitaxis: Nose bleed.

Erysipelas: Contagious skin disease due to Streptococci with vesicular and bulbous lesions. Synonyms: Rose, Saint Anthony's Fire (from its burning heat or, perhaps, because Saint Anthony was supposed to cure it miraculously).

Extravasted blood: Rupture of a blood vessel.

Falling sickness: Epilepsy.

Fatty Liver: Cirrhosis of liver.

Fits: Sudden attack or seizure of muscle activity.

Flux: An excessive flow or discharge of fluid like hemorrhage or diarrhea/dysentery.

Flux of humour: Circulation.

French pox: Syphilis.

Furuncle: A boil.

Gangrene: Death and decay of tissue in a part of the body--usually a lime, due to injury, disease, or failure of blood supply. Synonym: mortification.

Gathering: A collection of pus.

Glandular Fever: Mononucleosis.

Gleet: See catarrh.

Gravel: A disease characterized by small stones which are formed in the kidneys, passed along the ureters to the bladder, and expelled with the urine. Synonym: kidney stone.

Great pox: Syphilis.

Green fever/sickness: Anemia.

Grippe: An old term for influenza

Grocer's Itch: Skin disease caused by mites in sugar or flour.

Heart sickness: Condition caused by loss of salt from body.

Heat Stroke: Body temperature elevates because of surrounding environment temperature and body does not perspire to reduce temperature. Coma and death result if not reversed.

Hectic fever/Hectical complaint: A daily recurring fever with profound sweating, chills, and flushed appearance,- often associated with pulmonary tuberculosis or septic poisoning.

Hematemesis: Vomiting blood.

Hematuria: Bloody urine.

Hemiplegy: Paralysis of one side of body.

Hip Gout: Osteomylitis.

Hives: A skin eruption of smooth, slightly elevated areas on the skin which is redder or paler than the surrounding skin. Often attended by severe itching. Also called cynanche trachealis. In the mid-nineteenth century, hives was a commonly given cause of death of children three years and under. Because true hives does not kill, croup was probably the actual cause of death in those children.

Horrors: Delirium tremens.

Hospital fever: See typhus.

Hydrocephalus: Enlarged head, water on the brain. See dropsy.

Hydroperticardium: Heart dropsy.

Hydrothorax: See dropsy.

Hydrophobia: Rabies.

Hydrothroax: Dropsy in chest.

Hypertrophic: Enlargement of organ, like the heart.

Icterus: See jaundice.

Impetigo: Contagious skin disease characterized by pustules.

Inanition: Exhaustion from lack of nourishment; starvation.

Infantile paralysis: Polio.

Infection: In the early part of the last century, infections were thought to be the propagation of disease by effluvia (see above) from patients crowded together. "Miasms" were believed to be substances which could not be seen in any form, emanations not apparent to the senses. Such Miasms were understood to act by infection.

Inflammation: Redness, swelling, pain, tenderness, heat, and disturbed function of an area of the body. In the last century, cause of death often was listed as inflammation of a body organ, such as, brain or lung, but this was purely a descriptive term and is not helpful in identifying the actual underlying disease.

Intestinal colic: Abdominal pain due to improper diet.

Jail fever: Typhus.

Jaundice: Yellow discoloration of the skin, whites of the eyes, and mucous membranes, due to an increase of bile pigments in the blood. Synonym: Icterus.

Kidney stone: See gravel.

Kings evil: A popular name for scrofula. The name originated in the time of Edward the Confessor, with the belief that the disease could be cured by the touch of the King of England.

Kruchhusten: Whooping cough.

Lagrippe: Influenza.

Living in: Time of delivery of infant.

Lockjaw: Tetanus, a disease in which the jaws become firmly locked together. Synonyms: trismus, tetanus.

Lues disease: Syphilis.

Lues venera: Venereal disease.

Lumbago: Back pain.

Lung Fever: Pneumonia

Lung Sickness: Tuberculosis.

Malignant fever: See typhus.

Malignant sore throat: Diphtheria.

Mania: Insanity.

Marasmus: Malnutrition occurring in infants and young children, caused by an insufficient intake of calories or protein.

Membranous Croup: Diphtheria.

Meningitis: Inflammation of the meninges (brain and spinal cord) characterized by high fever, severe headache, and stiff neck or back muscles. Synonym: brain fever.

Metritis: Inflammation of uterus or purulent vaginal discharge.

Miasma: Poisonous vapors thought to infect air.

Milk fever: Disease from drinking contaminated milk, like undulant fever or brucellosis.

Milk leg: Post partum thrombophlebitis.

Milk sickness: poisoning resulting from the drinking of milk produced by a cow who had eaten a plant known as white snake root or other poisonous weeds.

Mormal: gangrene.

Morphew: Scurvy blisters on the body.

Mortification: Gangrene of necrotic tissue.

Myelitis: Inflammation of the spine.

Myocarditis: Inflammation of the heart muscles.

Necrosis: Mortification of bones or tissue.

Nephrosis: Kidney degeneration.

Nepritis: Inflammation of kidneys.

Nervous prostration: Extreme exhaustion from inability to control physical and mental activities.

Neuralgia: Sharp and paroxysmal pain along the course of a sensory nerve. Discomfort such as headache was Neuralgia in head.

Nostalgia: Homesickness.

Palsy: Paralysis or uncontrolled movement of controlled muscles. It was listed as "cause of death".

Paristhmitis: See quinsy.

Paroxysm: Convulsions.

Pellagra: Disease caused by eating spoiled maize.

Pemphigus: Skin disease of watery blisters.

Pericarditis: Inflammation of heart.

Peripneumonia: Inflammation of lungs.

Peritonotis: Inflammation of abdominal area.

Petechial fever: Fever characterized by skin spotting. See typhus.

Phthiriasis: Lice infestation.

Phthisis: Chronic wasting away or a name for tuberculosis. See consumption.

Plague/Black Death: Bubonic Plague.

Pleurisy: Inflammation of the pleura, the lining of the chest cavity. Symptoms are chills, fever, dry cough, and pain in the affected side (a stitch).

Pneumonia: Inflammation of the lungs

Podagra: Gout.

Poliomyelitis: Polio.

Potter's asthma: Fibroid pthisis.

Potts Disease: Tuberculosis of the spinal vertebrae.

Pox: Syphilis.

Puerperal exhaustion: Death due to child birth.

Puerperal fever: Elevated temperature after giving birth to an infant.

Puking fever: Milk sickness.

Putrid fever: Typhus Fever, Ship Fever, Diphtheria, transmitted by the bite of fleas and lice.

Putrid sore throat: Ulceration of an acute form, attacking the tonsils.

Pyemia: Blood poisoning from pus in the blood.

Pyrexia: See dysentery.

Quinsy: An acute inflammation of the tonsils, often leading to an abscess. Synonyms: suppurative tonsillitis, cynanche tonsillaris, paristhmitis, sore throat.

Remitting fever: Malaria.

Rheumatism: Any disorder associated with paint in joints.

Rickets: Disease of skeletal system.

Rose cold: Hay fever or nasal symptoms of an allergy.

Rose-Rash: Roseola or "false measles".

Rotanny fever: Child's disease??

Rubeola: German measles.

Sanguineous crust: Scab.

Scarlatina/ Scarlet fever: A contagious disease noted by red rash.

Scarlet rash: Roseola.

Sciatica: Rheumatism in the hips.

Scirrhus: Cancerous tumors.

Scotomy: Dizziness, nausea and dimness of sight.

Scrivener's palsy: Writer's cramp.

Screws: Rheumatism.

Scrofula: Primary tuberculosis of the lymphatic glands, especially those in the neck. A disease of children and young adults. Synonym: king's evil.

Scrumpox: Skin disease, impetigo.

Scurvy: Lack of vitamin C. Symptoms of weakness, spongy gums and hemorrhages under skin.

Septic: Infected, a condition of local or generalized invasion of the body by disease-causing germs.

Septicemia: Blood poisoning.

Shakes: Delirium tremens.

Shaking: Chills, ague.

Shingles: Viral disease with skin blisters.

Ship fever: Typhus.

Siriasis: Brain inflammation due to sun exposure.

Sloes: Milk sickness.

Small pox: Contagious disease with fever and blisters.

Softening Of The Brain: cerebral hemorrhage/stroke.

Sore throat distemper: Diphtheria or quinsy.

Spanish influenza: Epidemic influenza.

Spasms: Sudden involuntary contraction of muscle or group of muscles, like a convulsion.

Spina bifida: Deformity of spine.

Spotted fever: Typhus or meningitis.

Sprue: Tropical disease characterized by intestinal disorders and sore throat.

St. Anthony's fire: Also erysipelas, but named so because of affected skin areas are bright red in appearance.

St. Vitas dance: Ceaseless occurrence of rapid complex jerking movements performed involuntary.

Stomatitis: Inflammation of the mouth.

Stranger's fever: Yellow fever.

Strangery: Rupture.

Sudor anglicus: Sweating sickness.

Summer complaint: Diarrhea, usually in infants caused by spoiled milk. See cholera infantum.

Sunstroke: Uncontrolled elevation of body temperature due to environment heat. Lack of sodium in the body is a predisposing cause.

Suppuration: The production of pus.

Swamp fever: Could be malaria, typhoid or Encephalitis.

Sweating Sickness: Infectious and fatal disease common to UK in 15th century.

Teething: The entire process which results in the eruption of the teeth. Nineteenth century medical reports stated that infants were more prone to disease at the time of teething. Symptoms were restlessness, fretfulness, convulsions, diarrhea, and painful and swollen gums. The latter could be relieved by lancing over the protruding tooth. Often teething was reported as a cause of death in infants. Perhaps they became susceptible to infections, especially if lancing was performed without antisepsis. Another explanation of teething as a cause of death is that infants were often weaned at the time of teething; perhaps they then died from drinking contaminated milk, leading to an infection, or from malnutrition if watered-down milk was given.

Tetanus: An infectious, often fatal disease caused by a specific bacterium that enters the body through wounds. Synonyms: trismus, lockjaw.

Thrombosis: Blood clot inside blood vessel.

Thrush: A disease characterized by whitish spots and ulcers on the membranes of the mouth, tongue, and fauces caused by a parasitic fungus. Synonyms: Aphthae, sore mouth Aphthous stomatitis.

Tick fever: Rocky mountain spotted fever.

Toxemis of pregnancy: Eclampsia.

Trench mouth: Painful ulcers found along gum line. Caused by poor nutrition and poor hygiene.

Trismus nascentium or neonatorum: A form of tetanus seen only in infants, almost invariably in the first five days of life.

Tussis convulsive: Whooping cough.

Typhoid fever: An infectious, often fatal disease, usually occurring in the summer months, characterized by intestinal inflammation and ulceration. The name came from the disease's similarity to typhus (see below). Synonym: Enteric fever.

Typhus: An acute, infectious disease transmitted by lice and fleas. The epidemic or classic form is louse borne; the endemic or murine is flea borne. Synonyms: typhus fever, malignant fever (in the 1850s), jail fever, hospital fever, ship fever, putrid fever, brain fever, bilious fever, spotted fever, Petechial fever, camp fever.

Variola: smallpox.

Venesection: Bleeding.

Water on brain: Enlarged head.

White swelling: Tuberculosis of the bone.

Winter Fever: pneumonia.

Womb fever: Infection of the uterus.

Worm fit: Convulsions associated with teething, worms, elevated temperature or diarrhea.

Yellow fever/Yellowjacket: An acute, often fatal, infectious disease of warm climates, caused by a virus transmitted by mosquitoes.

EPIDEMICS:
In case you ever wondered why a large number of your ancestors disappeared during a certain period in history, this might help. Epidemics have always had a great influence on people - and thus influencing, as well, the genealogists trying to trace them. Many cases of people disappearing from records can be traced to dying during an epidemic or moving away from the affected area. Some of the major epidemics in the United States are listed below.

1657 Boston: Measles
1687 Boston: Measles
1690 New York: Yellow Fever
1713 Boston: Measles
1729 Boston: Measles
1732-33 Worldwide: Influenza
1738 South Carolina: Smallpox
1739-40 Boston: Measles
1747 Conn, NY, PA & SC: Measles
1759 North America (areas inhabited by white people): Measles
1761 North America & West Indies: Influenza
1772 North America: Measles
1775 North America (especially hard in New England) - Epidemic (unknown)
1775-76 Worldwide: Influenza (one of worst flu epidemics)
1783 Delaware (Dover) "extremely fatal" bilious disorder
1788 Philadelphia & NY: Measles
1793 Vermont: Influenza and a "putrid fever"
1793 Virginia: Influenza (killed 500 people in 5 counties in 4 weeks)
1793 Philadelphia: Yellow Fever (one of worst)
1793 Pennsylvania (Harrisburg & Middletown) many unexplained deaths
1794 Philadelphia: Yellow Fever
1796-97 Philadelphia: Yellow Fever
1798 Philadelphia: Yellow Fever (one of worst)
1803 New York: Yellow Fever
1820-23 Nationwide: "fever" (starts on Schuylkill River, PA & spreads)
1831-32 Nationwide: Asiatic Cholera (brought by English emigrants)
1832 New York & other major cities: Cholera
1837 Philadelphia: Typhus
1841 Nationwide: Yellow Fever (especially severe in South)
1847 New Orleans: Yellow Fever
1847-48 Worldwide: Influenza
1848-49 North America: Cholera
1850 Nationwide: Yellow Fever
1850-51 North America: Influenza
1852 Nationwide: Yellow Fever (New Orleans 8,000 die in summer)
1855 Nationwide (many parts) Yellow Fever
1857-59 Worldwide: Influenza (one of disease's greatest epidemics)

1860-61 Pennsylvania: Smallpox

1865-73 Philadelphia, NY, Boston, New Orleans, Baltimore, Memphis & Washington DC: A series of recurring epidemics of Smallpox, Cholera, Typhus, Typhoid, Scarlet Fever & Yellow Fever

1873-75 North America & Europe: Influenza

1878 New Orleans: Yellow Fever (last great epidemic of disease)

1885 Plymouth, PA: Typhoid

1886 Jacksonville, FL: Yellow Fever

1918 Worldwide: Influenza (high point year) More people hospitalized in World War I from Influenza than wounds. US Army training camps became death camps - with 80% death rate in some camps. Finally, these specific instances of cholera were mentioned:

1833 Columbus, OH

1834 New York City

1849 New York

1851 Coles Co, IL

1851 The Great Plains

EPIDEMIC TIMELINES AND CHRONOLOGIES

Epidemics in the U.S. 1657-1918: http://people.delphi.com/pamyates/epidemic.htm

U.S. Epidemics: http://www.infoplease.com/ipa/A0001460.html

Plagues & Epidemics (from Plumber.com): http://www.theplumber.com/plague.html

Some Historically Significant Epidemics: http://www.botany.duke.edu/microbe/chrono.htm

THIS AND THAT GENEALOGY TIPS ON E-MAIL AND THE INTERNET

Attachments are a great way to exchange information via e-mail when they work. They are a great source of frustration when they do not work.

In order to open or view an attachment, you must have installed on your computer the very same software that was used by the sender to originally write the file. If you do not have the same software as the sender, you are probably not going to be able to open or view the attachment. Sometimes it will require that you not only have the same software on your computer, but it will require that it be the same version. A newer version will usually open an older version, but an older version will not open a newer version.

Te key to attachment are the extensions used, that part of the name of the file that follows the period. All files written for PCS have a file name that ends in a period and then three characters. These last three characters are called the file name extension. Every piece of computer software writes files with different extensions. In order to open/read the file will require that you have a software that writes those same extension, and in most cases that means having the very same software as the sender.

Attachments are a wonderful tool and with a little knowledge and some detailed communication they can add greatly to your genealogical research.

E-MAIL:
Unreadable e-mails are a common problem when trying to send lineage, census and other highly formatted documents via e-mail. In addition to being frustrating, it surely makes for the possibility of errors creeping in during the reconstruction. To solve the problem, you have to consider sending the information as an attached word processing file. E-mail is in ASCII (ask' ee) format, which is a stripped down character set that is supported by most software programs and platforms. There are only 254 characters in ASCII. And since everything digital takes up a character, even a period and a space, there is no tab or table, bold, underline or anything fancy in ASCII. TXT or text files are also in ASCII and will, like e-mail, destroy your formatting. Sending anything in block paragraphs works great, but when you get to formats that include tabs, tables or columns it can be very difficult to reconstruct after transmitting in ASCII. There are a couple of alternatives:

The first thing to do is to exchange available software information with the receiver. If you are each using the same word processor you can send your formatted file as an attachment in the native format of that word processor. This is the very best way to preserve the formatting you have done in your genealogy files.

The second alternative would be to send the information as an attachment in as a RFT (Rich Format Text). This is a format that has been around for several years and is supported by all of the better word processors. This will come close to having the same word processor and sending in native format.

Even if you are not using the very same software, there may still be a way to exchange the files and preserve the formatting. Most better word processors will "read/write", "open/save as" in an emulated native format of several other word processors. If you do not have the same word processor, each of you can check to see if the word processors you do have might share the ability to write/read an emulated native format that you share. In other words, if you have Microsoft Word and your recipient has a software program that will not import MS Word .DOC files but will import WordPerfect files, you can send in the emulated WordPerfect native format from your Word and the recipient will be able to open the formatted document in their word processor even though neither of your are using WordPerfect. Go into the SAVE AS on your word processor and check all the emulated formats that you word processor will save files. This is pretty much a trial and error method of exchanging files, but if all else fails it's worth a shot.

The other thing to consider, regardless of which of the three alternatives you chose is the font that you use for your genealogy information. If the recipient does not have the same font installed on his computer their word processor will substitute another font. This is not big deal, but sometimes another font will throw off formatting and make your document difficult to read. This can usually be corrected by the recipient with a little bit of difficulty. For that reason it is a good rule of thumb to use New Times Roman or Arial for all of your genealogy files. These both come with windows and any Windows user should have them.

THIS AND THAT GENEALOGY TIPS ON ENGLAND, SCOTLAND, IRELAND

ENGLAND - AMERICAN AND WEST INDIAN COLONIES BEFORE 1782:
The British colonies on the western shores of the Atlantic were founded and developed in a variety of circumstances during the seventeenth and eighteenth centuries: as a result their legal status and administrative arrangements followed no common pattern. Control by the authorities in London was seldom close and in some colonies, at some periods, almost nonexistent. Local government was generally conducted by officials of the colonies themselves, and the records thereof are preserved, if they survive, in the appropriate state archive, where any inquiry should first be pursued.

The responsible authorities in London were the Secretaries of State and the Board of Trade. Of the two Secretaries, it was the Secretary of State for the Southern Department who was primarily, if not exclusively, charged with the oversight of colonial administrations, except for the period between 1768 and 1782, when a third Secretary of State, the Colonial or American Secretary, was appointed. For much executive action, advice and routine administration, however, the Secretaries were dependent on the Lords of Trade and Plantations, commonly known as the Board of Trade. The Board was founded in 1696 to succeed a variety of bodies with similar titles and overlapping jurisdictions which had existed at various periods since 1660. Its functions were originally purely advisory, but came in time to include much of the administration of the colonies, and to its offices at Plantations House were addressed many of the papers now in the Public Record Office.

PRINTED GUIDES:
The prime source of information about the records held in the Public Record Office is C M Andrews Guide to the Materials for American History to 1783 in the Public Record Office (2 vols, Carnegie Institution, Washington, 1912). Some of the references given are now obsolete, but can be keyed to those in current use.

A complete history of the records with guidance on their use, giving the references in their modern form, is to be found in R. D. B Pugh The Records of the Colonial and Dominions Offices, (PRO Handbook No 3, HMSO 1964).

Documents in the Public Record Office and elsewhere not mentioned by Andrews are described in B R Crick and M Alman eds. A Guide to Manuscripts Relating to America in Great Britain and Ireland (Mansell Publishing 1961) a revised edition of which has been prepared by John W. Raimo and published, under the same title, by Meckler Books/Mansell Publishing (1979).

Documents relating to the Caribbean are noted in H C Bell, D W. Parker and others Guide to British West Indian Archive Materials, in London and in the Islands, for the History of the United States (Carnegie Institution, Washington 1926); and P Walne ed. A Guide to Manuscript Sources for the History of Latin America and the Caribbean in the British Isles (Oxford University Press, 973).

PRINTED TEXTS:
The texts or abstracts of many documents from 1574 to 1738 can be found in Calendar of State Papers Colonial (HMSO, 1859 onwards).

Documents of the period from 1770 to 1783 are being similarly published as K G Davies ed. The Documents of the American Revolution (21 vols to date, Irish University Press 1972 onwards).

ARRANGEMENT OF THE RECORDS:
The arrangement of the earlier records does not reflect the respective roles of the Secretary of State and the Board of Trade. The class Colonial Papers: General Series (CO 1) was brought together by W N Sainsbury, first editor of the Calendar of State Papers Colonial: it contains, in chronological order, all the papers printed in the Calendar and dated not later than 1688, the original terminal date of the publication.

From 1688, and in a few instances before, until 1807, the records relating to the American colonies are combined in America and West Indies: Original Correspondence etc (CO 5). The records are arranged by colony: Carolina (Propriety);

North Carolina;
South Carolina;
Connecticut;
East Florida;
West Florida;
Georgia;
Maryland;
Massachussets;
New England (Massachussets, Rhode Island, New Hampshire and Pennsylvania);
New Hampshire;
New Jersey;
New York;
Pennsylvania;
Rhode Island;
Virginia and the Proprieties (including the Bahamas, Carolina, Connecticut, Maryland, East and West New Jersey, Pennsylvania and Rhode Island).

In spite of its title, the class does not include records of the colonies of Canada and the West Indies and includes only one, the Bahamas, which did not come to form part of the United States.

For each colony there are five main types of record: the Original Correspondence with the Secretary of State and with the Board of Trade; Entry Books of both; collections of Acts, and of Sessional Papers, of the colonial legislature. In addition there are for some colonies Naval Officers' Returns of shipping, collections of land grants and other materials, and military and naval dispatches. Documents concerned with Indian affairs and other, more general matters, are arranged in separate series.

The records concerned with:

Antigua and Montserrat;

Bahamas;

Barbados;

Bermuda;

former French colony of Canada;

Dominica;

Grenada;

British Honduras;

Hudson's Bay;

Jamaica;

Leeward Islands (including Antigua, St Kitts, Montserrat, Nevis and the Virgin Islands);

Montserrat;

Nevis;

Newfoundland;

Nova Scotia and Cape Breton Island;

Prince Edward Island;

St Kitts;

St Lucia;

St Vincent;

Tobago;

Trinidad; and

Virgin Islands

are arranged in the same way, but each series forms a separate class. The class numbers are listed by Pugh and Andrews and can also readily be identified in the Current Guide in the Reference Room.

Some records deal with matters concerning the Colonies in general. They are in the classes:

Colonies General: Original Correspondence
CO 323

Entry Books
CO 324

Board of Trade: Original Correspondence
CO 388

Board of Trade: Entry Books
CO 389

Board of Trade: Miscellaneous
CO 390

The class Board of Trade: Minutes (CO 391) includes the Journal of the Board of Trade. Entries before April 1704 appear in the Calendar of State Papers Colonial, and those for the period April 1704 to May 1782 in:

Journal of the Commissioners for Trade and Plantations (14 vols HMSO 1920-1928).

ORIGINAL CORRESPONDENCE:
There are collections of reports and papers from, and orders and instructions to, the responsible officials in each colony, especially the governors. The correspondence of the Secretaries of State and the Board of Trade are in separate sequences. Each contains not only correspondence with the colonies but also with other officials and private individuals in the United Kingdom and between the Secretary of State and the Board.

From 1703 to 1759 manuscript calendars of the correspondence of the Board with each colony were compiled: these are in General Registers (CO 326) pieces 1 to 51.

From 1759 to 1782 a single, annual, calendar was prepared for all colonies: this series is CO 326 pieces 52-74.

ENTRY BOOKS:
These are letter books containing copies of dispatches, letters, reports, petitions, commissions and instructions, either in full or in abstract. Before 1700 papers received as well as papers despatched are noted.

The Entry Books served as the primary record of outgoing correspondence, in particular royal commission, instructions and warrants: they were not intended as means of reference to the correspondence as a whole.

ACTS AND SESSIONAL PAPERS:
Copies, either printed or in manuscript, of the Acts and proceedings of colonial councils and legislatures were forwarded to the Board of Trade, having been approved, or rejected, by the Privy Council. Other copies were retained in the colony itself where, as a rule, they are still to be found.

NAVAL OFFICERS' RETURNS:
The Naval Officers were officials of the Board, in practice usually Customs Officers acting in a second capacity, and they discharged certain statutory duties under the Navigation Acts. They compiled lists of the merchantmen entering and clearing their ports: these returns, at their fullest, give dates, the names of master and vessel, tonnage, when and where built, whence and whither bound, and the nature, consignor and consignee of the cargo. Only a proportion of the lists survive: comparable records can also be found in Treasury Board Papers (T 1) and Miscellaneous (BT 6).

MILITARY AND NAVAL DISPATCHES:
The dispatches collected in CO 5 relate mainly to fighting against the French and various Indian tribes, which could not conveniently be divided by colony.

Original Correspondence: West Indies (CO 318) also contains some military dispatches. The majority of records concerning naval operations will be found among the ADM classes in the Public Record Office, and many concerning military operations, including a proportion removed from the papers of the Secretary of State and the Board of Trade, are in the WO classes. A detailed index to these papers is given in Alphabetical Guide to the War Office and other Classes (PRO List and Index Series vol LIII, HMSO 1931; reprinted by Kraus Thomson Organization 1963).

TREASURY AND CUSTOMS RECORD:
The extensive and varied records of the Treasury contain much material relating to the colonies: all have been mentioned by Andrews in volume II. Those records of the Board of Customs which survived a fire in 1814, chiefly statistics of trade, are likewise described by Andrews in the same volume.

LAND GRANTS:
In early colonial America the ownership of the land was considered to be vested in the Crown by right of discovery and settlement by its subjects. The Crown granted land to companies and to proprietors to organize settlements and also to some individual subjects as a reward for services. The matter is more fully described in O T Barck Jr. and H T Lefler Colonial America (Collier 1968)

The system whereby recipients of royal grants in turn gave or sold land varied. In some colonies, notably in New England, the legislatures established by the colonists assumed jurisdiction over the allocation of company lands. They made some direct grants to individuals for 'adventuring' money in the companies, but the greater part went to groups or communities to establish townships and to apportion the surrounding land.

In the southern counties, the 'headright' system of land distribution was the most common method followed during the seventeenth century. An individual who provided transport to the colony for any immigrant was thereby entitled to at least fifty acres of land. During the same period, however, larger tracts were given by the Crown, the proprietor or the company to favorites, to those who performed outstanding service to the company or, as in Maryland, to those who transported five or more persons to the colony. The 'headright' system led to many frauds and abuses, and by the early years of the eighteenth century most of the land was distributed by purchase or by taking out a patent signed by the governor of the colony for new, unpatented land.

Although grants were nominally made in the name of the Crown, most were made and recorded locally rather than in London. Of those grants which were reported to the Secretary of State or the Board of Trade no index exists. However, many are noted in Andrews and in the Calendar of State Papers Colonial.

INDIAN AFFAIRS:
There are collections of papers concerning Indian affairs in general, and relating to large tribes and confederacies not dwelling in any one colony in CO 5. The class includes some treaties, but there is no index to them and no easy means of locating those not mentioned by Andrews or in the Calendar.

OTHER RECORDS:
Separate leaflets are available on request on the service records of officers and men of the British Forces serving in the Army, Navy and Royal Marines; on emigre loyalists, on emigration and on merchant shipping records (Registrar General of Shipping and Seamen).

SCOTLAND:
"My Ain Folk: An Easy Guide to Scottish Family History",. by Graham S. Holton and Jack Winch. paperback, 150 pp. Available from Barnes & Noble @ $5.98 Includes info on accessing public records, using the Internet, etc.

Scottish Groups website pages at: http://www.homestead.com/scottishresearchgroup/sfrg.html

Scottish Names Research website: http://www.spiderweb.com.au/~frasbett

IRELAND:
To find out what county your family came from in Ireland, go to: http://www.goireland.com/Genealogy

If you are looking for townland names in Ireland - here is a large database for you. The URL is: http://www.seanruad.com/ and if you enter a county name and the province its in, you will get a huge file containing Townland name, what that townland is also know as (AKA), how many acres of land it covers, which Barony its in, which Parish its in and the name of the Poor Law Union. If you ask it to sort your request by Barony name - that will cut down on the file size by a great deal.

A great article on genealogy research travel to Ireland is available at: http://globalgazette.net/gazkb/gazkb39.htm

THIS AND THAT GENEALOGY TIPS ON EUROPE

JEWISH SURNAMES:
Visit these sites: Consolidated Jewish Surname Index: http://www.avotaynu.com/csi/csi-home.html for a database of more than 200,000 Jewish surnames found in 23 different sources. Key in the surname and the system will display all surnames that have the same Soundex code as the name you are searching. The Soundex system used is the Daitch-Mokotoff Soundex system which is used in all Jewish genealogical databases and is gaining popularity in genealogical circles in general.

E-mail the JewishGen webmaster at webmasters@jewishgen.org

Next to each spelling variant of the name are up to 23 codes which identify which of the sources contain the surname. Scroll down for a description of each source and a Web link to additional information about the source.

Some other valuable research tools include:

-- JewishGen Family Finder. This is a searchable database on the Internet which lists more than 25,000 Jewish surnames being researched by some 12,000 genealogists worldwide. It you get a hit, the JewishGen site will give you the postal and/or e-mail address of the submitter.

-- "Dictionary of Jewish Surnames from the Russian Empire" and "Dictionary of Jewish Surnames from the Kingdom of Poland." These two books list more than 80,000 different Jewish surnames from czarist Russia at the turn of the century. It includes the names etymology, where in the empire the name appeared, and all known variants of the name. If you are non-Jewish with ancestors from the Russian Empire, if the name in not in either of these books, it is unlikely the surname is Jewish.

-- "First American Jewish Families." This book attempted to document all descendants of Jews who arrived in the U.S. prior to 1838. If you have colonial ancestors who you think may have been Jewish and the surname is not in the book, do not be disappointed. There is some evidence the book may have only captured half the possible people. In addition, the author did not include any Jews who came to America and brought up their children as non-Jewish; there had to be at least one generation of Jewish-Americans in the family.

-- "Gedenkbuch." For non-Jews trying to determine if their German ancestors were Jewish, it is a good source of German-Jewish surnames. The book's origin is steeped in tragedy. The Gedenkbuch is a list of 128,000 German Jews murdered in the Holocaust. From a genealogical standpoint, it can be thought of as a list of virtually all German-Jewish surnames (about 25% of the Jews of Germany were murdered during this period). If your surname is not in the list, it is unlikely your ancestor is Jewish.

For non-Jewish researchers, be cautious of the source of information; a few databases include non-Jewish surnames. For example, the Jewish Genealogical People Finder is a database of Jewish family trees. Clearly it includes non-Jewish persons who married Jews. Similarly, "First American Jewish Families" noted above, is also a database of family trees that definitely includes non-Jewish surnames (many of the earliest Jewish families assimilated into the Christian American environment).

Another consideration is that many surnames are shared by Jews and non-Jews alike. The origins of surnames are often occupations or place names, either of which can occur in families independent of religion. The third most common Jewish surname in the United States (Cohen and Levy are the first two) is Miller.

Gary Mokotoff is the publisher of "Avotaynu, the International Review of Jewish Genealogy" - http://www.avotaynu.com or send e-mail to info@avotaynu.com - co-author of "Where Once We Walked: A Guide to the Jewish Communities Destroyed in the Holocaust" and "How to Document Victims and Locate Survivors of the

Holocaust," co-author of the Daitch-Mokotoff Soundex Code, and creator of numerous databases of interest to Jewish and Eastern European genealogists, including the Jewish Genealogical Family Finder, Jewish Genealogical People Finder, and the Consolidated Jewish Surname Index.

INTERNATIONAL REPLY COUPONS:

When writing to someone outside of the United States, IRC coupons are usually sent to cover the cost of replying to your letter. You can't send them U.S. stamps as they are unacceptable for postage in other countries. IRCs are issued by the Universal Postal Union (UPU) in Bern, Switzerland and one coupon can be exchanged in any post office in the world (except South Africa) for stamps sufficient to reply to your letter by surface mail. However, it usually takes three IRCs to cover the cost of air mail postage. IRCs can only be applied against the cost of overseas postage, one coupon per mailing and they are fast becoming useless for replies because of restrictions placed upon them. The cost of a "Standardbrief" (standard-weight [air mail] letter from Germany is now DM 3.00. Two IRCs, exchanged at DM 2.00 each, would have been more than sufficient, with change in stamps for the DM 1.00 overage. Under the restricted application that now apply, a correspondent in Germany not only can not get stamps in change any longer, but has to pay DM 1.00 in order to come up with a total of DM 3.00 in postage. IRCs cost Americans $1.05 each, and are available at full-service post offices throughout the country.

Alternatives to IRC might be - when writing to Europe, if it's an official agency such as an archive or government office, don't send money, either for anticipated services or for postage. In your initial inquiry ask to be billed and request the cost of mailing and handling be included in the invoice.

If you are writing to a private party, parish offices, etc., send a small amount of cash $2.00 or $3.00 to cover postage.

CELTIC LANGUAGES AND CULTURE:
  Gaelic and Gaelic Culture: http://sunsite.unc.edu/gaelic/
  Gaelic Language: http://link.bubl.ac.uk/gaelic
  Gaelic-English Dictionary: http://www.sst.ph.ic.ac.uk/angus/Faclair/
  Scots: http://www.snda.org.uk/scothist.htm
  Scottish Gaelic Language: http://www.editpros.com/scottish.html

LESS COMMON LANGUAGE RESOURCES: http://www.susx.ac.uk/langc/others.html
Among the links at this site are The Abyssinia CyberSpace Gateway (resources for Ethiopia, Eritrea, Somali/Somaliland, and Djibouti); The WWW Virtual Library: Middle East Studies; Al-Mashriq -- Levant Cultural Multimedia Services (Arabic); two Basque Web pages; Belarusian dictionary; Bengali; Bulgarian Electronic Resources; Catalan language lessons; Cheyenne (with links to other Native American languages); Croatian language; Dutch newspapers; Esperanto; Finnish language; Gaelic; Greek (modern Greek language lessons through the Internet); Hebrew, a Living Language; How to View Hebrew on the Internet (including special Web Hebrew fonts); Hungarian language course online; Icelandic language page and Icelandic phrases (with audio); major Indian languages; Korean through English (online tutorials); Medieval Latin; Old English; Portuguese (online beginner's course); Culture of the Andes (songs, stories, poems, and jokes in Quechua with translations in Spanish and English, with audio); Kiswahili (lessons, grammar, links to more Internet resources); The Internet Living Swahili Dictionary (with pronunciation and grammar guides); Introduction to Swedish (with English-Swedish dictionary); Swedish Lessons from Uppsala University; Learning Practical Turkish, for example, business, computing, and culinary terms (with RealAudio); Welsh language course from Brown University (includes dictionaries, a spellchecker, and links to more Welsh resources on the Internet); an online Welsh grammar at Brighton University; and The Virtual Shtetl (Yiddish language and culture).

FREE TRANSLATION SERVICE:
Genealogy Exchange & Surname Registry site has a list of Free Volunteer Genealogy translators! There are many languages available, including German to English. The URL for Genealogy Exchange & Surname Registry: http://www.genexchange.com/index.cfm

There is a free automated translator of plain texts. Copy and paste or type your text into the input box, set the translator from foreign language to English or whatever you desire and hit the "translate" button. The translation comes back in the box above the input box. It does not reformat syntax perfectly, and sometimes it mistranslates words (e.g., the surname "Zulauf" gets translated "inlet"). When this automated translator knows it cannot translate a word, it leaves that word in the original language. Go to: http://babelfish.altavista.digital.com/cgi

RESEARCH WEBPAGES:
http://www.CyndisList.com/   (Cyndi Howell's Genealogy Links list)

http://www.jewishgen.org/ShtetlSeeker/loctown.htm (Town locator for West Europe)

http://www.geocities.com/Heartland/Plains/2739/   (Kaj Malachowski's homepage)

http://hum.amu.edu.pl/~rafalp/GEN/gen-eng.html   (Genealogical information by Rafal Prinke)

http://www.rand.org/personal/Genea/   (Rand genealogy club)

THIS AND THAT GENEALOGY TIPS ON GEDCOMS

Not sure what a GEDCOM is? GEDCOM is the acronym for GEnealogical Data COMmunication, created by the Church of Jesus Christ of Latter-day Saints (Mormons) to facilitate the exchange of genealogical data among different software programs. A GEDCOM is a text file that is created automatically in a special format from information that is in a genealogical software program's database -- no need to rekey. Most, but not all, genealogical software programs have GEDCOM capability. For more information, see: http://helpdesk.rootsweb.com/help/wc2.html#1

GEDCOM - HOW TO READ IT - HOW TO USE IT:
GEDCOM was originally designed by the LDS Church for their PAF (Personal Ancestral File) Program. It is the international language that allows my Personal Ancestral File to talk to your Family Tree Maker, Family Origins, Roots, or Brother's Keeper.

Hopefully I can help you learn how to upload it, how to download it and if in a compressed state (.zip) how to uncompress it and if received in .txt format, how to convert it. Important to remember is that if you are going to receive these via e-mail , the person sending must send in the same format that you use (for instance IBM-compatible PCS use MIME while Macintosh use Bin-Hex).

It is a good idea to tell the person sending this GEDCOM to you what you use. I use PAF 2.31 so my instructions may not work exactly the same for you if you use some other application. If you use something else, please tell me how you do it.....

MAKE A GEDCOM:
Most genealogy programs have the capability of making a GEDCOM, and when created it always ends in .ged extension (i.e. hornbeck.ged). To create a GEDCOM, open your genealogy program and look in the menus for GEDCOM, GIE, EXPORT or SAVE AS or FILE - SAVE AS. You should have an option to make and export and save a GED or GEDCOM file. You will also have an option to select the drive you want it placed in, the directory you want it placed in, and an opportunity to give it a different name.

TO SEND A GEDCOM:
Prepare your GEDCOM and either save it to a floppy or somewhere on your hard drive where you can find it.

Then, write a NEW message to the person you want to send the .ged file to. Do not hit REPLY to send this file.

On your tool bar in your mail application, you will have an item "ATTACH FILE". Hit this and then send it. It should arrive as a .ged file not as text - however if it does, give them the following instructions on how to use it.

RECEIVE A GEDCOM:
When I receive a GEDCOM, whether by E-mail or by snail mail on disk, and it is a ---.ged file, the first thing I do it make a subdirectory in my PAF directory called "TEMP". I then transfer the - - --.ged to that directory and proceed to convert it to FR following instruction in PAF on how to do that.

These instructions are for PAF so if you use some other genealogy application, you may have to experiment a little. After you receive an attachment by e-mail as a .txt file or the text is embedded in the e-mail itself, here is one of the easy ways to use it.

1. If it came embedded in the e-mail message as text, then in your mail application such as Eudora, which is what I use, go to FILE and click SAVE AS and save the message to a TEMP directory. If you don't have a TEMP directory, make one. You will use it often for lots of things (I have a C, D, E, F hard drives and I have TEMP directory in all of them). If the GEDCOM came as an attachment and is already in your ATTACHMENT directory

go to #2.

2. If it came as a .ged file, you can skip this part. If it came as a .txt file or embedded in the e-mail, go to File Manager or Windows Explorer and find the file in your TEMP directory. Open it by double-clicking on it.

3. If there is anything before HEAD and after TRLR, delete it being, careful not to delete TRLR itself.

4. Click on FILE and SAVE AS to a floppy disk in A drive renaming it so it ends in .ged instead of .txt.

5. Assuming you have your genealogy application set up for multiple family record directories, make a new directory for this GEDCOM naming it whatever you like.

6. Move the .ged file to the directory you just created.

7. Now follow the directions in your genealogy program to convert this GEDCOM into family records.

If you receive a GEDCOM file that is split between two or more files, one with .ged as the extension and the others with .G00, .G01, G02, etc. - there are several ways to use these files. If it arrived through e-mail and the first .ged file is embedded in a message, you must follow instructions above to open and get rid of the text before HEAD and after TRLR in the first file. It is easy to work with these files if you put each one on a different floppy. Following your application's instructions, proceed to start the conversion to family records. It will ask for the next file (.G00) so insert that disk, then .G01, .G02, etc.

If you receive this file as a .zip file, go to File Manager and move it to a TEMP directory. Double click on it and unzip it to that same directory. It probably will be one or more .ged files. Follow instructions above on what to do next.

DO NOT ADD THE GEDCOM TO YOUR OWN FAMILY RECORDS FILE UNTIL AFTER YOU HAVE VIEWED IT TO SEE WHAT YOU HAVE. AND before you add it to your own family record files, first make a GEDCOM of your files, or back them up, SO IF SOMETHING GOES WRONG, YOU CAN GET BACK TO WHERE YOU WERE!

If you are using PAF 2.31 or PAF 3 and have either Word Perfect or WORD, you can use the application called GEN-BOOK to generate a booklet. After you have entered your Family History data into your genealogy software, GEN-BOOK can read your data directly from Personal Ancestral File (PAF 2.31/3.0), or Ancestral Quest (AQ) and generate a BOOK. GEN-BOOK can read a GEDCOM file from Family Tree Maker (FTM), Brothers Keeper (BK), Reunion, Family Origins (FO), Roots, The Master Genealogist (TMG), or any other genealogy software that will make a GEDCOM file. GEN-BOOK can extract the information and format it into a WordPerfect or WORD file. Your family history information is put into readable book format along with a Title Page, Table of Contents, Chapter Headings, event notes, sources, and a two- or three-column Index of Names. You can generate a book of the descendants or ancestors of any person in your database. This program allows beginners to prepare a completely indexed and organized book from their genealogy data by only answering a few personal choice questions such as the starting person and the number of generations to be included. For the advanced users, the capabilities of WordPerfect or MS Word offers unlimited manipulation and design of text to create the masterpiece you have always wanted to create. Then I print out the book (if it is not too many pages) and enter the data manually into my PAF files. I never add the GEDCOM directly into my records. There are many options to GEN-BOOK including making an Index but it does NOT index your notes. You must index your notes manually. GEN-BOOK has a home page at: http://www.foothill.net/~genbook/

For those using PAF 4 - you can purchase Companion directly from LDS and generate a book using that application. I have not yet done this so can't offer suggestions.

IBM AND MAC GEDCOMS - BY Ben H. Lashbaugh at howe@nccn.net:
My nephew and I both work in Family Tree Maker -- he on a PC and I on a Mac -- and the method of transferring GEDCOM files is MUCH simpler than you describe, at least on the Mac end.

In Family Tree Maker, in order to convert an .ftw file to a .ged file, all you have to do is Copy/Export Family File and save it in GEDCOM format --that's one of the selections you get. The file can then be sent as an e-mail attachment. (I have never tried incorporating it into e-mail because it would lose most or all of its formatting.)

Then, after receiving the file as an e-mail (Eudora) attachment, all I have to do to open it is to have Family Tree Maker open and go to the File menu, select Open Family File, and locate the new GEDCOM file which I now find in the Eudora Attachments folder. It's that simple. FTM automatically converts the GEDCOM file and you can save it wherever you want as an .ftw file.

An option from John Nairn - John.Nairn@kagi.com for working with GEDCOM files for Power Macintosh users is to get a copy of the new genealogy application called GEDitCOM. This applications can be downloaded from: http://www.xmission.com/~geditcom/ - it is available free as a GEDCOM file viewer and shareware as a GEDCOM file editor. Unlike most commercial packages, GEDitCOM uses GEDCOM as its internal data standard. Thus you never "import" and "export" GEDCOM files, you simply read them, make changes, and save them again. GEDitCOM is 100% compatible with all feature of GEDCOM. Thus, there is never any possibility of GEDCOM data getting lost or corrupted. Note, although many commercial programs claim to be GEDCOM compatible, they actually are only partially compatible. It is common for importing procedures to ignore GEDCOM data, misinterpret unusual GEDCOM data structures, or misfile data in generic note records.

Besides GEDitCOM being 100% compatible with GEDCOM, the entire user interface of GEDitCOM is customizable by the user. No one has to settle for the rigid forms and data entry methods provided by typical commercial packages. You can create your own genealogy interface and you can even switch interfaces at will depending on your needs that day.

GEDCOM UTILITIES:
See Randy Winch's page GEDCOM Utilities - http://www.rootsweb.com/~gumby/ged.html - The following utilities are available for download:

GEDSplit.exe - Windows 95 program to split any GEDCOM file in useful ways GEDSplit help file .

Analyze.exe - Windows 95 command line program to display the unconnected individuals in any GEDCOM file.

GEDPlace.exe - Allows editing of places in a GEDCOM file.

Addnote.exe Windows 95 Beta version - addnote.exe - Adds a user specified note to each individual in a GEDCOM file.

Addsour.exe Windows 95 Beta version - addsour.exe - Adds a user specified source to each individual in a GEDCOM file.

Gedcaps.exe Windows 95 Beta Version - changes the capitalization of names and/or places in a GEDCOM file.

gedcaps.exe - Changes the capitalization of the surnames in a GEDCOM file. Can convert to/from uppercase.

GEDLivng.exe Native Windows 95 version 16 bit gedlivng.exe (runs in a dos box or at the dos prompt) 32 bit gedlivng.exe (Must run in a Windows 95/NT dos box) Privatizes a GEDCOM file. (beta testing)

THIS AND THAT GENEALOGY TIPS ON GERMANY

UMLAUT:
A "double dot over a letter". The double-dot (called a diuresis; the letter-symbol combination is called an umlaut) is the correct, German way of writing the word; the ue, oe or ae letter combinations are a way of representing the umlaut in non-Germanic alphabets which lack the umlauts.

DOUBLE "S":
The English equivalent of the character that looks like "B" embedded in names is actually a separate character in German that stands for a double s as "ss".

GERMAN SURNAME SUFFIXES FOR FEMALES- from Carla Heller - carlah@earthlink.net:
" A special suffix comprised of the letters "-in" is often seen in old German records, added to the surnames of females, and is simply a German language grammatical practice which feminizes the name in question. When you see the "-in" suffix added to a German surname, it is intended to demonstrate that the surname was borne by a female.

"When the "-in" suffix is added in this way, it DOES NOT MATERIALLY CHANGE the existing surname itself. If you see your female ancestor denoted as "Katharina SCHNEIDERIN," for example, Katharina's actual surname would still be SCHNEIDER for all intents and purposes in your research. It is also important to note that the use of the feminine suffix on a surname in German DOES *NOT* INDICATE whether the female was unmarried or married. It was used for BOTH single and married females, identically.

"This is a standard, centuries-old German grammar practice, more common to old records than current ones. Since, unlike English, every noun has a GENDER in German, the use of the feminizing suffix for surnames of females was in keeping with the structure of that language. Even today, German grammar still adds the letters "-in" to the end of feminine NOUNS, such as "Freundin," meaning "female friend" ("Freund" being "male friend"), and "Lehrerin," meaning "female teacher" ("Lehrer" being "male teacher.")

"Note that while this suffix commonly occurred in earlier centuries, it was NOT used UNIVERSALLY throughout Germany---you may find German records which completely OMIT the use of the suffix for feminine surnames. Some researchers will never encounter this form. The use in German of the feminizing "-in" suffix on surnames of females has greatly diminished in modern times."

OTHER HELPFUL INFORMATION:
EVANGELISCHE in Germany means virtually the same as "Lutheran" (followers of Martin Luther), but in Switzerland "Evangelische" means virtually the same as "Reformed" (followers of Zwingly and Calvin). Historically, in both of these areas "Evangelische" was a term adopted by the Reformers to distinguish their "Protestant" positions from that of the Roman Catholic Church which they were opposing.

LANDKREIS/KREIS:
Landkreis, short just "Kreis" is the administrative body one notch above "village" or "town".

From the top to the bottom:
(a) Country, like "Kingdom of Prussia"
(b) State or Province, like "Provinz Posen" or older "Departement Posen".
© Gubernatorial (or: Administrative) District (This has no equivalent in the USA administrative organization), like "Regie-rungsbezirk Bromberg"
(d) County, like "Landkreis Meseritz" or just "Kreis Meseritz"
(e) Town, Township or Village, like "Stadt Betsche"

A 'Kreis' is, in essence, a county. It literally is a 'circle or ring' and refers to 'sphere' of influence. It is usually translated very generically as 'district', but with Prussian 'administrative districts' being comprised of several Kreise, it gets confusing to refer to them as districts.

It is getting very confusing when using "district" as a translation for "Kreis", especially when you look at the current German structure, were "Gubernatorial District" (Regierungsbezirk) is the next bigger administrative government level above the county level, but one level below the state level.

When you deal with former East Germany, the confusion will be total, as the "Deutsche Demokratische Republik" abolished the states and was organized in subdivisions of Bezirke (Districts), which in turn were subdivided into Kreise.

So, never ever use "district" as a translation for "Kreis" or for "Landkreis". I've heard purists claim that they are not really counties, but in that they are the smallest district that includes several towns. Those purists are WRONG. If and when several tiny villages join forces administratively, they are not called "Distrikt", but "Verbandsgemeinde". The closest thing in the USA to a Verbandsgemeinde in Germany would be a Township, like the Township of Ulysses in upstate New York, which you won't find in Rand McNally, but instead of Ulysses, you find the "member towns", like Trumansburg and others. Administratively, Verbandsgemeinden kind of merged their administration. Instead of a Town House, a Mayor, a Vital Statistics Officer, a Comptroller, a ... for each of the let's say ten hamlets, they only need one of each. The advantage: Monetary savings, and some of the hamlets in Verbandsgemeinden are so small, that the tax revenue just would not suffice to pay all the salaries, not to think of financing the public service tasks.

Whenever you check a phone book server and find an address, in which the town is hyphenated, chances are, that you look at a Verbandsgemeinde. The first word before the hyphen is the Verbandsgemeinde-name, the part after the hypen is the original name of the hamlet. In more recent times, with the new postal code often discerning a location down to an eighth of a square mile, the original village name is omitted. But there are still some of the hyphenated ones out there. Like "Modautal-Hoxhohl", which has about 250 residents, while the whole Verbandsgemeinde Modautal (a merger of 10 formerly independent villages) has 4,450 residents ... "Modautal" in this example is the name of the Verbandsgemeinde, "Hoxhohl" is the original name of the village.

Some Landkreise in modern Germany even go by their antiquated name. When you talk COUNTY in English, you have good reason to expect that County to be ruled by a Count. Actually, some of the German petty states somehow managed to keep their borders intact as county lines, and also to preserve their ancient name.

English .... "Count" = German "Graf"; English (British, that is) "County" = German "Grafschaft.

A handful of counties in Germany not go by "Kreis such-and-such", but as "Grafschaft such-and-such", like "Grafschaft Hoya" which actually is a Landkreis. And (at least) one goes by the formal name of "Landschaftsverband". But I don't think, that with civic administration in the Prussian province of Posen, one would encounter anything other than:

(basic level)   "Dorf (or) Stadt (or) Gemeinde"
(county level)   "Kreis" or "Landkreis"
(regional level)   "Regierungsbezirk" or "Bezirk" in the
(provincial level) "Provinz" or "Departement" Posen of the
(country level)   "Koenigreich Preussen"

The "Grenzmark Posen-Westpreussen", that pops up for a few years in this century is "provincial level", and it was uniting the little that was left of the former provinces Westpreussen and Posen into one administrative body.

I think the translation as 'county' is accurate. They are perhaps smaller than most US counties. I'm not real sure what a township is, but I think the typical Kreis would be of a larger scale.

It is not exactly "accurate", but it is the closest you can get, if you consider, that some of the administrative tasks performed by counties in the USA, are performed at town (Dorf, Gemeinde, Stadt) level in Germany.

(Posted originally as a reply from Siegfried Rambaum to James Birkholz as a follow-up to an article in the Posen-L mailing list). Siegfried Rambaum - siram@lightlink.com

GENEALOGICAL INQUIRIES AT THE BADEN ARCHIVES - From Bruce NOE, brucenoe@cybercable.tm.fr
- Baden Archives in Karlsruhe - Below is a translation of the bulletin of the Generallandesarchiv Karlruhe (Archives for the former state of Baden) regarding genealogical inquiries:

The research of a family history is a common request of many who turn to the State Archive either in writing or in person. However, unrealistic wishes and expectations often exist regarding the sources available, the means of help, and the archive personnel. Therefore, this introductory overview should show you the possibilities and limits of genealogical inquiries at the State Archive. It should first be noted that the State Archive has no extensive and complete name indexes, the archival records are rarely arranged according to names, and the archivists cannot within the framework of their service devote themselves to genealogical tasks or genealogical inquiries.

The State Archive stores written and printed material of the state authorities or its predecessors from the territories within the boundaries of the state of Baden as it existed before 1945. A general survey is presented in the "Gesamtübersicht der Bestände des Generallandesarchives Karlsruhe" [An Overview of the Holdings of the State Archive in Karlsruhe], edited by Manfred Krebs (Stuttgart 1954/57). A revision of this publication of 10 volumes is in the progress; 3 volumes (1988-1992) are now available. Therefore, we have, with a few exceptions (areas west of the Rhine in Pfalz, the Speyer Seminary and the Margrave of Baden), neither documents of areas outside of Baden nor documents which resulted from cities, municipalities (e.g. citizen books, civil protocols) or churches (e.g. church books before 1810). The publication "Minerva Handbuch. Archive im deutschprachigen Raum" [Minerva Handbook. Archives in German-speaking Territories] (2nd Ed., Berlin/New York 1974) gives an overview of the other archives which are responsible for other domains.

Before you undertake genealogical research in the archival records, you should always consult the available literature. This is not only good advice for methodic research, but in some cases you may benefit from information which has already been researched. Genealogical publications and genealogical journals, local family history books and emigrant lists are a few worth mentioning. Furthermore, there are source publications which are also suitable for genealogical evaluations such as document books, indexes, periodicals and guides.

Finally, there are name lists for official purposes such as directories or state manuals. Full descriptions of literature and source publications are found in the "Handbuch der Genealogie" [Handbook of Genealogy], edited by Eckart Henning and Wolfgang Ribbe (Neustadt A.D.A., 1972). The publications of this kind, which deal specifically with Baden, are listed in the "Bibliographie der Badischen Geschichte" [Bibliography of the History of Baden], edited by Friedrich Lautenschlager and Werner Schulz (Karlsruhe/Stuttgart 1929-1984), and additionally in the "Landesbibliographie von Baden-Württemberg" [State Bibliography of Baden-Wuerttemberg], edited by Werner Schulz and Guenter Stegmaier (Stuttgart 1978 ff.). These can be found in the reading rooms of the state libraries in Karlsruhe and Stuttgart.

Probably the most important sources for genealogical research are the church books. They contain the data for births and/or christenings, marriages and deaths. They mention parents of a child to be baptized or the origin of the people to be married or of the deceased. Between 1810 and 1870, the clergy of Baden had to maintain the church books as civil documents of the citizenry and every year deliver duplicates to the district officials. These duplicates for all municipalities of the contemporary government district (only 1810 - 1870!) of Baden are today stored with us here in Karlsruhe. The duplicates for the government district of Freiberg are in the State Archive of Freiberg, Colombistr. 4, 79098 Freiberg. The originals of these church books and the earlier (before 1810) and more recent church books (after 1870) are normally at the individual clergyman's offices of the respective denomination or the Archiepiscopal Archive, Herrenstr. 35, 79098 Freiberg and/or the Evangelic Church Archive, Blumenstr. 1, 76133 Karlsruhe. You can find a list of the surviving church books in the book by Hermann Franz, "Die Kirchenbücher in Baden" [The Church Books in Baden] (3rd Ed., Karlsruhe 1957). Before you resort to other sources, you should make the most of the church books since they are the only source which contains the complete information which makes it possible to trace a family from generation to generation.

The written information in the archives resulted from the "administrative course of events". Regarding family research, that means that information about individual persons is only available as far as the person came in contact in some way with the "authorities". Only in the rarest cases will you find all of the desired data mentioned in the source. The references are mostly limited to the mention of a name.

Within this constraint, archival sources for genealogical research offer the possibility to go back into the 14 or 15th century, when the use of surnames emerged in the civil proceedings. Early written records are only sparse. Moreover, their evaluation presupposes a considerable scientific knowledge, including Latin or Middle-High-German. However, from the 18th century on, written records become more numerous, and you should limit your research to the sources which you can expect to contain relevant familial information. As a priority, consider the tax lists, which can be found in department 66 (Beraine), and also in the topographical file department among the topics "Renovationen, Schätzungen, Zehntwesen" [Renovations, Assessments, Tax Dispositions].

In addition, you should refer to the homage lists in which are listed the subjects who had to make an oath of allegiance in the event of a new ruler. These lists are located under the topic "Landesherrlichkeit".

Finally, we should mention the inheritance files, personnel files (servant acts), serf lists, military enlistment lists, purchase records, emigration and naturalization files, although this list is not exhaustive. Other topics are also worth considering on an individual basis. If you know that the person you are researching is named Müller [miller] you should also check under the subject of "Mühlen" [mills] and so forth. A full list of the relevant sources can be found in the manual of genealogy previously mentioned.

All of these sources are arranged according to governmental and territorial aspects in the State Archive. Therefore, no inquiries can be pursued in a purposeful way into the official written or printed material if you do not know in which place the person in question lived or ended up. If however you have traced back a line of ancestors by means of the church books, you normally know the place for which other information may exist, and you can search in a well directed way among the other possible references for the specific place.

If the place is not known, research is more difficult. A generally valid search strategy cannot be given for this case. You can consult the available card index for the occurrence of surnames in Baden, which despite its volume, only contains information from a part of the files of the 18th and 19th century and therefore certainly does not offer a complete picture. However, you may be able to determine a place in which the name in question occurred.

The State Archive personnel offer aid in determining what reference material should be checked for specific genealogical questions, and they deliver the archival records to the reading room for use. The review and evaluation of the archival records are up to the user. Archive employees do not do genealogical investigations within the framework of their service. Also, help reading records can only be offered on a very limited basis. The response to written inquiries is limited to indications of which archival records may be worth checking. In this case, the previously mentioned card index of surnames remains out of consideration since its information can usually only be verified by further extensive research. Without an exact location and a definite scope, research and proper processing of written inquiries are not possible. This also applies to the providing of information from the duplicate church books of 1810 to 1870, which are stored here. The determination of the archival records and the answer to written inquiries is subject to a fee (at present 16 DM per quarter hour or portion of). Use of the reading room is - with the exception of commercial purposes - free of charge.

Successful genealogical study requires training in the proper methods and in deciphering old documents, a lot of patience and therefore a lot of time. Associations which offer aid for such research exist, and there are commercial contractors who undertake genealogical investigations for a fee. The State Archive, upon request, will provide a list of addresses.

LOCATE GERMAN ANCESTRAL HOME:
Occasionally we have the surname for an ancestral German with no idea of his or her home area or where to look for records in Germany. Most of us know the LDS (Mormon) International Genealogical Index (IGI) is a superbly useful tool to identify concentrations of an old surname in Germany. Another way is to analyze current phone listings, and many researchers have never tried to do this. Researching telephone listings works surprisingly well because German society has not been as mobile as that in the USA, and surnames have tended to remain in the same area for very long periods of time. Identifying current surname concentrations in Germany can point to where an ancestor lived centuries earlier. It is worth a try if simpler, easier methods have failed to locate your ancestor's hometown.

GERMAN DEFINITIONS:
vater = father
mutter = mother
junge (or knabe, or bu) = boy
busche = more than one boy
madchen (matel or madel) = girl
junger = disciple
geehrtes = your favor of
Geburtsorte = birthplace
Geburtsurkunde = certificate of birth
geboren = born
wirtshaus = public place of worship
platz = place
pfaff = vicar
mein = mine
mir = myself
bar = fearful
kind, kinder, kindchen = baby, child, infant
darin = in it or in that, therein
bringen (bringet, also can be brachte or gebracht) = bring or take
Frudyte - truth
und = and
werb = advertise
werben = recruit, propaganda
wert = worth
wirt = host or landlord
fruchte = fruit
Johannes = John
Wilhelm = William
du = you
forstay = understand
sprechen = speak or language

COUNT:
eine = 1
zwei = 2
drei = 3
vier = 4
funf = 5
sechs = 6

sieben = 7
acht = 8
neun = 9
zehn = 10
elf = 11
zwolf = 12
dreizen = 13
vierzen = 14
etc. add zen to numerals to indicate + ten, i.e. vier four zen ten = fourteen
zwanzig = 20
einundzwanzig = 21
Dreifzig = 30
vierzig = 40 etc.
hundert = 100
tausend = 1000

FREE TRANSLATION SERVICE:
There is a free automated translator of plain texts at: http://babelfish.altavista.digital.com/cgi-bin/translate?
Copy and paste or type your text into the input box, set the translator from foreign language to English or whatever
you desire and hit the "translate" button. The translation comes back in the box above the input box. It does not
reformat syntax perfectly, and sometimes it mistranslates words (e.g., the surname "Zulauf" gets translated "inlet").
When this automated translator knows it cannot translate a word, it leaves that word in the original language.

GERMAN IMMIGRANT QUERIES, FAMILY REUNIONS OR FESTIVALS AND BOOKS ABOUT GERMAN
MIGRATION AND GERMAN GENEALOGY can be found at: http://www.germanmigration.com

Translations by Arthur Teschler's German Genealogy Group:
http://w3g.med.uni-giessen.de/gene/www/abt/translation.html

The Ships List Digest's On-Line: http://www.cimorelli.com/ShipsList/digest/

Professions, Occupations and Illnesses: http://www.genealogy.com/brigitte/occupat.htm

Germany/Prussian Mailing Lists: http://members.aol.com/gfsjohnf/gen_mail_country-ger.html

To identify a town in Germany go to: http://www.orte.de/ click on the Orteveitzehnis - go to the first letter of the
town/city after a couple of clicks you will be there.

http://www.webcom.com/german/welcome.html - German American Corner

http://www.bawue.de/~hanacek/info/earchive.htm - Archives in Germany

THIS AND THAT GENEALOGY TIPS ON GERMAN RECORDS

After the fall of the Roman Empire, the Holy Roman Empire was formed and lead by Germanic people for several centuries leading to stable trade and general prosperity. However as European trade lead to world trade, Germanic forces fell behind the French, English, Spanish, Portuguese, and Dutch, who used ocean exploration as well as land.

It was during the latter part of this period that records of individuals and families began to be kept by various churches and was the main source of government information. It was also during this latter period that religious differences contributed to economic ones in causing the eventual breakup of the Germanic domain during the Thirty Year's War beginning in 1618-1621. Political disruption coupled with a sharp economic setback, partly due to the devastation and tremendous depopulation from the Thirty Year's War (some sources say that disease, war and emigration lead to a 2/3 drop in Germanic population that did not recover until the mid 1800's) and a long term shift in European economic bases saw the Germanic kingdom divided into 360+ small states and free cities by 1648. These small states went by the names of Achbisopric, Bishapric, Duchy, County, Electorate, Landgraviate, Margaviate, City, and Principality, so being confused about names is certainly understandable. Today's Germany is about twice the size of the state of Wisconsin. Bavaria (Bayern) was one of the largest land pieces and one of the few to retain a relatively stable governing family for 1000 years. Other larger ones were Wurttemberg, Saxony, Brandenburg (later Prussia), Pomerania, Munster, and Mecklenberg.

The general population was living as "serfs" and were under the direct authority of the ruler in this feudal system. Laws were different in each state and changed at the will of the leader(s) in most cases. A person or family often had to request permission to move or even visit outside of their place of residence and report to authorities upon leaving and arriving. Education was restricted. Religion of the population was determined by the state leader(s) and often depended on political alliances.

Since the size of each state was small, revenue was generated through taxes and fees on all goods that were transported through the state to markets. This sometimes meant that several times more taxes and fees were paid than the actual value of the product, leading to economic stagnation.

It was during this period that emigration from Germanic lands began of a serious nature, at first to neighboring countries such as Hungary, Romania, Poland, Russia, and later, as transportation improved and became available to the general public, the Americas, Australia, India, Africa among others.

Wars between these small states and with major powers such as France, Austria, and Russia, both political and religious, continued throughout the 1700's and early 1800's, leading to further disease, death, economic depression, and serious emigration. In the early 1800's the entire area was conquered by Napoleon Bonoparte who seized power in France from 1799 to 1814. It was during this time that the Napoleonic Settlements of 1797-98 was developed and combined the then 234 independent Germanic states into 40 and a separate Austria. Poland was again made an independent state as well for the first time since the early 1600's. Other changes were a society based on wealth and merit rather than prescription and privilege which was introduced into the Rhineland (west side of the River Rhine). German states that remained independent such as Prussia, Brandenburg, Hanover, Saxony, Thuingian states, Hesse, Pomerania and Oldenburg made some important changes in this direction. The feudal system was collapsing and there was gradually more individual freedom making emigration somewhat easier and more available.

After the fall of Napoleon, Prussia, through economic and military development, became the dominant power in the Germanic states and eventually unified the country in 1871 into what we see as modern day Germany. Today the country is divided into areas called Lower Saxony (northwest), NorthRhine-Westphalia (west central), Rhineland-Palatinate (west), Baden-Wurttemberg (southwest), Bavaria (southeast), Hesse (westcentral), Thuringia (central), Saxony (eastcentral) Brandenburg (northeast), Saxon-Anhalt (northcentral), Mecklenburg-Western Pomerania (northeast, and Schleswig-Holstein (north).

Germans arrived in America during 3 broadly-drawn periods:

1683-1820

This emigration was largely caused by religious persecutions following from the changes wrought by the Thirty Years War, and by economic hardship. Many were Protestants from the Palatinate area of Germany.

1820-1871

Economic hardships, including those caused by Unemployment, crop failure and starvation, was the primary cause of emigration during this period, in combination with wars and military service. Most of the emigrants came from Alsace-Lorraine, Baden, Hessen, Rhineland, and Württemberg.

1871-1914

Emigration became more affordable during this period, as well as much more common. All areas of Germany contributed, including Prussia.

The following is the address to write for information on German immigrants coming from Hamburg, Germany: Historic Emigration Office, c/o Tourist Information AM Hafen, Bei den St.Pauli Landungsbrucken 3, D-20359 Hamburg, Germany. When you request genealogical information they will include tourist brochures and a note stating how much it will cost. When I requested it the charge was $30 for each year researched so needless to say, the closer you can come to the date your ancestors immigrated the better. You may receive a copy of the ship's manifest showing their names, the city in Germany where they lived, the ship's captain's name, the ship's name, and port of entry in the US.

Research in Germany is a complex matter requiring study of methods and history. Germany was made up of various principalities prior to about 1870 when Prussia began to consolidate larger areas. The Family History Library has many microfilms of German records which you can access once you know where your ancestor was born, married or left from to come to America.

You must know which town in Germany your ancestors came from AND THE KINGDOM OR PRESENT DAY STATE. If you don't, then start at the passenger lists. If there passage occurred between 1850 and 1887, there is a collection of indexed passenger lists called Glazier and Filby "Germans to America" probably available at most genealogy libraries. If your ancestors came through Hamburg, they may have stayed there a few days and if so, were required to register with the German police. Those records still exist and the town of origin is often mentioned.

Once you know when your ancestors arrived in America, add five years and start looking for their Naturalization Certificate and/or the Declaration of Intent. Sometimes the declaration has more details than the Naturalization Certificate and may list the town of origin.

If your ancestor obtained a Social Security number, get the original application Form SS-5 from the Freedom of Information Office and possibly you will find something there to help you.

In the 1850's Bavaria was a separate kingdom as was Baden and Wurttemburg. This is some what analogous to our referring to the states of New York, and Ohio and Kentucky. In the years 1850 to 1860 Wurttemberg was an independent kingdom inside Germany. Later it is combined with the duchy's of Baden and Hohenzollern to the actual state Baden-Wurttemburg in Germany.

Beginners should do two things first: interview elderly or infirm relatives and read a good book on genealogy. The importance of talking to relatives before they pass away cannot be over emphasized. Your local library probably has several books on genealogy. Check out the ones that seem best to you and read them.

Then you should gather and organize all the information you have from various sources. You may already have enough to induce you to get some genealogical software to help in organizing your information. Document all your sources. Organization allows you to develop an overview of what you have so that you can better direct your research.

Next locate your local LDS (Mormon) FHC (Family History Center). The genealogical collection of the LDS Family History Library (FHL) is unsurpassed, and much of it can be used at your local FHC. You need not be Mormon. You can probably find the LDS church in your phone book.

Eventually your major information sources are likely to be German civil records and German church registers. German civil records start in the Napoleonic times in regions west of the Rhine River, in 1874 in Prussia, and 1876 in all of Germany. German church records start as early as the 15th century, but for many areas extant records start only after the end of the 30 Years War in the 17th century, or later. Many church registers existed in original (Kirchenbuch) and a nearly contemporaneous copy (Kirchenbuchduplikat). Many church registers and some older civil records are available through the LDS FHC. For those that are not, you must write to the German Standesamt (civil records office) or parish of interest or to the appropriate archive.

Other important sources include Ortssippenb"ucher, which list all the families in a town, typically using church records as the source; the IGI, which is an index of extracted records; passenger lists; the ASTAKA, a collection of German genealogies; German state censuses; and Geschlechterb"ucher, which is a series of published genealogies.

Further documents are also available in German archives. Examples of available documents include tax rolls, emigration papers, land registers, wills, and court cases. Most of these have not been filmed by the LDS and are available only at the appropriate archive. Catalogs of the holdings of some archives are available in printed form in some US research libraries.

Keep in mind a general rule of genealogy is to go from the known to the unknown, and not the other way around. For example, if your name is Bauer, you should concentrate on expanding the tree of Bauers related to you by examining documents that refer to them. You should probably not research the genealogy of some other Bauer to see if he is related to you, because the chance of success is slight. Note that this general rule does not apply if you are researching a rare surname, or if you can pair the surname with a town or another surname.

Another general rule is to do as much research as possible locally. Use your local LDS FHC, library, interlibrary loan, genealogical society, etc. to their fullest extent before you write or travel to distant archives or churches. It is usually cheaper and often more efficient, and it will make subsequent research more productive.

Prussia was part of Germany. In fact Prussia became the Germany of 1871 when Bismarck was able to get Bavaria, Hesse, Baden, Wurttemberg, Hannover, Oldenburg completely absorbed into the German Empire either through political, conquest or deception.

Posen was a separate province of Prussia as was West Prussia (Westpreussen). The portion that became part of Russia and Poland was East Prussia (Ostpreussen). West Prussia was partially cut up after WWI then after WWII Poland took all that was West Prussia as well as the eastern part (Hinter-Pommern) of Pomerania, which explain why the western part (Vorpommern) is still in Germany.

Silesia, the other province was completely absorbed by Poland after WWI. Poland also took Galicia from Austria after WWI but lost much of it to Prussia in 1945 along with large part of it's own territory.

Memel was located in East Prussia, now part of Lithuania.

Konigsburg is Kallinburg now - still the part of Russia, the only part not attached to Russia because of Lithuania.

Danzig was set off as Free City that last between WWI and WWII then after 1945 changed to Gdansk.

Portion of Brandenburg also was taken by Poland after WWII.

Prussia's provinces before 1871 were: Pommern, Brandenburg, Hesse-Nassau, Rheinland, Posen, West Prussia, East Prussia, Waldeck, Westfalen (Westphalia) and Silesia.

All traces of "Prussia" was abolished by the Allied Powers after WWII in an attempt to wipe out the Prussian military mentality which fueled both WWI and WWII.

GERMAN RECORDS and Where They May Be Hiding:
If you know the city, town, or village of origin for your ancestor in Germany, you should check with your local branch of the LDS (Mormon) Family History Library to see if there are available microfilms of records for that locality. This information is accessible by visiting the branches (the Family History Centers) throughout the United States and elsewhere abroad. (It is not currently possible to determine this by using the World Wide Web, Internet, or E-mail.)

If you do not know the exact city, town, or village of origin for your ancestor in Germany (which is ESSENTIAL to further research in German records), you need to continue your U.S.-based research until you can determine this information. Guidelines and suggestions for this type of research are available at the following Web site: http://w3g.med.uni-giessen.de/gene/faqs/sgg.html#origin

As to the question of whether particular records for a particular locality have survived, the answer takes a bit of research as well. Many, many German records have survived (even those dating back many centuries); and some have not. However, if the LDS does NOT have microfilms of the records for the German locality you seek, it does not necessarily mean that there are no existing records for that place!

There are at least three other reasons why you may NOT find LDS microfilm of a given German locality:

1. The place in question did not have its own parish church for the denomination you seek. The LDS films parish records, not records from every single individual village or town. You must determine whether your ancestors' village or town was the same place where the church they attended was located----these are not always in one and the same place. A single parish church (Catholic or Lutheran) often served parishoners in multiple nearby communities. Check historical gazetteers (available in the LDS Family History Centers) such as Meyers-Orts (ask the staff to direct you to it, it's on microfilm) which will tell you whether or not your ancestors' village or town had a church in it of the appropriate denomination. Other gazetteers (such as "Die Kirchebücher in Baden," also available at the LDS FHC) for a given region of Germany will tell you where these parishes were located. (These are available for Wuerttemberg, Prussia, etc. as well.)

2. The LDS may not have obtained permission to film records in a particular locality, for whatever reason. Sometimes, the church or civil authorities in a given place are not especially cooperative in this regard. Try writing directly to the church in question instead.

3. The LDS may not have yet filmed the records of the community you seek. Though a large number of German records have been filmed, not all of them have. You would need to consult (by phone or mail) the main LDS Library branch in Salt Lake City, Utah, for specific details about what may be slated for filming in the future.

If you have not first checked with the LDS library about films of available records, I strongly recommend that you do. If you are having trouble locating films at the LDS, keep the above points in mind, and try again. If you have significant problems with the library staff (who are usually volunteers, and can vary in knowledge and experience), ask to speak to your local FHC branch director, who is a paid professional. Do not give up on or overlook the LDS library resources if you can help it---their collection is the best and most extensive anywhere in the world.

If you know the locality you need but can't find LDS film on it (for whatever reason), you can still try writing to the church in question for the information you seek. See the following Web page for further information: http://w3g.med.uni-giessen.de/gene/faqs/sgg.html#letter

If you lack precise information about the locality (meaning the town, city, or village---not just the region, which is not sufficiently specific) from which your German ancestors came (or lived in, or were married, etc., in) you are not yet at a point in your research where you can successfully make the jump across the Atlantic---very sad and disappointing, I know, but quite true. See the Web page suggested at the beginning of this letter for suggestions.

THIS AND THAT GENEALOGY TIPS ON HOLIDAYS

PILGRIMS REMEMBERED:
Thanksgiving and the Pilgrims seem to go together like the turkey and stuffing that many of us enjoy at our holiday feasts.

The first national Thanksgiving Day, proclaimed by President George Washington, was celebrated on Nov. 26, 1789, and Thanksgiving has been an official annual holiday in America since 1863, when President Abraham Lincoln set the date as the last Thursday in November.

However, this American holiday dates back to the beginning of our country's settlement by the English -- to the Pilgrims who settled at Plymouth, Mass., in 1620, and to those settlers who stepped shore Dec. 4, 1619, at what became Berkeley plantation near present-day Charles City, Virginia. In accordance with the Berkeley proprietor's instructions that ``the day of our ships' arrival ... shall be yearly and perpetually kept as a day of Thanksgiving,'' these Virginia settlers celebrated what actually was the first Thanksgiving Day in this country by more than a year before the Pilgrims arrived in New England.

While a great deal of information is known and has been published about first settlers of Massachusetts, scant genealogical information has survived pertaining to those pioneers of Virginia who first celebrated Thanksgiving there. Settled in 1619 as Berkeley Hundred, this small community was wiped out by the natives in 1622. This area later became part of Charles City County.

To find a list of those so-called ancient planters of Virginia -- those who are known to have come to Virginia before the end of 1616, and who survived the 1622 conflict, consult the introduction in Volume I of Nell Marion Nugent's `Cavaliers and Pioneers," where a list of those living in Virginia in 1624-5 appears. For genealogical accounts of all known pre-1620 Virginians, see "Adventurers of Purse and Person, Virginia, 1607-1625," by Annie L. Jester and Martha W. Hiden, widely available in libraries.

If your ancestry leads you back to Plymouth Colony, then you will want to read "Plymouth Colony: Its History & People, 1620-1691," by Eugene Aubrey Stratton. In it, the author reveals that of the 99 Mayflower passengers who stayed, only 52 were still living when the "Fortune," which was the next ship to the colony, arrived there in November 1621.

Although Spanish families were in St. Augustine, Florida, before 1600 and in the Southwest as early as 1615, and while the Jamestown settlement in Virginia dates from 1607, the Pilgrims who came on the Mayflower are probably the best-known progenitors of those tracing their early American roots because so much has been written about them. These settlers are fully listed in Governor William Bradford's ``History of Plimoth Plantation, 1620-1647."

Of the Mayflower passengers, only 23 families or individuals survived that difficult first winter and left American descendants, while at least one other passenger -- Moses Fletcher -- left progeny in Holland. However, it is estimated that the contemporary progeny of these Pilgrims probably numbers more than 30 million.

For genealogists who can make the connections across nearly 400 years and 10 to 14 generations to an ancestor who came on the Mayflower, the historical adventure into American records can be rewarding. But regardless of when your ancestors came to America, remember them as you enjoy your Thanksgiving Day feasts. If you have access to the World Wide Web, you can read "The Truth About the Pilgrims and Thanksgiving" at: http://pilgrims.net/plymouth/index.htm

THE MAYFLOWER AND THE FIRST THANKSGIVING:
The Mayflower carried 102 passengers and a crew of 26 plus the captain. There were 32 children aboard. During the trip one person died and one was born. What were the accommodations aboard ship like some 350 years ago? Here

are a few ideas.

For 30 days of the 66 day voyage, passengers had to stay huddled below, between the decks. They could not use candles or lanterns because of fire hazard. They could not cook between decks unless it was a calm day. Cold food might be biscuits, pickled eggs, salted or smoked meat, fish, dried fruits and vegetables. Adults and children alike would drink a weat beer called "small beer". There was no privacy. No one ever bathed or changed clothes.

Of the Mayflower passengers, only 23 families or individuals survived that difficult first winter and left American descendants, while at least one other passenger, Moses Fletcher, left progeny in Holland. It is estimated that the progeny of these Pilgrims probably number more than 30 million today.

Passengers on the Mayflower with living descendants today are John Alden, Isaac Allerton, John Billington, William Bradford, William Brewster, Peter Brown, James Chilton, Francis Cooke, Edward Doty, Francis Eaton, Edward Fuller, Samuel Fuller, Stephen Hopkins, John Howland, Richard More, Degory Priest, Thomas Rogers, Henry Sampson, George Soule, Myles Standish, John Tilley, Richard Warren, William White and Edward Winslow. There are also American descendants of some of the members of the Mayflower crew but their descendants are not entitled to membership in the Society of Mayflower Descendants. John White of Virginia was one such crewman.

George Enregt Bowman (1860-1941) founded the Society of Mayflower Descendants and became the first editor of the Mayflower Descendant.

The first national Thanksgiving Day, proclaimed by President George Washington, was celebrated on Nov 26, 1789 and Thanksgiving has been an official annual holiday in America since 1863 when President Abraham Lincoln set the date as the last Thursday in November.

Thanksgiving is an American holiday with roots dating back to the beginning of this country's settlement by the English, to those settlers who stepped ashore Dec 4, 1619 at what became Berkeley Plantation near present-day Charles City, VA and to the better-known group who settled at Plymouth, MA in 1620. In accordance with the Berkeley proprietor's instructions that "the day of our ships' arrival.... shall be yearly and perpetually kept as a day of Thanksgiving," those Virginia settlers celebrated what was the first Thanksgiving Day in this country by more than a year before the Pilgrims arrived in New England. Even though Spanish families were in St. Augustine, FL before 1600, and in the Southwest (New Mexico) by 1615, and the Jamestown, VA settlement from 1607, it is the Mayflower families who are intertwined with this annual November celebration.

http://members.aol.com/calebj/mayflower.html - MAYFLOWER WEB PAGE - where you will find a complete list of the "Mayflower" passengers, links to every passenger's genealogical and biographical information plus some early Plymouth passenger lists such as the "Fortune" in 1621 and the "Anne" in 1623. There is also a history of the "Mayflower", its dimensions and images as well as information about the crew and much more.

A NATIONAL THANKSGIVING:
Whereas it is the duty of all nations to acknowledge the providence of Almighty God, to obey His will, to be grateful for His benefits, and humbly to implore His protection and favor; and Whereas both Houses of Congress have, by their joint committee, requested me "to recommend to the people of the United States a day of public thanksgiving and prayer, to be observed by acknowledging with grateful hearts the many and signal favors of Almighty God, especially by affording them an opportunity peaceably to establish a form of government for their safety and happiness":

Now, therefore, I do recommend and assign Thursday, the 26th day of November next, to be devoted by the people of these States to the service of that great and glorious Being who is the Beneficent Author of all the good that was, that is, or that will be; that we may then all unite in rendering unto Him our sincere and humble thanks for His kind care and protection of the people of this country previous to their becoming a nation; for the signal and manifold mercies and the favorable interpositions of His providence in the course and conclusion of the late war; for the great degree of tranquillity, union, and plenty which we have since enjoyed; for the peaceable and rational manner in which we have been enabled to establish constitutions of government for our safety and happiness, and particularly the national one now lately instituted; for the civil and religious liberty with which we are blessed, and the means we have of acquiring and diffusing useful knowledge; and, in general, for all the great and various favors which He has been pleased to confer upon us.

And also that we may then unite in most humbly offering our prayers and supplication to the great Lord and Ruler of Nations, and beseech Him to pardon our national and other transgressions; to enable us all, whether in public or private stations, to perform our several and relative duties properly and punctually; to render our national government a blessing to all the people by constantly being a government of wise, just and constitutional laws, discreetly and faithfully executed and obeyed; to protect and guide all sovereigns and nations (especially such as have shown kindness to us), and to bless them with good governments, peace, and concord; to promote the knowledge and practice of true religion and virtue, and the increase of science among them and us; and, generally, to grant unto all mankind such a degree of temporal prosperity as He alone knows to be best.

Given under my hand, at the city of New York, the 3d day of October, AD 1789
-- George Washington

CHRISTMAS TRADITIONS:
Few Americans are aware that large groups of colonists objected to Christmas during the 17th and 18th centuries. Christmas came to the American colonies while it was the subject of strenuous controversy in England. For the Church of England, the Feast of Nativity was one of the most important of the year, even though the English puritans condemned it. New England Puritans also shared this hostile attitude toward observing Christmas. Their opposition culminated in an act of Parliament in 1647 which abolished the observance of Christmas and Easter.

This was echoed in 1659 when Puritans of the American colonies enacted a law in the General Court of Massachusetts to punish those who kept Christmas. One of the Puritan doctrinal objections to Christmas was the belief that Church government should not ordain anything contrary to, or not found in the Scriptures, because the Bible did not prescribe special religious feasts. Therefore, the strict Puritans discarded as "devises of men" all feasts, except the Sabbath, the Liturgy with its required prayer and Bible reading, and the use of vestments and ornaments. This view excluded the religious observance of Christmas.

With the adoption of the Constitution in 1791, the separation of church and state was established, and the Puritan and Evangelical churches were less inclined to oppose the celebration of Christmas when it no longer symbolized the religious and political dominance of the Church of England.

HOLLY AS A CHRISTMAS DECORATION
The custom dates back to the time of the ancient Romans who used holly in connection with the celebration of their Saturnalia which occurs about the same time as Christmas. Since the leaves of the holly tree were always green and it was most beautiful at a time of the year when other trees were barren, some believed it to be sacred. It was believed that holly was hateful to witches because of its thorns and was therefore used to keep evil spirits away, and down thru the years it has become one of the leading symbols of well-being at Christmas. In the spiritual sense it has come to represent the crown of thorns worn by Christ when he was crucified.

THE YULE LOG
Burning of the yule log is an ancient Christmas ceremony handed down from the Scandinavians, who used to kindle huge bonfires in honor of their God, Thor. The bringing in and placing of the ponderous log on the hearth of the wide chimney in the baronial hall was the most joyous of the ceremonies observed on Christmas Eve. It was drawn in triumph from it's resting place amid shouts and laughter, every wayfarer doffing his hat as it passed, for he well knew that it was full of good promises, and that its flame would burn out old wrongs and heartburnings. On its entrance into the hall, the minstrels hailed it with song and music or in the absence of minstrels, that each member of the family sat upon it in turn, sang a Yule song and drank to a Merry Christmas and a Happy New Year; after they had as part of

their feast, Yule dough, or Yule cookies, on which was impressed the figure of the infant Jesus.

THE CHRISTMAS TREE
The Christmas Tree seems to have originated in Germany, and can be traced back to the year 1604. There is a pretty legend in connection with it which makes St. Winfred the inventor of the idea. In the midst of a crowd of converts he hewed down a giant oak tree which had formerly been the object of their Druidic worship. As it fell backward like a tower, groaning as it split asunder in four pieces, there stood behind it, unharmed by the ruin, a young fir tree, pointing a green spire toward the stars. Winfred let the ace drop and turned to speak to the people. "This little tree, a young child of the forest, shall be your holy tree tonight. It is the wood of peace, for your houses are built of the fir. It is the sign of an endless light, for its leaves are evergreen. See how it points upward to heaven! Let this be called the tree of Christ-child; gather about it, not in the wild wood but in your own homes; there it will shelter gifts of love and rites of kindness."

The Christmas tree was introduced into the Court of St. James about 1840 and the custom spread rapidly among the aristocratic families of London, and was almost immediately adopted by all classes throughout England. It was a young German immigrant, August Ingard, a youth of 21, who introduced the Christmas tree to America. He and his family made their home in Wooster, Ohio. They decided to have a Christmas tree, as was their custom in Bavaria. Young August went into the woods outside Wooster and chopped down a spruce tree. From the village tinsmith he obtained a star fashioned of tin. Paper decorations were made and America's first Christmas tree blossomed out in all its glory in the Ingard home December 24, 1847. The tomb of August Ingard stands on Madison Hill in Wooster. This year, as always, a lighted tree will stand at it's door, a tribute to the man who first brought to America the symbol of peace, love and hope that is Christmas.

CHRISTMAS GREETINGS
Sending of Christmas cards seems to be strictly an Anglo-Saxon custom, originated in England about 1844. They were introduced in America by the artist Louis Prang of Boston about 1875.

LEGEND OF THE CHRISTMAS CANDLE
Long ago an old shoemaker lived in a cottage on the edge of a village. Although he was poor and had little to share, each evening he placed a candle in his window as a welcome sign for travelers. War came, yet his light never wavered and somehow, in all the villages only the shoemaker was at peace with the world. "But how can peace come from a candle?" they asked. "The candle is a symbol of peace", he replied, "because light and peace are one". Christmas Eve came and the people, longing more than ever for peace, remembered the shoemaker's candle. Every Villager placed a candle in his window and on Christmas morning, as if by a miracle, a messenger brought new of the war's end. The custom of the bayberry candle originated in North America during the colonial days. It is considered a symbol of good luck for the ensuing year.

THE POINSETTIA
It was the custom of the early inhabitants of Mexico at the Christmas season to have in their chapel a manager in which lay an image of the Infant Saviour. We are indebted to Joel R. Poinsett of South Carolina, for the discovery of this colorful Christmas plant. In March, 1825, he was appointed the first American Minister to Mexico. It was he who brought the poinsettia to the United States.

SANTA CLAUS
Nicholas, was an authentic historical figure, who served as Bishop of Myra in the Eastern Church during the 4th century. He represented the spirit of sharing, and rewarded the good children with gifts, and brought switches for the bad. Traditionally, he rode upon a white horse, which accounts for the fact that hay was invariably left at the fireplace.

It was Clement Moore, in his famous immortal poem, "The Night Before Christmas" which caused St. Nicholas to lose his Ecclesiastical appearance for the jolly old elf, St. Nick, and to transform the white horse to the immortal eight reindeer.

(Christmas Symbols by Mr. Gertrude H. Hagerty, James Alexander Chapter DAR) Reprinted from Clinton Co., Indiana Roots December 1988

110

THIS AND THAT GENEALOGY TIPS ON IMMIGRATION AND PASSPORTS

CITIZENSHIP REQUIREMENT ACTS 1790 AND 1796:

The first naturalization law was passed March 26, 1790. Naturalization was an option, not a requirement. Prior to 1906 naturalization records were seldom uniform from one court to another and from one era to another. Furthermore these records were created by many different courts and now may be housed in many different repositories. While the rules for naturalization have changed, the basic format has generally been a two step process of "intent" followed by a final "petition", except for veterans of certain wars, who were allowed to do both at once. Minors residing here for five years prior to their 23rd birthday could also complete both steps at once between 1824 and 1906. Naturalization records were not collected by one single entity. A person could "declare intent" in one court and file "petition for citizenship" in a different court. To add to the complexity various courts kept records of differing detail. Some declarations of intent my contain some genealogical data such as original country or place of birth. These records may not contain details about family members. The courts holding naturalization records could be at the county, state or federal level. Children became citizens when their fathers did. Wives, until 1922, likewise became citizens when their husbands did. Further the names of wife and children may not be listed on either application. In general if you are not reasonably sure if, when and where a declaration might have been made, a search is likely to be time consuming and difficult.

The order of the forms filed was Declaration of Intention, Petition for Naturalization, then if the test were successful they received there Naturalization Certificate and were citizens. The waiting period to file a Declaration was 1 or 2 years, the Petition was 5 years, then the test. If your family member was naturalized before September 1906, the records are at the courthouse in the county where they were naturalized. Now if your grandparents were married and he became naturalized before 1922, your grandmother would have automatically become a citizen. Any foreign born children would become citizens also. This was the law. If he was naturalized after 1922, then she would have had to file also.

Modern Records:

Starting in 1906, copies of naturalization papers were collected by the Immigration and Naturalization Service (INS). These records include both immigration and naturalization records. They are more standardized than records of previous eras and include the names of spouses and children, whether they were citizens or not. INS immigration records date from 1897 onward. You can request these files directly. The form needed is G639 and can be requested from your local or regional Immigration and Naturalization Service office or by calling 1--800-870-3676.

Verbal information can be sought at 202-514-2607. The more information you have the more likely your ancestor will be identified even if they were not naturalized. There is no cost for the INS record search. You will need to provide full name and address (or addresses) as a minimum. Further, critical dates, social security number, birthday and place of birth will help insure a creditable search. The address of the Washington, D.C. INS office is: Immigration and Naturalization Service, 425 I (eye) Street NW, Washington, DC 20536.

Most aliens became citizens within 10 years of the time they were eligible. Before 1906 the records were kept by federal, state and local courts. There is a book that summarizes these records on file for each state: "Locating Your Immigrant Ancestors: A Guide to Naturalization Records" by James C. and Lila Lee Negles. You can obtain this from Everton Publishers, Inc. or your local intra-library loan program.

To become a citizen of the United States by Acts of 1790 and 1796, one had to live in the United States for 5 years and in the state or territory for one year; and had to make a Declaration of Intent three years prior to becoming a citizen. However, naturalization was not required, and many people lived their lives here without naturalization, or after making D of I, not continuing with the procedure. It was purely voluntary. It was not until 1906 that appearance in Federal Court was required - prior to that any court of record could naturalize

As to children, when the father was naturalized, his wife and children were automatically citizens. If a person had lived in the United States for at least 3 years prior to age of 21, he could apply for naturalization directly, without waiting to file the D. of I. A reference source for changes in laws is Gettys, Luella: The Laws of Citizenship in the United States 1934, University of Chicago Press, Chicago, Illinois.

Remember, naturalization is voluntary and not all immigrants were/are naturalized. You find many naturalizations dated in the 1940's during WWII when many aliens had to be naturalized to stay in USA.

In your search for your immigrant ancestor, look for Certificates of Citizenship issued to individuals who had completed all the requirements of entry. They were often saved and passed down in families. This certificate may show no more than the name of the immigrant, the country from which he relinquished citizenship, the date of the event and the name of the court where naturalization was finalized. The location of the court is the key to finding additional papers which may provide more detail. Not all aliens were naturalized but if they were, the documents in court records will provide information necessary to trace your ancestor's Americanization. You may find additional information including port of arrival and name of the vessel. Naturalization laws were not made uniform until 1906. Prior to this time, aliens could naturalize in any court but information varied from court to court.

The National Archives and its eleven branches are natural starting places for obtaining naturalization information. It should be noted that it was usually required that an alien be a resident of this country for at least five years. The Declaration of Intention or "first papers" were completed and filed with a court soon after the immigrant arrived in this country. You might find these in port cities. After the five years stay in America, the immigrant was required to go to court once more and file his "final papers". It was not necessary to do this in the same court as the "first papers". Certain groups of people were naturalized without filing a Declaration of Intention. Wives and children of naturalized males generally became citizens automatically. Those who served in the U. S. military forces also became citizens after an honorable discharge. Military records then become another source of information.

Over a million immigrants came to the colonies before 1820 but few were recorded on passenger lists. Most of the known lists have been published and many have been indexed in Filby's Passenger and Immigration List Index and Supplements (11 volumes) but you must know the full name, approximate age and date of arrival, also their nationality.

Passenger Lists are available at the National Archives and at some of its branches. They consist of custom passenger lists, transcripts and abstracts of customs passenger lists, immigration passenger lists and indexes to these lists. The Family History Center and most large genealogical libraries will have the Index to the Passenger Lists. The records were created by captains or masters of vessels, collectors of customs and immigration officials at the port of entry. They document a high percentage of the immigrations between 1820 and 1914 when most immigrants came to the U.S. Most came through the port of New York and Ellis Island and there is an Index to Passenger Lists of Vessels Arriving at New York 1897-1902 however there is no index for New York arrivals for the period 1847-1896. An Alphabetical index of passenger lists for 1902-1943 has been microfilmed. Unless an exact date of arrival is known, it may take many hours of searching the lists of ship arrivals.

For more specific information on passenger lists, naturalization records, military records and other collections, consult the Guide to Genealogical Research in the National Archives. To search the U. S. Customs Passenger Lists in the National Archives after 1820, you must know the full name, age, approximate date of arrival and port of entry. You may find in these records the name, age, sex, occupation, country of origin, port of departure, destination, date of arrival, name of the vessel. Immigration lists or "ship manifests" which began being used in 1883 give more detailed information. You can request a search of the Passenger Arrival Records by requesting Form 81 from the National Archives or e-mail your request for the form to: Inquire@nara.gov

The National Archives has custody of millions of records relating to persons who have had dealings with the federal government. Including but not limited to: Censuses, Land Records, Naturalization Records (after 1906), Passenger Lists, Passport Applications, Claims for Pensions and Bounty Land, etc. You can learn more about NARA at: http://www.nara.gov

http://www.nara.gov/publications/microfilm/immigrant/immpass.html

http://w3g.med.uni-giessen.de/gene/faqs/sgg.html#passengers

Go here for information on Emigration, Ship Lists and other resources on the Internet:
http://freespace.virgin.net/alan.tupman/sites/ships.htm

Go here for information on Naturalization and Related Records in the NY State Archives:
http://unix6.nysed.gov/holding/fact/natur-fa.htm

Naturalization records consist of many papers since this was a three step process and you must request all the papers.
Here is what I request either via e-mail or snail mail to the proper Regional Archive (listed below):
Alien Records
Declaration of Intention (first papers)
Petition
Oath of Allegiance
Certificate of Naturalization (Final papers)

You must tell the Archives the following about your ancestor and this can be done via e-mail (see below list):
Name of Ancestor and variations of name:
Birth date or close estimate:
Country of Birth:
Date of Entry:
Port of Entry:
Name of Spouse: if known
Names of Children: if known
Your full name and address.

They will search their records and get back to you within one or two days to let you know the cost to send you the copies. (No cost if they do not find anything). (Usually $5.00 per person searched and found)

Here are the addresses (Mid-Atlantic Region covers Allegheny and surrounding counties plus..WVA and other areas):
National Archives-Northeast Region (Boston), 380 Trapelo Road, Waltham, Massachusetts 02154-6399, Phone: 617-647-8100, Fax: 617-647-8460
Hours: 8:00 a.m.-4:30 p.m., Monday-Friday, 8:00 a.m.-4:30 p.m., 1st Saturday of each month
Connecticut, Maine, Massachusetts, New Hampshire, Rhode Island, and Vermont
- --
National Archives-Northeast Region (Pittsfield), 100 Dan Fox Drive, Pittsfield, Massachusetts 01201-8230, Phone: 413-445-6885, Fax: 413-445-7599
Hours: 9:00 a.m.-3:00 p.m., Monday-Friday, 9:00 a.m.-9:00 p.m., Wednesday
Microfilm only
- --
National Archives-Northeast Region (New York), 201 Varick Street, New York, New York 10014-4811, Phone: 212-337-1300, Fax: 212-337-1306
Hours: 8:00 a.m.-4:30 p.m., Monday-Friday, 8:30 a.m.-4:00 p.m., 3rd Saturday of each month.
New Jersey, New York, Puerto Rico, and the U.S. Virgin Islands
- --
National Archives-Mid Atlantic Region, 900 Market Street, Room 1350, Philadelphia, Pennsylvania 19107-4292, Phone: 215-597-3000, Fax: 215-597-2303
Hours: 8:00 a.m.-5:00 p.m., Monday-Friday, 8:00 a.m.-4:00 p. m., 2nd Saturday of each month
Delaware, Maryland, Pennsylvania, Virginia, and West Virginia
- --

National Archives-Southeast Region (Atlanta), 1557 St. Joseph Avenue, East Point, Georgia 30344-2593, Phone: 404-763-7477, Fax: 404-763-7033
Hours: 8:00 a.m.-4:00 p.m., Monday, Wednesday, Thursday, Friday, 8:00 a.m.-8:00 p.m., Tuesday
Alabama, Florida, Georgia, Kentucky, Mississippi, North Carolina, South Carolina, and Tennessee
- --
National Archives-Great Lakes Region (Chicago), 7358 South Pulaski Road, Chicago, Illinois 60629-5898, Phone: 312-353-0162, Fax: 312-353-1294
Hours: 8:00 a.m.-4:15 p.m., Monday, Wednesday, Thursday, Friday, 8:00 a.m.-8:30 p.m., Tuesday
Illinois, Indiana, Michigan, Minnesota, Ohio, and Wisconsin
- --
National Archives-Central Plains Region (Kansas City), 2312 East Bannister Road, Kansas City, Missouri 64131, Phone: 816-926-6272, Fax: 816-926-6982
Hours: 8:00 a.m.-4:00 p.m., Monday-Friday, 9:00 a.m.-4:00 p.m., 3rd Saturday of each month
Iowa, Kansas, Missouri, and Nebraska
- --
National Archives-Southwest Region (Fort Worth), 501 West Felix Street, Building 1, P.O. Box 6216, Fort Worth, Texas 76115-3405, Phone: 817-334-5525, Fax: 817-334-5621
Hours: 8:00 a.m.-4:00 p.m., Monday-Friday
Arkansas, Louisiana, Oklahoma, and Texas
- --
National Archives-Rocky Mountain Region (Denver), Denver Federal Center, Building 48, P.O. Box 25307, Denver, Colorado 80225-0307, Phone: 303-236-0817, Fax: 303-236-9354
Hours: 7:30 a.m.-4:00 p.m., Monday, Tuesday, Thursday, Friday, 7:30 a.m.-5:00 p.m., Wednesday
Colorado, Montana, New Mexico, North Dakota, South Dakota, Utah, and Wyoming
- --
National Archives-Pacific Region (Laguna Niguel), 24000 Avila Road, 1st Floor East, P.O. Box 6719, Laguna Niguel, California 92607-6719, Phone: 714-360-2641, Fax: 714-360-2644
Hours: 8:00 a.m.-4:30 p.m., Monday-Friday, 8:00 a.m.-4:30 p.m., 1st Saturday each month (Microfilm research only)
Arizona, Southern California, and Clark County, Nevada
- --
National Archives-Pacific Region (San Bruno), 1000 Commodore Drive, San Bruno, California 94066-2350, Phone: 415-876-9009, Fax: 415-876-9233
Hours: 8:00 a.m.-4:00 p.m., Monday, Tuesday, Thursday, Friday, 8:00 a.m.-8:00 p.m., Wednesday
Northern California, Hawaii, Nevada except Clark County, the Pacific Trust Territories, and American Samoa
- --
National Archives-Pacific Alaska Region (Seattle), 6125 Sand Point Way NE, Seattle, Washington 98115-7433
Phone: 206-526-6507, Fax: 206-526-4344
Hours: 7:45 a.m.-4:00 p.m., Monday-Friday, 5:00 p.m.-9:00 p.m., 1st Tuesday of each month
Idaho, Oregon, and Washington
- --
National Archives-Pacific Alaska Region (Anchorage), 654 West Third Avenue, Anchorage, Alaska 99501-2145, Phone: 907-271-2441, Fax: 907-271-2442
Hours: 8:00 a.m.-4:00 p.m. Monday-Friday, Call for Saturday hours
Alaska

Through the Freedom of Information Act (FOIA) you can write to Immigration and Naturalization in Washington, DC and request a file on anyone who was born before 1897 and naturalized after September 1906. You need to call this telephone number, and ask for one or two copies of Form G-639:   1-800-870-FORM. When you get the form in the mail, make a photocopy or two, then if you need one sometime you will have it. You can copy just the front of the form for what you are needing. The form has many questions on it but all that is necessary is full name, date of birth (exact or approximate) and place of birth (country). Any other information you receive will just aide in the search, the more the better. After you mail it, you will receive a letter from INS telling you they have received your request. Keep the letter, it has a CO number on it and if you need any further correspondences with INS, you need this number. After about 3 months, you will receive the file if it is found or another letter that states the file was not found.

Summary:
Records after 1906 for naturalization and 1897 for immigration are held by the INS. You may request copies of these files via mail with form G639. Early naturalization records (pre 1906) were maintained at various courts in all states. The type of information in these early records is not standard. These files are more difficult to locate because they may be part of records held by numerous judicial entities. In some cases these records have been moved to other repositories. Please visit the National Archives web page on naturalization records for more detail about their holdings: http://www.nara.gov/genealogy/natural.html

It is very important that family historians understand that they can retrieve post 1906 records by mail. They need not employ anyone. Records prior to 1906 are generally much more complex to find. I have prepared a document to answer these questions and act as a guide.

CASTLE GARDENS AND ELLIS ISLANDS:
The history of immigration spans American history. This movement of people ultimately brought 42 million immigrants into this country. The government passed no immigration laws until 1819 and even then they only covered the standard for steerage conditions on sailing vessels and made provisions that limited immigration records must be kept. Not until 1882 were immigration regulations made at all uniform. During the peak years of immigration, from about 1900 to 1914, as many as 5,000 people a day were processed through Ellis Island.

Prior to 1855, ships carrying passengers to the United States simply left them at the wharf, stranded, to be attacked by thugs and criminals and made prey by con men. The public feared the diseases that the immigrants brought with them and immigrants were ousted by society in general.

Before Ellis Island, Castle Garden, an old fort on the lower southern tip of Manhattan (now Battery Park), was designated in 1855 as an immigrant receiving station under state supervision. This center enabled the U.S. Government to keep better track of its immigrants. Clerks would record the names, nationalities, and destinations of immigrants. Physicians would give routine checkups and physicals to ensure that the immigrants were healthy.

When the new federal law was passed in 1882, Castle Garden continued to operate under contract to the U. S. Government, but by 1890, it's facilities had long since proved to be inadequate for the ever-increasing number of immigrant arrivals.

After a government survey of potential locations, a 27 acres parcel of land called Ellis Island was the site chosen to establish an entirely new U. S. immigration station. The history of Ellis Island tells us that the Dutch had originally purchased the land from the Indians and established the colony of New Amsterdam. It had a succession of owners before the American Revolution when Samuel Ellis bought and linked his name to it. New York purchased Ellis Island in 1808 and in turn sold it to the federal government who wanted to build a fort on it. Fort Gibson was fortified just before the War of 1812 but it saw little action during the war. It was used primarily as a munitions depot until it was transformed in 1892 into an immigration center. Construction began in 1890 and hundreds of workers labored at a large three-story reception center, hospital for the ill and quarantined immigrants, laundry facility, a boiler-house and an electric generating plant. Smaller buildings included a dormitory, restaurant and baggage station. Over the years, ballast from ships dumped near Ellis Island built it up, and the landfill and completion of sea walls brought it to it's present size. When it was completed and dedicated on Jan 1, 1892, it was a self-contained city.

Annie Moore from County Cork was the first person processed at Ellis Island from the SS NEVADA and she was presented with a ten dollar goldpiece. The ships CITY OF PARIS and the VICTORIA were also processed that day. Passenger lists for these and hundreds of other vessels which entered New York and other American ports have been preserved on microfilm and are available for those who wish to trace their ancestor's passage to America.

The life of the first station at Ellis Island was short. All the pine-frame buildings burned to the ground in a disastrous fire on June 15, 1897. Construction began immediately to replace the structures with fireproof buildings of brick, ironwork and limestone trimmings. It took 2-1/2 years to complete and the station reopened again in Dec 1900.

Emigration became a topic of conversation in communities all over Europe. The United States promised fulfillment of grand dreams which could no longer be kept alive in their native lands. For some it meant religious or political freedom; for others, freedom from conscription. For the majority it meant opportunity and the chance to improve their economic conditions. However, rumors had circulated about those who were denied entry because they looked suspicious or did not promptly answer the questions of immigration inspectors. The joy and excitement of reaching the "promised land" was mingled with the terrible dread of being rejected. Most had sold all their possessions and property, often going into debt to finance their journey. Yet they came by the millions.

Passengers of "means" escaped the rigors of the Ellis Island ordeal by being processed aboard the vessel itself, then delivered directly to Manhattan. The poorer classes sat sometimes three to four days in the crowded harbor awaiting their ship's turn to disembark passengers. Once on the island, they were closely observed by Inspectors who looked for the ill and infirm, empty stares indicating feebleminded and shortness of breath of those who climbed the stairs to the registry hall. The room looked like a stockyard with it's metal pipe partitions which were later exchanged for benches.

The Registry Hall was frequently referred to as the "Hall of Tears". It was filled to the walls with would-be Americans wearing numbered tags pinned to their clothes awaiting the battery of legal and medical examinations and hoping to be allowed to stay. Some family members might be accepted and others rejected. The painful decision to stay or return with a loved one had to be made on the spot. Some could not face the disgrace or ruin of deportation and it is estimated that as many as 3000 immigrants committed suicide. To enter the U. S. the immigrants knew that one must be disease-free and create the impression that they could make a living.

The first doctors they saw made a quick examination and noted any suspicions with a chalk mark on the right shoulder of the immigrant. People thus marked were held back for further examinations by a second group of doctors. Trachoma, a potentially blinding and highly contagious eye disease, was the most common reason for detaining an immigrant. Most though got a clean bill of health and only about two percent were turned back.

Once the doctors had passed an immigrant, they then proceeded to the registration clerks where names were always a problem. This is where names were twisted as most immigrants could not spell their name so clerks jotted down names as they sounded. Some name changes were deliberate when immigrants took new names for themselves knowing they had a better chance of getting a job. Once they were passed through here, they went to the baggage room to claim their belongings. Then they went to the money exchange desk where they exchanged their money for American dollars. Next to the railroad agent where they purchased a ticket to their destination. If they were bound for other than New York, they traveled by barge to New Jersey rail stations and from there they entered the mainstream of America.

At the end of WWI, many Americans were eager to see immigration restricted. The Immigration Act of 1917 carried a demand for a literacy test and reduced significantly the number of arrivals but only for a short time. The number of arrivals in New York soon climbed again and 500,000 immigrants entered through the Port in 1921. The government then enacted newer and more powerful methods of exclusion in 1921 and again in 1924. Soon the traffic through Ellis Island subsided to a trickle. A final revision of the "National origins" quota system went into effect in 1929 and the maximum number of all admissions was reduced to 150,000. As a result, in Nov 1954, the last immigrant and the last detainee left Ellis Island and the immigration center was declared as surplus property by the General Services Administration (GSA).

Ship arrival records had to be filed with the local Custom House. It is estimated that only about 40 percent of those records have survived and were turned over to the National Archives. All ships passenger lists which have survived have been microfilmed. Those microfilm copies for the Port of New York between 1846 and 1907 are not indexed.

All other ports are indexed. Many immigrants before 1891-92 entered through cities such as Boston, Philadelphia, Charleston, New Orleans and cities on the west coast of the U.S.A.

Restoration of Ellis Island began in 1982 with the renovation of the Great Hall. A genealogy exhibit where visitors will be able to search for immigrant information is planned. A computer will retrieve data on individuals including the name of the vessel on which they arrived, port of origin, arrival date in New York and other relevant details. It is expected that the number of tourists visiting the reborn Ellis Island will be the same each day as the average number of immigrants who passed through its days of operation as a receiving station.

The genealogical treasure house of the world, the Genealogical Department of The Church of Jesus Christ of Latter-day Saints (Mormon) is engaged in the most active and comprehensive genealogical program known to the world. Micro filming is the center of this genealogical operation. Trained specialists throughout the word are micro filming documents; land grants, deeds, probate, marriage, cemetery, parish registers and have accumulated over a millions rolls thus far. They are available in Salt Lake City and through branch libraries across the country. At the present time there is an extraction program being worked on by the Church of Jesus Christ of Latter-day Saints where the subject is the records of Ellis Island from 1892-1924. The finished product will become part of Family Search which is the program that includes the IGI, Ancestral File etc. held at Family History Centers. The LDS extraction statistics for 1997 show Ellis Island had 3,553,067 individual entries. Approximately 28% of the Ellis Island project has been completed. The Family History Library has microfilm copies of county naturalization before 1930 for many states and it has most federal court naturalization records before 1930.

If an immigrant ancestor arrived at the port of New York before 1892 (from 1855 on), they would have been processed through the existing facility at Castle Garden, since Ellis Island had not yet opened (which it did in 1892).

Passenger lists are only partially available at Ellis Island as what Ellis Island has at the historical site on their computer is only a fraction (by comparison) of the holdings at the U.S. National Archives (NARA) regional branches. Each regional branch of NARA has microfilms of those existing passenger lists which originated at a location geographically nearest that branch---in other words, the Boston records are in the Massachusetts regional branch, the New York records are in New York, etc. You can certainly visit or contact Ellis Island and search their computer for records, but if anyone wants to do more wide-ranging passenger list research (to insure that your ancestor is not overlooked), visiting the Archives is strongly recommended.

Please note that whichever processing facility served the immigrant, if the records were still in existence when the Archives did their filming, they will be in the appropriate Archives' branch. You don't need to worry whether it happened to be Ellis Island, Castle Garden, or some other port altogether (and there were several on the East coast alone).

Where records are available, it is quite possible to reconstruct the history of an entire family. Finding these records, however, is only the beginning of the project. If the person whose ship you are looking for became naturalized, then you should be able to find the name of the ship from that persons naturalization papers. (Remember, women became naturalized citizens with their husbands prior to 1923.)

If your ancestor was naturalized prior to 1906, you may have to search several places before you find naturalization papers. Before that date, a person could apply to a local, state or federal district to become naturalized. Contact the local courts, state courts and federal district courts in the area where your ancestor lived. In some cases, the court will still have the records, in others, the records may have been transferred to a local library or archive. Federal District Court Records may have been transferred to the National Archives.

After September 27, 1906, copies of naturalization papers were sent to the Immigration and Naturalization Service (INS) in Washington, DC. If your ancestor was naturalized after this date, you can write to: INS, 425 Eye Street NW, Washington, DC 20536.

For emigrants through Ellis Island and Castle Gardens - check out these sites:
http://gopher.nara.gov:70/1/about/publ/micro/compre
http://geocities.com/Athens/Acropolis/1709/Alfano1b.htm#paxmembers.tripod.com/~L_Alfano/immig.htm
http://www.nps.gov/cacl/
http://cmp1.ucr.edu/exhibitions/immigration_id.html
http://www.ellisisland.org/hotlinks.html
http://www.fortunecity.com/littleitaly/amalfi/100/ellis.htm

The Statue of Liberty-Ellis Island Foundation, Inc. plans to complete The American Family Immigration History Center in 2000. It will be housed in the Ellis Island Immigration Museum and will use state-of-the-art interactive computer technology to bring the immigration records of ancestors who came to this country as long as a century ago to one's fingertips. This ambitious project is gathering information on the more than 17 million people who immigrated through the port of New York from 1892-1924, the peak years of Ellis Island processing. The data is being taken directly from the ship's passenger manifests, which are currently on microfilm at the National Archives and Records Administration. It is being electronically transcribed through the generous efforts of The Church of Jesus Christ of Latter-day-Saints (the Mormons). These valuable documents are easily accessible. You will be able to find the immigrant's given name and surname, name of the ship he/she arrived on and their port of origin, date of arrival, age, gender and marital status, nationality and last place of residence.

Thanks to Carla Heller, carlah@earthlink.net for the following: "Below are some links to various Web sites which offer information on Ellis Island, some of which also have details on the Castle Garden immigrant processing facility in New York City, the predecessor to Ellis Island. Here are a few historical facts on both facilities.

(Please note: both Ellis Island and Castle Garden are the names of "immigrant receiving facilities," NOT port locations. Both served only passengers arriving at the port of New York. Contrary to popular misconception, New York·was not the ONLY East Coast port of arrival for European immigrants---though it was certainly the busiest and most popular. In terms of East Coast arrivals, immigrants might also have arrived from European ports at Philadelphia, Boston, and Baltimore, Maryland in addition to New York.

U.S. PASSENGER ARRIVAL RECORDS AND INDEXES ARE AVAILABLE FOR RESEARCH THROUGH THE U.S. NATIONAL ARCHIVES (NARA) REGIONAL BRANCHES AND THE LDS FAMILY HISTORY LIBRARY. Records are kept ACCORDING TO THE PORT CITY OF ARRIVAL: New York, Boston, Philadelphia, Baltimore, etc. It makes no different whether your ancestor was processed through the receiving facilities at Castle Garden or Ellis Island, or arrived before these facilities were in operation, or arrived elsewhere than New York. RECORDS for all of these are still found through NARA and the LDS Library's worldwide branches.

For immigrants arriving prior to 1855, there was no official reception facility. Until Castle Garden was ready to receive them in 1855, disembarking passengers were permitted to leave the ships directly into the Manhattan wharf area where the ships docked.

Castle Garden was the name given to a circular, fortress-like building located on the tip of Manhattan Island, in an area known as "the Battery." It had originally been a military station some years prior to its conversion to an immigration processing facility, which received its first immigrants 1 August 1855. It continued to receive and process immigrants arriving in the port of New York until mid-April, 1890.

From 19 April 1890 until 31 December 1891, immigrant processing and reception was temporarily transferred to the New York Barge Office, until the newly-built Ellis Island, situated separately within New York Harbor, opened its doors on 1 January 1892. (The Barge Office again temporarily fulfilled this task from 14 June 1897 through 16 December 1900, due to a fire which burned the new, wooden Ellis Island structure to the ground on 14 June 1897. A more fire-resistant Ellis Island was rebuilt over this 3-year hiatus and reopened 17 December 1900, continuing to serve as an immigration reception center until 1924. It was then used for other purposes (such as detention and deportation) until it officially closed altogether in 1954. Today, the facility at Ellis Island has been completely restored and is open to the public as a historical site. "

The following are Web sites contain information about either or both:
http://ourworld.compuserve.com/Homepages/M_Ziefle/famcom6e.htm
http://www.ellisisland.org/

BURIAL OF IMMIGRANTS IN NEW YORK CITY:
There were no burials on Ellis Island (1892-1954), and none at Castle Garden (1855-1892) (which was located on the southern tip of Manhattan at Battery Park). However, there was evidently an island elsewhere in the New York harbor area which was the site of a "State Immigrant Hospital," and there was an adjoining burial ground. The island where this hospital was located was called "Ward's Island" (now called "Great Barcut Island" in New York). The State Immigrant Hospital and burial grounds on Ward's Island were operating at least during the latter part of the Castle Garden era, from about 1880. It may have been operating before that. Starting in 1892, since Ellis Island had its own hospital located within the buildings which housed its immigrant processing facility, the Ward's Island hospital may have no longer been used. Ward's Island was given as a name for what is now or also called Randall's Island, which is at the juncture of the Harlem River and East River. It is one of the anchor points for the Triborough Bridge, and has a stadium on it. It is unlikely that the hospital or access to the former burial ground still exist (unlike the facilities at Ellis Island, which were restored and turned into a museum open to the public).

If you are interested in obtaining death records for persons who died in the New York City area (including Ward's Island), existing records for the time period in question are available through the New York City Municipal Archives. See their Web site at: http://www.ci.nyc.ny.us/html/serdir/html/xdoris01.html

Included in these records are persons who died before 1948 in New York City (Manhattan), one of the four surrounding boroughs (Brooklyn, Kings, Queens and the Bronx), or the islands in New York Harbor under the jurisdiction of the city of New York---such as Ward's Island. Note that the New York City Municipal Archives handles early records; records of deaths occurring after 1948 are maintained separately by the New York City Department of Health. For these, see the Web site at: http://www.ci.nyc.ny.us/html/doh/html/vr/vr.html

PLEASE NOTE THAT THESE AGENCIES HAVE NOTHING TO DO WITH PASSENGER LISTS OR IMMIGRATION INFORMATION. Contact them only if you are seeking copies or a search of vital records (such as death certificates).

If you remember "I" for "into" is Immigration and "E" for Exodus is Emigration - then you will know whether you are coming or going.

A group of volunteers have been transcribing passenger lists and posting them to a website. Go here to see them - http://istg.rootsweb.com/index1.html - Ships Passenger Lists. It is their goal to post passenger lists to this site in an attempt to allow researchers to access them online.

THE SHIPS LIST:
If you subscribe to and post your questions to: TheShipsList-D-request@rootsweb.com , you will receive directions from the various list owners and members as to how to find your information. Just send the word   Subscribe   to that address.

PASSENGER LISTS/SHIPS:
http://www.primenet.com/~langford/gen_page.htm (Passenger Lists)
http://members.aol.com/dcurtin1/gene/winthrop.htm (Passenger List of the Winthrop Fleet 1630)
http://members.aol.com/dcurtin1/gene/lyon.htm (Passenger List for the Lyon 1632)
http://members.aol.com/dcurtin1/gene/grifin34.htm (Passenger List for the Griffin 1634)
http://members.aol.com/dcurtin1/gene/planter.htm (Passenger List for the Planter 1635)
http://members.aol.com/dcurtin1/gene/martin38.htm (Passenger List for the Martin 1638)

http://members.aol.com/rprost/passenger.html (Passenger Lists on the Internet)
http://members.aol.com/calebj/mayflower.html (Mayflower)
http://freespace.virgin.net/alan.tupman/sites/ships.htm (Passenger Lists)
http://www.qrz.com/gene/www/emig/ham_pass.html (Hamburg Passenger Lists)
http://home.att.net/~arnielang/ship04f2.html
http://www.ristenbatt.com/genealogy/shipind.htm (PA-Germans)
http://www.sixranch.com/help/shipslists.html
http://members.tripod.com/~rosters/index-16.html
http://www.geocities.com/Heartland/5978/Emigration.html
http://www.hal-pc.org/~dcrane/txgenweb/passenge.htm (German-Texas Immigrant Passenger List)
http://www.Cyndislist.com/ships.htm
http://pixel.cs.vt.edu/library/ships/
http://genealogy.org/~palam/ia_index.htm
http://dcs1.uwaterloo.ca/~marj/genealogy/thevoyage.html
http://www-personal.umich.edu/~cgaunt/pass.html
http://www.ancestry.com (Check free lists at their web site; For paid members-has several shipping and immigration
          lists including Wurttemburg Emigration Index-7 volumes from 1780-1900)
http://www.rootsweb.com/~ote/indexshp.htm (Olive Tree-especially early colonists)
http://homepages.rootsweb.com/~george/johnsgermnotes/germhis1.html (Germanna Immigrants to Virginia in 1714
          and 1717)
http://istg.rootsweb.com (Where you'll see the results of the transcription guild's labors as well as links to other sites.)

Cunard's Archives - ship/passenger record - http://www.liv.ac.uk/~archives/cunard/chome.htm

To Request a search of the Passenger Arrival Records in USA email your request for Form 81 from the National
Archives - NARA - to: Inquire@nara.gov -They need your postal mail address

Steamship Historical Society of America Collection,
          University of Baltimore Library,
          1420 Maryland Avenue,
          Baltimore, MD 21201,
          http://www.sshsa.org
          Photos of ships can be ordered from the Library for a nominal fee.

More Information is available at: http://www.ubalt.edu/www/archives/ship.htm

Researchers who are seeking arrival records for passengers disembarking at the popular port of New York for a
particular period DO NOT HAVE ACCESS TO AN INDEX for these records. This makes it extremely difficult to
track down the arrival records you may seek, unless you are already aware of a specific date of arrival for your
ancestor of interest. For the period of New York arrivals from 1847 until June 16, 1897, it is my understanding
(gleaned from U.S. National Archives publications on the subject) that NO INDEX OF ARRIVAL RECORDS HAS
BEEN CREATED, and researchers will thus face the task of having to study the voluminous individual pages of the
arrival records themselves to locate an entry for an ancestor. To the best of my understanding, names in the arrival
records DO NOT appear in alphabetical order. I believe the records are organized according to date of arrival, port
of arrival, and (likely) ship of arrival.

Certain indexes ARE available for New York for both earlier and later arrivals than the period 1847 to mid-June
1897. The lack of indexes for other years might not be a matter of major concern to researchers, were it not for the
significant proportion of immigrant arrivals in the port of New York. While it was not the ONLY East Coast port of
arrival for European immigrants, it certainly was the busiest one. With lack of any index for a 50-year period of
arrivals, we are speaking of a considerable obstacle to one's research, unless a specific date of arrival is already
known.

U.S. arrival records DO NOT frequently include the name of the specific town of origin in Europe for a passenger. Michael Palmer, who is a recognized authority on this subject, recently posted a message stating that, "The port of departure is almost always given on original passenger arrival manifests..." Though obviously referring to ports of departure, Mr. Palmer does not mention whether a place of origin (meaning, a person's hometown or place of birth) is commonly specified in U.S. arrival records. I am of the understanding that, while place-of-origin information is often found in European departure passenger lists, it does not commonly appear in U.S. arrival lists.

For researchers who DO NOT KNOW a specific date of arrival during the above-stipulated period in New York for an ancestor, having to locate an arrival record without the aid of an index would be far more difficult and time-consuming than simply "taking a stab" at researching the Baden Emigration Index on LDS microfilms for ancestors who are known to have emigrated from Baden. The Baden Emigration Index on microfilm is arranged in alphabetical order by surname, and also according to a particular range of years---either BEFORE or AFTER 1866. The films are therefore considerably easier to search than an unindexed set of passenger records which are not organized in a similar manner.

Please maintain an awareness of possible obstacles with which someone researching U.S. arrival records may be faced. If one already knows WHEN an ancestor arrived, or does not mind the necessity of labor-and time-intensive research if there is no record index available, such obstacles will not be of concern to you.

Thanks to Carla Heller for help on this subject. Be sure to visit Carla's web page at: http://www.geocities.com/Heartland/Park/9485/ - How to Use LDS Family History Library Microfilm of the Baden Emigration Index

DEFINITIONS OF IMMIGRANT GROUPS:

HESSIANS: German Troops used by the British in the Revolutionary War, many of whom deserted and remained in America.

HUGUENOTS: French Protestants that fled from persecution mainly from 1685 onward. They went to Prussia, the German Palatinate and then came to America. Those in the French West Indies escaped to the southeastern coast of America, others went to England and Ireland.

MENNONITES: A Swiss Protestant group founded in 1525 and migrated by way of Alsace, England and Russia to America. They settled in Pennsylvania, Minnesota and Kansas.

MORAVIANS: The United Brethren is a Protestant group formed in Bohemia about 1415 and spread to Poland, Prussia, Germany and England.

PALATINES: In 1688 Louis XIV of France began persecuting German Protestants on the west bank of the Rhine River. Queen Ann of England helped a group to come to America in 1708. More than 2,000 arrived in New York in 1710 and settled along the Hudson and Mohawk Rivers.

QUAKERS: The Society of Friends was founded in England in 1648. Early restrictions brought them to New Jersey in 1675 and some 230 English Quakers founded Burlington, N.J. in 1678. 1681 was the year William Penn was granted the territory of Pennsylvania and within two years there were about 3,000 Quakers there.

SCOTS-IRISH: The descendants of the Presbyterian Scots that had been placed in the northern counties of Ireland by British rulers in the early part of the 17th century. Most came to America from 1718 until the Revolution. Settling in Pennsylvania first, the movement was then to the south and then westward with the frontier.

WALLONS: From southern Belgium, the language of the Wallons is a French dialect. Cornelis May of Flanders, Holland and about 30 to 40 families came to America in 1624 and Established Fort Orange, now known as Albany, NY.

SOME RESOURCES:
Temple - Balch Center for Immigration Studies, Philadelphia, PA , (scholarly immigration archive founded by Philadelphia Orphans Court in 1971 to fulfill Balch family wills; mission to document and interpret American immigration history and other ethnic life with photographs, foreign language newspapers; originals of NY passenger arrival lists (being published as Germans to America, Italians to America and Migration from the Russian Empire).

Germans to America currently ranges from Vol. 1 - January 1850 to Vol. 58, April 1890. New volumes are published as the work is completed.

Italians to America begins January 1880 and will eventually go to 1899. Vol. 9, through June 1896 is out.

Migration from the Russian Empire for arrivals at NY, currently cover Jan 1875 through May 1889. They will eventually go through 1910. The Genealogical Publishing Co. of Baltimore is publishing this series.

All of these books are essentially arranged by ship, from what port and port of arrival, date of arrival; name of immigrant, age, occupation, place of origin, and destination. Very few place of origins include a town, they generally are a state (Bavaria) or country (Germany, Russia). The relationships of people of the same name traveling together are not given, nor were they asked for when the lists were made.

Note that the Germans and Russian Empire books cover all the territory where Polish people lived. By Germans, they mean all people originating in Austria and the German Empire. I've looked at the Germans series, and there are lots of Polish surnames in them. The same goes for the Russian Empire series.

When using the books, remember to look under all spelling variations of the surname, and check several years around the date you may have found in the Census for date of arrival.

If your local library doesn't have these books in their genealogy collection, ask that they purchase them! The main LDS Library in Salt Lake City has these books. They are not currently on microfilm, as they are still being published. For those in the Chicago area, the Wheaton Public Library has them.

Most aliens became citizens within 10 years of the time they were eligible. Before 1906 the records were kept by federal, state and local courts. There is a book that summarizes these records on file for each state: "Locating Your Immigrant Ancestors: A Guide to Naturalization Records" by James C. and Lila Lee Negles. You can obtain this from Everton Publishers, Inc. or your local intra-library loan program.

To find the ship or port, check the Index to the Passenger Lists available at your local Family History Center and most large genealogical libraries. You can request a search of the Passenger Arrival Records by requesting Form 81 from the National Archives or e-mail your request for the form to: Inquire@nara.gov - be sure you give them your postal mailing address.

IMPORTANT DATES REGARDING NATURALIZATION:
1790
Citizenship required a two year residency in the U.S. and one year in the state, to be of good character, and to be performed in a court of record.

1795
Additional requirements were added of a 3-year residency to file a declaration of intention, a 5-year residency requirement (with 1-year in the state of residence) to file final papers, and required renunciation of titles of nobility and foreign allegiance. This act provided derivative citizenship for wives and minor children.

1798
Additional requirements stated that a copy of the return was to be sent to the Secretary of State, and the residency

was increased to fourteen years. This was repealed in 1802.

1804
Widows and children of an alien who died before filing his final papers were granted citizenship.

1824
The residency time between filing a declaration and final papers was shortened to two years.

1855
An alien female who married a U.S. citizen was automatically naturalized. This was repealed in 1922.

1862
Aliens over 21 who performed military service in the Army could become citizens after one year's residency.

1868
African Americans became citizens by passage of the Fourteenth Amendment.

1872
Alien seamen serving three years on a U.S. merchant vessel could be naturalized without fulfilling a residency requirement.

1882
Chinese were excluded from becoming citizens. This was repealed in 1943.

1891
The Office of Immigration was established. Polygamists, and those convicted of certain crimes or who carried certain diseases were excluded from citizenship.

1894
Aliens serving in the Navy or Marine Corps could be naturalized under the same conditions of the 1862 law.

1906
The Bureau of Immigration and Naturalization was established. Alien registration was required. Residency requirements were changed to two years to file intent, and five years for final papers. Derivative citizenship was still practiced.

1907
A female U.S. citizen who married an alien lost her U.S. citizenship and took on the nationality of her husband. This was repealed in 1922, but citizenship was not restored until 1936.

1918
Aliens serving in U.S. Forces during World War I could be naturalized without any residency requirement.

1921
The first Immigration Act to establish quotas of immigrants based on national origin was enacted.

1922
Women 21-years of age and over were entitled to citizenship. Derivative citizenship was discontinued. The residency requirement to file a declaration of intention was waived.

1924
The Citizen Act of June 2, 1924 provided that "all non-citizen Indians born with the territorial limits of the United

States be, and they are hereby declared to be, citizens of the United States." This included Indians living on tribal reservations.

1940

The Alien Immigration Act required registration and fingerprinting at a local post office within 30 days of arrival.

1952

The Immigration Act Amendment abandoned the national origins system of setting quotas on ethnic groups.

Note: Naturalization is voluntary. According to Census Bureau - of the foreign born persons listed on the 1890 through 1930 censuses, 25% had not become naturalized or filed their "first papers."

WESTERN COURT DISTRICT OF PENNSYLVANIA:

The Western Court District of Pennsylvania was established by Congress in 1820, with its seat at Pittsburgh. The US circuit and district courts that met there from 1820 to 1906 generated the declarations of intention and petitions for naturalization that are now in the custody of the FARC Philadelphia. These records are filed chronologically either by the date of the declaration or, if the naturalization action was completed by the same court, by the date of the petition. It should be noted that some of these documents are missing.

The indexes here microfilmed refer only to those aliens who sought naturalization in the US Circuit and the US District Court (1820-1906) for the Western District of Pennsylvania, which were located in Pittsburgh. However, an alien could seek citizenship through any court of record. Therefore, it was possible for an alien living in Pittsburgh to seek naturalization through the city or county courts in Pittsburgh. The city of Pittsburgh stopped the naturalization of aliens in 1906 and the county of Allegheny also relinquished naturalization jurisdiction in 1906. Both courts turned the function over to the Federal Courts. Therefore, these indexes do not contain the names of all those naturalized in the city of Pittsburgh or Allegheny County but only those naturalized in the Federal courts in Pittsburgh from 9 Oct 1820 through 28 Sep 1906. Researchers who wish to seek information on naturalization records from the city of Pittsburgh or Allegheny county should consult: A List of Immigrants Who Applied for Naturalization Papers in the District Courts of Allegheny County, PA 1798-1906. This 7-volume work was published by the Western PA Genealogical Society during the period 1978-1982.

BADEN EMIGRATION LIST INDEX from Carla Heller, carlah@earthlink.net - web page: http://www.geocities.com/Heartland/Park/9485/

The exact title of the publication on LDS microfilm is shown (in German) in their card catalogue as "Auswanderer, 17. bis 20. Jahrhundert," which roughly translates as "Emigration, 17th-20th Century." The author is shown as "Karlsruhe (Baden). Auswanderungsamt, which, again roughly translated, refers to the office(s) where residents of Baden (the former grand-duchy) registered when leaving the country and emigrating elsewhere. The microfilms are of original records in the Badischen Generallandesarchiv Karlsruhe, and were filmed by the LDS Family History Library in 1978.

This is a multi-film (38-roll, 35 mm) series of "card indexes and emigration lists for Baden, Germany to all parts of the world," (to give the language taken directly from the LDS Library's description). In general, the films are of good quality, and most of the data is typewritten or machine-printed, and therefore relatively easy to read.

The film series begins with Film # 1180096 and, as noted, contains an additional 37 rolls with separate numbers---not all of them in strict numerical sequence. To know which film(s) to view, a researcher needs to have an idea of whether an ancestor emigrated from Baden either before or after the year 1866 (the file is divided using that year as a separation point), and the films are in alphabetical order by surname or initial letter of the surname. For example, the first film in the series is for the period before 1866, and covers the alphabet from the letter "A" through the surname "DREHER."

There are also films in this series of emigration data for persons leaving Baden after 1866 (until 1911, the cutoff date for the filming), which are organized either alphabetically by surname and/or according to the location of the emigration office where the individuals registered---at Baden-Baden, Karlsruhe, Kehl, Altenheim, etc. There are also films in the same series with completely different sequence numbers which cover emigration from Baden and the nearby region of Elsass-Lothringen (Alsace-Lorraine), and films which contain some bibliographic material. It is necessary to carefully check the description and numbers of the available films to make sure you are ordering the particular roll(s) which may include the surnames, region, and time period you are seeking.

These films are of the Baden Emigration List index----an alphabetical card index with names and various degrees of information about the emigrants---not the actual emigration records themselves. The card index, is, though, quite helpful in many cases. Keep in mind that if you are researching a common German surname (such as SCHMIDT, MÜLLER, BAYER, MEYER, HOFFMANN, HARTMANN, MILLER, SCHNEIDER, SCHWARTZ, etc., etc., etc.), you are likely to encounter dozens and dozens of persons with not only the same surname, but the same given name---so you are well-advised to have some kind of other substantiating information about your Baden-origin ancestor, such as a birth or emigration date, parents' names, place of origin, etc. Remember, too, that German (and other) surnames which may seem unusual to those of us outside Germany are often quite common within Germany itself. Be prepared to do some detective work to more precisely identify any individuals whom you suspect might be your ancestors---both before and after you take the time to research the Baden Emigration List Index. No one wants to discover that they have been painstakingly researching the wrong family---especially years down the line!

The Baden Emigration List Index films are catalogued on the LDS FHC computer (and their conventional card catalogue) under the following headings (they cross-reference each other, but point to the same films:

1. Germany, Baden - Emigration and immigration
2. Germany - Emigration and immigration
3. Germany, Baden, Karlsruhe - Emigration and immigration
4. United States - Emigration and immigration
5. Germany, Elsass-Lothringen - Emigration and immigration

Current loan fees for LDS films vary slightly from one FHC branch to another. It can be $3.00 to $3.50 per roll plus 15 cents per roll additional for postage (as they are sent to the local branch from the main LDS library in Salt Lake City, unless certain rolls are already on permanent loan to the local branch). Check with your FHC branch staff for fee details. The usual current initial loan period for each film is 8 weeks, and they can be renewed (for an additional nominal fee per roll) at least twice. Researchers view LDS films within the local LDS Family History Center branches on the microfilm reading machines available there.

NATIONAL ARCHIVE PASSPORT APPLICATION RECORD INFORMATION:
Since 1798 the Department of State has issued passports to United States citizens traveling abroad. The Department did not, however, have sole authority to do so until an Act of August 18, 1856 (11 Stat. 60), for the first time regulated the issuance of passports.

There was no statutory requirement that Americans obtain a passport for travel abroad until World War I, although an order by Secretary of State William H. Seward prohibited departure from or entry into the United States without a passport during the period August 19, 1861 - March 17, 1862. Many persons did obtain passports, however, because they were required by the countries to which they were traveling or because the traveler wanted the protection a passport might provide. On November 14, 1914, the State Department issued a requirement that American citizens must have a valid passport for travel abroad. This was followed by Executive Order 2285 of December 15, 1915, which gave presidential authorization to the same requirement. Then, the Travel Control Act of May 22, 1918, made the requirement a matter of statutory law. A Joint Congressional Resolution of March 3, 1921, technically ended the wartime restrictions of travel, including the passport requirement. An Act of June 21, 1941, reimposed the statutory requirement, and the "Immigration and Nationality Act" of June 27, 1952, made it unlawful to depart from or enter the United States without a valid passport.

State Department passport records in the custody the National Archives include applications dated October 27, 1795 - November 30, 1812; February 22, 1830 - November 15, 1831; and May 13, 1833 - December 31, 1905; emergency applications submitted abroad 1877 - 1907; originals and copies of passports 1794 - 1901; and applications for special (diplomatic) passports 1829 - 1897. Applications dated 1906 - 1925 are in our Civil Reference Branch in Suitland, Maryland.

Finding aids for these records are incomplete. There is an alphabetical card index for applications dated 1850 - 1852 and 1860 - 1880. For the years 1810 - 1817 and 1834 - 1904 there are also registers and indexes which vary by arrangement. Some are chronological and some are alphabetical by the first letter(s) of the applicant's surname.

For post-1923 applications, please contact the Passport Office, Bureau of Consular Affairs, FAIM/RS, Room 1239, Department of State, 22nd & C Street, NW, Washington, DC 20520. The State Department maintains passport applications starting in 1925, and a name index that begins in 1923. If the passport application you seek was made between 1923 and 1925, the State Department will provide you with an application number, which you should in turn send to the National Archives.

The alphabetical card index for passport applications dated 1850 - 1852 and 1860 - 1880 is held in the Family History Library at Salt Lake City. The computer number in the catalog is 437973, the actual microfilm numbers are 1429876 - 1429903.

Textual Reference Branch National Archives and Records Administration, 7th and Pennsylvania Avenue NW, Washington, DC 20408

Hamburg Passenger Lists 1850-1934 website: http://www.hamrick.com/names/

http://members.aol.com/rprost/passenger.html - Passenger Lists on the Internet

http://home.att.net/~arnielang/ship04f2.html - Guide to Immigration Records and Ship's Passenger Lists Research Guide

URL's on what the boat conditions were like and the expectations of the immigrant, etc. The sites are:
http://www.hamburg.de/Behoerden/Pressestelle/emigration/englisch/welcome.htm
http://www.bergen.org/AAST/Projects/Immigration/index.html

Library of Congress - Immigrant Arrivals - a reference guide to published sources:
http://lcweb.loc.gov/rr/genealogy/bib_guid/immigrant.html

THIS AND THAT GENEALOGY TIPS ON LAND

LAND SURVEY:
There are two types of land survey which vary chiefly by the part of country in which you are located.

1. Along the Atlantic coastal states land surveys were at one time strictly by metes and bounds. Thus you will see: "Beginning at an oak tree in the bank of X creek, proceed North by East 27 degrees for 16 chains, 6 links, to a large stone; thence ......" This entire system derived from the fact that people moved into the frontier and claimed land, marked by natural boundaries, which were later surveyed.

2. The other system is based on the Geodetic Survey and makes use of the latitude and longitude lines. This was in existence by the time US land grants were being made (but not the British).

a. This system breaks down the area into squares within squares. The largest square after latitude and longitude is located by Range (East or West from a Meridian) and Township which are North or South of a line).

b. Each of these squares is broken down into sections, numbered in a prescribed order.

c. Each Section is one square mile.

d. Now divide each Section into four equal parts with a + at the center. Label these NE, SE, SW & NW.

e. Now divide each 1/4 into four equal parts the same way. Each will contain 40 acres. Now lets describe the 40 acres in the NE corner of the section: "NE 1/4 of the NE 1/4, Section 16, Range 2 West, Township 3 North." A larger plot might be described as: "N ½ of the NE 1/4......" or "SE 1/4 of the NE 1/4 and NW 1/4 of SE 1/4 of...." Multiple 1/4's are each described before naming the section.

f. This is not to say that a surveyor might not at times follow other lines but he was required to orient the plot by this system, and his starting point will always be one of the corners in the system. In many parts of the country the four major corners of the section are marked with a concrete marker, properly labeled.

g. Fortunately most of the US now uses this system. This also explains why most of the lesser roads in a community run N-S or E-W with square corners. The other side is that they did not have as many hills and streams to go around.

With a deed and a topographical map, using the 2nd system you can walk directly to the spot described. (In the former, you get into all kinds of platting, and hope with enough research and knowledge of the neighbors, you can find it.)

One problem is that the deed maker did not always spell out all the words. Thus it helps if you know what he was abbreviating. Any good topographical map dealer can help you get on the right map and point you to the section.

POLES, RODS, LINKS AND CHAINS:
Long Measure - 1 mile......80 chains/ 320 rods/ 5,250 feet

1 chain....4 rods or perches/ 66 feet/22 yards/100 links

1 rod.......varies from 5 ½ yards to 8 yds./16.5 feet/ 25 links . May also be used to describe an area equal to 1/4 of an acre.

1 link.......7.92 in./ 25 links in a rod/ 100 links or 4 yds. in a chain/ 0.66 feet

1 pole.....16.5 feet.

1 perch...16.5 feet/5.5 yds/1 rod. It is sometimes called a "pole" or a "rod".

SQUARE MEASURE:
1 sq mile......640 acres/ regular section

1 mile..........5280 ft./ 80 chains/320 rods or 8 furlongs

1 acre..........10 sq. chains/ 160 sq. rods/ 43,560 sq. ft

1 sq. rod......30 1/4 sq. yds/ 272 1/4 sq ft.

1 sq. ft.........144 sq inches

1 furlong.......660 ft./220 yds/10 chains/

1 square chain...16 square rods/ 1/10 of an acre

FEDERAL SOURCES - REVOLUTIONARY WAR BOUNTY-LAND WARRANT APPLICATION FILES:
Bounty-land warrants, which entitled their holders to free land in the public domain, were given to veterans or their survivors for wartime service performed between 1775 and 3 March 1855. Bounty-land warrant application files, which provide evidence of military service, are part of Record Group 15, Records of the Veterans Administration.

Since most bounty-land warrants were transferable, an approved bounty-land warrant application is not evidence of land ownership. Bounty-land warrants surrendered for land in the public domain, usually by someone other than the veteran who applied for the warrant, document ownership of land at a given time and place. These surrendered warrants are part of Record Group 49, Records of the General Land Office.

A bounty-land warrant application is especially valuable in an instance where the veteran or his widow did not apply for a pension. Not all Revolutionary War veterans and widows met the qualifications for pensions during their lifetimes, and some who did qualify did not apply. Since there was no need requirement for bounty land, many of these veterans and widow did apply for bounty-land warrants.

In addition to his rank, military unit, and period of service, a bounty-land warrant application by a Revolutionary War veteran will give his age and place of residence at the time of the application. An application by a widow will normally give, in addition to her age and place of residence, the date and place of her marriage to him, and her maiden name. An application by a survivor may list all of the veteran's heirs at law.

BOUNTY LAND LEGISLATION:
In 1776, the Continental Congress promised land to officers and soldiers who engaged in military service and served until the end of the Revolutionary War or until discharged and to the survivors of those killed in the war. The amount of land varied with rank. Privates and noncommissioned officers were to receive 100 acres, ensigns 150, lieutenants 200, captains 300, majors 400, lieutenant colonels 450, and colonels 500. In 1780 the law was extended to generals, granting brigadier generals 850 acres and major generals 1,100. This was the basic law under which bounty land was granted for Revolutionary War service until 1855.

In 1788 Congress directed the Secretary of War to begin issuing warrants to eligible veterans upon application. This law provided that the veteran could transfer his warrant to another person, and most of the warrants issued under this and succeeding acts were assigned at least once before being surrendered for land.

Actual patenting of land in exchange for bounty-land warrants did not begin until about 1800. Until 1830 the U.S.

Military District of Ohio was the only place a Revolutionary War bounty-land warrant could be used. Beginning in 1830 a bounty-land warrant could be exchanged for scrip which was receivable at any land office in Ohio, Indiana, and Illinois. In 1842 all federal bounty-land warrants were made good at any land office.

In 1855 Congress amended the basic law governing bounty land granted for Revolutionary War service by making the minimum entitlement 160 acres regardless of rank and reducing the service requirement to fourteen days or participation in any battle during the war. A veteran or survivors who had previously received fewer than 160 acres could apply for the balance. In 1856 the benefits of the 1855 act were extended to Revolutionary War naval officers and enlisted men and their heirs. Many applications for bounty-land warrants were made under the 1855 act by persons who met the service requirement for the first time.

Claimants for bounty-land warrants based on Revolutionary War service forwarded their applications to the Secretary of War until 1841, to the Commissioner of Pensions in the War Department from 1841 to 1849, and to the Secretary of the Interior after the Pension Office was transferred to that department in 1849. Some applications were accompanied by affidavits testifying to the military service performed, marriage records, and other forms of evidence. When an application was approved, a warrant for a specified number of acres was issued to the claimant or his assignee. The holder of the warrant then selected the portion of the public domain he wished to have in exchange for the warrant and surrendered the warrant at the appropriate district land office. The papers were forwarded to Washington where the Treasury Department and, after 1849, the Interior Department issued a patent for the land.

BOUNTY-LAND WARRANT APPLICATION FILES:
Bounty-land warrant applications and related papers approved before the War Department fire of November 1800 are presumed to have been lost in that fire. These lost files are represented by 10" x 14" cards that show the name of the veteran, his rank, the state or organization for which he served, the symbol "B.L.Wt." followed by the warrant number and the number of acres granted, the date the warrant was issued, and the name of a person other than the veteran to whom the warrant was delivered or assigned. This information was transcribed from surviving registers of bounty-land warrants issued before 8 November 1800.

Files for bounty-land warrants applications approved after 8 November 1800 are in envelopes that have headings consisting of the name of the veteran, his widow's name if she applied for the warrant, the state or organization for which he served, the symbol "B.L.Wt." followed by the number of the warrant, the number of acres granted, and, in the case of applications made under the act of 1855, the number "55". Records in the files may include applications, family Bible records, marriage records, affidavits testifying to the veteran's service, and other papers.

Envelopes containing rejected bounty-land warrant applications are marked "B.L.Reg." (for bounty-land register) followed by the register number assigned to the application.

Bounty-land warrant applications and related papers have been consolidated with pension application files based on the service of the same veteran. Frequently a widow's approved pension application is consolidated with her approved bounty-land warrant application under the act of 1855. A veteran's pension application and bounty-land warrant application may be in the same file. Rejected pension application files may also contain approved or rejected bounty-land warrant application papers.

MICROFILM PUBLICATION:
The Revolutionary War pension and bounty land warrant application files have been microfilmed on 2,670 rolls of National Archives Microfilm Publication M804. The files are arranged alphabetically by the surnames of the veterans. A pamphlet describing the contents of this publication roll by roll is available free of charge from the National Archives.

Microfilm Publication M804 is available to researchers at the National Archives in Washington, D.C. and at the eleven National Archives field branches. Individual rolls can be borrowed for you by your local library through the Census Microfilm Rental program. The publication is also available at the LDS Genealogical Department Library in Salt

Lake City and through its branch libraries. Microfilm rolls can be purchased from the National Archives.

As an alternative to using the microfilmed records, a copy of a Revolutionary War bounty-land warrant application file can be ordered by mail from the National Archives using NATF Form 80, Order for Copies of Veterans Records. Check "Bounty-Land Warrant Application" on the form and provide the name of the veteran, the war in which he served, the state from which he served, and, if you have it, the bounty-land warrant application file number.

"Index to Revolutionary War Pension Applications in the National Archives," published by the National Genealogical Society gives the name of the veteran, the state from which he served, the bounty-land warrant application file number, and, in the case of a widow's application, the given name of the widow. This index is available in many libraries and can be purchased from the Society.

Information found in a bounty-land warrant application file for your evolutionary War ancestor should be properly identified in your family records. A citation should include the following: (Descriptive title of the document), (name of the veteran), Revolutionary War Bounty-Land Warrant Application File (symbol and numbers), Records of the Veterans Administration, Record Group 15, National Archives Microfilm Publication M804, roll (number.)

A good page for US Public Land Survey methods: http://users.rootsweb.com/~mistclai/landsurv.htm

Bureau of Land Management (BLM), Eastern States, General Land Office (GLO) Records Automation web site. This site provides live database and image access to more than two million federal land title records for the Eastern Public Land States, dating back to 1820: http://www.glorecords.blm.gov/

If you get a 'hit' on a surname, then you will have the township, range and other numbers for the parcel of land. Now go back to the Search page and enter these numbers and do another Search. You will get an alphabetical listing of all the people given land patents in the area. Search the list carefully for like-sounding names or the surnames of in-laws. If you get a map of the area from one of the Internet map sites, you could enter all the surrounding property owners and get a better picture of the area at the time and see who were your family's neighbors and where marriage partners often came from.

From Land And Property Research in The United States by E Wade Hone:
The requirements for public land transaction (federal lands or BLM land) differed from act to act. There were certain basic elements involved in almost every public land transaction. When your ancestor desired a tract of land he went through these steps. (These are only for public domain lands; Ohio , Illinois , Arkansas plus many more).

Step One: Application or entry: This step is accomplished through several different methods, depending on the area and time period involved. Sometimes payment itself was considered adequate for successful application. One requirement for eligibility was the need for the applicant to have been native born or declare an intention to become a citizen of the U.S. This applied to most federal land purchases except military bounty land warrants, some preemption or private land claims.

Step 2: Once the application was completed, cash was paid or arrangements made for credit, and a receipt was issued. The receipt may be all that is in the file of the earliest cases.

Step 3: Warrant for Survey was issued for the specified land entry.

Step 4: The survey was recorded in the township plat books.

Step 5: The information was filed in a Tract book by the registrar. This paperwork , together was all other records created by the Applicable acts of Congress was then transferred to the General Land Office (today, Bureau of Land Management). These are called land-entry case files and MIGHT contain the following: Testimonies, declarations of Intent, affidavits, receipt copies, bounty land warrants, and proof of citizenship and naturalization. Specific birth dates, birthplaces, military rank, and enlistment information can be found, depending on the type of lands acquired. Case files also exist for those whose land claims were rejected, revoked, contested, or canceled. These are often more graphic in historical content than those readily accepted.

THE OFFICIAL LAND PATENTS RECORD SITE: A STARTING POINT By Michael John Neill

Land ownership has long been a part of the American Dream. It motivated countless Americans to move within the country and countless other people to emigrate to the United States. Before 1900, a significant proportion of adult males owned real property. Because land records cover a high proportion of the pre-1900 population, they constitute a significant genealogical resource. Federal land records are a part of this resource.

The Official Land Patents Record Site contains an index to land patent records for eleven states (Illinois is due to come on line in December of this year). The following states are currently represented in the Official Land Patents Record Site: Alabama, Arkansas, Florida, Indiana, Louisiana, Michigan, Minnesota, Mississippi, Missouri, Ohio, and Wisconsin. The one distinct advantage to this site is the ability to immediately obtain a digital copy of the patent. Individuals who wish to order an actual photocopy of the record can also do that directly from the web site. Users of the site need to have an overview of the terminology and the federal land acquisition process in order to make effective use of the site.

TERMINOLOGY CONSIDERATIONS:

Our discussion here is somewhat limited. Readers desiring more detailed information on the land acquisition process and terminology should refer to "The Source's" section chapter on land records or Wade E. Hone's book "Land and Property Research in the United States"

The patent is the official title to a piece of property, indicating that the acquisition process is complete. The patent is the first deed to a piece of property, where the government transfers ownership to a private individual. Subsequent deeds transfer ownership between private individuals and are local, not federal, records.

The warrant is an authorization for surveyors to mark or plat the property and to formally record a description of the piece of property. It was the result of a successful and completed application, not the result of the completion of the entire Federal land acquisition process. It is the patent that is the final document, not the warrant.

Patentee vs. warrantee. The patentee is the individual who received the land patent. The warrantee is the person for whom the land was surveyed. These individuals were not necessarily the same person.

Aliquot parts. This refers to the position of the property within a specific section of a township.

WHERE EXACTLY IS THE LAND?

In Federal land states (such as those in the BLM site), original tracts of land were usually originally rectangular or square in shape. A piece of property is described in reference to its position relative to base lines and meridians. Base lines run horizontally and meridians run vertically. Some states have more than one base line and more than one meridian. The survey system in Federal land states attempted to place a grid upon the area of the country being surveyed.

The largest region is the township, generally a square of land six miles on a side. The township is described relative to its position to the base line and meridian. Townships are described as either north or south of a base line and east or west of a meridian. A description of T3N8W, means the township is 3 townships north of the base line and eight townships west of the principal meridian. There are many base lines and meridians. Wade Hone's book contains several maps indicating which base lines and meridians were used in which locations.

Congressional townships are townships that are a part of the meridian grid system. Land patents and deeds generally refer to these townships. Civil townships are a governmental region, and occasionally are confused with congressional townships (for understandable reasons). Civil townships may coincide with a congressional township, include just part of a congressional township, or include multiple congressional townships. Congressional townships are for surveying purposes and civil townships are for governmental purposes. Census records, or any record that provides an address which includes a township, most likely refer to a civil township and not to a congressional township.

Townships are broken up into 36 sections; a section contains 640 acres and is one mile on a side. Sections are divided into four quarter-sections, the Northwest, the Northeast, the Southwest, and the Southeast. Each quarter-section contains 160 acres. The thirty-six sections in a township are numbered beginning in the Northeast corner of the township, going west, going south one section, and then back east, working horizontally and continuing down until the final section is reached (in the southeast quarter to the township). Obtaining plat maps of the area being researched is a good idea for the researcher. A modern plat map will provide the general lay of the land and should provide the congressional township numbers for townships in the county. Genealogists who know the township names where their ancestors lived also need to become familiar with the township numbers as well.

Melissa Calhoun's site on the township range system provides an excellent graphic representation of the system. http://www.outfitters.com/genealogy/land/twprangemap.html

SEARCH INTERFACE:
The Bureau of Land Management's search interface allows users to enter in all or parts of the following information:

From the Patent Description:
~ Document Number
~ *Patentee last name, first name, and middle initial*
~ *Warrantee last name, first name, and middle initial*
~ County Name (one or all counties)

From the Legal Land Description:
~ Section Number
~ Township Number/Direction (or any township)
~ Range Number/Direction (or any range)
~ Meridian Name (or all meridians within the state)

SEARCH OPTIONS:
Users can search for information on this site in more than one way. The most elementary way is to search for a specific name. One limitation is that searches can be conducted only one state at a time. For more researchers this is not a serious limitation. There are ways searches can be refined and customized.

By specifying search parameters, users can obtain a listing of all individuals who received patents/warrants in certain counties, certain townships, or even in specific sections, regardless of the name of the patentee/warrantee. Researchers can also search for specific names (or surnames) in specific geographic locations.

HOW DO I FIGURE OUT WHAT SECTION/TOWNSHIP IS "BELOW?"
Broadening the search to adjacent townships or sections requires the user to work with the numbering scheme for townships and sections. Searching for the township "above," "below," to the left, right, etc. can be done if the user is aware of the township numbering scheme. Printed maps on paper or graphic images of the maps will assist the user in determining adjacent townships and sections. While they are not absolutely necessary, theoretical maps (available on Melissa Calhoun's site and the BLM site) are especially helpful.

As an example, township 3N5W has the following townships that border it. To the north is 4N5W (one more "unit" north); to the south is 2N5W (one less "unit" north); to the east 3N4W (one less "unit" west); to the west 3N6W (one more "unit" west).

Township number must also be taken into account. For example, section 15 in a standard township is bordered by section 10 on the north, section 22 on the south, section 14 on the east and section 16 on the west. Searchers should not solely focus on the bordering sections, but should include those relatively close to the section of interest.

It should be remembered that sections on the edge of the township will have bordering sections in adjacent townships. Searching for adjacent sections in this case will require searching in adjacent townships.

As another example, section 1 township A directly borders four sections:
~ Sections 2 and 12 in township A
~ Section 6 in the township to the east of township A
~ Section 36 in the township to the north of township A

SEARCH RESULTS:
The site provides results in one of two formats: Genealogical Search Results and Title Search Results. A search for entries under the surname of "LAKE" in Chariton County, Missouri, is illustrative.

GENEALOGICAL SEARCH RESULTS:
The following data was extracted from the results page after using the Genealogical Search Results Option:

"There were 2 matches to your request. This is page 1 of 1. Click on the Patentee Name to view the Land Patent Report. You may begin the order process by clicking the 'Order' button associated with the patent."

PATENTEE NAME	SIGNATURE DATE	DOC. NR.	ACCESSION NR.
LAKE, JOHN - -	04/01/1857 - -	5729 - -	MO5020__.320
LAKE, SAMUEL - -	02/11/1819 - -	4951 - -	MO6180__.034

Clicking on the patentee name will bring up more information obtained on the document and a link to view or download a scan of the actual patent. Users who do not have a graphics viewer are provided with a link to obtain one. The graphics can either be viewed within the web browser (using a plug-in) or downloaded to a hard drive and viewed with a stand-alone program. The scans are reasonably good, easy to view, and will print fairly well on a decent laser printer.

TITLE SEARCH RESULTS:
The following data was extracted from the results page after using the Title Search Results Option and again searching for "LAKE" in Chariton County, Missouri:

"There were 3 matches to your request. This is page 1 of 1. Click on the Aliquot Parts to view the Land Patent Report. You may begin the order process by clicking the 'Order' button associated with the patent.

E1/2NW - -	30	56-N - -	17-W - -	5TH PRINCIPAL MERIDIAN	MO5020__.320
NWNW - -	30	56-N - -	17-W - -	5TH PRINCIPAL MERIDIAN	MO5020__.320
NW - -	11	56-N - -	20-W - -	5TH PRINCIPAL MERIDIAN	MO6180__.034

Information is listed in the following order: aliquot parts, section, township, township, range, meridian, accession number. On the title search results page, clicking on the aliquot parts pulls up more information about the patent. In this case, since the first two references have the same accession number, it appears that the two first parcels appear on the same patent.

Users who obtain search results (both for title searches and genealogical searches) will obtain them in tabular format in their browser. There is a limit to the total number of matches that can be displayed (200) and users get 20 matches per page. Users can save these files to their hard drives as text files and incorporate the data into a database (see Ancestry Daily News 7 October 1998 - - http://www.ancestry.com/dailynews/10_07_98.txt to learn more about converting Internet search results into spreadsheet format.

The following information was returned when the aliquot parts section was clicked on:

MO5020___.320
Canceled: N
Document Nr. : 5729
Misc. Document Nr. :
Patentee Name: LAKE, JOHN
Warrantee Name:
Authority: April 24, 1820: Cash Entry Sale (3 Stat. 566)
Signature Present: Y
Signature Date: 4/1/57
Metes/Bounds: N
Survey Date:
Subsurface Reserved: N
Land Office: MILAN
Comments:

MO6180___.034
Canceled: N
Document Nr. : 4951
Misc. Document Nr. :
Patentee Name: LAKE, SAMUEL
Warrantee Name: LAKE, SAMUEL
Authority: May 6, 1812: Scrip-Warrant Act of 1812 (2 Stat. 728)
Signature Present: Y
Signature Date: 2/11/19
Metes/Bounds: N
Survey Date:
Subsurface Reserved: N
Land Office: MISSOURI
Comments: HEIRS

A complete listing of various aliquot parts is not possible here due to space considerations, but a few examples will serve to illustrate:

NWNW--the northwest quarter of the northwest quarter
N1/2 NW--the north half of the northwest quarter
SWSE--the southwest quarter of the southeast quarter

It should be noted that the aliquot parts description always begins with the smallest part of the description. The maps on Melissa Calhoun's site will explain with pictures what at times is difficult to do with words.

IS THERE MORE?
Researchers should note that the patents on this web site are not the only records that may be available. This is true for two reasons.

The first is that there are other records contained in the land-entry case file for each patent. The patent is not the only record that was created. Materials in these files can vary, depending upon what type of land was being obtained and the act under which the claim was filed. But the case file should be referenced if you determine that your ancestor obtained a patent. It's too bad Samuel LAKE is not the ancestor. Since it is indicated that his heirs completed the land acquisition process, information on them may be contained in the land-entry case file.

Additionally, subsequent land transactions (between private individuals) are filed at the county level. The patents obtained on this site are "first" land sales from the Federal government, where property transferred hands from Federal to private ownership. Records of subsequent land transfers frequently are at the county level, occasionally in a state or regional archives (Ancestry's Red Book would provide this information for the counties of interest to the reader). If the property in question was owned by successive generations, analyzing subsequent land transfers may provide more information. The BLM site does not have records on transactions between private individuals. It should be noted that these private transactions represent the vast majority of land transactions that have taken place in the United States.

Researchers should not limit their searches to Federal land records. Unfortunately, local records of subsequent transfers do not contain the detail that one may find in the land-entry case file. It should be noted that there are significant numbers of genealogists whose ancestors never obtained a Federal land patent (including me!). Just because you don't find your ancestors didn't obtain a land patent does not mean that land records will not help your research.

For more information on land records, readers should refer to "Land & Property Research in the United States," by E. Wade Hone. This book is especially strong on Federal land records. Ancestry's "The Source" also contains a wonderful chapter on land records.

The more I searched the site and learned about Federal land records, the more I wished at least one of my ancestors had obtained a land patent.

Michael John Neill, is the Course I Coordinator at the Genealogical Institute of Mid America (GIMA) held annually in Springfield, Illinois, and is also on the faculty of Carl Sandburg College in Galesburg, Illinois. Michael is the education columnist for the FGS FORUM and is on the editorial board of the Illinois State Genealogical Society Quarterly. He conducts seminars and lectures on a wide variety of genealogical and computer topics and contributes to several genealogical publications, including Ancestry and Genealogical Computing.

THIS AND THAT GENEALOGY TIPS ON LDS (LATTER DAY SAINTS) and FHC (FAMILY HISTORY CENTERS)

FHC, LDS, ANCESTRAL FILE AND IGI:
The Ancestral File is a "working" file and it not meant to be a completed file. That's why there are constant updates and an "edit" function key. Its purpose is to coordinate your research with others, share your genealogy, link your genealogy to what's in the file. The church does not verify the information. It is up to you to document your hard work in order to maintain the integrity of the files. If you submit your information, keep it current. Make corrections, change your address, document your sources, etc.

The LDS librarians (as opposed to non-member librarians who are almost always experienced genealogists) are apt to be people the local church leaders have asked to work in the library in order to learn how to do genealogy. They do want to be helpful and they have keys to let you in. They are eager to learn, but are at different stages in that process. On the other hand many have a great deal of experience. Nevertheless, each of us has our own areas of expertise. Ask lots of questions. The librarians need to know to help people.

FHCs have three kinds of things:
1. Reference materials: hard copies and microfilm. The book collection varies from one FHC to the other. But each should have certain basic materials. On paper there are Resource Outlines for each state and province of Canada and several countries and special subjects. These cost a small amount. Good for reference. Browse the shelves. Every FHC has a collection of 200 basic reference works on microfiche. Ask the librarian where the directory to this is. Browse through the microfiche collection. Every time someone orders fiche it stays in the Center forever.

2. The Family History Library Catalog (FHLC). The FHLC is the catalog of what is in the Salt Lake Library. You can order microfilm and fiche (but not books) and use them in the FHC. Browse the FHLC. See if you can find the resource outline about how to use it. The headings in the state Resource Outlines are the same headings that are used in the FHLC. You can search it by author/title, the quickest way to find a specific book. Or you can search it by locality. At the beginning of each country or state there is a list of places for which they have material. It's an easy way to find out what political jurisdiction a town or city falls under. Or you can search the surname section for material about a specific family. This is a great index to "hidden genealogies," things on one surname buried in a genealogy of a different family. Or you can search by subject. The catalog is also on the FamilySearch computer, but it works a little differently. You cannot search by author or title, but you can enter a film number and identify it.

3. Databases on the FamilySearch computer and also on microfiche. The databases on the computer are the IGI, Ancestral File, the Social Security death index, Scottish Parish Registers (OPR) and Korean and Vietnam War deaths, as well as the catalog. Read the instruction manual and/or get copies of instructions to take home. The databases on fiche are census indexes 1790-1850, Scottish Old-Parochial Records and some others. See if the FHC has a copy of a huge book called THE LIBRARY.

Here are main points regarding how to make the best use of one's time at FHC:
> 1)You can download from LDS site research guides for localities you are interested in.
> 2)You can buy guides at reasonable cost at LDS FHCs.
> 3)Check them over and get an idea of what kinds of material is available.
> 4)You can download CD material at FHCs using your own disks. Remember, the sources used by someone submitting their data to the FHC isn't always clear and may not be verified.
> 5)Call FHC before hand to reserve computer time.

Things to download:
1. Information from FH Library Catalog--locality guide and surname index for most important current research.
2. Information from IGI regarding people with particular surname -- wise to use filter regarding localities or you

might get too much to handle--helps as guide, don't take as gospel.
3. Contributions to Ancestral File of your ancestors--helps as guide, don't take as gospel.

Order films for further research--remember to check whether index is on separate film. If so order it too!

Regarding the International Genealogical Index (IGI) - it is an index, a finding tool, however, it is not like an index in a book. In order to make good use of it, you must make some effort to understand how it is put together. It is primarily an index to temple work for individuals, which explains why there are often multiple entries for the same person. Names are often submitted for temple work to be done without having first found out whether it has been done before. There are various reasons why this has been very difficult to do in the past. The new IGI addendum goes a long way toward making it easier than ever before.

There seems to be a general recognition that there are two main kinds of entries in the IGI, those submitted by individuals and those extracted directly from original records. We tend to trust the latter entries, and it is relatively easy to check out the original source. If using the IGI on microfiche, these extracted entries usually have a batch number beginning with C or M or occasionally another letter, but some begin with numbers. The CD-ROM edition gives pretty complete information for each entry. But if you're using the IGI on fiche there is no substitute for reading detailed instructional material about this.

Basically discussed here are the individual entries, as these are the ones that give people the most trouble. In order to evaluate the entry, you need to get hold of the material "behind" it, i.e., the piece of paper submitted by the person to initiate the temple work. And what you most need from that is the source(s) used by the submitter. Submission has been done differently at different times. The four eras are:
1. Pre-1942   3. 1969-ca. 1990
2. 1942-1969   4. 1990 to the present

When you find an entry, look at the dates of temple work to identify which era the entry falls under (b =3D baptism; e =3D endowment, s =3D sealing to spouse or parents). Sometimes there will be a combination.

1. Before 1942 the resources referenced in the IGI are the temple books, the chronological records kept by the temples of the work done each day. These are on the films indicated on the IGI microfiche when there is a number in the batch number column and the word "film" in the sheet number column. Many of these films can be ordered at Family History Centers (FHCs), but check the fiche listing restricted films. If they cannot be ordered, they may still be in the open cabinets in the reading room in Salt Lake. You will need to find an agent to look if you can't go yourself. A few are in what is called the Special Collections room. (Ask at the FHC what this means).

What is more useful is the index to these early records. The Temple Index Bureau (TIB) is a series of index cards, now on microfilm, which often give additional information. These too are in Special Collections, but you can access them by using a Temple Ordinance Index Request (TOIR) form which should be available at an FHC. They are free from the Church Distribution Center. If you send in a TOIR (cost $1 for each search) and they find an index card, they may also find a family group sheet from the next era for you.

2. In 1942 individuals began sending in family group sheets. These too are indexed in the TIB and can be accessed by using TOIRs. Or you can look at these on microfilm. There are several other series of family group sheets, so look in the subject section of the FHLC (Family History Library Catalog) under "Mormons - Genealogy - Sources" and roam around until you find a series beginning with film #127. The sheets are arranged strictly alphabetically by the head of the household (sometimes an unmarried woman) and then by birth date of people with the same name. Many FHCs like to get these on indefinite loan to build the collection.

Besides getting more data on the family and an individual's outdated name and address, THE IMPORTANT PIECE OF INFORMATION ON THESE IS THE SOURCE OF INFORMATION. Hopefully you will be able to interpret it and go to a book you would never have dreamed of looking at for information on your family, i.e., the index (IGI) has worked! Note: this is the main point of this little dissertation. If you cannot interpret the source, play with the FHLC first if you have a clue to author or title. Then call the Family History Library (801-240-2584) and ask for the first floor library attendants' window. They can convert old call numbers to new. They will be appreciative if many of you do it.

3. The IGI began in 1969. At the same time submitters began using new forms, called Individual Entry and Marriage Entry Forms. Sometimes family group sheets were still used. (These were assigned batch numbers beginning with F, 50 or 60). The value of seeing these is not only the source. The submitter's address may still be current and there may be additional information. But WHAT YOU MOST WANT IS THE SOURCE! You get copies of these entry forms in either of two ways:

a. When received, they were assigned a batch number, with 99 sheets in a batch. (The first two digits of batch numbers beginning with 7 and 8 tell you the year they were submitted.) Then they were filmed. You can order the microfilm of them (about $3 apiece). If using the IGI on fiche you need to find out the film number (also called "Input Source") by using another set of fiche, the "Batch Number Index."

b. Or you can use the photo duplication form to get copies of 8 forms for $2. (Again, read the small print. Some batch numbers with the 4th, 5th and 6th digits higher than 365 refer to extractions from New England vital records. The films can be tricky to use. On the other hand, one film might have a great many useful entry forms on it. If you find a group of people with the same batch number, try it.

4. About 1990 FHC began using a new type of family group sheet (8 =BD x 11 instead of 8 =BD x 14). These are available by the same method as above. About the same time, the church began using Temple Ready to process submissions on disk. While this has been extremely useful in many ways, no longer are names and addresses and sources available. We are referred to the Ancestral File. This situation may eventually change, but for the present, we cannot get "behind" the IGI on these entries.

For many years there has been a project to extract the old pre-1970 records and add them to the IGI. Most of the pre-1942 baptismal records are in the 1993 CD-ROM edition. Many of the 1942-69 records are in the new Addendum.

One final hint, if you find a submitter listed on an old family group sheet, try looking for them in the Ancestral File. Then look for the submitter's name and address. You may find the current family historian.

Tips for Using LDS Disks:
1) Use them only as an outline.
2) Act as a roadmap to lead to location of documentation.
3) Older ones were typed - there's room for error.
4) They're only as correct as the person who sent them in.
5) Person who submitted info - F9 key gets you to submitters.
6) Submitter's address included; code next to the name =3D date of submission.
7) Write to submitters for documentation, if the date is recent.
8) Before 1982 submission was a one shot thing; i.e. no further info.
9) Church encouraged recent submissions; current info more likely to be supported.
10) Index part: Before you enter pedigrees - hit ENTER, you get the green screen tells you more about the person.
        At first glance, your ancestors may not seem to be in program.
11) They may be hidden; Check extra spouses, etc.
12) Remember to check a 20 year span of when you "know" they were born. Submission date may have been a guess
        by submitter (20-20 RULE).
13) If you don't find support for an ancestor, double check data.

Please note that the LDS has issued a Research CD-ROM disk with their research guides. It is reasonably priced and available from 1-800-537-5950 in the USA.

The IGI can be a wonderful aid for finding your ancestors, but not all of the information is correct. It is an index of LDS temple work, and nothing more. The names and the dates and the places are extremely important to members of the LDS church, particularly the dates that fall under "B,E,S" in the microfiche version, or the Ordinance Index on the computer. If you don't believe in the mission and the purpose of the LDS Church, don't let those dates bother you.

Names in the IGI come from 3 major sources:
1. Extracted records - microfilmers have filmed and people have extracted names from civil and church christenings, birth and marriage records. Half of the names on the IGI have come from this source. Example: If you have a marriage date for you g-grandparents that differs from the IGI, look at the batch #. If it begins with an "M", it was filmed from the actual marriage records in that county that is listed. You might want to examine where you got your info a little more closely. Death and burial records are usually not extracted.

2. Records submitted by LDS members - your date may differ from what is entered. You may have the family bible, but the other person may have a marriage document. The batch # will be an all digit # - such as 9024205. That info was submitted in 1990. You cannot correct what is on the IGI. Even if the date is wrong, it does not affect the validity of the temple ordinances. That's LDS policy.

3. Membership records - some of the names are deceased members of the LDS church.

Regarding sources:
1. Always, always record the batch #. This will lead you to the original source. Beside it is the serial sheet #. Copy it, too.

2. If you found it on the computer, press enter to get the details. It will give you a microfilm # that you can order in.

3. If you found it on microfiche, ask the librarian where the "Batch # Index" is located. It's usually near the IGI, and there are not many fiche. Look it up and write down the number under "printout". That is a microfilm # you can order in.

4. A few of the common batch #'s look like this:
> *Batch #9024245 - submitted in 1990 by an LDS Church member. Looking up the sheets that were filmed may give you more info on siblings, sources, the person who submitted it. Names submitted after May 1991 do not list the submitter.

> *Batch #C503781 - info taken from the actual extracted birth or christening record. Again, you might want to order it in. A christening record from a church may give you all kinds of info on the family that worshiped there.

> *Batch #M501001 - extracted from the actual marriage records of the county it was filmed in. I probably wouldn't order it in. I would go to the Locality File and order in the records from the county myself.

Once your film comes in:
1. Keep that batch # handy. You will need it to locate the exact sheet on the roll of microfilm that may have over 10,000 sheets on it. The serial sheet that is located right beside the batch # in the IGI will help you find your info.

2. They are usually filmed in batches of 100. Slowly roll through until you see a handwritten paper with a batch # on it. That will give you a ballpark idea of how far you'll have to roll.

3. When you get to your batch #, scan through till you find the serial sheet. You may get a family group sheet, or a

single individual or marriage entry. There should be a name and address, as well as documentation.

Most of this information came from printed sources of the LDS Church:
1. Using Ancestral File - #34113
2. Contributing to Ancestral File - #34029
3. Correcting Information in Ancestral File - sorry, my number's faded
4. International Genealogical Index on Microfiche - #31026
5. International Genealogical Index on Compact Disc - #31025
6. Finding an IGI Source - #31024

Ask for these publications, as well as any others by calling: Distribution Center - 1-800-537-5950. They are free and contain much more information than I have given here. Also, ask for a sheet that contains all items published for family history. I can't remember the exact title, but they can tell you what it is. Many are free, some are cheap. The Research Outlines are the best I've seen. Order them in for the states or countries you are researching in. They're only about 50 cents.

You can now search some of the LDS records online at: http://www.familysearch.com

THIS AND THAT GENEALOGY TIPS ON MICROFILM

REASONS FOR POOR MICROFILM QUALITY:
1. MICROFILMS PRODUCED DURING THE EARLIEST DAYS OF MICRO FILMING TECHNOLOGY. In the late 1930s through the 1950s, with a new technology and an entire world of records to choose from, agencies such as the Family History Library and various national archives began their filming. Naturally, the most-used and most valuable records were filmed first, when the quality was at its worst. However, both the LDS Church and the U.S. National Archives have done some selective re filming. Perhaps some other agencies have also. Just don't expect any agency to undertake re-filming on a massive Basis.

2. FADED INK. Some census takers economized by using ink of poor quality or by watering it down.

3. POOR TYPEWRITERS AND RIBBONS. Some records were typed on poorly-maintained typewriters using ribbons whose useful days were long gone.

4. BRITTLE PAPER. A good quality of paper is normally used in the printed books designed for recording of official records. However, many of the most valuable genealogical records were not kept in such volumes. Local governments on the U.S. frontier were sometimes fortunate to have any kind of consistent paper supply. Some records were kept on paper that has a high acid content. As the years passed, this paper becomes brittle and unless treated, will eventually fall to pieces.

5. POOR ARCHIVAL CONDITIONS. Archives, particularly state and local ones, are chronically under funded. That means their holdings are often poorly housed in regard to dust, light, moisture, mold, and overly compacted conditions Due to under staffing, problems that arise must often be ignored. Some of the "archival" conditions that exist in the United States are enough to make you cry. The situation in less prosperous countries is often worse.

6. POOR CONDITION UPON RECEIPT. The records may have been received in water-stained, faded, fragmentary or worn condition when they arrived at the archives.

7. POOR MICRO FILMING CONDITIONS. Some of the Family History Library's records were microfilmed under circumstances that should be told in a good movie or book. The same may be true for some Microfilmers working for other organizations. Imagine carting a film camera, cans of microfilm and other materials and a portable power generator by donkey to a village in the mountains of Italy. Then it's up several flights of stairs to an unlit, unventilated (and it's the middle of the summer) attic in an old building. Now, set up your power generator and have at it!

8. RESTRICTIVE ARCHIVAL REGULATIONS. Some tightly bound volumes were filmed at archives that would not allow the volumes to be unbound for filming, due to the cost, the extensive labor involved, or the fragile condition of the volumes. The result, of course, is microfilmed pages that are hard to read at the center of the volume.

9. RECORDS AVAILABLE ONLY BY PURCHASING EXISTING MICROFILMS. The Family History Library and other organizations often purchase microfilms rather than producing them themselves. This happens for a variety of reasons: The archives may do its own micro filming or have it done by a commercial microfilmer. In these situations the archives may be unwilling or contractually unable to allow an additional filming to be done as long as it is possible to read the existing films.

10. HASTY FILMING. Some microfilmers are paid by the page or frame. This is done to ensure value for the money, but can tempt some microfilmers beyond what they can bear. Excessive haste is more likely to be a problem when the original records are loose papers housed in packets tied up with string. The filmer must undo the string, take out the records, arrange them on the micro filming surface in the order in which they were housed in the packet, then do the filming, then stack the records in the same order, reinsert them in the packet and tie it back up.

11. POOR QUALITY CONTROL WHEN DEVELOPING THE MICROFILM OR REPRODUCING COPIES FROM THE MASTER NEGATIVE. Organizations such as the National Archives and the Family History Library have quality control standards, but people do sometimes make mistakes.

SUGGESTIONS:
1. Take your time and re-read. When you can't make out an entry, it sometimes helps to leave it for awhile and come back to it.

2. Use a magnifying glass.

3. If the image is out of focus, try a machine with a less powerful lens. The image will be smaller but it may also be clearer.

4. Some film readers have a stronger and a weaker light setting; try both.

5. Try placing a sheet of colored paper on the projection surface.

6. Try using a reader that is located in the darkest part of the room.

7. Check the glass plates on the film reader. They may be scratched or dirty.

8. Get permission to turn out the lights near you if this is possible.

9. Check with a staff member to see if a better quality copy can be obtained.

10. If none of these work, you may need to hire a researcher who has access to the original volumes (unfortunately not possible with U.S. census films and some other records).

READING MICROFILM:
Here's a simple aid to make microfilm reading easier: On a sheet of light blue stationary (white paper "disappears" when you put it on the white surface of the reader), draw a single line the long way of the paper with a yellow or pink Hi-Liter, about two inches in from the edge.

Put this on the microfilm reader and position the paper and film image so that the desired line of the image is highlighted. It looks just like the highlighting was on the film! A little weight, like an eraser, is enough to hold the paper from slipping around or sliding off onto the floor.

Makes it much easier to focus back on the correct line after you turn away to write on the sheet you are copying data to.

If you are trying to read light or blurred writing - you might also try putting a yellow, green or blue (or use all three of different combinations) colored plastic pages you used to use to put your reports in high school, against the screen that you are reading from. You can get these in different colors with a side slide to hold the papers and they cost about $1.00. It will also help with bringing out faded writing by putting the sheets down on the photocopy machine then put your pages down that you cannot read. If you enlarge the copy it makes a great difference too. Experiment by using different colors and layers.

MICROFILM RENTAL:
You can order a starter kit from the National Archives Microfilm Rental Program, PO Box 30, Annapolis Junction, MD 20702-0030 or go to their web page and print out an order blank: http://www.nara.gov click on the genealogy page and go down to the Microfilm Rental Program. The starter kit is $28.00. You'll receive a membership card, order forms and two free bonus coupons for free rentals, a complete set of census catalogs 1790-1920, order forms

for Ship Passenger Arrival and Veteran's Records as well as a description of selected genealogical publications available through this program.

http://www.censusmicrofilm.com - Census Microfilm: A place which sells census microfilm (you can donate it to your local library) for $10.95 per roll which I am told is a fraction of cost of National Archives.

THIS AND THAT MISCELLANEOUS GENEALOGY TIPS

OLD STYLE DATES:
The "why" of old-style vs new-style is addressed by the document at this URL:
http://www.genuki.org.uk/big/dates.html

Old style dates do NOT refer to how the date is written. (EXAMPLE: day/month/year vs month/day/year). It has to do with converting from the Julian calendar to the Gregorian calendar. Up until 1752, the Julian calendar was used by England and her colonies. The first day of the year was Mar 25. To confuse this more, the whole month of March was listed as month # 1. (Oct, Nov and Dec were named such because they are the 8th, 9th and 10th months under this system.) When the Gregorian calendar was used, the first day of Jan was the legal first day of the year. Also there was an 11 day difference that had to be made up. So that the day after Sep. 2, 1752 was Sep 14, 1752. This was because the makers of the Julian calendar did not take into account that the year is slightly longer than 365 days. We have leap years to do that now. The 400 year rule says that every 400 years you have to add a day to make up for the differences that are too small to make up otherwise.

Some European countries switched to the Gregorian calendar as early as 1600. Because of the confusion over whether the first month was Jan or Mar depending on which calendar was used, the practice became to either name the calendar used. OS meant OLD STYLE for the Julian and NS meant NEW STYLE for Gregorian) or to give any date between Jan 1 and up to and including Mar 24 a double year. (For example: 01 Feb 1710/11.) This is because it could either be the last month of 1710 OLD Style or the second month of 1711 NEW Style. From Mar 25 to Dec 31, no correction would be needed so the date would be as is (Example: 25 Mar 1710).

QUAKER PRACTICE - Prior to 1752, the 12 months of the year were numbered beginning with March and ending in February. After 1752 they were numbered beginning in January and ending with December. Example: 18th of the 5th mo. 1750 (O.S.) becomes 29 Jul 1750 (N.S.) N. S. is the Gregorian Calendar and the O.S. is the Julian Calendar. The Quakers refused to use the names of the months (as they were pagan names) and used numbers instead so you get dates like 3-1-1710/11. Unless they said the 3rd month or month 1 or something similar, it got confusing. The American way of saying month/day/year was not the European way which was day/month/year. This is a good argument for always writing out the month (or using the first 3 letters.)

The dates when various countries changed over varied, so this has to be figured separately for each jurisdiction. England was relatively late. Scotland, being more advanced culturally than England, changed the date of the New Year in 1600, though they didn't subtract the days for excess leap years until 1752. Russia and Turkey changed to the Gregorian calendar in 1918, Greece in 1928.

The first dates prior to 14 Sep. 1752 must be assumed to be the Old Style Dates, unless there is an indication that they were converted to New Style. To convert Old Style dates to New Style dates, add 11 days.

In determining the age of a person who was born 14 Sep 1752 and who lived after that date, one must take into account of the 11 days that we last in Sep 1752, otherwise the person will appear to be 11 days older than he actually was at any given time after the calendar change. In order to determine the Old Style (O.S.) birth date when age of death is given for a person who was born before the calendar change and died after 1752, 11 days must be subtracted.

DAY OF THE WEEK FORMULA:
Step 1: Begin with the last 2 digits of the year.

Step 2. Add 1/4 of this number, disregarding any remainder.

Step 3. Add the date in the month.

Step 4. Add according to the month

January	1	(for leap year, 0)
February	4	(for leap year, 3)
March	4	
April	0	
May	2	
June	5	
July	0	
August	3	
September	6	
October	1	
November	4	
December	6	

Step 5. Add for the:

18th Century	4
19th Century	2
20th Century	0
21st Century	6

Step 6. Total the numbers.

Divide by 7. Check the remainder against this chart to find the day of the week:

1=Sunday
2=Monday
3=Tuesday
4=Wednesday
5=Thursday
6=Friday
0=Saturday

CALCULATE BIRTH DATES:
If you have the date of death and the age at time of death (as sometimes found on a tombstone). This method allows the computation to be done on a calculator and eliminates the laborious and tricky subtraction we used to do on paper.

To start, if the death date was for instance 1889, May 6 - enter 18890506. If the age at death was 71 years, 7 months, 9 days - subtract 710709. You should get a result of 18179797. You must now subtract 8870 to correct the months and days. You now have 18170927 or 1817, Sep 27, the correct birth date.

8870 FORMULA:
The following is quoted in part from p184 of the May-June 1993 GENEALOGICAL HELPER: "Mrs. Boyer wrote to remind us that the "8870" formula does not always give the proper results, and to point out that there are ways to modify it so that it will. Briefly, the formula is:

```
18890506 = Date of death (6 May 1889)
 710709 = Age at death (71 years, 7 months, 9 days)
--------
18179797
   8870 = "The Formula"
--------
```

18170927 = Date of birth (27 Sep 1817)

Another example: The person died on March 10, 1873 and was 52 years, 4 months, and 19 days old. 18730310 (Year of death, month, and day) subtract 520419 (Age at death years, months, and days) total 18209891 subtract 8870 (Formula number) 18201021 (Date of birth). This person was born on October 21, 1820.

However, if the death year is a leap year, you should use 8871, rather than 8870. And if the month previous to the death had 31 days, you should use 8869, rather than 8870."

BIRTH DATE CALCULATOR WEB PAGE calculates birth date from death date and age at death: http://enws347.eas.asu.edu:8000/~buckner/bdform.html

DETERMINING AGE:
In determining the age of a person who was born 14 Sep 1752 and who lived after that date, one must take into account of the 11 days that we lost in Sep 1752, otherwise the person will appear to be 11 days older than he actually was at any given time after the calendar change. In order to determine the Old Style (O.S.) birth date when age of death is given for a person who was born before the calendar change and died after 1752, 11 days must be subtracted.

CALCULATING AGE AT DEATH:
Example - Date of death   May 6, 1889, age 71 years, 7 months, 9 days.

First - Subtract 1 from the year 1889 which will give you 1888.
Second - Add 12 to the month (fifth month) - which will give you 17 - then subtract 1 giving you the number 16
Third - Add 30 to the day (the 6th of the month) which will give you the number 36.

Therefore your numbers are - 1889 - 16- 36

Fourth - Subtract 71 yrs from 1889 = 1817
Fifth - Subtract 7 months from 16 giving you the 9th month which is September.
Sixth - Subtract 9 days from 36 which gives you the 27th of the month.
Result - A birth date of Sep 27, 1817

Computed dates of birth should be verified by adding the stated age to the answer. The result should be, of course, the date of death.

FOOLPROOF PRE-1850 AGE CALCULATIONS:
You can often combine age data from several pre-1850 censuses to narrow the age range for an ancestor who died before the 1850 census came along and you were able to get his actual age. Most of us have a bit of a struggle getting all the age brackets straight in our heads so that we make accurate refinements in our ancestor's age - so I offer here a relatively easy and foolproof way to make these age refinements.

The first thing you need is a pre-1850 census age bracket cheat sheet. I use a short document that lists for each pre-1850 census the census day, the age bracket for each column and the range of birth years covered by each column in each census. This does away with simple math errors because it's pre-calculated.

Next you need some way to represent in a clear and simple fashion the possible years of birth for your ancestor from each census. The clearest and easiest way I know of to do this is to graph the years on a sheet of graph paper. If your male ancestor was listed in the 5th column in the 1820 census, then, according to the cheat sheet, he was born between 1775-1794. This is a pretty big spread. Graphed, it would be a line covering the 20 years from 1775 to 1794.

Now suppose you found him again in the 1830 census and his age was listed in the 6th column making him born

1790-1800. It is immediately obvious that he must have been born 1790-1794. This drops the possible age spread from 20 years to 4 years -- a big improvement.

The overlap of the two lines is the new, refined age spread. This looks almost too simple to bother graphing so let's look at a little more complicated case.

Suppose your ancestor was 40-50 in 1830, was listed as under 16 in 1790, and was 16-26 in the 1800 census. What age bracket do you get when you combine these data? To find out, go to your cheat sheet and find the spread of birth years represented by each column in each census and graph the data.

You can see easily that he was actually born between 1780-1784 and that he fits the data in the 1790 census as well.

Well, these have been simple examples but more complex examples abound out there in genealogy. Sometimes you can actually narrow it down to the exact birth year if everything works out just right. This simple technique, however, works just as easily on those harder examples.

Here's a Census Chart to help you figure the birth year: http://vax1.vigo.lib.in.us/~jmounts/cendates.htm

MARRIAGE RECORDS:
During the colonial period, the law required a true and perfect parish register. After 1780, ministers were required to report all marriages to the county court clerk whose duty it was to see that the returns were entered in a book kept for that purpose. In 1783 the law recognized that the scarcity of ministers in the western counties had produced a situation whereby not only dissenting ministers, but some magistrates and others had been induced to solemnize marriages. The amended act of 1784 removed the four ministers per denomination per county restriction for marriages and permitted any ordained minister to perform marriages. Also Quakers and Mennonites were permitted to marry under their own customs, but the clerk of the meeting was to make a return to the county clerk. The county record books which have survived are sometimes titled "Marriage Records" or " Marriage Registers," although they might contain only the entry of the marriage bond and not the actual return.

HANDFAST:
H/F after a person's name on birth and marriage records means "Handfast". Basically it is a sign of the confirmation of a type of "uncanonical, private or even probationary form of marriage". Handfasting was for announcing a union between a man and woman who wished to live together as husband and wife before receiving the blessing of the church.

The couple would stand before a group of their peers, hold their clasped hands above their heads and state their intentions. The agreement was good for a year and a day or until the preacher came to perform the rites of the church. If at the end of the specified time, each wished to go his own way, they could do so with no ties. No matter what happened, any child born of a Handfast would inherit.

INFLATION CALCULATOR:
If you know what it cost then - figure what it would cost now: http://www.westegg.com/inflation/

SYMBOLIC CROSSROADS WEDDING:
A crossroads wedding was one in which the marriage was held at a crossroads after the sun had set with the bride wearing only her shift. This was done to show she had no debts to bring to the marriage.

WHAT'S IT ALL MEAN...LINEAL...COLLATERAL...ALLIED?
LINEAL means ascending or descending in a direct line. Example - If your surname/maiden name is Brown, your Brown line is your direct lineal line.

COLLATERAL means descended from the same ancestor but not in a direct line of descent.

ALLIED families are families related usually through marriage.

SASE:
Enclose a SASE (self-addressed stamped envelope) when requesting information from ANY source, individuals, Court House, Library, etc. You stand a much better chance of a reply if you do. Otherwise, your query may go into the trash pile.

YEOMAN AND FREEMAN:
In England, the terms "Yeoman" and "Freeman" mean the same thing. There were roughly six social classes in early England: the peers or noblemen; the gentry; knights of the shire who lived off the rents from their lands; lawyers, merchants, professional people; Yeoman farmers and then the common people. A Yeoman farmer was a freeholder having quite a lot of land and employing others to help him farm it. The terms in New England probably meant much the same thing.

PHOTOS OF SHIPS:
Some organizations sell photographs of passenger ships that carried immigrants from Eastern Europe in the first two decades of this century.

The Steamship Historical Society of America, University of Baltimore, 1420 Maryland Ave., Baltimore, MD 21201 and The Steamship Historical Society, 415 Pelton Ave., Staten Island, NY 10310.

The Steamship Historical Society of America Collection at the University of Baltimore Library is a great source of information about ships. They have more than 100,000 ship photos and more than 30,000 negatives. Send the name of the ship to Librarian at SSHSA Collection, University of Baltimore Library.

You can send to the Mariner's Museum and get an 8 x 10 black and white photograph and other information about the ship such as when, where built, when dismantled, size, tonnage, etc. for $5.00. You do need to know the name of the ship. They have 350,000 photographs of ships. There was a great article in the "Genealogical Helper" for July-August 1995 about it. They don't have passenger ship lists, but they do have immigrant stories of their trip. They also have a FAX, it's 1-804-591-7310. The Mariner's Museum, 100 Museum Drive, Newport News, VA 23606-3759.

BOAT OR SHIP:
Boat - as used by seamen the term does not apply to a vessel, but to a small craft. Boat as distinguished from the general term ship, is constructed of bent frames and a vessel of ship of sawn frames. (This is the opinion of a shipbuilder.)

Ship - Strictly a vessel, square-rigged, on all masts from three up. The term is used loosely and applied to quite generally to all vessels. A seaman speaks of his vessel as "the ship" regardless of rig or power.

TELL THE WORLD WHO YOU ARE:
The effort to achieve identification is as old - yet as contemporary - as man. Primitive man gave himself a distinguishing identification by means of tattoos, scars, bone piercing, hair cuttings and other markings. Indian tribes adopted special facial colorations and markings, and stylings for the head and hairpiece. African tribesmen pierce their nose with weird bone structures. These markings and mutilations all tend to identify the individual as belonging to a tribe or clan under one cause. Costume is another means of differentiating one group from another, i.e. the sari of India, the kilt of the highlander, the tunic of ancient Rome. We still see that today with groups, clubs and even gangs and their attire and tattoos.

Soon after the Crusades in Europe, many people began to feel the need for family names which would identify them. The nobles were the first to adopt surnames, usually from the names of the lands they owned. Soon others did the same. Surname can be classified in four categories: Local surnames, kinship surnames, pet names and nicknames, occupational surnames. The local surname was derived from the place where the man once held land or where he once lived. Kinship names derived from the father is common in most countries. The addition of -son to a name would identify the offspring of a person. Pet names and nicknames were given to someone with some noticeable characteristic so he would be remembered, i.e. "Red", "Shorty", etc. Occupational surnames refer to the services one might offer such as Carpenter, Miller, etc.

Another method of identification arose in the Middle Ages to identify one from another. During the Crusades, the knight, completely covered from head to toe with his armor, came to identify himself with his shield and his Coat of Arms. Many families can associate themselves with coats of arms dating back to medieval times.

Coats of arms were granted to persons by the King. Originally a Coat of Arms was a surcoat (i.e., the cloth coat worn over armor to keep off the sun and rain) with symbols painted on it to distinguish which individual was wearing said armor, in the hope of avoiding friendly fire. The crest was the device worn on the helmet for the same reason. Rules vary from country to country as to who can or cannot use a particular set of arms. The crest is part of the arms. Arms were never issued to entire families, but to an individual and inherited by the eldest son. Until his father died, a son could only display the crest.

Grant of arms reposed in the king in most, if not all, countries, but was generally delegated to the College of Arms (England) or equivalent. In many jurisdictions anyone can register arms with the appropriate authority.

CRESTS from William L Pratt - prattw@nevada.edu:
Crests were granted to persons by the King. Crests were, and are, part of an achievement of arms. Originally a Coat of Arms was a surcoat (i.e., the cloth coat worn over armor to keep off the sun and rain) with symbols painted on it to distinguish which individual was wearing said armor, in the hope of avoiding friendly fire. The crest was the device worn on the helmet for the same reason. Rules vary from country to country as to who can or cannot use a particular set of arms. The crest is part of the arms. A common usage is that arms are inherited by the eldest son. Younger sons) may display the crest alone. I believe right to display the crest is not inherited by issue of the daughters and younger sons. In Scotland, I think, only the chieftain (eldest son of the Chief) may display the crest of the chief's arms undifferenced, though any clansman may bear the crest surrounded by a "belt and buckle" {the clans man's badge).

Grant of arms reposed in the king in most (all?) countries, but was generally delegated to the College of Arms (England) or equivalent. In many jurisdictions anyone can register arms with the appropriate authority. In Scotland the Lord Lyon King at Arms also registers tartans. In Scotland it is a misdemeanor to display someone else's arms (I think, it may just be actionable in a civil suit). In England it is a gaffe, but legal. Other countries will have other regulations.

Arms were never issued to entire families, but to an individual and inherited by the eldest son (until Papa died, he could only display the crest) (English usage). In Scotland, today, clan membership is generally figured on the basis of surname, so one can use the tartan and display the clans man's badge of the appropriate clan (your father's) based on surname.

EVIDENCE AND PROOF:
All evidence is relative in its value; none that I know of is absolute. There are three kinds of facts: those for which you have abundant proof, those which you believe to be true but for which you do not have overwhelming evidence, and assumptions which you use as leads, hoping to find more evidence or a strong reason to abandon it. The problem comes when two pieces of evidence do not agree completely, or when we are not absolutely certain that the evidence we have applies.

Here are some guiding principles:
1. The nearer the recording is to the event, the more likely it is to be correct. For example, a birth certificate is probably more accurate than a tombstone.
2. Legal documents tend to be more accurate than family notes or traditions. They were probably prepared by a third

party and people tend to be more careful with legal matters.

3. The census is not a legal document. It is only as accurate as the census taker and the person giving the information. Names may be spelled incorrectly. Included may be nieces or nephews with the same last name being mistaken for children, and children may not be listed if they were away at the time of the census.

1. With Family Bibles, ask the following:

a. What is the date of the publishing edition on page 2? Is it such that the family purchased it early in their marriage, or did an enterprising child fill it in later?

b. Is the handwriting the same for all entries (someone "caught up" the record at one sitting)? Even if the same person wrote it all, if it was done over a period of years, their handwriting will vary, certainly the pen and ink will.

2. With birth certificates:

a. The date and place is probably correct, though in very olden days, the doctor or midwife may have done the paperwork later and there may be a day or two difference.

b. The mother's name is probably correct though the spelling may be off. The doctor knew who his patient was.

c. Likewise the spelling of the child's name can vary. Be especially careful of transcribed copies of lists made before the days of birth certificates.

d. The biological father is probably correct but not as sure. The doctor can only record what the mother told him.

3. With tombstones:

a. Don't be surprised if dates vary from other records. The stone mason may have made a mistake, but more often the family member providing the information was doing so from memory.

b. If the data doesn't fit, look for another explanation.

4. Wills:

a. A good source of information but don't draw too much from them.

b. If older children are missing from the list, don't be alarmed. Instead turn to land deeds and see if the father may have helped the older son buy land at an earlier date, or even have deeded some of his own land to him.

c. Very rarely a person may have mentioned a brother, sister, niece, or nephew by name but without identification as to relationship.

5. The more facts we have about a person, the more he/she becomes a unique individual. Nothing is absolute and you may have to judge between conflicting facts.

WITCHES AND WIZARDS:

Salem, MA accused and imprisoned many of its citizens in the spring of 1692 and many went to their deaths on the gallows protesting their innocense. Among the twenty alleged witches and wizards who were executed in 1692 were: Bridget (Playfer) Wasselbe Oliver Bishop, the first to die. She was hanged in Salem on Jun 10, 1692. Other women were (known maiden names are in parentheses) - Rebecca (Towne) Nurse; Sarah (Solart) Poole Good; Martha Rich Corey; Mary (Towne) Easty; Sarah (Averhill) Wildes, Susannah (North) Martin; Alice Parker; Ann Greenslade Pudeator; Wilmot Redd; Elizabeth (Jackson) Howe; Martha (Allen) Carrier; Margaret (Stevenson) Scott and Mary (Ayer) Parker. Six men were executed as wizards: George Jacobs, Sr.; John Willard; John Proctor; Rev. George Burroughs; Samuel Wardwell and Giles Corey who was pressed to death. George Jacobs is said to have been 80 years old but this could be incorrect. Also charged with witchcraft was his son George Jacobs, Jr.; his daughter-in-law Rebecca (Andrews) Frost Jacobs; his granddaughter Margaret Jacobs and George Jacobs, Jr's brother-in-law Daniel Andrews.

If you have New England roots, you may find you have ancestors who were involved in these infamous witch trials. Millions of Americans are descendants of the victims, the judges, the juries, witnesses and the accusers.

If you have an ancestor who was judged a witch, you may be interested in Daughters of American Witches Co., c/o Mrs. Kline L. Engle, 1800 E. Missouri Ave., Phoenix, AZ 85014.

CERTIFIED GENEALOGISTS/SEARCHERS/SPECIALISTS:

C.G.R.S. - Certified Genealogical Record Searcher, proven ability to search original and published records and to provide information from these. He/she has not had to show ability to construct a pedigree or prepare a history, although the researcher may be able to do so.

C.A.L.S. - Certified American Lineage Specialist has shown competence to prepare and authenticate a line of descent (such as for a lineage society).

C.A.I.L.S. - Certified American Indian Lineage Specialist is able to work with records, such as tribal records, dealing with American Indians.

C.G. - Certified Genealogist has shown capability for researching primary and secondary records and also to solve genealogical problems based upon investigation and analysis of the sources.

C.G.I. - Certified Genealogical Instructors and

C.G.L. - Certified Genealogical Lecturers have fulfilled requirements to show competence in instructing and lecturing.

RECORDS MISSING AT COUNTY COURTHOUSES:

When the county courthouse reports "records missing", write to the State Archives. With changes in county clerks, they are not always informed when records have been moved, usually as space limits their capacity for storage. Remember when working on county records to check for formation of the county as many counties were split off and formed from other counties.

FINDING MAIDEN NAMES:

In the lower left-hand corner of most deeds, you will find signatures of two to four witnesses. The first one is always from the husband's side. The next one is always from the wife's side. This is to protect her 1/3 dower right under the law. Nothing you will ever use will give greater clues to maiden names than witnesses to old deeds!

Also in the 1800's and before, it was traditional when the daughter got married, as part of her dowry, the father either covered the loan or carried the note for his son-in-law. If you know the husband's name but not the wife's maiden name and you can find out to whom they were making their mortgage payments, about 70% of the time it was her father.

LEGAL TRIVIA

When land was sold, the spouse had to be listed in the land record. Land records should be searched after a death as often a list of heirs will be shown during partition of the estate and even sometimes a map.

If there is a will, it is probated by an Executor - if there is no will, the estate is cared for by an Administrator appointed by the court.

"IN RE" concerning adoptions means "in regards to" something. You can often find adoptions listed in record books where divorce and probate records are filed. Instead of putting adoptions in under the letter "A" they may place them under "I" for "in re". Under this category you will find petitions to change name, petition to adopt, etc.

BONDS:

Bonds are a type of "guarantee" that the bondsmen will perform the responsibilities granted them and if they default, the value of the bond will be forfeited. Bondsmen were often family members or close friends.

Marriage bonds insured that the marriage would occur according to agreement and that there was no impediment to the marriage such as an existing marriage.

Executor's bonds insured that the executor of a deceased person's estate would administer the estate according to law.

Bail bonds insured that the accused would appear for trial.

Bastardy bonds might be required of the father of an illegitimate child to insure that he would be responsible for the child's support.

Professional bonds are similar to today's malpractice insurance.

LOST TOWNS IN AMERICA:
If you are looking for "lost towns", try writing to U. S. Board of Geographic Names, 523 National Center, Reston, VA 22092.

HOW TO SAVE A PORTION OF ROOTS:
Highlight the portion of ROOTS you want to print or save using the EDIT feature on the tool bar. To do this, place the mouse cursor at the beginning of the text you wish to save, and hold down the left mouse button as you move the cursor to the end of the text.

Copy the highlighted portion to the clipboard. To do this, press CTRL C, or on the menu bar click on EDIT|COPY. (The clipboard is an unseen portion of memory that stores information to be copied elsewhere.)

Go to MESSAGE or whatever it is called in your mail application. This is where you "reply to" or send an e-mail. In Eudora it's called MESSAGE. Then go to NEW. Don't put any ADDRESS in as you are not going to send this but do put in a SUBJECT. Then drop down to the body of the message and hit PASTE. The portion you want should now be there.

You can either go to FILE and print it out.... or SAVE AS.... (wherever you want) or transfer it to one of your mailboxes. I have a ROOTS mailbox and I save all these little tidbits there.

HOW TO PRINT A PORTION OF A DOCUMENT:
Highlight the lines you want to either save or print by holding down the mouse button and dragging the mouse across the portion you want to print. Once it is highlighted, hit CONTROL and P. The print screen comes up giving three choices as to how many pages or what to print, one of these is "selection". Choose that, and hit "Print". If it is "Save "you want, there is a place for marking "to file", and the "print to file" screen comes up, fill in the pertinent info and hit "OK".

Another way is to drag and hold down your mouse button to highlight the portion of anything you want to print out. Once it is highlighted, hit CONTROL and P and print it out. Or, if you like, paste it into a new message and print it out - then save it with a subject.

USING JUNO - submitted by j-psmith@juno.com:
On Juno to copy & paste - there are two screens. On the left, the Read screen and beside it , to the right is the Write screen. When you have a ROOTS message on the Read screen and see a section you want to save.- Highlight the message by pulling your courser down on the left side of the screen as far as you want to copy. If you raise your courser and lose the highlighting just go back and start over. As you get to the bottom of the page it will automatically scroll up so just keep your finger down on the mouse until the complete message you want, is highlighted. You are on the Read screen. Click on Edit. When the window comes down click on Copy. Go to the Write screen and Click on Edit again. When the window comes down Paste will be highlighted. Click on it. Your copy will appear on the screen and you can print it or put it on a floppy disk.   Then go back to the Read screen and read the rest of the ROOTS messages. If the Edit button does not work well use the right mouse button the same as you would the edit.

TO COPY/PASTE FROM PAF:
If you are using Eudora or other mail servers, you must run PAF through Windows. You get your PAF program to Windows the same way you put any program there, from the DOS prompt. If in doubt, just follow the *how-to* information in your Windows book.

1. Open a new message in Eudora; enter addressee, subject, etc.

2. At the point in your message where you want to add data from PAF/FR program, MINIMIZE Eudora.

3. Open PAF/FR and bring-up the Pedigree Search screen; go to the person who's information you want to copy.

4. Press ALT-ENTER, making PAF screen into a window.

5. Click on small box in upper left of window.

6. Click on Edit

7. Click on Mark

8. Press left button of mouse and HOLD it down while moving from the little yellow box and dragging the yellow across the screen to cover every thing you want to copy; release mouse button

9. Press ENTER

10. MINIMIZE PAF/FR

11. Reopen Eudora; place cursor where you want to put the data

12. Click on Edit

13. Click on Paste

14. MINIMIZE Eudora again

15. Reopen PAF/FR

16. Press ENTER

17. If you have further pages to copy, repeat from #5, above, through #16 until you have copied everything to your Eudora message page.

18. To clear PAF/FR, while in PAF, press ALT-ENTER, to return to a regular screen (from the window)

19. Exit PAF your usual way

20. Reopen your message, and finish it your usual way

OR - PRODUCE A TEXT REPORT THIS WAY:
If you need to attach a PAF report to an e-mail message especially for a recipient that does not have genealogy software you should use plain text. This is also true if you do not know what word processing software the recipient has. Plain text can be read by any word processor. To do this you should install a generic printer. This is not actually a printer - but rather a universal way of printing text. The following instructions assume you are using

Windows 95 or 98:

1. Click on Printers, under My Computer.

2. Click on Add Printer.

3. Go down the list of Manufacturers and click on Generic.

4. You will need your Windows CD-ROM or diskettes to obtain the necessary printer drivers.

5. The next time you print a text file change the printer Name to Generic Printer and check the Print to file.

6. Indicate the file name you want and where you want the text file saved on you PC.

7. You can right-click on the new file name and Send To your e-mail program as an attachment or you can open the text file, in your word processor, and "Copy & Paste" into your e-mail message.

PAF4 "HOW TO" PAGE: http://www.rootsweb.com/~flvcgg/PAF40/paf40idx.htm

You can download PAF4 directly from the LDS site at: http://www.familysearch.org/ - click on Search for Ancestors.

You can download the User's Guide free from:
http://www.ldscatalog.com/cgi-bin/ncommerce3/CategoryDisplay?cgmenbr=1402&cgrfnbr=1678&RowStart=1&Loc
Code=FH - select "Software doe\wnloads -Free - OR

If you go to the LDS web site: http://www.familysearch.org/ - then click on "order family history resources" (on the left side of the screen), then click on "software downloads - free", then select item number 36100998 "Personal Ancestral File 4.o Users Guide (English)" or the one immediately below that for Spanish. Then you will download it into your hard drive. From there you can read it on the screen or print it out. It is free.

QUERY THE NEWSPAPERS:
There are tens of thousands of people doing genealogical research on the Internet but there are tens of thousands more who have never touched a computer? Do you know how to get your queries in front of these people? How about newspaper genealogy columns? The Mobile (Alabama) Genealogical Society's web site has a page called THE NEWS STAND that provides information. In many cases you can even e-mail your query to the columnist right from the web page! They charge nothing for this service. If you already know about THE NEWS STAND and haven't visited, or haven't visited lately, you need to check out our latest updates. Go to the MGS Cyber Lobby at: http://www.siteone.com/clubs/mgs - Scroll down to (and click on) THE NEWS STAND. Currently, there are listings for almost 40 different columns which appear in newspapers in 3 Australian States, 3 Canadian Provinces and 20 United States.

OLD STYLE HANDWRITING:
The internal "s" in pre-mid-nineteenth century hand writing resembled a lowercase "f". Our modern "s" form was used for an initial s, and for the second "s" of an internal pair. Thus, properly written, an internal "s" pair was written, by our standards, as "fs". But not everybody wrote them correctly, so the internal pair would often be written as "ff". Another problem arises when the second "s" of a correctly written internal pair is sloppy. The pair can then be read as a lowercase "p". Sometimes this happens even if the Second "s" is well formed. This problem particularly bites us in the case of transcribed records and indices. Modern data entry techs are often completely unaware of these orthographic problems, so we find "ss" transcribed as "ff", or if correctly written, as "p". A related problem is the use of internal "s" in printing at the time. There was an internal "s" character, which looked like a lowercase "f" without a crossbar. But printers who ran out of lowercase "s" would substitute lowercase "f". And some didn't bother even to stock lowercase "s" in their type case. The orthographic convention which seems to have been used

154

by 18th century and earlier printers was to use the internal "s" character, or lowercase "f", for both of an internal "s" pair, so in printing you will usually find it as "ff".

RAILROAD RETIREMENT INFORMATION:
1. The Railroad retirement pension went into effect about the same time as social security in the late 1930's. Therefore only those relatives who worked for the railroad after this time will a record.

2. Railroad social security numbers start with 700-XX-XXXX. If you have a social security number starting with 700 it's a dead give away that they worked for the railroad. If they have a 700 number they should have a copy of the original social security applications.

3. They began destroying the railroad pension files after a certain length of time. My great grandfather's pension record for example, has been destroyed, but they had the social security application on microfilm. My great grandfather died in 1944.

4. If they have a pension file, it contains a wealth of information about the person you are researching. It may contain information about his spouse, marriage, work record, etc.....It's well worth the $16 fee they now charge. I believe the charge now helps to maintain the files from further destruction.

For everyone who is interested, the URL for the RR retirement board: http://www.rrb.gov/geneal.html

HOW TO REPAIR THE SPINE OF A BOOK:
There are times when the spine area of the cover is worn and needs help. Cut a piece of clear book tape 1 =BD" longer than the cover and 1 =BD" wider than the spine. Make two =BE" long cuts in the tape at top and bottom. These cuts should align with the fold of the cover. Lower book spine onto tape, being sure it is centered.

Gently roll spine from side to side for a good tape-to-spine bond. Do not roll the spine over so far that it adheres to the rest of the book tape! Using the edge of the bone folder, lift the tape up over the edge (ledge) of the book and into the crease (run bone folder up and down the crease--where the cover folds back when book is opened a couple or three times) before smoothing onto book cover. Otherwise, the book will not close properly!

Open cover and contents away from the cover which is lying flat on the work surface so that the inside of the cover is exposed. Fold the corresponding strip of tape over and onto the inside back cover. Using a bone folder, smooth onto cover surface. Fold the other end of tape to the inside in the same manner. Close book. Repeat procedure for other cover/contents. The last step is to hold the book in one hand and, using a bone folder, fold down the top and bottom center flaps into the inside against the back of the book cover (in open area between book cover and spine.

GENEALOGICAL BOOK URLS:
Advanced Book Exchange: http://www.abebooks.com/

Amazon Books: http://www.amazon.com

Ancestor Publishers: http://www.firstct.com/fv/ancpub.html

Ancestor's Attic: http://members.tripod.com/~ancestorsattic/index.html

Appleton's Genealogy: http://www.moobasi.com/genealogy/

Back Tracks Genealogy Books: http://www.naxs.com/abingdon/backtrak/catalog.htm

Barnes & Noble: http:/barnesandnoble.com/

Blair's Books Service: http://www.glbco.com/

Borders.com: http://www.borders.com/sections/section_11807.html

Books We Own List: http://www.rootsweb.com/~bwo/index.html

Broad View Books, Used Genealogy Books: http://broadviewbooks.com/

Broken Arrow Publishing: http://clanhuston.com/books.htm

Compuology: http://www.compuology.com/

Cyndi's List-Books, Microfilm & Microfiche: http://www.cyndislist.com/books.htm

Essex Genealogy Books: http://www.essexbooks.com/

Everton American Books: http://www.everton.com

Family Line Genealogy Publications: http://pages.prodigy.com/Strawn/family.htm

Family Tree Bookshop, Easton MD: http://www.bluecrab.org/famtree

Frontier Press-Genealogical and Historical Books: http://www.doit.com/frontier/frontier.cgi

Genealogical Publishing Company: http://www.genealogybookshop.com/genealogybookshop/index.html

Genealogy Books: http://www.bakingmasters.com/bookstore/gen.htm

Genealogy Books, Disks, CD-ROMs for sale: http://www.genealogy-books.com

Genealogy Online-Iberian Publishing: http://www.iberian.com/frames

Genealogy Records Service: http://www.ancestrycorner.com

Genealogy Shoppe: http://members.aol.com/GenShoppe/genshoppe.htm

Genealogy Unlimited, Inc.: http://www.itsnet.com/home/genun/public_html

Golden West Marketing: http://www.greenheart.com/rdietz

Gorin Genealogical Publishing: http://members.aol.com/kygen/gorin.htm

Hearthstone Bookshop: http://www.hearthstonebooks.com

Heritage Quest Genealogy Books: http://www.heritagequest.com

Higginson Book Co.: http://www.higginsonbooks.com

History House Books: http://www.historyhouse.com

MacBeth Genealogical Services: http://www.macbeth.com.au

Making of America: http://www.umdl.umich.edu/moa/index.html

McDowell Publications, Genealogy & History & Publications: http://members.aol.com/sammcpub/index.html

Park Genealogical Books: http://www.parkbooks.com

SK Publications: http://www.skpub.com/geni/

Tattered Cover Book Store: http://www.tatteredcover.com/cgi-bin/tcpages.pl

Tuttle Antiquarian Books: http://abaa-booknet.com/alldlrs/ne/05701tut.html

Westland Publications Genealogy: http://www.theriver.com/westlandpubn/index.html

Willow Bend Books: http://www.willowbend.net/default.asp

Ye Olde Genealogie Shoppe: http://www.yogs.com/

To download free genealogy charts and forms: http://www.genrecords.com/forms.htm

MAP WEBSITE - They have maps of just about every area imaginable:
http://oddens.geog.uu.nl/index.html

This site will locate cities across the nation and the world, will calculate milage between two cities, and will show a map of the two locations: http://www.indo.com/distance

Find what county a city is in at the Geographic Name server: http://www.mit.edu:8001/geo

US SURNAME DISTRIBUTION LIST - get a map of the US showing distribution of people with a particular surname within the 50 states: http://www.hamrick.com/names

HISPANIC SURNAMES: This site gives the origin of each name and often describes a coat of arms:
http://www.ciudadfutura.com/apellidos/origin/

ITALY INFORMATION: http://www.punto-informatico.it

TAX LISTS:
Most colonial counties and towns taxed adult males with what was called a Poll Tax which, depending on the area, were due when a young man reached either sixteen, eighteen or twenty-one and stopped when he reached fifty or sixty - again depending on the area. Sometimes his father became liable for a son's tax when the son reached sixteen to twenty and the tax lists showed them as unnamed tallies under the father's name. Poll and property tax lists can be used as a substitute for the census. Sometimes the county or town clerks added useful descriptions of the common names such as Henry Baker (one arm), Henry Baker (baker) and Henry Baker (blacksmith). A search of these lists can be helpful in identifying men with common names and can indicate when men entered or left the area. Women, children, slaves, indentured servants, landless men over the poll tax age, paupers, ministers, justices of the peace, militia officers, tax assessors and any men that were granted exemption (for whatever reasons) were usually not on the lists.

The Quitrent Tax was a land tax that went either to the crown or to the proprietors. It began in England as a land obligation that was due to the manor and was an annual money payment. The American Revolution ended the quitrents.

Federal Direct Tax, starting in 1798 and through 1917, was used to raise money for armies. In the early years it was levied against real property and slave owners and produced extensive name lists. During the Civil War and later, these taxes were levied as income tax, property taxes and license fees. Most of the early surviving lists have been microfilmed and most are in the state historical societies. The lists from the Civil War and later are being microfilmed by the National Archives.

If you're trying to obtain a copy of a birth, death, marriage or other certificate, check out: http://www.vitalrec.com - Vital Records Information Page for United States. This page contains information on obtaining vital records in every county, state and territory in the U.S. along with some great links.

Do you know the name of the town but not the county, go to the Geographic Names Information System at: http://mapping.usgs.gov/www/gnis/gnisform.html - to get it! Or try http://www.mit.edu/geo?location - Geographic Nameserver.

http://govinfo.kerr.orst.edu/usaco-stateis.html to locate counties in the U. S. and get info on them - Maps depicting counties and their locations and lots of other information from U.S. census records. Detailed information on each county in the USA is available at the above listed web page.

Go here for The Obituary Links Page: http://www.geocities.com/Heartland/Bluffs/7748/obit/obituary.htm - to access hundreds of online obituary links and related information - divided by state and counties.

And try http://www.geocities.com/Heartland/Bluffs/7748/obit/famobit.htm - Family Surname Obituary Archives Online and the incredible http://www.geocities.com/Heartland/Bluffs/7748/obit/links.htm - Obituary Links with search engines.

HELPFUL TIP:
If you remember "I" for "into" is Immigration and "E" for Exodus is Emigration - then you will know whether you are coming or going.

DAR ONLINE:
The library of the Daughters of the American Revolution, one of the most valuable research facilities in the country, has just put its catalog online. The web site says: "The DAR Library was founded in 1896 as a collection of genealogical and historical publications for the use of staff genealogists verifying application papers for the National Society of Daughters of the American Revolution. Shortly after 1900, the growing collection was opened to the public and has remained so ever since."

Non-members of the Daughters of the American Revolution, the Sons of the American Revolution, the Sons of the Revolution or the Children of the American Revolution pay a small daily user fee to help maintain and to expand the library's collections.

The library is one of the nation's premier genealogical research centers and was recently (1998) ranked the third-most important national institution based on the uniqueness of sources in a listing by publisher Heritage Quest. In late 1998, the library's book collection numbered some 150,000 volumes. Approximately 5,000 new titles enter the Library in any given year.

Many thousands of volumes of genealogical compilations, record abstracts and other materials are available only at the DAR Library. DAR members and the public have contributed these sources, building a collection of great research depth covering all periods of American history. The period of the American Revolution is naturally a major focal point, but the colonial era and the nineteenth century receive detailed coverage as well. Through the efforts of local DAR members and chapters nationwide, approximately 15,000 volumes of Genealogical Records Committee Reports have entered the Library and constitute a unique source for family histories, cemetery record transcriptions, and Bible records.

You can search the catalog at: http://dar.library.net/index.htm - This page also contains some very helpful tips for using the catalog, including how to search for place names, information on historical periods in American history, family names, authors and titles of books, the use of call words, and searching for a particular record type. The catalog will be a huge help for those planning on visiting the facilities in Washington, DC, but those who cannot travel to Washington can also benefit by utilizing the mail search service offered by the library. For details and restrictions on this service, visit the web page at: http://www.dar.org/library/libsearch.html or write to: The DAR Library, 1776 D Street, N.W., Washington, DC 20006-5392, Tel: 202-879-3229

FREE FORMS DOWNLOAD:
Ancestry.com has made available several quality charts and forms for you to use in your research efforts. Keeping track of your research efforts will help you stay organized. Simply download the forms you need and print out as many copies as you wish! You are licensed to download and print these forms for unlimited personal, non-commercial use. Ancestry.com recommends that you print these forms on acid-free paper in order to slow physical deterioration. The Ancestry.com Forms download page is at: http://www.ancestry.com/download/forms.htm

Forms available include:
~ Ancestral Chart
~ Research Calendar
~ Research Extract
~ Correspondence Record
~ Family Group Sheet
~ Source Summary

THIS AND THAT GENEALOGY TIPS ON MYTHS

NINE MYTHS ABOUT OUR AMERICAN ANCESTORS

Myth 1 - When our American ancestors moved they always moved West.
Fact: While most early settlers came to the eastern shore of North America, it was logical for most expansionist movements to flow westward. However, there are many documented cases showing movement northward, southward or back to the East after pioneers became less than enchanted with raw frontier.

Myth 2 - Because of travel conditions, prior to the railroads, families rarely moved more than once or twice in a lifetime.
Fact: A study of Revolutionary War pension applications reveal that many of these veterans moved six or more times and quite often lived in as many different states.

Myth 3 - Our ancestors usually moved, like Abraham, not knowing where they were going.
Fact: In-depth study into the migratory habits of our ancestors shows that in most cases they had received many reports on an "ideal" location by which they were convinced they would better themselves by moving. Sometimes, they relied on reports from relatives or neighbors who had already moved, but often a member of a family would make a preliminary trip to check out the new territory. The move usually involved several families making the trip together.

Myth 4 - Most American men were devoutly religious at the time of the American Revolution.
Fact: While most colonists gave nominal adherence to Christian values in the late eighteenth century, some historians have estimated that no more than 15 percent of the men were church members.

Myth 5 - Immediately following the American Revolution, most Southern churchmen were either Baptist or Methodist.
Fact: Following the Revolution War, the majority of Southerners of Anglo-Saxon heritage who were church members still belonged to the successor of the Anglican Church in America, the Protestant Episcopal Church. The second largest number of churchmen were the Scotch-Irish Presbyterians. The great movement to the Methodist and Baptist Churches came in the early part of the nineteenth century.

Myth 6 - Most Southern families were slave owners just prior to the Civil War.
Fact: The majority of the white Southern heads of households never owned a slave. This is substantiated through a study of slave census records.

Myth 7 - Most of the wealth of America was in Northern states just prior to the Civil War.
Fact: While industrial growth in the North had exceeded that in the South, the southeast had experienced an era of economic prosperity in the middle of the nineteenth century and, as a result, six of the ten wealthiest states in the Union in 1860 were below the Mason-Dixon Line.

Myth 8 - Due to the lack of major industry, there were no large cities in the South at the outbreak of the Civil War.
Fact: It is true that most of the large cities in the country were along the eastern seaboard during the 1850's. However, according to the 1850 census, New Orleans was the fifth largest city in the U. S., ranking just behind Philadelphia. The population of this major Southern port city at the time was 116,375.

Myth 9 - Most American males were involved in some kind of military action between the American Revolution and the Civil War.
Fact: There were a number of wars on Southern soil, between 1783 and 1865, including battles of the War of 1812, the War with Mexico and several Indian Wars. However, the majority of males in this country never participated in any kind of military action beyond a militia drill during this time period.

THIS AND THAT GENEALOGY TIPS ON NAMING PATTERNS

NAMING PRACTICES:

In the early colonies, the law of primogeniture was in effect. It is an exclusive right of the eldest son to inherit the father's estate. To ensure that the eldest son inherited, in the event the father died intestate, the eldest son was generally given the same name as his father. The second son was often given the first name of one of his uncles, generally the father's oldest brother. Later, families devised their own system to ensure that their offspring inherited. ie., giving all children the same middle name, denoting the fact that all with that name could inherit, and not just the oldest son.

As many families were very large, it is possible to find collateral kin, and thus an earlier ancestor by studying the names of your ancestors siblings. You can often make connections by studying the collateral kin.

As stated above, the eldest son usually had the same name as his father, the second son, the first name of one of his uncles. (paternal usually, unless the father had no brothers, then a maternal uncle). The middle name was either his mother's maiden name, or grandmother's maiden name. Basically, as more children were born, more maiden names were used, but generally those in the direct line. Great grandmothers, great great grandmothers, etc. Interestingly, after the fifth child, there will be names of famous people. Second generation immigrants often deviated from the original family names. They often named their children after local heroes. It is not uncommon for a southern family to name male children after famous southern political personalities, such as Robert E. Lee, Francis Marion, Jackson, Jefferson Davis, etc. However, the following generation often returned to the names of the previous generation. Therefore, when you find a generation of "local heroes", don't be discouraged. Ignore the names and try to concentrate on the more common names. This will help guide you back to the earlier ancestors.

Women's names follow the same practices as men's names, but generally follow the maternal line. The eldest daughter is often named for her maternal grandmother. Once again maiden names are often used as middle names. Sometimes, if the family is very large, you will only find one or two of the daughters with a maiden name as a middle name. Ironically, to find your female ancestor, you might have to take the first name of the eldest daughter, and the middle name of the second son.

Another interesting tidbit regarding women's lines - if you have the marriage record of your ancestor, and have no information about the wife other than her name, make a note of the person that married them. Many times the minister who performed the wedding is a relative. Her name may be different because she was a widow, thus being referred to by her first husband's name, instead of her maiden name.

It is often difficult to prove identity when there are several individuals with the same name. Aside from analyzing the family thru the naming trends, one should attempt to learn everything about their ancestor; wife, children, children's spouses, minister, debtors, creditors, occupation, religion, neighbors, siblings, politics, etc. Find his neighbors by studying the description of every parcel of land that he owned. Try to learn as much about his neighbors as possible.

There are some key principles to remember when researching collateral lines. First, names may change, particularly with women, but the relationships will remain, no matter how often the name changes. The strongest kin ties appear between women. The most enduring bond occurs between mothers and their grown daughters. This means that you may find more information by looking for a different surname than the direct line you are researching. Ties to the wife's kin are generally stronger than those to husband's, unless male ties are crucial to the husband's occupation. It is therefore necessary to learn the occupation of your ancestor.

Social relationships among kin are not broken by geographic mobility. This is important because you may be looking in an area where the records have been destroyed. You may find your information from one that is geographically removed from the destruction.

161

Genealogical organizations and literature are based on surnames. Too often, female lines are neglected. Be sure you understand the meaning of kinship terms in the period in which you are working. In colonial times, "in-law" referred to the relationships that we now call "step".

KINSHIP TERMS:

Affinity - relationships which exist because of marital ties. The contemporary term for these relations is "in-laws."

Augmented family - extension of nuclear family to include people bound together by law, rather than blood; eg. half siblings, adopted children, step-parents, step-siblings, etc.

Aunt - in American society, this term can refer to a woman in four different relative positions: father's sister, mother's sister, father's brother's wife, mother's brother's wife.

Brother - in addition to obvious meaning may also include:
(1) the husband of one's sister
(2) the brother of one's wife
(3) the husband of one's sister-in-law
(4) half-brother
(5) step-brother

Genealogists must also be aware "brother" may refer to a member of one's church.

Collateral family - referring to relatives who are "off to one side" i.e. not in the direct lineal ancestry, but who share a common ancestor. In western society, these people are called aunts, uncles, cousins, etc.

Consanguinity - refers to persons who share common descent or biological heritage.

Senior and Junior - The use of Sr. and Jr. after a name did not necessarily imply a father and son relationship as it does today. They may have lived in the same vicinity or they could have been an uncle and nephew. It could even be two unrelated individuals with the same name but of different ages. In order to help distinguish between them, "Sr." or "Jr." would be "tacked" on and it merely meant the older and the younger respectively.

Cousin - a very general term in American society referring to someone with whom you share a common ancestor. This term was widely used to mean an "extended family". If this person is in a different generation, the term "removed" is used giving the number of generations apart.

Extended family - when families of more than two generations compose a household or relationship.

Full sibling - one who has the same biological mother and father (thus the same ancestry) as oneself A half sibling has one of the same parents (and therefore shares only one side of the lineage) as oneself.

In Law - in contemporary society, term used to designate someone to whom you are related by your own marriage or that of a sibling. In colonial society, this term also referred to relationships created by the marriage of a parent, currently called "step" relationships. Thus a "mother-in-law" in the 17th century, may have been a father's second wife.

Natural child - when the term "natural" is used the researcher should not jump to a conclusion that it denotes an illegitimate relationship. It is meant to indicate a relationship by blood rather than one by marriage or adoption. An illegitimate child may be called "my base son" or "my bastard son."

Nephew/Niece - one who is the child of a sibling (or a half-sibling, or step-sibling, or a spouse's sibling, or your spouse's spouse's sibling. Since the term derives from the Latin term, "nepos" meaning grandson, it is possible an early colonial reference may have this meaning.

"Now wife"- often assumed that the testator of a will with this term had a former wife. While this may be true, it is more likely the testator is indicating the bequest is intended only for his present wife and not necessarily to any subsequent wife he may have. Donald Lines Jacobus wrote, ".... it is to be doubted whether any other legal phrase has fooled so many of our most experienced genealogists."

Nuclear family - a family group consisting of mother, father and dependent children.

Step-sibling - one related by virtue of a parent's marriage to an individual with children by a former marriage or relationship. While no relation by blood, there can be strong ties of emotion and tradition between step-siblings.

Uncle - in American society this term can refer to a man in four different relative positions: father's brother; mother's brother; father's sister's husband; mother's sister's husband.

The Illinois US Gen Web has an excellent Web Page that includes a helpful section "Surnames what's in a name". Its URL is: http://www.rootsweb.com/~ilgenweb/

THE OLD JONES NAMING PATTERN:
The first son is named after the father's father
the second son is named after the mother's father
the third son is named after the father himself.
the fourth through end son is named after a favorite brother or friend (usually of the fathers)

the first daughter is named after the mother's mother
the second daughter is named after the father's mother
the third daughter is named after the mother herself
and the fourth through end daughter is named after a favorite sister or friend (usually of the mothers)

Of course in order for it to work you would have to know the first and second name of all involved. There are exceptions of course, like if the naming pattern was already satisfied. For instance say the mothers name was Martha and she was named after her mother Martha. Then she names the first girl Martha after her mother, the second she names after the fathers mother, and the third girl's name is now open to other possibilities because she already named a girl after herself, or she could use her middle name. The same is true for the sons also. Especially watch if a child dies with an important name and they rename the baby the same name; usually you would try to put that name into the place where the child died as to follow the naming pattern.

This is true for naming patterns of the Welsh and Irish, except the third son is named for a brother or friend, not the fourth.

Nicknames can be VERY important clues. Record any nicknames you know and ask elderly relatives about other people's nicknames. Middle names can also be a lot of help -- or can be quite misleading if the person you're searching for has been known by middle name. One of the things I've learned the hard way is that if no one knows the middle name of a person only a few generations back, that may be because it was the middle name that was used.

Family tradition stories can provide great clues but isn't infallible. To make the best use of it, look at how many times the story has been passed down and how long it's been since you heard it. Each and every clue is important. So when in doubt, I urge you to save that questionable piece of information.

19TH CENTURY NAMING PATTERNS:
First son: named for his paternal grandfather.
Second son: named for his maternal grandfather.

Third son: named after father or father's paternal grandfather.
Fourth son: named after father's oldest brother or mother's paternal grandfather.
Fifth son: named after mother's eldest brother or father's material grandfather.
Sixth son: named after father's second oldest brother or for mother's maternal grandfather.

First dau: named for maternal grandmother.
Second dau: named for her paternal grandmother.
Third dau: named after mother or for mother's maternal grandmother.
Fourth dau: named after mother's oldest sister or for father's paternal grandmother.
Fifth dau: named after father's eldest sister or for mother's paternal grandmother.
Sixth dau: named after mother's second oldest sister or for father's paternal grandmother.

With people being what they are, there were all sorts of variations, some covered by rules and some by family decision. It was customary to name the next daughter/son born within a second marriage for the deceased husband/wife. If a father died before his child was born, the child was often named for him. If a mother died in childbirth, that child, if a girl, was usually named for the mother. Another child was commonly named for a child who had died within the family.

DUTCH NAMING PATTERNS: The custom was that the lst son be named for paternal grandfather; 2nd son named for his maternal grandfather; lst daughter for her maternal grandmother; 2nd daughter for her paternal grandmother. If 4 children were born then all 4 grandparents are known.

GERMAN NAMING PATTERNS:
The custom of Germans was to give, at baptism, two names. The first was a spiritual or a saint's name in honor of a favorite saint. In my own German family, I see Johann Adam, Johann George, Johann Jacob Hetzel and some favorite female names were Anna Barbara and Anna Margaret Hetzel, all within the same family! The second or middle name was the name the person was known by within the family. German girls were often given their mother's name plus one of their own, the latter name usually for a godmother.

It was common practice in some German families to name the first born son after the child's paternal grandfather and the second born son after the maternal grandfather.

The suffix "in" or "en", added to the end of a name, such as Anna Maria Hetzelin denoted female, often an unmarried female.

The definitive URL for German patterns is by Kerchner at:
http://www.kerchner.com/germname.htm - 18th Century Pennsylvania German Naming Patterns

SCOTCH NAMING PATTERNS:
According to the book "In Search of Scottish Ancestry" the general naming pattern in Scotland was to name:
The eldest son after the paternal grandfather.
The second son after the maternal grandfather.
The third after the father.
The oldest daughter after the maternal grandmother.
The second daughter after the paternal grandmother.
The third daughter after the mother.
One variation of above was for the eldest son to be named
after the mother's father and the eldest daughter after the father's mother.

Since given names change over the years someone doing research on their line would need to know the approximate time period when their ancestor was born and in what country.

FEMALE GIVEN NAMES & NICKNAMES:
Abigail - Abby, Nabby, Gail
Adelina - Addie, Addy
Adelaide - Addy, Adele, Dell, Della, Heidi
Agatha - Aggy
Agnes - Aggy, Inez, Nessa
Aileen - Allie, Lena
Alberta - Allie, Alla, Bert, Bertie
Alexandra - Alex, Alla, Sandy
Alfreda - Alfy, Freda, Freddy, Freida
Alice/Alica - Alce, Alicia, Allie, Ally, Elsie, Lisa
Almira - Mira,
Amanda - Mandy, Mendy
Almena - Allie, Mena
Amelia - Emily, Mel, Millie
Anne - Annie, Nan, Nancy, Nanny, Nina
Antoinette - Ann, Net, Netty, Tony
Arabella - Ara, Arry, Bel, Bella, Belle
Arlene - Arly, Lena
Armeda - Arry, Meda
Armena - Arry, Mena
Armilda - Arry, Milda, Milly
Artelia - Artie, Telia
Asenath - Assene, Natty, Sene
Augusta/Augustina - Aggy, Gussie, Tina

Barbara - Bab, Babs
Beatrice - Bea, Trisha, Triasie, Trissy, Trix, Trixie
Belinda - Bella, Belle, Linda
Bertha - Birdie, Bert, Bertie, Berty
Bessie - Elizabeth
Bridget - Biddie, Biddy, Bridie

Camille -Cammy, Millie
Caroline/Carolyn - Caddie, Carrie, Carol, Cassie, Lynn
Cassandra - Cassie, Sandra, Sandy
Catharina/ Catharine - Cassie, Cathy, Kate, Katie, Katrine, Kit, Kitty, Trina
Cecilia or Cecily - Celia, Cis, Cissy, Sis, Sisley
Charlotte - Char, Lotta, Lottie, Lotty, sometimes Sherry
Christiana/Christine - Chris, Chrissie, Crissy, Christy, Tina
Chrinstina - Chrissie, Xina
Cicely - Cecilia
Cinderella - Cindy, Ella
Clara - Clare
Clarissa/Clarinda - Clara, Clare, Cissy
Constance - Connie
Cordelia - Cordy, Delia
Cordessa - Cordy, Essa
Cornelia - Corny, Nelle, Nelly
Cynthia - Cindy

Darcus - Darkey

Darlene - Darry, Lena
Deborah/Debra - Deb, Debby, Lil, Lila
Delilah - Dell, Della, Lil, Lila
Delores - Dell, Lola, Dolly
Dorinda same as Dorothea
Dorothea/Dorothy - Dol, Dolly, Dot, Dotha, Dotty

Edith - Edie
Eleanor - Ella, Elaine, Ellen, Ellie, Lanna, Lenora, Nell, Nellie, Nelly, Nora
Elizabeth/Elisabeth - Bess, Bessy, Beth, Betsy, Betty, Elsbeth, Elsie, Eliza, Libby, Lisa, Liza, Liz, Lizzy
Ellen - Helen
Elmira - Ely, Mira
Emeline - Em, Emily, Emma, Emmy, Milly
Emma - Emm, Emmie, Emily
Estelle - Essy, Stella
Esther - Essie
Eugenia - Genie
Euphemia - Effie
Eustacia - Stacia, Stacy
Evaline - Eva, Lena
Eve - Eva
Eva - Eveline, Eveline, Evelyn

Faith - Fay
Fidelia - Delia
Florence - Flo, Flora, Floss, Flossie
Frances - Cissy, Fanny, Fran, Frankie, Sis
Frederica/Fredericka - Freda, Freddie, Ricka

Gabrielle - Ella, Gabby
Genevieve - Eva, Ginny
Geraldine - Dina, Gerrie, Jerry
Gertrude - Gert, Gertie, Gerdrutta, Gerda, Gertraut, Truddy
Griselda - Grissel
Gwendolyn - Gwen, Wendy

Hannah - Anna, Nan, Nanny
Harriet/Harriot - Hat, Hatty
Helen/Helena - Ella, Ellen, Eleanor, Elena, Elnora, Ellie, Lena, Nell, Nelly, Nora
Heloise - Eloise, Lois
Henrietta - Etta, Hank, Hetty, Nettie
Hermione - Hermie
Hepsibah - Hipsie
Hester/Hesther - Esther, Hessy, Hetty, Hitty
Honora/Honoria - Norah, Nora

Irene - Rena
Isabel/Isabella - Elizabeth, Belle, Bella, Bib, Tibbie

Jane - Janie, Jean, Jennie, Jessie, Joan
Janet - Jane
Jeannette - Etta, Janet, Jean, Jessie, Nettie

Jemima - Mima
Jesicca - Jess, Jessie
Joan/Joanna/Johanna - fem of John, Nonie
Joanna/Johannah - Joan, Jody, Hannah
Josepha/Josephine - Jo, Jody, Joey, Josey, Fina, Pheny
Joyce - Jo, Joy
Juanita - Nettie, Nita
Judith - Judy
Julia/Julie - Jill
Juliet - Julia

Kate - Catharine
Katharine/Katherine - Catharine, Katie, Kay, Kit, Kittiy
Keziah - Kizzie

Letitia - Lettie, Lettice, Titia, Tish
Lillian - Lil, Lilly, Lolly
Louise/Louisa - Lou, Vicey
Lucretia - Creesey
Lucinda - Cindy, Lucy
Lula - Lou
Lydia - .Liddy

Ladosca - Doaky
Laura - Laurinda
Lavinia - Viney
Lena - Helena or Madaline
Lenora - Lee, Nora
Letitia - Lettie, Lettice, Titia, Tish
Lillian - Lil, Lily, Lolly
Lorinda - Laurinda
Lorraine - Lee
Louisa/Louise - Lou, Louie, Vicey
Lucia - fem of Lucius
Lucretia - Creesey
Lucinda - Cindy, Lucy
Lula - Lou
Lydia - Liddy

Mabel - Amabel
Madalene - Maud, Maun
Magdalena - Lena, Maggie, Molly
Malvina - Mal, Vinnie
Margaret - Gritty, Mag, Maggy, Margo, Meg, Meggy, Metta, Peg, Peggy
Margery/Marjory - Madge, Margie
Marian - Marianne
Marion - Mary
Martha - Mat, Matty, Pat, Patty, Patsy
Mary - Marie, May, Moll, Molly, Poll, Polly
Mathilda/Matilda - Mat, Matty, Patty, Tilda, Tillie
Minerva - Nurvy, Minnie
Minnie - Mary

Mintora - Mintie, Minte, Minty
Miriam - Mary
Myrtle - Myrtie, Myrt

Nancy - Nannie, Nan, Nance, Agness
Nellie/Nelly - Ellen, Helen, Eleanor
Norah/Nora - Honora, Leonora, Eleanor

Octavia - Tave, Tavy
Olivia - Livvie, Liv

Paula - fem of Paulus
Paulina - Pauline
Phillis - Phyllis
Philipana - Pena, Penny, Peney
Polly - Mary, Pol
Priscilla - Prissy, Sissy

Rebecca/Rebekah - Becky, Beck, Reba
Rhoda - Roady
Rosina - Rosey, Rose
Roxana - Roxy

Sarah - Sal, Sally
Sibbilla - Sibby
Sophia - Sophy, Suffy, Sop
Sophronia - Fina, Sop
Susan/Susahhan - Anna, Sue, Suke, Sukky, Susie, Susy
Sylvia - fem of Sylvanus

Temperance - Tempe, Tempie
Theodora - Dora
Theresa - Terry, Tracy
Thomasa/Thomasine - Tamzine

Ursula - Suly

Valeria - Valerie
Verona - Runnie, Rennie
Virginia - Jenny, Jen, Jane

Wilhemina - Mina,Minnie, Minella, Wilma, Wilmett, Wilmot
Winifred - Winnie

MALE GIVEN NAMES & NICKNAMES:
Cornelius - Neal
Elisha - Eli, Lish, Eeel, Elisa
Frederick - Eric, Friedreich, Fred
Jehiel - Hile.
John - Johannes, Jack, Hans, Hance, Johan, Jacques
Jonathan - John, Nathan
Howard - Howie

Lawrence - Laraus, Lars, Lassey, Laurie
Matthew - Mathias, Matt, Thiess
Nathaniel - Nathan, Nat
Nicholas - Nick, Claus, Clase
Richard - Ricky, Dick, Ricardo
William - Billy, Ole, Wolle, Wilhelm, Will, Willie

GERMAN NAMING PRACTICES:

A large percentage of German males were named Johann. I have found my own grandfather called Johann George Hetzel, John George, George John and just plain John or George. Many German males had the first name of Johann, then a middle name. Additionally, most were referred to by their middle name, not their first name. It seems that the name a person "goes by" every day is called a "rufname" This name does not necessarily have to be their first name - It can be any one of the given names at birth or baptism that the individual chooses to use as his "rufname."

THIS AND THAT GENEALOGY TIPS ON THE NATIONAL ARCHIVES

National Archives Genealogy page: http://www.nara.gov/genealogy/genindex.html

NARA site relating to the regional repositories: http://www.nara.gov/regional/nrmenu.html

NARA books: http://www.nara.gov/nara/bookstore/books.html

The following guides are for sale through the NARA: http://www.nara.gov/publications/micro.html
The 1790-1890 Federal Population Censuses
The 1900 Federal Population Census
The 1910 Federal Population Census
The 1920 Federal Population Census
Immigrant & Passenger Arrivals
Genealogical & Biographical Research
Military Service Records
Black Studies
American Indians
Diplomatic Records

The National Archives is actually many facilities under the administration of the National Archives and Records Administration (NARA). Of special interest to genealogists are the repositories in Washington, DC and the twelve regional locations around the United States. The NARA is, among other things, concerned with maintaining historic records for the federal government. Some of the records maintained by the NARA are of critical importance to family historians.

1. Federal Census Returns (each 10 years, 1790 to 1920) most of 1890 census lost to fire in 1921

2. Ship Passenger Lists (from about 1820 to 1957 for most ports, some ports/years are not indexed, some indexes very hard to read)

3. Military Service Records as follows:
Volunteer Soldiers, compiled service records (1775-1902)
Regular Military enlisted (1789-1912), registers of enlistment, muster rolls
Regular Military officers (1789-1917), registers of enlistment, personnel records after 1863, muster rolls In general it is much easier finding information about volunteer soldiers.

4. Military pension applications and Bounty Land Claims (for service between 1775 and 1916). Most pension records were turned over to the NARA by the Veterans Administration early in the 20th century, pension files that were active at that time are still with the VA. Pension files are usually full of genealogical information.

Excerpt from "Genealogical Records in the National Archives" General Services Administration, Leaflet #5, Washington, DC 20408:

The National Archives has incomplete series of customs passenger lists and immigration passenger lists of ships arriving from abroad at Atlantic and Gulf of Mexico ports. For the Port of Philadelphia, the Archives have customs passenger lists from 1800-1882, Immigration passenger lists from 1883-1945, and Indexes from 1800-1948. A customs passenger list normally contains the following information for each passenger: name, age, sex, and occupation; country from which he came; and the country to which he was going; and if he died in passage, the date and circumstances of his death. The immigration passenger lists that are more than 50 years old (those less than 50 years old are not available for reference purposes) vary in informational content but usually show the place of birth and last place of residence in addition to the information found in the customs passenger lists. Some of the immigration passenger lists include the name and address of a relative in the country from which the passenger came.

NATURALIZATIONS 1793 - 1930:

The naturalization process usually includes two steps: the declaration of intention and the petition for naturalization. The declaration of intention may be taken at any time after the alien has arrived within the United States. The information contained within the declaration was very detailed before 1828-1838, often with the name of the declarant, place and date of birth, port and date of emigration and immigration, approximate age, and name or title of the monarch whom he is renouncing given. At various dates between 1828 and 1838, the individual courts witched to a shorter declaration form requiring only the name of the declarant, approximate age, and name or title of the monarch to be given.

The petition for naturalization occurred at least two years after the declaration of intention and after the alien had resided within the United States for at least five years. Uniformly, the petition for naturalization will give no biographical or genealogical information before 1906.

There were two major exceptions to the rules cited above. Minors, those children who arrived in this country under the age or 18 or 21, only had to reach their majority and reside within the country for five years before making a final petition for naturalization. The requirement that a declaration be filed was waived. These petitions will give the year and port of entry for the petitioner. Military service in the Union or United States forces and an honorable discharge allowed aliens to omit both the declaration and four years of residency requirements. Only one year of residency within the United States was required. The military petitions will given the length of service and the unit in which the petitioner served.

Starting in 1906, the United States Immigration and Naturalization Service issued a standard form to be used by all courts in the United States. The declaration of intention would give a detailed physical description of the applicant as well as important genealogical information about date and place of birth. The petition required the name of the ship, port and date of entry, and names of family members, ages, and places of birth.

With rare exceptions, no woman was naturalized prior to 1923, after the passage of the 19th amendment which granted women the right to vote.

As a word of warning, however, do not expect that the naturalization records will provide the genealogist with all of the biographical information which she or he is seeking. The various courts in Philadelphia, once freed from the restraints imposed upon them under the original Naturalization Acts of Congress, slowly slipped into a standard form for both the declaration and intention which provides the genealogist with clues, but not actual data regarding the date of birth of the applicant, port and year of entry, or names of the members of the family who either accompanied him at the time of his arrival or who composed the family at the time of his naturalization. Many of these categories were incorporated into the standard Bureau of Labor Naturalization form required of all courts starting in 1906.

Secondly, few women appear in the naturalization records prior to 22 September 1922, after they had achieved the right to vote. Of the over 200,000 naturalizations contained in the files at the Philadelphia City Archives, possibly fifty involve the naturalization of a woman prior to 1922.

According to the federal naturalization laws, any court of record within the United States had the power to conduct naturalization proceedings. These proceedings usually involved two steps. A man, (or, very rarely, a woman,) visited the court to swear or affirm his intention to renounce his allegiance to his native country and monarch. This was known as the Declaration of Intention. After a waiting period of three years, later reduced to two years, he could enter any court in the country, produce a copy of the declaration, prove that he had resided in the United States for a period of not less than five years, have a person vouch for his character, and present a petition for full citizenship. This paper is known as the Naturalization Petition. If he fulfilled all of these obligations, the court would issue a certificate of citizenship and would retain, as part of its records, the applicant's copy of the declaration and the petition for naturalization. The court would not retain a copy of the actual Certificate of Citizenship. This belonged to the newly enfranchised citizen.

DECLARATIONS OF INTENTION:
The first document of the citizenship/naturalization process is known as the Declaration of Intention. When first developed in Philadelphia, this document would provide much information helpful for genealogical pursuits. Generally, the information contained within the Declaration had the date of the declaration, name, birthplace, birth date, and approximate age of the declarant, nativity, name of the monarch, port of embarkation, port and date of arrival, and declarant's signature or mark. Between 1828 and 1838, the various courts abandoned this form in lieu of a shorter form which has only the date of the declaration, name and approximate age of the declarant, nativity, name of monarch, and declarant's signature or mark. There is no other information contained on the declarations filed in the Philadelphia county courts until 1906.

The declarations starting in 1906 contain the following information: name; occupation; age; description, including color, complexion, height, weight, hair color, eye color, other marks; birthplace; birth date; place of residence; port and vessel of embarkation; foreign residence; name of monarch; port and date of arrival; signature or mark of declarant; and date of declaration. There is no other information contained on the declarations filed in the Philadelphia county courts until 1906.

EXCEPTIONS TO FILING A DECLARATION:
All persons who wanted to initiate naturalization proceedings in the 19th century had to file a declaration, with two major exceptions:

MINORS - Those people who arrived in the United States under the age of either 18 or 21 (the law changed) had only to wait the five-year residency requirement and achieve their majority before filing a petition to become a citizen. The law waived the necessity of minors having to file a declaration of intention. However, before 1850, both the Quarter Sessions Court and the Common Pleas Court would often have an applicant fill out the declaration docket as well as a minor's petition in order to have some proof of the applicant's age and signature.

MILITARY SERVICE- Persons serving in the United States armed forces (the Union forces during the Civil War), only had to present their honorable discharge and reside in the country for a period of only one year, not five, in order to file for naturalization.

PETITIONS FOR NATURALIZATIONS:
The petition for naturalization, important as proof of your ancestor's successful bid to become a citizen of the United States, contains no genealogical information before 1906. It will state the date and court before which the applicant made his declaration, the applicant's desire to become a citizen, a voucher from an existing citizen as to the applicant's moral character, date of the petition, and the applicant's signature or mark.

Minor's petitions will provide the year and port through which the applicant arrived. Before 1850, in the Common Pleas and Quarter Sessions Courts, one will usually find a declaration for the minor filed on the same day within the declaration records of the respective courts.

Military petitions will provide the name of the company and regiment, length of service, and date of honorable discharge.

After 1906, the petition for naturalization provides the following information: name; address; occupation; birth date; birthplace; emigration date and port; port and date of arrival; date and court of declaration; name, age and birthplace of wife, if any; name, birth dates and birthplaces of children, if any; affidavits of petitioner and witnesses; oath of allegiance; order of court admitting petitioner; and number and date of certificate of naturalization.

172

At no time in American history did a person have to return to the same court in which he filed his declaration of intent in order to file his petition for naturalization. One will find in the petition files of the various courts declarations taken before courts from Maine to California.

THE 5-YEAR RULE:

A person had to reside in the United States for at least five years before filing for his final petition for naturalization. Generally, he also had to reside in the State of Pennsylvania for one year before this action.

During the 19th century, no maximum time period existed for the filing of naturalization petitions. Nor did anyone have to become naturalized in order to own property, hold a job, or any thing else that he wanted to do, except vote. Cases exist in which a person might have arrived before 1800 but not filed for naturalization until after 1850. The provision that a person had to be naturalized before casting a vote accounts for the fact that the peak years for naturalization are those of presidential campaigns.

As noted above, military service was taken in lieu of both a declaration of intention and four of the five years of residency.

THE 2-YEAR RULE:

A person had to wait a minimum of two years between the action of declaring his intent to become a citizen and actually filing his final petition for naturalization. Before 1828, this period of waiting was three years.

Again, the only exception that the Archives staff has noticed occurs when a person has signed the declaration document and proven that he arrived as a minor which allows him to file his final petition on the same day.

INTERPRETING DATA FROM NATURALIZATIONS:

The tricky part of using the naturalizations is understanding how the little data which is given on the form can be used to determine information about your forebear. To do this, one should always remember the rules stated above. One can sometimes estimate an approximate date of arrival by realizing that a person had to be 18 before he was required to file a declaration, (otherwise he would file a "minor's" petition) and that at least five years had to pass between arrival and petition.

To give a random example. Henry Axt filed his declaration of intention in the Supreme Court of Pennsylvania on 1 April 1856 and his final petition in the Philadelphia County District Court on 16 April 1860. He stated that he was 23 years old on his declaration of intention. This would put his birth date approximately 1832 or 1833. His 18th birth date would probably have occurred in either 1850 or 1851. Since he filed his petition in 1860, he could not have arrived after 1855. Therefore, his probable arrival date would be 1851-1855.

Another example is that of Ernst Albert, who stated that he was 21 at the time of his declaration on 1 January 1856. He filed a petition on 18 April 1860. Again, using the same formula, we assume that his birth date falls in 1834, and using the 5-year rule, could not have arrived after 1855. Therefore, he arrived in the United States between 1852 and 1855.

Determining the port of arrival, if it is not mentioned on the declaration or petition, requires searching through the ship passenger lists of each port. Using the formula above will cut the amount of time and records which will have to be searched. A survey of 15,394 naturalizations filed in the Common Pleas and District Courts from 1850-1857 revealed that 33.8% of the petitions had the port and/or the date of immigration. New York had the highest number of arrivals with 48%, followed by Philadelphia with 45%. The next four, in order of incidence, were Baltimore, Boston, New Orleans, and Wilmington, Delaware. [Three people reported that they entered the United States through Quebec, and one person through St. Louis, Missouri.]

SOME FINAL NOTES:

The Immigration and Naturalization Service (I. & N.S.), Washington, D.C. 20536, has duplicate records of all naturalizations that occurred after 27 September 1906. Inquiries about citizenship granted after that date should be sent on Form G-639. Contact the I. & N.S., 26 Federal Plaza, New York, N. Y. 10278 or your local Immigration Office for a copy of this form. I. & N. S. will charge a fee of $15.00 to complete your request.

The 1900 United States Census has three codes in its Naturalization column. NA means that the person has been naturalized (again, women were not naturalized but could be considered naturalized if their husband was); AL means that the person is still an alien and has not begun the naturalization process. PA stands for Papers Applied for, not Pennsylvania, which means that the person has started the naturalization process by filing a declaration of intention but has not completed it at the time of the census visit. Contact the local county court for naturalization records as an alien could apply for naturalization in ANY court: city, county, state or federal.

NATURALIZATION REQUESTS:
To clear up the method for requesting information on a particular individual from NARA-Mid Atlantic States regarding naturalization. The following is the response you get from them if you request information and not forms. You can copy and complete the form listed below and e-mail it to NARA as directed. Or just put the requested information in an e-mail if you cannot copy the form. The Mid-Atlantic has the records from Federal agencies and U.S. Courts in the states of Delaware, Maryland, Pennsylvania, Virginia and West Virginia You cannot request information on any other region at this address.

NATURALIZATION REQUEST FORM - Type or print clearly! A search can not be made without the completion of essential information that has been marked with a star (*).

*REQUESTING PARTY'S POSTAL MAILING ADDRESS
Date:

Name:

Address:

1. Petitioner's Name (and spelling variations):

2. Date of Naturalization and/or Arrival into the U.S.: (A search can be made of a ten year time period if exact date is not known)

3. Naturalization Court or Place of Residence (county) 5 years after arrival:

4. Naturalization Petition Number:

5. Date of Birth:

6. Country of Birth:

7. Port of Entry into the U.S.:

8. Spouse's Name:

8a. Date of marriage:

9. Children's Name(s) & Date(s) of Birth:

Remember: Naturalization is not now (and never was) a requirement. An alien can live in the United States without becoming a naturalized citizen. Therefore, your ancestor may have never gone through this process.

Do not send any money until you receive a bill. You will be notified of the results in the search for your requested records.

Please return the completed form by E-mail:
archives@philarch.nara.gov or postal mail at National
Archives-Mid Atlantic Region, 900 Market St, Rm 1350,
Philadelphia, PA 19107-4292.

MEDICAL RECORDS:
If an ancestor's military records indicate he received a medical discharge or was wounded, resubmit the form to the National Archives and request the complete medical records by writing on top of the form in large letters "SEND COMPLETE MEDICAL FILE". Medical records are not part of military records and will not ordinarily be with military records sent to you.

PHOTOCOPIES:
The National Archives will provide you with photo copies of some documents. Their fee is very small and I recommend that you consider using their request forms if you are concerned about project costs. You may request:
1. Veterans Records, use NATF Form 80. Certain military records, pension files and bounty-land applications can be requested with this form. One file for one person will cost about $10.00. You must provide them with as much information as possible. The minimum is: name, branch of service, state from which he served, war, whether union or confederate. Additional information: such as unit in which he served and place and date of birth, certainly would insure a favorable result. If your soldier was named Jones or Smith you should have very detailed information before requesting the file. They, in general, will not do research for you. Often they will not photo copy the entirety of a large file unless you make a specific request.

2. Passenger Arrival Records use NATF Form 81. One record will cost $10.00. They will search existing passenger indexes and then provide you with a copy of the ships list. The availability of indexes is quite complex and I will not attempt to characterize their abilities. The NATF Form 81 explains in detail what they will do and what information you need to provide.

3. Census Records, use NATF Form 82. One household will cost about $6.00. They will provide you with copies of specifically identified pages of Federal population census schedules. You must provide them with the following information:

census year
state or territory
county
township or other subdivision
name of head of household
page number
enumeration district (for 1880, 1900, 1910 and 1920 only)

Form 82 states, "The National Archives does not search census indexes, nor do we provide census research service by mail."

The National Archives has finding aids online for Census Records, Veterans Records and Passenger Arrival Records. Their web site is: http://www.nara.gov

To obtain the forms described above you should write to:
Textual Reference Branch, National Archives and Records Administration, 7th and Pennsylvania Avenue NW., Washington, DC 20408

Forms can also be ordered by sending an e-mail to:
inquire@nara.gov or use their e-mail reference and information service inquire@arch2.nara.gov operated by the staff of the Customer Services Division. "Inquire" is intended to provide timely responses to reference requests, or at least get the process started quickly by referring your message to the appropriate office or person. They also answer general inquiries about the National Archives and Records Administration (NARA). If you have not visited NARA's web page, we recommend that you do because there is much useful information about the agency and its records holdings and services.

The numbers and subjects of forms are:

Form 80 (Military service and pension records prior to World War I, including the Revolutionary War, War of 1812, the Mexican War, Civil War, and the Spanish-American War)

Form 81 (Passenger Arrival Records)

Form 82 (Copies of Census Records -- requiring your knowledge of the publication, roll, and page number, as we do not conduct searches of Census Records for you)

Form 83 (Eastern Cherokee Applications)

Form 84 (Land Entry Papers -- for Federal lands only), and

Form 180 Military Service Records, World War I and later -- the form can also be downloaded directly from the following Internet location: http://www.nara.gov/regional/mpr.html

Give them the FORM NUMBER, the QUANTITY needed and YOUR POSTAL MAILING ADDRESS.

NARA'S NATIONAL PERSONNEL RECORDS CENTER for MILITARY PERSONNEL RECORDS:
9700 Page Avenue, St. Louis, MO 63132-5100
Tel: 314-538-4243 (Air Force records)
Tel: 314-538-4261 (Army records)
Tel: 314-538-4141 (Navy, Marine Corps, Coast Guard records)
Fax: 314-538-4175
E-mail: center@stlouis.nara.gov (General information only, no e-mail requests for records.) -
http://www.nara.gov/regional/stlouis.html - NARA WEB PAGE

The National Personnel Records Center (NPRC) is one of NARA's regional records services facilities. The center receives, stores, and services federal, military, and civilian personnel records at two facilities in St. Louis, Missouri: the Civilian Personnel Records (CPR) Building (which will be featured tomorrow) at 111 Winnebago Street, on the south side of the city of St. Louis and the Military Personnel Records (MPR) Building at 9700 Page Avenue in St. Louis County.

The Military Personnel Records Building houses military personnel and medical records as well as the dependent medical records of former members of the United States Navy and Marine Corps.

A July 12, 1973, fire at 9700 Page Avenue destroyed nearly all of the records pertaining to persons discharged from the Army before 1960 and about two-thirds of the records pertaining to persons discharged from the Air Force before 1964. Alternate record sources are used to attempt to document the service of such persons.

Although stored and serviced by NARA, the military personnel records remain under the legal control of the Department of Defense and information from the records in released following rules set by the military services, not by NARA.

Records held by the center include millions of military personnel, health, and medical records of discharged and deceased veterans of all services during the 20th century, medical treatment records of retirees from all services, and records for dependent and other persons treated at Navy medical facilities.

The military personnel records include:

Air Force: Officers and Enlisted beginning Sep. 25, 1947.

Army: Officers separated beginning Jul. 1, 1917;
Enlisted separated beginning Nov. 1, 1912.

Coast Guard: Officers separated beginning Jan. 1, 1929;
Enlisted separated beginning Jan. 1, 1915.

Marine Corps: Officers and Enlisted separated beginning Jan. 1, 1905.

Navy: Officers separated beginning Jan. 1, 1903;
Enlisted separated beginning Jan. 1, 1886.

(Earlier records are at the National Archives in Washington, D.C.)

Medical records include:
Inpatient and outpatient clinical records for selected time periods (see http://www.nara.gov/regional/mprmpm.html for dates and a description of the records included).

Inpatient, outpatient, dental, and mental health treatment records for military retirees, dependents, and others created at military health care facilities (see: http://www.nara.gov/regional/mprmtr.html for more information).

The July 12, 1973, fire destroyed about 80% of the records for Army personnel discharged between Nov. 1, 1912, and Jan. 1, 1960, and about 75% of the records for Air Force personnel with surnames from "Hubbard" through "Z" discharged between Sep. 25, 1947, and Jan. 1, 1964. NARA has more information about the fire at: http://www.nara.gov/regional/mprfire.html

Records available to veterans. Copies of most military personnel and medical records at NPRC are available to veterans or the next of kin free of charge. Requests must contain enough information to identify the record from among the more than 70 million on file at the center. The information needed to locate a record includes full name, military service number, branch, and approximate dates of service. Unit(s) of assignment and date and place of birth may also be helpful. For additional information on obtaining personnel records, see: http://www.nara.gov/regional/mprpub1a.html

For further information on obtaining inpatient medical records, see: http://www.nara.gov/regional/mprpub2a.html

Records available for genealogy. Only limited information can be released to the general public without the written authorization of the veteran or next of kin, and NARA may charge fees for copies sent to other than the veteran or next of kin. Information that may be released includes name, age or date of birth, dates of service, source of commission, rank/grade and date attained, marital status, promotion sequence number, city, state, and date of last known address, serial or service number (but not social security number), places of induction and separation, duty assignments, dependents, (including name, sex, and age), unclassified records of court martial trials, military education and schooling, information about decorations and awards, and for deceased veterans, the places of birth, death, and burial. For more information, see: http://www.nara.gov/regional/mprpub1b.html

Standard Form 180, Request Pertaining to Military Records, which is recommended but not mandatory, can be downloaded from NARA at: http://www.nara.gov/regional/mprsf180.html

Requests from federal agencies and veterans (or next of kin) take precedence over requests from the general public. Because of the workload, NARA requests "Please do not send a follow-up request before 90 days have elapsed as it may cause further delays."

MILITARY LINKS & RESOURCES:
List of Case Files (1888-1933) from the Sawtelle Disabled Veterans Home, Los Angeles:
http://www.nara.gov/regional/findaids/lagdav.html

Checklist of Archival Holdings Related to World War II at NARA's Pacific Region (Laguna Niguel):
http://www.nara.gov/regional/findaids/lagww2.html

Medals of Honor Index - (List of Medal of Honor recipients by conflict with information about each honoree):
http://www.army.mil/cmh-pg/moh1.htm

State-level Lists of Casualties from the Korean Conflict (1951-1957) State-level Lists of Casualties from the Vietnam Conflict (1957-): http://www.nara.gov/nara/electronic/korvnsta.html

Vietnam Casualty Search Page: http://www.no-quarter.org

Army Center for Military History
1099 14th Street, NW
Washington, DC 20005-3402
Tel: 202-761-5413
E-mail: cmhweb@cmh-smtp.army.mil
http://www.army.mil/cmh-pg/default.htm

Dept. of Veterans Affairs
810 Vermont Avenue, NW
Washington, DC 20420
Tel: 202-233-4000
800-827-1000
http://www.va.gov/foia/default.htm

Marine Corps Historical Center
Washington Navy Yard, Building 58
Ninth and M Streets, SE
Washington, DC 20374-0580
Tel: 202-433-3483
http://www.usmc.mil/

National Cemetery System
Department of Veterans Affairs
810 Vermont Avenue, NW
Washington, DC 20420
Tel: 202-273-5221
E-mail: ncscss@mail.va.gov
http://www.va.gov/cemetery/index.htm

Naval Historical Center
Washington Navy Yard
901 M Street, SE
Washington, DC 20374-5060

Library:
Tel: 202-433-4132
Fax: 202-433-9553
Museum:
Tel: 202-433-4882
Fax: 202-433-8200
Operational Archives:
Fax: 202-433-2833
Ships History Branch:
Tel: 202-433-3643
Fax: 202-433-6677
http://www.history.navy.mil/

U.S. Air Force Historical Research Agency
Mail:
HQ AFHRA/RSA
600 Chennault Circle
Maxwell AFB, AL 36112-6424
E-mail: AFHRANEWS1%RS%AFHRA@MAX1.au.af.mil
http://www.au.af.mil/au/afhra

U.S. Army Military History Institute
22 Ashburn Drive, Carlisle Barracks
Carlisle, PA 17013
Tel: 717-245-3611
E-mail: MHI-SC@carlisle-emh2.army.mil (Special Collections)
            MHI-WAR.@carlisle-emh2.army.mil (Archives Collection)
            MHI-HR@carlisle-emh2.army.mil (Historical Reference)
http://carlisle-www.army.mil/usamhi

U.S. Coast Guard Historian's Office (G-CP-4)
2100 2nd Street, SW
Washington, DC 20593
Tel: 202-267-0948
E-mail: rbrowning@comdt.uscg.mil
sprice@comdt.uscg.mil
http://www.dot.gov/dotinfo/uscg/hq/g-cp/history/collect.html

More Military Links can be found at NARA's Military Personnel Records Center Link page:
http://www.nara.gov/regional/mprhelp.html

THIS AND THAT GENEALOGY TIPS ON OCCUPATIONS

Accomptant -	Accountant
Almoner -	Giver of charity to the needy
Amanuensis -	Secretary or stenographer
Artificer -	A soldier mechanic who does repairs
Bailie -	Bailiff
Baxter -	Baker
Bluestocking -	Female writer
Boniface -	Keeper of an inn
Brazier -	One who works with brass
Brewster -	Beer manufacturer
Brightsmith -	Metal Worker
Bull-whacker -	Oxen driver
Burgonmaster -	Mayor
Caulker -	One who filled up cracks (in ships or windows) or seams to make them watertight by using tar or oakum-hemp fiber produced by taking old ropes apart
Chaisemaker -	Carriage maker
Chandler -	Dealer or trader; one who makes or sells candles; retailer of groceries
Chiffonnier -	Wig maker
Clark -	Clerk
Clerk -	Clergyman, cleric
Clicker -	The servant of a salesman who stood at the door to invite customers; one who received the matter in the galley from the compositors and arranged it in due form ready for printing; one who makes eyelet holes in boots using a machine which clicked
Cohen -	Priest
Collier -	Coal miner
Colporteur -	Peddler of books
Cooper -	One who makes or repairs vessels made of staves and hoops, such as casks, barrels, tubs, etc
Cordwainer -	Shoemaker, originally any leather worker using leather from Cordova/Cordoba in Spain
Costermonger -	Peddler of fruits and vegetables
Crocker -	Potter
Crowner -	Coroner
Currier -	One who dresses the coat of a horse with a curry comb; one who tanned leather by incorporating oil or grease
Docker -	Stevedore, dock worker who loads and unloads cargo
Dowser -	One who finds water using a rod or witching stick
Draper -	A dealer in dry goods
Drayman -	One who drives a long strong cart without fixed sides for carrying heavy loads
Dresser -	A surgeon's assistant in a hospital
Drover -	One who drives cattle, sheep, etc. to market; a dealer in cattle
Duffer -	Peddler
Factor -	Agent, commission merchant; one who acts or transacts business for another; Scottish steward or bailiff of an estate
Farrier -	A blacksmith, one who shoes horses
Faulkner -	Falconer
Fell monger -	One who removes hair or wool from hides in preparation for leather making
Fletcher -	One who made bows and arrows
Fuller -	One who fulls cloth; one who shrinks and thickens woolen cloth by moistening, heating and pressing, one who cleans and finished cloth.

Gaoler -	A keeper of the goal, a jailer
Glazier -	Window glassman
Hacker -	Maker of hoes
Hatcheler -	One who combed out or carded flax
Haymonger -	Dealer in hay
Hayward -	Keeper of fences
Higgler -	Itinerant peddler
Hillier -	Roof tiler
Hind -	A farm laborer
Holster -	A groom who took care of horses, often at an inn
Hooker -	Reaper
Hooper -	One who made hoops for casks and barrels
Huckster -	Sells small wares
Husbandman -	A farmer who cultivated the land
Jagger -	Fish peddler
Journeyman -	One who had served his apprenticeship and mastered his craft, not bound to serve a master, but hired by the day
Joyner / Joiner -	A skilled carpenter
Keeler -	Bargeman
Kempster -	Wool comber
Lardner -	Keeper of the cupboard
Lavender -	Washer woman
Lederer -	Leather maker
Leech -	Physician
Longshoreman -	Stevedore
Lormer -	Maker of horse gear
Malender -	Farmer
Maltster -	Brewer
Manciple -	A steward
Mason -	Bricklayer
Mintmaster -	One who issued local currency
Monger -	Seller of goods (ale, fish)
Muleskinner -	Teamster
Neatherder -	Herds cows
Ordinary -	Innkeeper with fixed prices
Pattern Maker -	A maker of a clog shod with an iron ring. A clog was a wooden pole with a pattern cut into the end
Peregrinator -	Itinerant wanderer
Peruker -	A wig maker
Pettifogger -	A shyster lawyer
Pigman -	Crockery dealer
Plumber -	One who applied sheet lead for roofing and set lead frames for plain or stained glass windows
Porter -	Door keeper
Puddler -	Wrought iron worker
Quarrier	Quarry worker
Rigger -	Hoist tackle worker
Ripper -	Seller of fish
Roper -	Maker of rope or nets
Saddler -	One who makes, repairs or sells saddles or other furnishings for horses
Sawbones -	Physician
Sawyer -	One who saws; carpenter

Schumacker -	Shoemaker
Scribler -	A minor or worthless author
Scrivener -	Professional or public copyist or writer; notary public
Scrutiner -	Election judge
Shrieve -	Sheriff
Slater -	Roofer
Slopseller -	Seller of ready-made clothes in a slop shop
Snobscat/Snob -	One who repaired shoes
Sorter -	Tailor
Spinster -	A woman who spins or an unmarried woman
Spurrer -	Maker of spurs
Squire -	Country gentleman; farm owner; justice of peace
Stuff gown -	(Also Stuff gownsman) Junior barrister
Supercargo -	Officer on merchant ship who is in charge of cargo and the commercial concerns of the ship
Tanner -	One who tans (cures) animal hides into leather
Tapley -	One who puts the tap in an ale cask
Tasker -	Reaper
Teamster -	One who drives a team for hauling
Thatcher -	Roofer
Tide waiter -	Customs inspector
Tinker -	An itinerant tin pot and pan seller and repairman
Tipstaff -	Policeman
Travers -	Toll bridge collection
Tucker -	Cleaner of cloth goods
Turner -	A person who turns wood on a lathe into spindles
Victualer -	A tavern keeper, or one who provides an army, navy, or ship with food supplies
Vulcan -	Blacksmith
Wagoner -	Teamster not for hire
Wainwright -	Wagon maker
Waiter -	Customs officer or tide waiter; one who waited on the tide to collect duty on goods brought in
Waterman -	Boatman who plies for hire
Webster -	Operator of looms
Wharfinger -	Owner of a wharf
Wheelwright -	One who made or repaired wheels; wheeled carriages, etc.
Whitesmith -	Tinsmith; worker of iron who finishes or polishes the work
Whitewing -	Street sweeper
Whitster -	Bleach of cloth
Wright -	Workman, especially a construction worker
Yeoman -	Farmer who owns his own land

THIS AND THAT GENEALOGY TIPS ON PHOTOGRAPHS & PHOTOGRAPHY

COPYING PHOTOGRAPHS:
When copying photographs on the photocopy machine, the quality can be improved by using a copy-screen. Copy-screens are available in the 65 line and 85 line sizes. Use of the screen (under the photo being copied) creates a dot matrix image and produces a copy with better detail and contrast balances. Such screens are available from larger art supply stores. It is reported that the difference in the copies is worth the small cost of the screen which can be kept and reused many times.

If you want to make a copy of the photograph yourself with your own camera - first you need a basic single lens reflex 35 mm camera - not the auto focus type. The basic lens on your camera, provided it is not less than a 50mm lens, will often focus close enough to copy large photos. For smaller photographs you will need a set of "close-ups". These are actually ring-shaped magnifying glasses that screw to the front of your lens.

You will need a way to hold your camera steady while you are making the exposure. A tripod or copy stand is helpful but is not a necessity. You may be able to position your photo on a table in front of the camera and get a good copy. Use books or other objects to adjust the height of your subject so you get the entire photo in the view finder and get it level with the camera. If you do not get them aligned properly your copy will be out of focus. A cable release will allow you to trip the camera shutter without movement or vibration.

Any black and white film will do so long as it has a low ISO rating. Your exposure will be longer but the finished product will look much better.

Be sure to have plenty of light on your subject and watch out for shadows and glare. A couple of lamps on each side of the copy should do nicely and diffused daylight coming through a window is ideal.

A slow shutter speed and a small lens aperture is preferable. An aperture setting of f16 or f22 will give better results. Fill the view finder with the entire subject.

If you use lamps with 60 watt bulbs, ISO 50 film and an aperture of f16, average exposure time should be about 1 second. If the subject is darker than most, exposure time should be longer.

Colored filters will help in case of stains or faded photos. Use a filter the same color as the stain. On faded photos use a blue filter to improve the contrast, possibly an 80A filter.

A good film lab should be able to process the film to your satisfaction.

In this day of computers and scanners, you might also consider scanning the photo and have it digitally enhanced.

CAMERA STAND:
A pattern for a good camera stand can be found on the Internet at: http://www.frontiernet.net/~rjacob/copystnd.htm

LIGHTING:
Try blue light bulbs.
Try using a blue filter on the lens and then regular light bulbs.
Try using sunlight if possible

OTHER TIPS:
Black-and-white photographs usually last longer than color photographs, so try to take at least one roll of black-and-white film. However, the black and white paper now being used is not as archival as the paper of yesteryear. In addition, some labs will print black and white film on color paper and make it look like black and white images.

You can have black and white photographs made from color negatives. Make sure your negatives are stored in light tight and waterproof containers. Color photographs are subject to loss of color from UV rays, so keep them out of the light. If you see a color photograph changing colors to a blue/green tint, get it copied on black and white film as soon as possible.

If you have an auto focus camera by all means use it. Be sure your aperture and shutter speeds are manual or at least your aperture and let the camera set the shutter. Stop to an f16 and fire away perfect copies every time. You can use Kodak T Max 400 speed film and go up to as big as 11X14 prints with no grain so with todays film both B&W and Color you can use fast film and get excellent results.

This tip was submitted by Margaret Scheffler - figaro@dreamscape.com
"Most important to the process is a BASIC 35mm CAMERA preferably with built in light meter that uses fixed focal length lenses (minimally a 50mm lens). The small point and shoot variety will not do. All that said, if I had a once in a life time chance to copy something I would not see again, I would give whatever camera I had available a chance.

"One can buy a used manual 35 mm for around $100, with a 50 mm lens a little more. I use a Minolta, but any standard 35 mm camera works the same. The key to my setup is a Tamron 90mm tele-macro lens. I later purchased the matched doubler so that I can make full frame a picture not too much bigger than a postage stamp. There are other similar lenses by reputable companies -- just ask for a 90 to 100 mm macro/portrait lens. You need to go to a major camera store that knows more than just about the latest cameras on the market. You want a fixed focal length lens that FOCUSES AT CLOSE distance -- about 15" or less. You DO NOT want a zoom lens with a macro feature. You may be able to find a used lens.

"All that said, if you have a manual 35 mm camera with a good 50 mm lens, you can probably buy a set of close-up attachments for less than $50 and give them a try -- not quite as good as a macro lens, but considerably cheaper, produce quite good results, and will give you an idea if you like copying photos before investing much money. I started out using close-up lenses. They produce acceptable results. Since the close-up lenses cover fixed focal differences you have to take them off and on the camera depending on the size of the picture and you cannot always "fill the frame". (The macro lens eliminates those problems). Another alternative is using bellows or extension tubes, but calculating the exposure is difficult and I would not recommend them for the beginner. With both the macro/portrait lens and the close-up lenses process, you can use the built-in light meter on your camera which makes the whole process easier.

"A "MUST" piece of equipment, is a sturdy tripod or copy stand on which to mount your camera facing the table. (People have used piles of books in a pinch). You can get copy lights which attach to the pole of a copy stand.

"I use strobes for lighting (flashes that screw into the copy light sockets like regular light bulbs), but you can use natural daylight or copy light bulbs that are the right temperature and color for the film you are using. Strobes are the easiest and produce the most natural colors. They cost only about $25 each (you need two) with a guide number of 60 for 100 speed film.

"As an alternative to a copy stand and lights you can try matching goose-neck type lamps which let you put the light at various angles.

"When copying you need to watch the shadows -- this pertains to both natural and artificial light. Outside lighting may cause a problem with shadows unless the day is overcast. Use a cable release, particularly if you are not using flashes, as the slightest movement can ruin your picture.

"If you are using natural light, you can use your light meter in the camera for proper exposure. When you use flashes, a flash meter is helpful.

"I frequently use 100 speed color film to get the brown tones of old photos. However, black and white pictures will last longer. I believe color film is expected to last about 40 years. B & W lasts much longer. Set your f stop to about f16 and use the light meter in the camera help you calculate the shutter speed which will be SLOW (thus the need for the cable release). If you are using black and white film you can get 50 & 125 speed film, also 400 speed B & W document film. You might try practicing with the 100 speed color film since it is cheaper and you can get it developed more quickly. I have had difficulty finding good quality black and white processing. Regular light bulbs cause color errors when used with color film but they can be used with b & w film.

"It takes most of us a while to acquire ones equipment. Initially I used a tripod to steady the camera, and a 50 mm lens with closeup attachments and natural light. I probably next added the copy stand. Then copy light bulbs -- then the flashes. Copy stands aren't too expensive and are much easier to adjust up and down than the tripod with the center pole reversed to face the camera towards the table. Obviously, if you are taking the equipment to a library or similar place, a tripod is more portable.

"You can copy a photo hanging on a wall if it is flat/parallel to the wall. (If the picture is hung and not parallel to the wall, you might use some of those pink or artgum erasers to bring the bottom out from the wall to make it parallel). You can copy photos that are in frames behind glass, although one has to be careful not to get glare from the glass. If the picture can easily be taken from the glass I do that. A polarizing lens may help reduce the glare. The polarizing filter can also help reduce that sheen that is on old photos that are starting to decompose.

"Old photos suffer (fade) from light exposure, so once you copy them, put them away in a dark place. The same goes if you scan them into your computer. Do it ONCE and then put them away. If you want your picture hung on the wall, have an enlargement made. At the very least put it in a darkened area of your room, not where bright light hits it.

"I've enjoyed copying old pictures -- made lots of mistakes starting out. Even now, if I have borrowed pictures, I get my copies developed before sending the originals back, as the copies might come out too light or dark, with light streaks, etc. If you only have one chance at seeing what you want to copy, vary the exposure settings (varying f-stop and shutter speeds), positions of the camera and lighting to maximize your success.

"To make sure the camera is parallel to the picture or document I want to copy, I use a little level that attaches to the camera (by flash attachment shoe) to make sure I have the camera level. There are some small levels in hardware stores you might be able to set on the back of your camera. Without the camera being perfectly level and parallel to what you want to copy, at close distances some parts of the picture may be in focus and other parts not.

"In summary, an alternative is the special kind of photocopier I have seen in high end photo processing centers. Some of them make almost as good quality pictures as the originals. The copies are quite expensive, but if one only wants one or two pictures it could be cheaper than buying expensive equipment. Another option is to send pictures out for a copy negative, but I would be reluctant to chance losing an original that way. What I have described is essentially the process for making copy negatives.

"Scanning and digital cameras are fine for adding photos to your genealogy program, but the resulting prints will have a short life. They are not the solution to saving old photos. Today's scanned images may go the way of the 8 track tape.

"This can be an interesting hobby in itself. For those who like photography, give it a try. Look for used equipment. It can save you a bundle."

PHOTO DAMAGE:
The absolute worst way to save pictures is in a "sticky-type" photo album. It is next to impossible to unstick them. You might try steaming up the bathroom & leaving a couple of pages in there to absorb some of the moisture...without getting the paper or pictures really damp themselves. This might loosen some of them without a lot of damage. If it works with a couple of them, you can try more of the book but just a very little at a time.

185

You might try to microwave the photos that are stuck together... just a very little at a time. DON'T COOK them.

Another method, tedious but it works, is to take a hair dryer on its lowest setting and carefully working from the edges inward, a little bit at a time, warm the photo's edge and lift. It will work BUT it takes time.

Before you try anything, take your paper album to Kinko's or some other coping business and make copies of the pages, or even scan your pages into your computer. Just in case your removal methods are not successful. These pictures are too valuable to take a chance with.

Photographing Photographs from Jerry Merritt - jerrym@beaches.net
A well taken photo can show just as much detail as was in the original document or photo being shot. "Well taken" is the key.

To get a good photo of a document or old photo you need a few things:

A single lens reflex (through the lens viewing) camera.

A close up lens -- either a macro lens or a set of inexpensive close up lens that screw onto the end of the camera's regular lens will work.

A stable platform to shoot from. A good tripod will work.

A fine grained film with plenty of contrast to bring out faded ink or faces. TMax 100 works great.

A means to hold the document or photo exactly perpendicular to the camera lens for low distortion and perfect focus over the whole document. The document or photo should also have as flat a surface as possible without damaging a curled object by bending it too much. Another person can hold the object in position, if they brace it against something solid to keep it from moving even a little bit. Otherwise you'll need some kind of jig made up ahead of time to keep the object being photographed rock steady.

A good light source. Indirect sunlight is excellent. An Ott light works well, too. Or, in a pinch, use any bright, diffuse light available.

Once all this is amassed, mount or otherwise orient the object being photographed so that it is well lit and stable. Then mount the camera on a tripod or other stable mount and get it oriented exactly perpendicular (head on) to the object. Now focus carefully and frame the object dead center to fill the view as much as possible e.g. get as close as possible so you pick up the most detail. Check to make sure no shadows or reflections fall on the object. It may seem like overkill to get the camera mounted on a tripod for a simple shot of an old photo but any movement of the camera (or the object) in a closeup will blur the image and you will lose the sparkle in great-grandma's eyes. Make sure you have a steady mount and a crisp, clear focus above all else. You may get only one chance to take a photo of an ancestor or of a valuable document so be prepared to do it right and you won't be disappointed in the results.

I've done over a 100 old photos this way and several old Family Bibles. Even on regular size prints, all of the writing in the old Bibles is completely legible. And copies of the old photos make great gifts to cousins who are sharing the family history with you.

I wouldn't recommend, however, trying to use a "point and click" type of camera. You'll get a picture but compared to the results obtained using a good 35mm or better camera the difference is like a fire fly to a lightning bolt -- to paraphrase Mark Twain.

THIS AND THAT GENEALOGY TIPS ON PRUSSIA AND POLAND

RECORDS IN POLAND:
Writing to Polish civil authorities, whether local or the centralized archives, should be a last resort, only after trying to find microfilms to use. Vital records were primarily kept by the churches until the second world war. Prussia established civil registration in 1874, but the church records are often more reliable. After WWII, Russians and Poles "cleansed" Posen of Germans and their "stuff". Protestant churches and cemeteries were destroyed or converted to other uses. The Prussian civil registration offices were probably converted to Polish counterparts, with the German records being destroyed or packed off to archives. German protestant church books either escaped with Germans who fled, or were destroyed or packed off to archives.

THE POLISH LANGUAGE by L. W. "Doc" L~epkowski - ROFDOC@aol.com:
The language of our ancestors is most difficult, and true translation is even more difficult, and sometimes literally impossible. To successfully translate one must be able to THINK in the language. I lived in pre-war Poland for a few years - and for the first year I was identified as an American as soon as I opened my mouth. Then one magic day my American identity disappeared, simply because I started thinking in Polish - not translating from one language to another. Polish is a very courteous language, replete with honorifics, titles and customs completely absent in English. One example: you do not ask anyone: "How old are you?" The simple inference that the individual is old is taken as insulting. You ask: "How many years do you have?". How often do you address an envelope to the "Honorable Doctor Mr XXX" ? Yet in Polish it is customary to address this envelope to: "Szanowny Panie Doktorze XXX"
....

Just remember this: The Polish language contains three genders, masculine, feminine and neuter. There are two cases, singular and plural, with seven declinations each. Word endings often identify gender. Diacritical marks appear on nine (9) different letters, making these letters difficult to pronounce by the average American. Here they are, with my version of the associated phonetics:

a - with a curl attached to the bottom pronounced with the tongue retracted and blocking the throat - a sort of OWN sound with nasal emphasis

c - with a slash on top - pronounced like CH

e - with a curls attached to the bottom - same pronunciation effort as for the a

a - sort of ennnh sound - nasal emphasis again

l - the letter L with a bar thru the capital or a curled bar over the lower case - pronounced like a W

o - the letter o with a slash on top - pronounced like the oo in wood or hood

s - with a slash on top - pronounced like ESH

z - with a dot on top, pronounced hard - clamp your teeth together, retract your tongue and trill it while you pronounce the z!!!! (easy -just takes practice)

z - with a slash on top - substitute the Z for the V in Viet and you've got it ZIET.

The final tip. Do you want to write letters in Polish? The best guide I know of is Rosemary A. Chorzempa's book Polish Roots. You can get it at Barnes & Noble, Amazon and so on. She has made this an easy task - you don't have to study Polish to accomplish your genealogical search - thanks to this book this daunting task is possible for the rank

& file. She deserves a big thanks from all.

POLISH-ENGLISH/ENGLISH-POLISH DICTIONARY:
For basic translation, you might try McKay's Polish-English/English-Polish Dictionary by Jim Stanislawski, 400 pages published by Random House, cost $17. The ISBN is 0-812-91691-3. It's reasonably priced and has a very decent amount of info in it, including a surprising number of entries on older terms that makes it rather good for genealogical translations.

POLISH HISTORY:
There are eight major periods of Polish History:

(1) The Kingdom Period- 960 -1138 - during which Poland became organized as an independent nation.
(2) The Duchy Period -1138-1320 - during which Poland dissolved into smaller units lacking a central power.
(3) The empire Period-1320-1572 - known as Poland's Golden Age, when the kingdom was unified, beginning with the reign of Casimir the Great. Poland then became the third largest nation in Europe.
(4) The Period of Elective Kings 1572-1772 - during which the county was weakened by the "liberium veto" in the Sejm(Parliament), allowing any deputy to stop the passage of a bill.
(5) The Partition Period 1772 to 1914 during which Poland lost its independence identity. The first partition of Poland between Russia, Prussia and Austria took place in 1772 and the second in 1792. The final partition was in 1795 and it wiped Poland from the map of Europe as an independent political state. During the period of foreign occupation both Russia and Prussia tried to de-Polonize the Polish people by forbidding the use of the Polish language, and by various attempts to get the people off of the land. The Austrians were more lenient but their area suffered from a great deal of poverty. As a result of the oppression and the poverty, extensive migration took place prior to World War I, mostly to the United States. The immigrants were political refugees, peasants and landless laborers.
(6) Two World Wars and the period of Independence 1914-1945 - Poland was liberated during the first World War and then experienced twenty years of instability. In 1939, under the heel of the Nazi invaders it was annihilated for the fourth time.
(7) Period of the People's Republic 1945-1989 - After World War II the county was stabilized as a "Peoples' Republic" allied with the Soviet Union.
(8) The collapse of Communism-1989

If your ancestors lived geographically in POLAND between 840 and today, here are the chronological sovereigns over Poland:
840 to 1231 A.D.--POLISH;
1231 to 1466 A.D.--Teutonic Knights ie German [Prussian];
1466 to 1772 A.D.--POLISH;
1772 to 1919 A.D.--Descendants of Teutonic Knights called themselves "Prussian"; 1919 to 1939 A.D.--POLISH;
1939 to 1945 A.D.--GERMAN;
1945 to TODAY--POLISH.

POLAND AND LITHUANIA:
Prior to the union of Poland and Lithuania, your ancestors may have been ethnic Lithuanians. Lithuania prior to the 1300's was the last pagan state in Europe. Poland had from time to time been invaded by the Lithuanians. (By Lithuanians, I mean residents of that country, not necessarily ethnic Lithuanians).

The Teutonic Knights, which had been founded during the time of the Crusades to the Middle East, had gotten permission to settle in Masovia, by the Duke of that territory. One of their missions was to Christianize the pagan tribes in the vicinity of the Baltic Sea, which included the Prussians and Lithuanians, which were causing problems for the various Polish borderland areas. These Prussians were a Balt tribe which were exterminated by the Teutonic Knights, who usurped the name - hence the name Prussia and Prussians, who were actually Germans. Anyway, the Knights became a threat to Poland and Lithuania, as they formed their own independent state, which was not the intention of the Duke of Mazovia at all. So, to fend off attacks, the Poles and Lithuanians joined forces to battle the

Knights. This was a huge scandal in the Christian world, - a Christian nation allied with a pagan nation! The German propagandists used this as an excuse to call Poland a pagan country, and that it was their goal to Christianize (re-Germanize) them!

So Poland decided that if the daughter of the King of Poland, and the Grand Duke of Lithuania married (in 1386) and they became king and queen of the unified country, and as part of the arrangement, the Lithuanians were converted to Christianity, this would create a large and powerful Christian nation, which could repulse invaders. Also part of the arrangement was that the Polish gentry accepted the Lithuanian gentry as brothers - which meant they assumed Polish names and coats of arms of the existing Polish gentry - in effect they were adopted. These people's descendants spoke Polish, and became Polonized, or assimilated.

Something else that most people do not know is that at that time, Lithuania included all of Belarus and Ukraine. The official language of this country was Old Byelorussian, NOT Lithuanian. The number of ethnic Lithuanians was only a small portion of that country. The people who retained that language and culture were the peasants. And peasants had a history of being oppressed, no matter of what ethnic group. The gentry of Poland/Lithuania made up 10% of the population. Ethnic Germans and Jews made up about 15%. The rest were peasants of various ethnic groups. The residents of the larger towns and cities were largely Jews, German merchants, and the Polish/Lithuanian gentry. In the countryside of ethnic Lithuania, the vast majority of the population (peasants) spoke only Lithuanian. Many residents of Lithuania for hundreds of years spoke Polish and considered themselves Lithuanian, because they lived there, but of the Polish nation. Also, these eastern territories were colonized by Poles from farther west. Many of the wealthier Polish gentry had huge estates in these areas - another explanation why there were Poles in these areas. The most famous of the Lithuanian/Polish gentry were the Radziwill family - Jackie Kennedy Onassis sister married into that family, her name is Lee Radziwill.

Old Poland/Lithuania had many things in common with the USA - the country had as residents people from numerous ethnic groups and many religions. As the USA has English as the common language, so Poland/Lithuania had Polish. Many countries during that time had multi-ethnic populations. It wasn't until the idea of nationalism developed in the early 1800's that this started to cause problems for European countries, and went to the extreme in WW2 and the Holocaust - and continues toady with ethnic cleansing. Can you imagine what would happen in this country if everyone had to become English, and repudiate their non-Anglo cultural backgrounds? Countries with one language and one ethnic group became the ideal.

The ethnic Lithuanians today have their own version of history which states that they were oppressed by Poland, but anyone who reads and understands the entire history of this area will have a more balanced view of the situation. After WW1, the Lithuanians were furious with Poland over Poland incorporating Vilnius, the historic Lithuanian capital, (in Polish, Wilno) into Poland, however, the vast majority of residents in the city spoke Polish and considered themselves Polish, hence they wanted to be a part of Poland, as they had been for 400 years before the Partitions.

KREIS:
A 'Kreis' is, in essence, a county. It literally is a 'circle or ring' and refers to 'sphere' of influence. It is usually translated very generically as 'district', but with Prussian 'administrative districts' being comprised of several Kreise, it gets confusing to refer to them as districts. I've heard purists claim that they are not really counties, but in that they are the smallest district that includes several towns, I think the translation as 'county' is accurate. They are perhaps smaller than most US counties. I'm not real sure what a township is, but I think the typical Kreis would be of a larger scale.

The divisions were: the Kingdom of Prussia was divided into provinces (like Posen), which were divided into Administrative districts (2 in Posen: Bromberg and Posen), which included the Kreise. The Kreise could be further broken down into civil registration districts of half a dozen villages per 'Standesamt'.

NAME SPELLING:
Doing genealogy, no matter of what ethnic group, involves dealing with spelling variations. Up until about 75 years ago, spelling was not even a subject studied in schools. Ben Franklin said that he wouldn't trust a man who didn't spell

his name at least three different ways.

Technically in Polish, there is an accepted spelling based on the sound of the name. Studying the language helps. When my father or aunts were asked how do you spell your name, they'd reply, "how it sounds!" This is true in Polish. Now if the recorder of the name was not Polish, as many government clerks and census takers, they would spell it the way they heard it, but based on English. And remember, in the early years, most Poles who came here could not read or write Polish, much less English! Even the Catholic Priests recording BP/M/D records in the early 1900's spelled names differently in the records.

People who identified as Polish, could have German, Russian, Lithuanian, or even English/Scot surnames, and still be Polish. There may have been one ancestor of these different backgrounds, but if they became assimilated into Polish culture/language, they're just as Polish as someone with a Polish name. Many people from other ethnic groups settled in Poland over the centuries - in that regard very much like the USA.

Also, in Polish and other Slavic languages, the last name reflected the gender of the person. Bonchowski would be the man's last name, but Bonkowska would be the woman's. Also there was a spelling difference for a single or a married woman (which I don't know the rules to). Perhaps a Polish speaker could explain this better.

INVESTIGATE SURNAMES:
An investigation of surnames can be initiated by clicking here: http://www.feefhs.org/feefhsei.html
Full Text [search engine] "hot link" Index of...

GERMANY/PRUSSIAN GENEALOGY MAILING LISTS:
http://members.aol.com/gfsjohnf/gen_mail_country-ger.html

RESEARCH WEBPAGES:
http://ciuw.warman.net.pl/alf/archiwa/index.eng.html (Polish Archives)

http://members.aol.com/genpoland/genpolen.htm (Genealogy in Poland)

http://members.aol.com/rechtman/posen.html (Posen, Poland Jewish Death Records 1831-1835)

http://www.jewishgen.org/cemetery/poland.htm (Information on Jewish cemeteries in Poland)

http://www.pgsa.org (The Polish Genealogical Society of America)

http://maxpages.com/poland (Poland Border Surnames)

http://www.wwdir.com/polres.html (Poland information)

http://www.poczta-polska.pl/kody/win/kody.html (Polish post office)

http://www.CyndisList.com (Cyndi Howell's Genealogy Links list)

http://poland.pl:80 (The official website of Poland)

http://www.wsdsc.poznan.pl/arch/archive.htm (Archdiocesan Archives in Poznan, Poland)

http://ciuw.warman.net.pl/alf/archiwa/mapa/mapa.html (Clickable map of State archives in Poland)

http://www.jewishgen.org/ShtetlSeeker/loctown.htm (Town locator for West Europe)

http://www.rubikon.net.pl/mroz/a/diec.htm (Polish dioceses in a clickable linked map)

http://wwwspp.perytnet.pl/informat.htm (Polish dioceses (names, addresses and links)

http://akson.sgh.waw.pl/~anthon/slownik.html   (English-Polish dictionary)

http://www.wwdir.com/polres.html (Poland information)

http://www.geocities.com/Heartland/Plains/2739 (Kaj Malachowski's homepage)

http://hum.amu.edu.pl/~rafalp/GEN/gen-eng.html   (Genealogical information by Rafal Prinke)

http://www.rand.org/personal/Genea/ (Rand genealogy club)

http://www.rootsweb.com/~polwgw/terms.html (Polish Terms)

http://www.rootsweb.com/~polwgw/namelist.html (Polish first names)

http://members.aol.com/pgsamerica/slownike.html (Polish Geographical)

http://conan.nova.org/EPG.htm (Polish to English Legal-Economics & Business Terms)

http://hum.amu.edu.pl/~zbzw/ph/pro/plpro.html (Polish Provinces)

Here is what appears to be a Polish Search Engine:
http://www.wp.pl - Try entering your last name. Unfortunately the whole site is in Polish.

THIS AND THAT GENEALOGY TIPS ON PUBLIC RECORDS - U. S. GOVERNMENT

PUBLIC RECORDS OFFICE:
PRINTED GUIDES
The prime source of information about the records held in the Public Record Office is C M Andrews Guide to the Materials for American History to 1783 in the Public Record Office (2 vols, Carnegie Institution, Washington, 1912). Some of the references given are now obsolete, but can be keyed to those in current use.

A complete history of the records with guidance on their use, giving the references in their modern form, is to be found in R. D. B Pugh The Records of the Colonial and Dominions Offices, (PRO Handbook No 3, HMSO 1964).

Documents in the Public Record Office and elsewhere not mentioned by Andrews are described in B R Crick and M Alman eds. A Guide to Manuscripts Relating to America in Great Britain and Ireland (Mansell Publishing 1961) a revised edition of which has been prepared by John W. Raimo and published, under the same title, by Meckler Books/Mansell Publishing (1979).

Documents relating to the Caribbean are noted in H C Bell, D W. Parker and others Guide to British West Indian Archive Materials, in London and in the Islands, for the History of the United States (Carnegie Institution, Washington 1926); and P Walne ed. A Guide to Manuscript Sources for the History of Latin America and the Caribbean in the British Isles (Oxford University Press, 973).

PRINTED TEXTS
The texts or abstracts of many documents from 1574 to 1738 can be found in Calendar of State Papers Colonial (HMSO, 1859 onwards).

Documents of the period from 1770 to 1783 are being similarly published as K G Davies ed. The Documents of the American Revolution (21 vols to date, Irish University Press 1972 onwards).

ARRANGEMENT OF THE RECORDS
The arrangement of the earlier records does not reflect the respective roles of the Secretary of State and the Board of Trade. The class Colonial Papers: General Series (CO 1) was brought together by W N Sainsbury, first editor of the Calendar of State Papers Colonial: it contains, in chronological order, all the papers printed in the Calendar and dated not later than 1688, the original terminal date of the publication.

From 1688, and in a few instances before, until 1807, the records relating to the American colonies are combined in America and West Indies: Original Correspondence etc (CO 5). The records are arranged by colony:

> Carolina (Propriety);
> North Carolina;
> South Carolina;
> Connecticut;
> East Florida;
> West Florida;
> Georgia;
> Maryland;
> Massachussets;
> New England (Massachussets, Rhode Island, New Hampshire and Pennsylvania);
> New Hampshire;
> New Jersey;
> New York;
> Pennsylvania;
> Rhode Island;

Virginia and the Proprieties (including the Bahamas, Carolina, Connecticut, Maryland, East and West New Jersey, Pennsylvania and Rhode Island).

In spite of its title, the class does not include records of the colonies of Canada and the West Indies and includes only one, the Bahamas, which did not come to form part of the United States.

For each colony there are five main types of record: the Original Correspondence with the Secretary of State and with the Board of Trade; Entry Books of both; collections of Acts, and of Sessional Papers, of the colonial legislature. In addition there are for some colonies Naval Officers' Returns of shipping, collections of land grants and other materials, and military and naval dispatches. Documents concerned with Indian affairs and other, more general matters, are arranged in separate series.

The records concerned with:

Antigua and Montserrat;

Bahamas;

Barbados;

Bermuda;

former French colony of Canada;

Dominica;

Grenada;

British Honduras;

Hudson's Bay;

Jamaica;

Leeward Islands (including Antigua, St Kitts, Montserrat, Nevis and the Virgin

Islands);

Montserrat;

Nevis;

Newfoundland;

Nova Scotia and Cape Breton Island;

Prince Edward Island;

St Kitts;

St Lucia;

St Vincent;

Tobago;

Trinidad; and

Virgin Islands are arranged in the same way, but each series forms a separate class. The class numbers are listed by Pugh and Andrews and can also readily be identified in the Current Guide in the Reference Room.

Some records deal with matters concerning the Colonies in general. They are in the classes:

Colonies General: Original Correspondence
CO 323
Entry Books
CO 324
Board of Trade: Original Correspondence
CO 388
Board of Trade: Entry Books
CO 389
Board of Trade: Miscellaneous
CO 390

The class Board of Trade: Minutes (CO 391) includes the Journal of the Board of Trade. Entries before April 1704 appear in the Calendar of State Papers Colonial, and those for the period April 1704 to May 1782 in:

Journal of the Commissioners for Trade and Plantations (14 vols HMSO 1920-1928).

ORIGINAL CORRESPONDENCE

There are collections of reports and papers from, and orders and instructions to, the responsible officials in each colony, especially the governors. The correspondence of the Secretaries of State and the Board of Trade are in separate sequences. Each contains not only correspondence with the colonies but also with other officials and private individuals in the United Kingdom and between the Secretary of State and the Board.

From 1703 to 1759 manuscript calendars of the correspondence of the Board with each colony were compiled: these are in General Registers (CO 326) pieces 1 to 51.

From 1759 to 1782 a single, annual, calendar was prepared for all colonies: this series is   CO 326 pieces 52-74.

ENTRY BOOKS

These are letter books containing copies of dispatches, letters, reports, petitions, commissions and instructions, either in full or in abstract. Before 1700 papers received as well as papers despatched are noted. The Entry Books served as the primary record of outgoing correspondence, in particular royal commission, instructions and warrants: they were not intended as means of reference to the correspondence as a whole.

ACTS AND SESSIONAL PAPERS

Copies, either printed or in manuscript, of the Acts and proceedings of colonial councils and legislatures were forwarded to the Board of Trade, having been approved, or rejected, by the Privy Council. Other copies were retained in the colony itself where, as a rule, they are still to be found.

NAVAL OFFICERS' RETURNS

The Naval Officers were officials of the Board, in practice usually Customs Officers acting in a second capacity, and they discharged certain statutory duties under the Navigation Acts. They compiled lists of the merchantmen entering and clearing their ports: these returns, at their fullest, give dates, the names of master and vessel, tonnage, when and where built, whence and whither bound, and the nature, consignor and consignee of the cargo. Only a proportion of the lists survive: comparable records can also be found in Treasury Board Papers (T 1) and Miscellaneous (BT 6).

MILITARY AND NAVAL DISPATCHES
The dispatches collected in CO 5 relate mainly to fighting against the French and various Indian tribes, which could not conveniently be divided by colony.

Original Correspondence: West Indies (CO 318) also contains some military dispatches. The majority of records concerning naval operations will be found among the ADM classes in the Public Record Office, and many concerning military operations, including a proportion removed from the papers of the Secretary of State and the Board of Trade, are in the WO classes. A detailed index to these papers is given in Alphabetical Guide to the War Office and other Classes (PRO List and Index Series vol LIII, HMSO 1931; reprinted by Kraus Thomson Organization 1963).

TREASURY AND CUSTOMS RECORDS
The extensive and varied records of the Treasury contain much material relating to the colonies: all have been mentioned by Andrews in volume II. Those records of the Board of Customs which survived a fire in 1814, chiefly statistics of trade, are likewise described by Andrews in the same volume.

LAND GRANTS
In early colonial America the ownership of the land was considered to be vested in the Crown by right of discovery and settlement by its subjects. The Crown granted land to companies and to proprietors to organize settlements and also to some individual subjects as a reward for services. The matter is more fully described in O T Barck Jr. and H T Lefler Colonial America (Collier 1968)

The system whereby recipients of royal grants in turn gave or sold land varied. In some colonies, notably in New England, the legislatures established by the colonists assumed jurisdiction over the allocation of company lands. They made some direct grants to individuals for 'adventuring' money in the companies, but the greater part went to groups or communities to establish townships and to apportion the surrounding land.

In the southern counties, the 'headright' system of land distribution was the most common method followed during the seventeenth century. An individual who provided transport to the colony for any immigrant was thereby entitled to at least fifty acres of land. During the same period, however, larger tracts were given by the Crown, the proprietor or the company to favorites, to those who performed outstanding service to the company or, as in Maryland, to those who transported five or more persons to the colony. The 'headright' system led to many frauds and abuses, and by the early years of the eighteenth century most of the land was distributed by purchase or by taking out a patent signed by the governor of the colony for new, unpatented land.

Although grants were nominally made in the name of the Crown, most were made and recorded locally rather than in London. Of those grants which were reported to the Secretary of State or the Board of Trade no index exists. However, many are noted in Andrews and in the Calendar of State Papers Colonial.

INDIAN AFFAIRS
There are collections of papers concerning Indian affairs in general, and relating to large tribes and confederacies not dwelling in any one colony in CO 5. The class includes some treaties, but there is no index to them and no easy means of locating those not mentioned by Andrews or in the Calendar.

OTHER RECORDS
Separate leaflets are available on request on the service records of officers and men of the British Forces serving in the Army, Navy and Royal Marines; on emigre loyalists, on emigration and on merchant shipping records (Registrar General of Shipping and Seamen).

THE WPA WORKS PROJECT:

When Franklin Delano Roosevelt took office in 1933, more than 13 million Americans were out of work. In the first hundred days of his administration, Roosevelt pushed through legislation for much of his New Deal, including the Works Progress Administration (WPA), which was responsible for the nation's relief program. It was first established as the Work Projects Administration by executive order on 6 May 1935 and in 1939 the agency's name was changed to Work Progress Administration. Before it's liquidation in 1942, it became the biggest relief program in U.S. history, providing employment for millions of people.

The WPA was initiated to give work to laid off workers during the great depression, repairing roads, sidewalks and sewers, cleaning and reading cemeteries and assisting small town governments in keeping the town functioning.

One of the important projects of the WPA was the "Historical Records Survey Program." In this program people were hired by the WPA to inventory all records both public and private, that were of historical value. The project was never completed, and not all of the records that were inventoried are of value to genealogist. However, where an inventory of the county records was completed they can be very useful. Where the county inventories exist they will list all records from the inception of the county until the time of inventory. Some of the inventories were published and some were not.

Massive bibliographies, inventories, indexes, and other historical materials were prepared by out-of-work historians, lawyers, teachers, researchers, and clerical workers. The intent of the program was to organize historical materials, particularly the unpublished government documents and records which are basic in the administration of local government and which provide invaluable data for students of political, economic, and social history. Archival guides were designed to meet the requirements of day-to-day administration by federal and local government officials, and also the needs of lawyers, businessmen, and other citizens who require facts from public records to conduct their affairs.

Inventories produced by the Historical Records Survey Program attempted to do more than merely provide lists of records - the program attempted to sketch the historical background of the county or other unit of government, and to describe precisely, and in detail, the organization and function of the governmental agencies whose records were listed.

Family historians continue to reap the benefits of these works, which survive in original, microfilm, and published forms in libraries and archives all over the United States. Listed below are but a few of the WPA records projects of genealogical value:

The Soundex Index to the U.S. population census is probably the most-used WPA work. While not error-free, Soundex indexes to the 1880, 1900, 1910, and 1920 censuses, microfilmed by the National Archives, have launched research projects for millions of family historians.

Other heavily used indexes created by the WPA and available through the WPA, through the National Archives (custodian of the original documents), and through the Family History Library operated by The Church of Jesus Christ of Latter-day Saints in Salt Lake City are naturalization indexes. The "Soundex Index to Naturalization Petitions for the United States District and Circuit Courts, Northern District of Illinois and Immigration and Naturalization Service District #9, 1840-1950," includes more than 1.5 million index cards for naturalizations that took place in Chicago and northern Illinois, as well as in parts of Indiana, Iowa, and Wisconsin. Other large and important WPA naturalization compilations are the "Soundex Name Index to New England Naturalization Petitions, 1790-1906," and the "Index to Naturalization Petitions of the United States District Court for the Eastern District of New York, 1865-1957."

The WPA operated at four organizational levels - the central administration at Washington, D.C., regional offices, state administrations, and district offices.

There are three WPA National Archives microfilm publications (Record Group 60): T935 "Index to Reference Cards for Work Project Administration Project Files, 1935-1937 (79 rolls); T936 "Index to Reference Cards for Work Project Administration Project Files 1938" (15 rolls); and T937, "Index to Reference Cards for Work Project

Administration Project Administration Project Files, 1939-1942" (19 rolls). Except for certain federally sponsored projects, state and local governments helped finance and supervise WPA work projects.

For family researchers in Indiana, there are WPA indexes to vital records in sixty-five of that state's ninety-two counties. Indiana county histories were indexed by the WPA, alphabetically by county name, up to and including the letter J. Since that time, others have taken up where the WPA left off and have completed the indexing of various other counties.

WPA RELATED SITES:
American Life Histories, Manuscripts from the Federal Writers' Project, 1936-1940 (American Memory Project, Library of Congress): http://lcweb2.loc.gov/wpaintro/wpahome.html

African American Mosiac - WPA, Library of Congress: http://www.loc.gov/exhibits/african/wpa.html

NARA: RG 69 - Records of the Work Projects Administration:
gopher://gopher.nara.gov:70/00/inform/guide/10s/rg069.txt

THIS AND THAT GENEALOGY TIPS ON PROBATE RECORDS AND WILLS

PROBATE RECORDS:

When possible, visit the courthouses in person because only you will recognize possible variations on your surnames. If you must write to the courthouse, expect them to do a limited search for the exact record you require and they may request a search fee. In most cases the search is free but you will be required to pay for copies of records. Be sure to ALWAYS enclose a SASE with any request.

Most probate offices have general indexes to their records which refer to original will books and estate papers. Some do not, so careful investigation of each volume's index is required. Probate jurisdiction has varied from state to state both in responsibility and the governmental level at which probating was hired. Some places in New England such as Connecticut and Vermont probated on a probate district level, comprised of one or more towns. Massachusetts and Maine functioned on a county level, while New Hampshire functioned on a provincial level before 1772 but on a county level after. Prior to the formation of the United States, New York County handled all probate matters for the state of New York, and it wasn't until after 1780 that the probate burden was shifted to the individual counties. During colonial times, probate matters were handled by the General Court, the Particular Court, or some other court, but many colonies, including Pennsylvania, set up special Probate Courts or Orphans Courts. In some Midwestern states in the 1800's, upon the death of an individual, his property was simply handed over to his spouse without any formal proceedings. Some counties today have such matters handled by the Probate Judge, the Clerk of the Circuit Court, or the County Clerk. In some Midwestern states in the 1800's, upon the death of an individual, his property was simply handed over to his spouse without any formal proceedings.

II find The Handy Book For Genealogists invaluable for addresses of courthouses and other very valuable genealogy information but there is also The Red Book which gives similar information. These books will tell you the location of records county clerk, clerk of court, probate judge, etc.), the time frame of the records, when the county was formed, and the address of the courthouse.

An estate is "testate" when a legal will is in existence and "intestate" when there is no will or the will, is not legal. The court must approve any will before it can be probated, and if it does not gain such approval, it becomes intestate. The maker of the will usually names one or more executors to carry out its provisions, but if one is not named, or he died before the testator did, then the court appoints an administrator. In intestate estates, the court appoints an administrator, whose duties are similar to the executor, and distribution is made according to local law. If the executor refuses to assume responsibility, a "renunciation" is made, and an administrator is appointed by the court.

The usual procedure for administration of probate is that after a person possessed of estate of any size dies, an interested party petitions the court to probate the estate. This person may be a friend of the deceased, the surviving spouse, other relatives, a creditor, or a public official. The petition usually contains the name of the deceased, date and place of his death, name and place of residence of the surviving spouse, and the names and residences of all known heirs. The petition is usually filed among related probate papers. Such records are referred to as the "files" or "packets" and contain all papers relating to the estate. Some files have been destroyed or moved to state archives, but most remain in their respective county offices.

After the petition for probate has been approved, further probating procedures take place. Courts generally require that the administrator be bonded, but in a few testate cases, the testator specifically indicates that the executor may act without a bond.

One of the first acts of the executor or administrator is to make a complete inventory of the property of the deceased and have it appraised prior to any settlements. The inventory rarely gives any valuable genealogical data, but it does give some idea of a person's financial status. The "inventory" lists all property, real or personal, and the "appraisal" lists their value. When sales are made, the names of the buyers should be examined closely, because quite often they are family members and close relatives. Some sales documents state the relationship.

On occasion, the court granted an allowance to the widow or minor children while the case was in probate, and documents related to this may be an excellent genealogical source. Allowance may be in cash or in kind, and records vary in detail.

When minor heirs exist, guardianship and apprentice records may be initiated, and these records can provide excellent data for the genealogist. The court usually appointed a guardian for minors under fourteen years of age, but those older than fourteen were sometimes allowed to choose their own guardian.

After certain administrative actions have been completed, which may be over a period of months or even years, property and monies belonging to the estate are distributed to heirs, devisees, and legatees, according to the will or, in intestate cases, state and local laws. Documents relating to the distribution of an estate are sometimes very helpful in determining kinship.

During the probate process the executor or administrator must keep an accounting of his actions and report to the court concerning his work. Letters may be received, depositions taken, affidavits signed, and other papers initiated which might help you solve a genealogical problem.

Be sure to read every paper in the file.

WILLS:
When you locate a will, dates are important to note. There may also be a codicil which is a change to the will that was made at a later date than the will. The oldest child is often listed first. Sometimes all the children are named in the order of their birth. Sons-in-law are often named instead of the daughter. Daughters-in-law may be mentioned if a son is deceased.

Scandals and disobedience are sometimes reasons to make exceptions in a will. Names of deceased children may be mentioned in instructions for burial plot locations. Brothers of the deceased person are sometimes named as overseers. Married sons are very often given money. Namesakes sometimes receive more of an inheritance than the other heirs do. Guardians are sometimes named for children under 21. However, a minor over the age of 14 may choose his or her own guardian. Misspelling is common. Do not overlook collateral lines when you have the opportunity to follow them.

When land was sold, the spouse had to be listed in the land record. Land records should be searched after a death as often a list of heirs will be shown during partition of the estate and even sometimes a map.

If there is a will, it is probated by an Executor - if there is no will, the estate is cared for by an Administrator appointed by the court.

When a will is proved, it is the first step in the probate process. Proved means the will is accepted by the court as being the authentic will of the deceased person. The person designated as executor either accepts or declines the role of executor. If he/she declines, the court decides what person will assume that role. The spouse usually is considered next in line if he/she was not designated in the will for that role. Once the will is proved the rest of the probate process takes place. Incidentally, when there is an administrator appointed during the probate process, it means there was no will, so an administration begins. In other words, the person's assets are disposed of according to the laws for that state at that time. Now and then, the term, administrator is mistakenly used when there is a will. In any case, when you write to a probate court for a will, be sure also to ask whether there is a will OR administration, just in case the person died without a will (that is, died intestate).

Sometimes administrations contain a lot more information than a will. The terms of a will are not always carried out. If they are not carried out, that is how it will be unless someone protests officially to the court. It is important to pay attention to all these factors or you can miss important information.

THIS AND THAT GENEALOGY TIPS ON RELATIONSHIPS

RELATIONSHIPS:
Relationships sometimes had different meanings then they do today. Conclusions about the relationship between any two people must rest on a preponderance of all the available evidence. Here are some relationships that you will probably run into sooner or later in your genealogy research:

Alias:
The use of two surnames, joined by the word "alias" in early American records usually indicates an illegitimate birth and that the person has joined the surname of his reputed father to that of his mother. However, there were other reasons for the adoption of two surnames. Sometimes when children inherited through their mother, they used both the father's and the mother's names. Sometimes the name of the natural father, who had died, was joined to that of a stepfather. In case of adoption, the original name and the name of the adoptive parent were sometimes used together.

Brother:
The term "brother" could indicate any one of the following relationships by blood or marriage: 1) the husband of one's sister, 2) the brother of one's wife, 3) the husband of one's sister-in-law, 4) a half-brother, or 5) a stepbrother.

Cousins Once Removed:
Cousinships have to do for persons in the same generation: 1st cousins have the same grandparents; 2nd cousins have the same great grandparents; 3rd cousins have the same great great grandparents. Now for the sticky part, the "removed" part, namely the generational differences. For example: My first cousin's children are removed a generation from me, hence are my "first cousins once removed." My first cousin's grandchildren are removed two generations from me, hence are my "first cousins twice removed." Keep in mind, when the word "removed" is used to describe a relationship, it indicates that the two people are from different generations.

Cousin:
The term "cousin" was once used generally to indicate almost any degree of relationship by blood or marriage outside the immediate family. In early New England the term was sometimes used to refer to a nephew or niece.

First Cousin:
Your first cousins are the people in your family who have two of the same grandparents as you. In other words, they are the children of your aunts and uncles.

Second Cousin:
Your second cousins are the people in your family who share one set of the same great-grandparents with you.

Third, Fourth, and Fifth Cousins:
Third, Fourth, and Fifth Cousins. Your third cousins share one set of great-great-grandparents, fourth cousins share one set of great-great-great-grandparents, and so on.

Great and Grand:
The sister/brother of your GREAT grand parent is your GREAT grand aunt/uncle. The sister/brother of your grand parent is your grand aunt/uncle. Technically, there is no such thing as a GREAT aunt/uncle.

In-laws:
The terms "father-in-law," "mother-in-law," "son-in-law," and "daughter-in-law" have always indicated a relationship by marriage rather than by blood. When you find these terms in early American records, they may have the same meanings we give them today. But they may also have very different meanings. "Father-in-law," and "mother-in-law," may refer to a step-parent and "son-in-law" and "daughter-in-law" may refer to a step-child. The terms "brother-in-

law" and "sister-in-law" are more likely to have the same meanings we give them today.

Nephew:
The term nephew derives from the Latin "Nepos" meaning grandson. Occasionally an early will refers to the testators grandchildren, both males and females as "nephews." However, for the most part the term was used as it is today to mean the son of a brother or sister and occasionally, the daughter of a brother or sister.

"Natural" Son:
When the term "natural" son is used the researcher should not jump to the conclusion that it denotes an illegitimate relationship. What it always indicates is a relationship by blood as distinguished from a relationship by marriage or adoption. In seventeenth century English wills, it was more common to refer to an illegitimate child as "my base son" or "my bastard son."

"Now" wife:
When this term is used in a will, it is often assumed that the testator had a former wife. This may be true but is not necessarily so unless he refers to children by a first wife and children by his "present" or "now" wife. When the term is used without reference to children, it more usually means the testator is indicating that the bequest is intended only for his present wife and should not go to any subsequent wife he may have.

Senior/junior: Prior to the nineteenth century, do not assume that the use of the terms SR and JR refers to a father and son. The relationship could have been that of an uncle and nephew or of cousins. Before the use of middle names, it was not uncommon to have two or more men in a family with identical names. The older man was known as Senior and the younger as Junior. A still younger person of the name might use "III" following his name. It is important for the researcher to keep in mind that a man known in his younger years as William Smith, Jr. may have been known as William Smith, Sr. after the death of the older man.

ANOTHER EXPLANATION:
First cousins share common grandparents.
Second cousins share great grandparents.
Third cousins share great-great-grandparents.
Fourth cousins share g-g-g-grandparents
etc.

The "once-removed", etc. occurs when two individuals differ in the number of generations from the common ancestor. If the great-grandparents of one individual is the great-great-grandparent of the second individual, the two are Second Cousins, Once-Removed.

To calculate the relationship, find the closest common ancestor. Determine the degree of "cousinship" from the above table or a continuation of it. Determine the number of generations that the more distant individual is further removed from the common ancestor. This is the number of "Times Removed".

Example 2: An individual's 4g-grandparent is the second individual's 6g-grandparents. They are Fifth Cousins, (share 4g-gp), Twice-Removed (6g-gp -- 4 g-gp).

MODIFIED HENRY SYSTEM OF NUMBERING:
Genealogies which number individuals using the Modified Henry System, permit calculating the relationship directly from the individual's numbers. In the Modified Henry System, each individual's number represents his family line in the family being discussed. The number of digits is the number of generations from the first listed ancestor. The value of a digit represents the birth order, (when known), with a, b, c, etc. representing children 10, 11, 12 (for larger families). Letters at the end of the alphabet may be used when birth-order is unknown. A "." is often used to provide a break every 5 generations to aid in counting.

Example: Two individual's # 143a6.84 and 14358.1246. They share the first three generations (to 143). # 143 is the 2g=gp of the older individual and the 4g-gp of the second individual. This makes them Third Cousins, Twice-Removed.

INSTRUCTIONS FOR USING A RELATIONSHIP CHART:
Pick two people in your family and figure out which ancestor they have in common. For example, if you chose yourself and a cousin, you would have a grandparent in common.

Look at the top row of the chart and find the first person's relationship to the common ancestor.

Look at the far left column of the chart and find the second person's relationship to the common ancestor.

Determine where the row and column containing those two relationships meet.

Relationship Chart

For a true "relationship" to exist, there must be an ancestor who is common to both individuals. If you examine the chart below, for example, the Common Ancestor is Box 1 on the horizontal scale (HS) as well as Box 1 on the Vertical Scale (VS).

Let us suppose that you have a **grandson** of that common ancestor, as seen in Box 3 of the HS, and you want to know that grandson's relationship to a great-granddaughter, who would be seen in Box 4 on the VS.

If you follow Box 4 (VS) down to where it meets the vertical pathway to Box 3 on the HS, then where those paths cross, it tells you the relationship -- they are **first cousins once removed**.

	1	2	3	4	5	6	7	8	9	10
1	Common Ancestor	Son or Daughter	Grandson or Daughter	Great Grandson or Daughter	2nd Great Grandson or Daughter	3rd Great Grandson or Daughter	4th Great Grandson or Daughter	5th Great Grandson or Daughter	6th Great Grandson or Daughter	7th Great Grandson or Daughter
2	Son or Daughter	**Siblings (Brother or Sister)**	Nephew or Niece	Grand Nephew or Niece	Great Grand Nephew or Niece	2nd Great Grand Nephew or Niece	3rd Great Grand Nephew or Niece	4th Great Grand Nephew or Niece	5th Great Grand Nephew or Niece	6th Great Grand Nephew or Niece
3	Grandson or Daughter	Nephew or Niece	**First Cousin**	First Cousin Once Removed	First Cousin Twice Removed	First Cousin Three Times Removed	First Cousin Four Times Removed	First Cousin Five Times Removed	First Cousin Six Times Removed	First Cousin Seven Times Removed
4	Great Grandson or Daughter	Grand Nephew or Niece	First Cousin Once Removed	**Second Cousin**	Second Cousin Once Removed	Second Cousin Twice Removed	Second Cousin Three Times Removed	Second Cousin Four Times Removed	Second Cousin Five Times Removed	Second Cousin Six Times Removed
5	2nd Great Grandson or Daughter	Great Grand Nephew or Niece	First Cousin Twice Removed	Second Cousin Once Removed	**Third Cousin**	Third Cousin Once Removed	Third Cousin Twice Removed	Third Cousin Three Times Removed	Third Cousin Four Times Removed	Second Cousin Five Times Removed
6	3rd Great Grandson or Daughter	2nd Great Grand Nephew or Niece	First Cousin Three Times Removed	Second Cousin Twice Removed	Third Cousin Once Removed	**Fourth Cousin**	Fourth Cousin Once Removed	Fourth Cousin Twice Removed	Fourth Cousin Three Times Removed	Fourth Cousin Four Times Removed
7	4th Great Grandson or Daughter	3rd Great Grand Nephew or Niece	First Cousin Four Times Removed	Second Cousin Three Times Removed	Third Cousin Twice Removed	Fourth Cousin Once Removed	**Fifth Cousin**	Fifth Cousin Once Removed	Fifth Cousin Twice Removed	Fifth Cousin Three Times Removed
8	5th Great Grandson or Daughter	4th Great Grand Nephew or Niece	First Cousin Five Times Removed	Second Cousin Four Times Removed	Third Cousin Three Times Removed	Fourth Cousin Twice Removed	Fifth Cousin Once Removed	**Sixth Cousin**	Sixth Cousin Once Removed	Sixth Cousin Twice Removed
9	6th Great Grandson or Daughter	5th Great Grand Nephew or Niece	First Cousin Six Times Removed	Second Cousin Five Times Removed	Third Cousin Four Times Removed	Fourth Cousin Three Times Removed	Fifth Cousin Twice Removed	Sixth Cousin Once Removed	**Seventh Cousin**	Seventh Cousin Once Removed
10	7th Great Grandson or Daughter	6th Great Grand Nephew or Niece	First Cousin Seven Times Removed	Second Cousin Six Times Removed	Third Cousin Five Times Removed	Fourth Cousin Four Times Removed	Fifth Cousin Three Times Removed	Sixth Cousin Twice Removed	Seventh Cousin Once Removed	**Eighth Cousin**

THIS AND THAT GENEALOGY TIPS ON RELIGIONS

QUAKERS:
When a couple desired to obtain a marriage certificate, they made two appearances before both the Men's Meeting and the Women's Meeting prior to the marriage. Subsequent reports were made by the Committees appointed to attend the ceremony. Then, the report of the Committee so appointed reported at the next (following) Meeting that the marriage had been accomplished----within a month.

If a man and woman were members of different Monthly Meetings, they made their declaration where the woman was a member, the man being required to bring a certificate from his meeting that he was a member in good standing.

The Minutes contained a great deal of information, particularly during migrations. They related to memberships received and issued and various disciplinary actions taken against members. Thousands of such disciplinary measures are in the records. Unless the offending member repented, he was disowned, and no further records appear of him.

THE SECOND GREAT AWAKENING:
Lorenzo Dow was a great American preacher of the movement called The Second Great Awakening in the late 18th and early 19th centuries. He was a traveling preacher of the late 1700's and early 1800's and his name appears often in the records of many states. He also is credited with inventing "camp meetings." It is reported that 20,000 children were named after this colorful preacher.

From the book   Pioneers and Preachers
Section: Emotional Religion and Frontier Sermons

Frontier life spawned some rather eccentric preachers, one of whom was Lorenzo Dow, known as "Crazy Dow." His odd behavior and extensive travels both in America and abroad brought him much publicity and fame. As a fortune teller; seer; miracle worker; professor of calamities, births, deaths, and illnesses; and interpreter of dreams; he was one of the most discussed and controversial preachers of his day. He could preach on virtually any subject and damned nearly everyone and everything. At times he shocked his congregations by preaching from obscene and sadistic portions of the Old Testament. Tall, slender and spare of frame, with sloping shoulders and just a hint of a stoop, Dow's physical appearance normally would have not seemed forbidding, except for the fact that his matted and unkempt hair hung almost to his waist; much of it hung down his back and on his shoulders, but some of it fell forward over his face and full beard. With a grave countenance and piercing eyes, he "glanced reproofs wherever he looked" and caused the hardest sinners to flinch. He was emaciated from lack of proper food and sleep, and he knew little about the benefits of a bath. He went hatless and shoeless, wearing torn and shabby clothes. Dow presented an odd sight even to the backwoodsmen. When he came in possession of any money, which was rare, he soon lost it to a swindler. When he bought a horse, it was usually a spavined, ill-looking brute, scarcely able to totter along the trails and roads. Trusting in God to send angels and ravens to feed him, he usually begged for food from door to door. Rumor said that when unable to find food, he ate grasshoppers. Dow had hidden powers of endurance. Dow's voice sounded more female that male, not loud but trenchant. He often dragged some of the syllables of his words to painful lengths making them disgusting and disagreeable to delicate ears. While preaching for several successive days at Pittstown, New York, some of the members of the congregation thought that he was either crazy or possessed of the devil. After hearing the strange man preach, many people cursed and swore, partly because of what he said, but mostly because of his peculiar speech and odd demeanor. Most people detested him -- some believed he was saucy and deserved to be knocked down. Eccentric to the extreme, Dow eventually evolved techniques through trial and error that often made him a very effective preacher. One Sunday morning while Reverend Jacob Young was preaching at a camp meeting. Dow lay sick in a tent nearby. A the close of Young's sermon the sick minister rose from his bed and walked up to the pulpit. Standing there in a stooped position, looking over his right shoulder, his lack back to the congregation, he said, "There is a notable robber in this country, who has done a vast deal of mischief, and is still doing it; and, in order that the people may be on their guard, I intend to give you a full description of his character and the instrument by which he carried our his work." The congregation was often plagued by outlaws and became alarmed.

Some people thought that Dow was referring to a Baptist minister who had been a Tory and a thief during the American revolution. This man had fled to escape punishment after the war to Spanish territory where he supposedly had become a respectable citizen. But, this was not so. Dow was only trying to grab the attention of the congregation. He turned his face toward the assembly and began talking slowly in a dark and mysterious manner, eventually giving the robber's name in Hebrew, in Greek, and in English.. The evil one was none other than the Devil. For the remainder of his sermon, Dow preached to a rapt audience and many conversions were gained.

In closing one sermon, Dow said, "If there is any gentleman in the congregation who has any objection to my sermon, let him come forward, take the stand and make it known." There were five Calvinist ministers in the congregation and Dow expected a rebuttal, but none came. After standing silently for a few moments, Dow continued, "Now, gentlemen, I am going to leave the country, and if you do not come forward and defend your doctrine while I am present, but attempt to contradict my sermon when I am gone, someone may compare you to the little dog that does not have the courage to bark at the traveler when he is opposite to the gate, but will run along and bark on his track after he is gone!" Dow closed the meeting with a prayer and left unceremoniously.

When Dow arrived at one camp meeting ground, several settlers moved toward him shouting in satisfaction that the "wild man" was coming. Dow did present a bizarre appearance. He wore a rapaulin hat cocked on his head, a tattered green military coatee without its shiny ornaments, and a pair of knee britches that did not conceal his knees. Dow was in a hurry and he was laden with a bundle of tracts and handbills. On each bill was printed in large letters the following words: "Hush! Hark! This afternoon at three o'clock, Lorenzo Dow will preach inder the Federal Oaks." Dow rushed past one man without giving him a handbill He stopped abruptly and appeared to search the innermost recesses of his soul for guidance, after which he handed out the first tract. He passed several other people ignoring them as if they lived on another planet. He continued this unusual and scattered distribution until all his bills were gone.

Although Francis Asbury believed Dow demented, he widely never interfered with the miracle worker. In time, when Asbury believed that Dow was not exercising a good influence on the people east of the Appalachian Mountains, he sent him to the western frontier. In the thinly populated western areas, Dow gained unusual fame and became venerated as a prophet of the Lord. It did not take long for a preacher on the frontier to learn the importance of emotional release to the frontier people. The successful ministers were able to sway the behavior of the congregation in ways which today would appear unusual. Falling and jerking were common. Because the frontiersmen were themselves an odd lot by today's standards, some eccentric preachers were quite acceptable on the frontier. Unusual pulpit behavior and offbeat sermons often resulted. But, as the frontier disappeared and organized churches moved into an area, it gradually became less acceptable for ministers to move their congregations to such physical and emotional levels.

CHURCH OF THE BRETHREN:
once called German Baptist Brethren, (nicknamed Dunkers), Mennonites and the Amish are all considered Pennsylvania Dutch. They are considered Low German, the Lutherans are High German. The Pennsylvania Dutch were those of German Ancestry in the Lancaster County region of SE Pennsylvania (including York, Berks and adjacent areas), who normally wear the Plain Garb, and speak the dialect, although some have changed in the past half century - (even to using computers) .

ANABAPTISTS from: Jennie Vertrees at backwood@netins.net
A group of people called the "brethren" at the time of Luther and Zwingli did not believe in immersion, but taught that baptism was symbolic of what had taken place inside each person baptized. On January 21, 1525, at the fountain which was in the square in Zuerich, Switzerland; George Blaurock, a former priest, asked another member of the "brethren", Conrad Grebel, to baptize him. It was not done by immersion, but Grebel then baptized a number of others. Later, this group decided immersion was the thing to do, so all were rebaptized by immersion this time. The idea of rebaptism drew criticism from Catholics and Protestants alike, who started calling these "rebaptizers", which is what Anabaptist means. The first members of the order were mainly scholars and pacifists, but this changed drastically. Some of the names involved in the movement are Melchior Hoffman, Thomas Muentzer (who predated the movement), John Matthys and John of Leiden were some of the leaders. The movement eventually became Mennonite

from its leader, Menno Simons. To find out who the Anabaptists are, read information about the Mennonites and Menno Simons. It is a long story in the 1500s, but is interesting and rather lengthy. What I have given you is merely a thumbnail sketch.

CAMBELLITES:
The Restoration Movement of the 19th century was led by several men. Thomas Campbell, an Irish-born Presbyterian who settled in Pennsylvania in 1807 (the father of Alexander Campbell) and Alexander Campbell, (also in Pennsylvania), Barton W. Stone, Baptist, in KY, and Walter Scott, Scottish immigrant in Pennsylvania were all leading proponents of this movement. However, A. Campbell became the best known. Alexander Campbell settled in the western panhandle of West Virginia and founded Bethany College in Bethany, West Virginia.

The Campbellites were anabaptists emphasizing the one "sacrament" of baptism (by emersion) as being sufficient for salvation. They also made the Eucharist (Lord's Supper) a central focus of their worship service insisting on observing this rite each Lord's day (Sunday). Their goal was to reject man's creeds. They advocated speaking only where the Bible speaks and being silent were the Bible is silent. The movement was intended to reform existing churches, but a belief that this was impossible led to the establishment of new groups of believers, often known only as Disciples or Christians.

Two groups eventually developed. One is the Disciples of Christ (Christian Church) which is generally organized and has a national headquarters. The other is the churches of Christ. They are not nationally organized and meet as independent congregations. Alexander Campbell is rejected as a founder and is considered only as a restorer of the first century church. The term "Campbellite" was never used by the churches of Christ. It is generally considered an offensive term today and I believe it was also considered the same in the 19th century.

ROMAN CATHOLICS:
In Europe, saints' feast days are commonly celebrated instead of a person's actual chronological birthday (as we do in the U.S.). A child's parents may have selected a saint whose feast day fell on the day of birth or baptism, or may have waited several days beyond that date to pick the child's saintly namesake. For information on Roman Catholic saints and their feast days, go to: http://catholic.org/saints/stsindex.html

METHODIST EPISCOPAL CHURCH:
Methodism reached the 13 colonies [from England] in 1760. By 1777 there were some 6,000 Methodists and by 1789 there were 15,000.

John Wesley was conservative and loyalist in his politics and issued a public appeal to the colonies urging submission to the King, but religious zeal overcame this. John Wesley did not intend that the Methodists be an independent church. The Methodists were a group "within" the Church of England. The Bishop of London had refused to ordain ministers for America, so two men John Wesley had appointed to superintend and ordain ministers, Thomas Coke and Francis Asbury, were soon called Bishops, and the Methodist Episcopal Church was founded.

Methodism grew rapidly as the population was starving for religion that was new, virile and hopeful. The Methodist preachers were men of the people, speaking the language of ordinary folk. Growth was predominantly in the rural sections and on the frontier. The circuit plan and the system of local and traveling preachers was admirably adapted to this type of work. Under the district superintendents, were circuit riders with assigned areas to cover, some as much as 500 miles. It had to be traversed by whatever conveyance was possible -- on horseback, by canoe or where these failed, on foot. The circuit riders spoke wherever they could gain a hearing. In log cabins, court houses, school houses, taverns or in the open air.... They preached and sang the love of God in Christ. They desired above all things conversions. In addition to the circuit riders there were local preachers, exhorters, quarterly meetings, which gathered the members from farms and villages for fellowship and camp meetings.

EVANGELICAL AND LUTHERAN:
Evangelische simply means Evangelical. When Lutherisch/Lutheran is also present then it means Evangelical

206

Lutheran. However, you should be careful because there are several types of Evangelical churches. In Germany, there was also an "Evangelische reformierter" which was Evangelical Reformed. So, many of these folks came to America and found a church that suited their beliefs or needs. In the very old days, you were of a certain faith because the ruling royal family of their area chose for typically political reasons one faith over the other.

The Evangelische church of Germany is not necessarily Lutheran. As a result of the Prussian Union, the Lutheran and Reformed/Calvinistic churches were forced to combine by Prussian King, Frederick William III.

Distinctively Lutheran services were now simply forbidden and conscientious Lutherans, like Professor Dr. J. G. Scheibel of Breslau, removed from office and persecuted in various incredibly ferocious ways - despite Prussia's claims that it followed an enlightened policy of religion! Nobelmen and merchants were fined heavily for allowing Lutheran services on their properties. Lutherans had to meet secretly in forests, cellars and barns. Judas-money was paid for the betrayal of faithful pastors. Midwives had to report the birth of all Lutheran children. Lutheran baptisms were declared invalid, and babies were sometimes forcibly rebaptized in the official union-church under police compulsion. Faithful pastors were imprisoned. In one village the faithful Lutherans were attacked on Christmas Eve by a military force of five hundred men, who drove the weeping women away from the church with swords and bayonets, forced open the church-doors, and "installed" the union pastor with his union liturgy. The army refused to end the occupation till the protesting parishioners would start attending the union services.

The Confessional Awakening...finally led thousands of Lutherans, from many walks of life, to emigrate to the New World, so that they and their children might be free to confess and practice their Biblical, Reformation faith without compromise.

Only after the death of Frederick William III (1840) was the hitherto underground Lutheran church allowed to exist in Prussia as an independent body (1845).

MEANING OF EVANGELISCHE from: "Ned H. Benson" - nbenson@stjohnschurch.org -
This would be better understood to be Lutheran if the complete American title would be used - Evangelical Lutheran. I came from an area in western PA where most of the Lutheran churches were careful to identify themselves as Ev. Lutheran.

The meaning of "Evangelische" is very important in Germanic genealogy research. In Germany since the early 1800s "Evangelische" has indicated "non-Catholic," or what Americans call "Protestant." Since the early 1800s there were two main streams of Christian faith: Evangelische and Katholisch. Later other smaller groups appear: Methodisch, Presbyterianisch, usw.

However, from the time of the Reformation until the early 1800s, there were two streams of "Evangelische:" Evangelische Lutheranische and Evangelische Reformierte, the former what we would call "Lutheran," and the latter designating "Reformed." "Reformed" indicated the Protestant stream with theological roots in the Swiss Reformation of Ulrich Zwingli in Zurich and John Calvin in Geneva. These distinctions were maintained by German immigrants to the USA after the two streams were forced by governmental authority to merge in Germany. No such pressure in the USA, so the separate streams remained intact well into the 20th century.

Though "friendly" with one another, the two streams must not be casually mushed together: they tried, without success, to reach common understanding, and the dividing issue was the nature of Christ's presence in Holy Communion. It is a development of major theological and ecclesiological significance that the major Lutheran body in the USA (the ELCA) and the major Reformed churches (Presbyterian, Reformed, United Church of Christ) reached common acceptance only this year (1998!), settling the theological dispute by mutual recognition, something Melanchthon (Lutheran) and the Reformed theologians didn't manage in the 16th century.

Western PA Lutherans identified their churches as Ev. Lutheran to distinguish them from Ev. Reformierte. My German ancestors from Wuerttemberg, from Hessen, and from Westffalen were definitely and decidedly Ev. Reformierte and they made it very clear that just because they spoke German and had German surnames they WERE NOT Lutheran! In the USA they were members of the Deutsche Ev. Reformierte Kirche -- which became the Evangelical and Reformed Church, which in the late 1950s merged into what is now the United Church of Christ.

So if you are searching for German church records in the USA, don't just look at Lutheran churches. Your ancestors may have been, like mine were, Reformierte. If so records will be in a current day United Church of Christ congregation, or at a UCC seminary - Lancaster PA in the east, Eden in St. Louis in the mid-west.

DUNKARDS:
According to the "Encyclopedia of Religion" edited by Vergilius Ferm and published in 1964 by Littlefield, Adams & Co., (paraphrased) the dunkards are also know as Dunkers or Tunkers (because of the German word "tunken" - which means, to dip). They settled predominately in Pennsylvania during the early 18th century, but have members in most of the states. The order suffered a schism in 1728, out of which "The Old German Baptist Brethren" (old order), "The Brethren Church" & and "The Church of the Brethren" were spawned.

THIS AND THAT GENEALOGY TIPS ON THE REVOLUTIONARY WAR

The Revolutionary War began April 19, 1775 at Lexington and Concord, MA between the local militia and British troops and ended with the signing of the Treaty of Paris in 1783.

There are many records on the approximately 250,000 military participants and several million wives and descendants of these veterans. Basically, there are three types of records: Service records, Pension records, and Bounty-land Warrants.

SERVICE RECORDS: Most of the original service records and the earliest pension records of the Revolutionary War were destroyed in fires in 1800 and 1814. However, substitute records were used to make the compiled service records, which are now part of Record Group 93 at the National Archives in Washington, D.C. Service records document a person's involvement with the military and can provide the unit to which he belonged. This information will make it easier to find and identify your ancestor in the pension records. There often are several men with the same or similar names in military records. Service records seldom provide genealogical information about the soldier or his family.

If your ancestor served in a military unit, he should appear on muster/attendance rolls. This will give his name, date and place of enlistment and muster. Some records may show his age, physical description, marital status, occupation, even place of birth or residence.

The federal government has compiled military service records for soldiers serving in volunteer units in wars since 1775. These records, on cards, have abstracts of information taken from unmicrofilmed original records at National Archives, such as muster rolls, pay lists, hospital records, record books, orders and correspondence found in Record group 94, Records of the Adjutant General's Office, 1780s-1917. A card was made for each soldier and put in an envelope along with some original documents. These files are arranged by state, military unit, then alphabetically by the soldier's name.

In addition to federal records, each state or colony kept service records for its own militia and volunteer regiments. These records are usually available at state archives, state historical societies or state adjutant general's offices. If a state unit was mustered into federal service, then the federal government might have sent copies of records to the office of the state adjutant general. Therefore it is usually necessary to search both federal and state records.

Check the following:
General Index to Compiled Military Service Records of Revolutionary War Soldiers (National Archives M860, 58 rolls); also available at the Family History Library (FHL films 882,841-98). This alphabetical index includes soldiers, sailors, members of Army staff departments and civilian employees of the Army and Navy (such as teamsters, carpenters and cooks). For each soldier or civilian, the index gives name, rank, unit and profession or office.

Compiled Service Records of Soldiers Who Served in the American Army During the Revolutionary War (National Archives M881, 1,096 rolls); also available at the Family History Library -- FHLC computer number 432762).

PENSION RECORDS - The federal government and some state governments granted pensions to officers, disabled veterans, needy veterans, widows or orphans of veterans and veterans who served a certain length of time. Pension records usually contain more genealogical information than service records. However, not all of our veteran ancestors applied for or received a pension.

Pension files for 1775 to 1916 are available at the National Archives in Record Group 15, Records of the Veterans Administration, and only those for the Revolutionary War have been microfilmed. Lists of federal and state military pensioners have been published for the years 1792 to 1795, 1813, 1817, 1818, 1820, 1823, 1828, 1831, 1835, and 1840. These are most likely ones to contain information about a Revolutionary War ancestor and most of these lists can be found in the U.S. Congressional Serial Set available at federal repository libraries and many university libraries. Some have been reprinted and can be found in genealogical collections at many libraries.

BOUNTY LAND:

The federal government and some states offered land to those who would serve in the military during the Revolutionary War. Bounty land could be claimed by veterans or their heirs. The federal government and some states reserved tracts of land in the public domain for this purpose.

A veteran requested bounty land by filing an application, usually at the local courthouse. The application papers and supporting documents were placed in bounty land files kept by the federal or state agency. These files contain information similar to pension files. If the application was approved, the individual was given either a WARRANT to receive the land or SCRIPT which could be exchanged for a warrant. Later laws allowed for the sale or exchange of warrants. Actually, few soldiers received title to bounty land or settled on it as most of them sold or exchanged their warrants.

Federal bounty land applications and warrants for the Revolutionary War have been microfilmed. They are available at the National Archives, its regional branches, and the Family History Library. Revolutionary War Pension and Bounty Land Warrant Application Files, 1800-1900; (National Archives M804).

Write to General Reference Branch (NNRG), National Archives and Records Administration, 8th and Pennsylvania Avenue N.W., Washington, DC 20408 and request several free copies of Form NATF-80. You also can request this form by: inquire@arch2.nara.gov

Fill out the forms as completely as possible for the search of either Service (military), Pension, and Bounty-land Warrants or all three. Each search will cost about $10. if files are found. Military (service) records will provide you with information about the unit(s) in which an individual served, battles in which he/she fought, and other details. However, it is the pension records that are the most valuable genealogically but not all veterans received a pension, and not all of their records have survived. Bounty-land Warrants should also be searched.

Be sure to also check the state militia records at the state archives of the state in which your ancestor lived.

Your library may have references on the Revolutionary War such as the DAR (Daughters of the American Revolution) Patriot Indexes or the Index of Revolutionary War Pension Applications (published by the National Genealogical Society in 1980); Genealogical Abstracts of Revolutionary War Pension Files (three volumes) by Virgil D. White [Waynesboro, TN, National Historical Publishing Co., 1990-92]; Rider's American Genealogical-Biographical Index. While the Daughters of American Revolution (DAR) indexes are valuable they are not complete. Your ancestor may have served and not be mentioned in these references. If you find your ancestor is mentioned as a patriot in their records, it means that someone has joined the DAR on this person. You may obtain a photocopy of an application paper of related members by writing to: Office of the Organizing Secretary General, NSDAR, 1776 D Street, N.W., Washington, DC 20006. Cost is $5 per record and the order must include: Date of request, your name and address, name of ancestor and page number in the DAR Patriot Index; The Centennial Edition of the Patriot Index (1994) is the most recently published and is in three volumes.

If you do not find a records of military service in the Revolutionary War for your ancestor, your ancestor may have been a member of a pacifist church, such as the Society of Friends (Quakers); they may have been ministers; they may have been German mercenaries or they may have been Tories or Loyalists. It is estimated that one-third of the Colonial population were Loyalists. A Loyalist was one who actively participated in the war to aid the cause of Crown, usually in British uniform. Tories were sympathetic to Great Britain and they were sometimes punished if they refused to take an oath of allegiance. Their property was not usually confiscated, and they were not generally charged with treason, as were the Loyalists. About 15,000 Loyalist militiamen organized themselves and chose their own officers during the British occupation of Georgia, North Carolina, South Carolina, New York and Maine. In many places Loyalists were harassed, expelled and/or their property confiscated. Approximately 100,000 Loyalists left America; but some of them eventually returned, and some switched sides during the war.

In addition to Canada and Florida, many Loyalists and Tories went to the West Indies, especially Jamaica, and some returned to Britain. About four-fifths of Upper Canada's (now Ontario) settlers came from the American colonies. There are many printed sources pertaining to Loyalists. See Val Greenwood's book The Researcher's Guide to American Genealogy and the index to "American & British Genealogy & Heraldry: A Selected List of Books," (Third Edition) compiled by P. William Filby (both available in many public libraries).

German mercenaries (about 30,000) fought with the British and participated in every major battle campaign. More than 5,000 of them deserted to remain in this country, while others received permission after the war to stay here. Although this group is loosely referred to as Hessians they actually came from several different areas of Germany. See Genealogical & Local History Books in Print: General Reference & World Resources Volume (5th edition) compiled by Marian Hoffman.

If your ancestor was a minister, see Soldiers of God: The Chaplains of the Revolutionary War by E. F. Williams and J. T. Headley's The Chaplains and Clergy of the Revolution.

If you are searching for African-Americans see Black Courage, 1775-1783: Documentation of Black Participation in the American Revolution by Robert Ewell Greene. It was published by National Society of the Daughters of the American Revolution in 1984.

Visit the web page of the Reference Branch, The U.S. Army Military History Institute, Carlisle Barracks, PA 17013 at http://carlisle-www.army.mil/usamhi/. Its staff will not do genealogical research, but will locate historical material about a military unit and loan books to your local library on interlibrary loan.

THIS AND THAT GENEALOGY TIPS ON SAVING

Save diaries, letters, old postcards, photographs, maps, drawings, recordings of family members - tapes, etc. for oral history, photographs, slides and rubbings of tombstones, quilts, deeds and contracts.

Do not save old newspapers! If you want the information saved in your files, photocopy the articles on good bond paper. Newspapers are pure acid and eventually crumble to nothing. There are other sources for information contained in newspapers. Most are on microfilm.

Ultra violet light cause deterioration of any memorabilia. Protection from light is the first and most important consideration in saving old items - or even current ones. Covering pictures, or anything made of paper, with a plastic film which filters out at least 97 per cent of the ultra violet rays is a must. This should be applied between the glass and picture of any item that is being framed. DO NOT LAMINATE. This is an irreversible process. Encapsulate, frame, but do not laminate.

Most glues used in scrapbooks, etc. are called "irreversible glue" - that is, they are permanent. Things glued this way to paper will be ruined by the acid in the paper. There are ways archivists use to loosen items glued in this way. If one needs help in saving such items, contact the archives in your area. They will be glad to help.

Items that have been stored in basements often become moldy. They can be restored by killing the mold, then washing. Any washing done to old items must be done with distilled water. Powdered chlorine bleach is a valuable tool in cleaning and preserving prints. Acid paper can be buffered to counteract the acid. It comes in liquid or spray. This should be done after the cleaning process. Then the item must be stored in an acid-free environment, protected from ultra violet light. Specific cleaning instructions should be obtained from an archives or other source.

Quilts should be saved but they should not be folded. You may hang them if you make a sleeve to hang them from using a waxed flax thread. Never hang them from the quilt material itself. To store them get a large cardboard roll and roll them, then make a muslin sleeve to cover them as protection from dust. The cardboard must be sprayed with the buffer mentioned above, then covered with cotton before rolling the quilt in it. To repair or hold old deteriorating quilts together, use fine silk and waxed thread.

PRESERVE OLD DOCUMENTS:
Encapsulate them in Mylar. Cut two sheets of Mylar, at least 1 " bigger than the document. Run adhesive transfer tape (available at art supply stores, I believe) around all 4 sides of one of the sheets, leaving about 1/8th inch free of adhesive at each corner.

Lay the document in the center of this sheet, being careful so that it does not come in contact with the adhesive.

Then roll the second sheet of Mylar on top, so that the adhesive forms an almost complete seal.

The Mylar is inert and will not leach any harmful acids onto or into the document. It also protects it from handling. The 1/8' inch left free of adhesive in each corner insures that air and moisture can freely pass in and out, and you will not have any mold or mildew (foxing) or dry rot.

If you are planning to frame, frame a copy. Store the original (after encapsulation) horizontally, in rag mats, window on top, uncut backing on the bottom. Use photo corners to affix the Mylar corners to the backing board.

Do NOT use lamination on any document you wish to preserve. The gasses the paper and ink produces will accumulate within the lamination, further eroding the paper, ink and lettering. You can also use Ph neutral paper to cover the clippings on both side, and SUPPORTING it (yes, even if they lay flat), as newspaper paper-quality does not hold its own support. If you decide to laminate anyway - your lamination film and adhesive MUST be free of anything that will contribute to yellowing. The item cannot "breathe" in this environment and if the chemicals present are destructive over time, the item will yellow badly. A better option that some archives use is micro-encapsulation. Using sheets of Mylar and acidfree/archival quality double sided adhesive, you sandwich the item between two sheets and seal all around the edge, leaving a tiny gap for breathing. Backing the document with a buffered sheet of lignin free paper or treating with a spray above will help arrest the deterioration. The item itself is not adhered in anyway, so the Mylar can be cut open to remove it at a future date. The Mylar lends great support to the paper as well. The Mylar sheets come in many sizes, small sheets for cutting to preserve clippings to big enough to encapsulate broadsides.

You can purchase acid-free album sheets, clear Mylar protectors and archival glue from a catalog company called Exposures in Oshkosh, WI (1 800 572-5750). The glue is sort of rubbery and you can actually remove a photo to replace it or to move it, provided it isn't fragile. You would not be able to move a newspaper clipping.

DO NOT treat the paper with various anti-acid solution without TESTING the effect this might have on the ink. Again, cheap ink was commonly used with newspaper.

DO NOT Xerox the clippings: the heat & exposure of the copy machine will harm the paper and accelerate its deterioration (YES, even a one time exposer does a tremendous amount of damage, in a 5-10 years period). If you wish to make a copy, us a camera.

READ more about this stuff. A good classic start up book is "An Ounce Of Preservation". Cheap, thorough and for non-professionals.

MEND TORN DOCUMENTS:
If you must mend torn documents or books, do not use cellophane tape as it will brown over time. Go to a good art store or library supply store and find tape made from Mylar "D" or Scotchpar film coated with a pH neutral adhesive. They do not have acid in them and will not brown like scotch tape.

OPINION ON PHOTOCOPYING OLD PHOTOS:
Photocopying old photos contribute to their degradation. Photos will deteriorate no matter what method is used to store them or to copy them. Some can be damaged by the bright light used in some copiers. Even though you don't see any appreciable difference right away, it can still damage the picture over a period of time.

If your ancestral photos are really old, and if you intend to make copies for distribution, it is best to have the professionally re-photographed by someone who knows what they are doing. A low light (NOT flash!), combined with either a wide lens opening and/or long shutter time, will give optimum results without subjecting the old photograph to damaging light rays. This will also give you a good negative from which you can make other copies, enlargements, compositions, etc.

Yes, this is the more expensive way to go but nobody ever said genealogy was a cheap hobby. And, it doesn't have to be all that expensive... a good single-lens reflex 35mm camera on a steady mount surface and a holder to put the original picture in while taking the photo is about all you need. It can be done in almost any well-lit room (avoid direct sunlight on the original photo, however). That, and the price of a roll of film being developed and printed is about all it takes.

STRAIGHTEN ROLLED DOCUMENTS:
If your document has been rolled up for many years and you want to straighten it out - get a sheet of rag matboard to act as a blotter, a sheet of rag paper and have handy a heavy piece of glass. Dampen the sheet of rag paper slightly with distilled water from a spray bottle. Have someone help you carefully unroll the document onto the matboard, lay the rag paper on top and cover it all with the piece of glass. Let sit for at least 24 hours. When uncovered, it should be flat. Let it dry thoroughly. If you have trouble unrolling the document - you might try this ..... place an open container of water near the document in a large plastic bag and seal tightly. Let it sit for at least 2 days until the paper

relaxes it's fibers so it may be unrolled safely.

DON'T DAMAGE DOCUMENTS: Some useful objects on your desk may destroy information stored on your paper records, photographs and computer diskettes. The adhesive on pressure sensitive tapes, such as Scotch tape and Magic Mend, contain a great deal of acid and literally eat paper. This damage is irreversible and, at the very least, will leave acid stains on the paper.

Self-stick notes, such as Post-It-Notes, are a handy and efficient way of leaving messages and marking documents. The sticky top edges of the notes, however, leave behind an adhesive when the note is removed. Also the colors of the notes tend to run when wet, so they should not be used on papers of value.

Magnet paper clip holders magnetize the paper clips that are stored in them. If these clips are then used to attach a note to a diskette, for example, the magnetized clip can damage or erase the information on the diskette.

PRESERVE OLD DOCUMENTS:
If you have an old document you want to preserve - if it is two sided, place it in a Mylar sleeve like the ones which have one side folded & you just slip the document in it. You might try the "L fold" ones but place it in very carefully. If it's one sided, still use the Mylar but place an acid free and buffered sheet of backing paper in to further prevent against migratory acid attack. In addition (before you do all this) you could de-acidify it, but don't use those home recipes you read about every now and then. The spray solutions on the market are quite safe and nonaqueous.

To display between pieces of glass, it is possible to have such things framed by a museum framing technique, which uses acid-free components and does not allow the glass to come in direct contact with the document. Any reputable framer should be able to do this. I have had this done, resulting in a beautiful and meaningful piece to display (away from direct light, please). If you want to do this yourself, materials are available. A catalog from University Products, Inc., 517 Main Street, P.O. Box 101, Holyoke, MA 01041-0101, provides a complete selection of archival materials for almost any preservation project one could imagine. They would send a catalog if requested.

If you are interested in preserving family papers and photos, the Library of Congress website has some good preservation information. The site is: http://lcweb.loc.gov/preserv/

THIS AND THAT GENEALOGY TIPS ON SOCIAL SECURITY

SOCIAL SECURITY:
Social Security was inaugurated in 1935 and they began issuing numbers but NOT to everyone. Only People who worked outside the home were issued numbers. Many women were not assigned numbers of their own . The number they used if there was ever a need for one ie. a pension or they became widowed was the number of their husband with a letter added to distinguish the two.

Since births were not generally required to be recorded prior to the early 1900's (almost everywhere in the US), it was determined that the 1880 census could be used as proof of age. Since persons born before 1870 were over 65 in 1935 and thus not eligible to sign up for Social Security, the Soundex created for the 1880 census was deliberately limited to those families who had children age 10 or under. Thus persons born after 1870 and before 1880 could use the census record as proof of their age.

The first deductions for SSI started in 1935, with the first payments to be paid after 1 Jan 1937. I believe the recipients had to be either donors or widows or underage children. So if any of your ancestors were over 65 and died in 1937 you should be able to find them in the index.

The records are filed by Social Security numbers and not by names. If you cannot provide the Social Security number when you request records, they can search for a person's records by using the full name, date and place of birth, and parents' names (including mother's maiden name).

MAKE SURE YOU CLEARLY STATE THAT THE PERSON IS DECEASED!

The fee for searching for the SS-5 application when the Social Security number is provided is $7.00 and when the number is unknown but identifying information is provided the fee is $16.50. The fee for searching for the claim file is $14, and photocopying material from the claim file is 10 cents a page, plus actual postage. The search fee will be charged even if they are unable to locate or disclose any information. The records are confidential and they do not disclose information about individuals unless they are deceased or they have their consent to do so. Send requests and a check or money order payable to the Social Security Administration and mail it to:

Social Security Administration
Office of Central Records Operations
FOIA Workgroup
P.O. Box 17772
300 N. Greene Street
Baltimore, MD 21290

SSA offers now the option to make the payment of fees by credit card. They accept MasterCard and Visa.

Representatives of the Office of Disclosure Policy, which handles requests of SS-5 application copies to Social Security Administration, report that they are experiencing a 3-to-6-month delay in responding because of a staffing shortage and a high volume of requests. Desiring to know the status of a request you can call that office at 410-965-1727 (a voice mail number where you can only leave a message) or write to:

Social Security Administration
Office of Disclosure Policy
3-A-6 Operations Building
6401 Security Boulevard
Baltimore, Maryland 21235

SOCIAL SECURITY NUMBERS:

The first three numbers identify the area where the individual was living when the card was issued. The second two digits are a "control" used by the government as a way to quickly identify fraudulent numbers. Within each area (i.e. the first three digits) the odd groups, 01 through 09, and then the even groups, 10 through 98, are issued first. Then the even groups 02 through 08 and the odd groups 11 through 99 are issued. The last four numbers are issued strictly in numerical sequence. The government can easily tell the place of issuance of a social security card, the year it was issued, and approximately at what time of the year it was issued. For example, a number beginning with 010-28 was issued in 1951 to someone living in Massachusetts, while 010-44, although still given to someone in Massachusetts, was not issued until 1968. If someone born in 1965 is using a number that was issued in 1955, this is an indication of a problem.

SOCIAL SECURITY ACCOUNT APPLICATIONS:

Social Security Administration is requesting that we use the following address when asking for copies of Social Security Account Applications (Form SS-5) under the Freedom Of Information Act.

Social Security Administration
Office of Central Records Operations
FOIA Workgroup
P.O. Box 17772
300 N Greene St
Baltimore MD 21290

It might be a good idea to send a copy of the ancestors death certificate and state your relationship to the person in your letter. The original applications give the name, address, place of employment and address, age, date and place of birth, full name of each parent including mother's maiden name. The applications are dated and signed by the applicant.

If you are not familiar with the SS-5, you may be missing a great source of information on recent generations of your family. The form is filled out at the time a person applies for their Social Security Account Number. After that person dies, their application becomes a public record available to any person who applies for a copy under the Freedom of Information Act. Since the application includes the full name of the person, their date and place of birth, the full name of their father and the full maiden name of their mother, plus their place of employment at the time the application was made, it can aid location and identification of past generations.

To request a copy of the SS-5, simply send the full name, Social Security Number, and date of death for the person, plus a check for $7.00 for each record requested, to the address above -- indicating that you are requesting their SS-5 under the Freedom of Information Act. No special form is required. To find the Social Security Number for most persons who died since the late 1960s, you can search one of the online data bases maintained by various genealogical publishers. The one provided for free by Ancestry, Inc. is at: http://www.ancestry.com/

SOCIAL SECURITY LETTER FORWARDING SERVICE:

To contact a living person whom you have lost, write a letter to the person, be sure to include your address and telephone number in the letter. Send the letter in an unsealed stamped envelope, along with a cover letter to the Social Security Administration, Letter Forwarding Unit, 6401 Security Blvd., Baltimore, MD 21235. If for some reason that comes back to you, try: Social Security Administration, Office of Central Records Operations, 300 N. Greene St., Room 1312, Tower Metro West, Baltimore, MD 21201.

Include in the letter as much as you know about the person: Name, Social Security number, birthplace, birth date, name of the person's parents. You do not have to know all of the information, but the process will be quicker if you give more identifying information. If the person you are seeking is listed in the SSA files, the letter will be forwarded to them and it's up to that person to contact you.

There may be no charge for humanitarian requests; other searches there is a charge.

DEATH MASTER FILE:

The Death Master File (DMF) from the Social Security Administration (SSA) contains over 59.7 million records created from SSA payment records. It contains the records of those for whom the lump sum death benefit was paid.

The $255. death benefit is not issued to everyone. Only where there are dependents. Children or a spouse. That lump sum benefit may have been requested by a family member, an attorney, a mortuary, etc. [NOTE: If someone is missing from the list, it may be that the benefit was never requested, there was an error on the form requesting the benefit or even an error in entering the information into the SSDI]. Not everyone who collected benefits is listed on the SSDI. The exceptions are to numerous to name but suffice to say not everyone is listed.

For more information, visit: http://www.ancestry.com/ssdi/q01hlp.htm

To search this database, go to: http://www.ancestry.com/ssdi/advanced.htm

or go to their main page at: http://www.ancestry.com

THIS AND THAT GENEALOGY TIPS ON STARTING GENEALOGY

TWENTY WAYS TO AVOID GENEALOGICAL GRIEF:
Here are some suggestions to help beginners prevent misfortune when learning how to do genealogical research. Many of these tips are "old hat" to experienced genealogists, but it is always worthwhile to remind ourselves of the basics of sound research.

1. Always note the source of information that you record or photocopy, and date it too. If the material is from a book, write the name, author, publisher, year of publication, ISBN or ISSN (if it has one), and also the library where you found it (or else photocopy the title page). Occasionally you'll find that you need to refer to a book again, or go back to great aunt Matilda to clarify something she told you.

2. Talk to all your older-generation relatives before they're all gone and you're the older generation! Even a distant relative can be a gold mine of information about your ancestors.

3. Make photocopies or keep backups of all letters and e-mail messages you send. This will save you from wondering which of your correspondents' questions you've already answered, and which of your questions they have or haven't answered.

4. Don't procrastinate in responding to letters or messages you receive. If you don't have time to write a detailed reply, send your correspondent a quick message or postcard to acknowledge receipt and tell her/him approximately when you'll send them a more complete reply. Then be sure to write back as you've promised.

5. Make frequent backups of your computer disks. Store your backups and photocopies of your irreplaceable documents where you work or at someone else's home.

6. When searching for relatives in records, don't pass over entries that are almost (but not quite) what you're looking for. For example, if you're searching for the marriage of John Brown and Mary Jones in 1850, make a note of the marriage of John Brown and Nancy Smith in 1847; this could be a previous marriage in which the wife died shortly after.

7. When writing to libraries or to genealogical or historical societies in your areas of interest, ask them for the names and addresses of out-of-print booksellers in the area. Write to the booksellers and ask if they have any old local histories or family histories pertaining to the area.

8. Remember that just because information is on computer or in print, it ain't necessarily fact! Information in recent family histories is often based on that from older published works. If the older books are incorrect, the wrong information simply gets repeated and further disseminated.

9. The earlier the time period in which you're researching, the less consistent our ancestors were about the spelling of their surnames. Also, some of them were illiterate and couldn't tell a record keeper how their names should be spelled.

10. Family traditions of close connections to famous people are usually false, but there may be a more obscure relationship involved. For example, perhaps the famous person spent a night at your ancestor's inn instead of (as the legend goes) marrying into the family.

11. Try not to let your research get behind. Establish a filing system for your papers (using file folders or 3-ring binders) and file each page of notes, document, photocopy, etc. as you acquire it. There are few things more disheartening than contemplating a foot-high stack of unfiled papers, wondering if the birth certificate you desperately need to refer to is buried somewhere in it.

12. Double-check all dates to make sure they are reasonable, for example, a woman born in 1790 could not have become a mother in 1800.

13. Be on the lookout for nicknames. A request for a birth certificate for Sadie White may be rejected by a record office if the name in their files is Sarah White.

14. Beware of mail-order promotions offering what might purport to be a personalized genealogy of your surname with a title like The Amazing Story of the BLANK Family, BLANKs Since the Civil War or Burke's Peerage World Book of BLANKs. These books are not properly researched and documented genealogies; instead they are often little more than lists of names from phone directories or other readily-available sources. Notify the Better Business Bureau, postal authorities and consumer advocate agencies if you receive one of these. For more about these, see the ROOTS-L FAQ file FAQ SCAMS. If you're looking for occurrences of a particular surname, national and international phone listings are widely available on CD-ROM and can be viewed in many public libraries or purchased.

15. Don't assume modern meanings for terms used to describe relationships. For example, in the 17th century a stepchild was often called a "son-in-law" or "daughter-in-law," and a "cousin" could refer to almost any relative except a sibling or child.

16. Remember that indexes to books rarely include the names of all persons mentioned in the book and, in addition, occasionally contain errors. If it appears that a book is likely to have valuable information, spend some time skimming its contents rather than returning it to the library shelf after a quick glance at the index.

17. Be precise when making notes and especially when sharing information with others. Write dates using an unambiguous format: Americans interpret 5/6/1881 as 6 May 1881, but in many other countries it would be read as 5 June 1881. Always capitalize or underline surnames, some of which can be mistaken for given names, e.g., HENRY, HOWARD. Note place names in full, including parish or township, county, state or province, and country.

18. You'll often encounter conflicting information, for example, you might discover that your paternal grandmother's birth date on her gravestone is different than her birth date as told to you by your father. Note the source for each piece of information, but don't feel you have to decide immediately which date is the correct one. In fact, both of them may be wrong! Further research may reveal a more credible birth date, for example, the one on her birth certificate. Take time occasionally to review and verify the conclusions you've reached concerning each of your ancestors' lives: this will prevent you from wasting time following blind alleys.

19. Boundaries and place names change constantly over the years. Always verify them in historical atlases or genealogical texts pertaining to the area. For example, the boundaries of Lancaster County, Pennsylvania have changed four times since it was first colonized.

20. Whenever you can, advertise the surnames you're researching by posting them electronically (for example, on the ROOTS-L Surname List) and submitting them to genealogical directories and surname lists published by genealogical societies that you belong to. This will put you in touch with others who are researching the same for a much longer time, and save you from re inventing the wheel. After all, the most rewarding genealogical research is the kind that no one else has already done!

This article first appeared in The British Columbia Genealogist, vol. 17 #1, Mar/88. It was reprinted with some changes by the Florida Genealogical Society in their Journal, vol. 24 #2, Oct/88, and in the Canadian Federation of Genealogical and Family History Societies Newsletter, vol. 6 #2, Oct/93. If you reprint this article, please credit the British Columbia Genealogical Society and send them a copy of your publication containing it. Their address is: BCGS, PO Box 88054, Lansdowne Mall, Richmond BC Canada V6X 3T6.

WHAT TO DO WHEN THE COURTHOUSE HAS BURNED AND YOU ARE ALL OUT OF MARSHMALLOWS! From a program for the Oklahoma Genealogical Society, February 4, 1985, given by Mrs. Lois

M. COPLE:

1. The courthouse may not have burned totally. Some records may have been saved because they were in an annex or wing that didn't burn. Don't always rely on what the 'Handy Book for Genealogist' or the court clerk says.
2. There may be/have been 2 courthouses in the same county.
3. The records may have been reconstructed or re-recorded, and remember that deeds sometimes are not recorded for years after the transfer. (Also check with county abstract offices).
4. Check neighboring counties for deeds, probate records and marriages. It may be necessary to go out a second or third county away for a marriage record.   People who elope do not go to their own town courthouse for the license.
5. Check everything in the courthouse where the family went to and the county where they came from if the county is known. Many sold land to relatives before moving on.
6. Check the parent county/counties Land records and the State Land Records for those counties. In the case of territory claimed by two states, check both state records. If your problem is in the Fire Lands or a Military District, check the parent States records.
7. Check the progeny (those that were formed from your county) county/counties for Land records that may have been recorded at a much later date.

FEDERAL RECORDS:

1. Census Records
2. Mortality schedules.
3. Military records and Pensions.
4. Federal Land Grants, Homestead States.
5. Immigration and Naturalization.
6. DECENNIAL Digest. This index covers the years 1658 to 1906 and is found in most law libraries. It indexes cases that went to appellate or higher courts.
7. Federal court records. (Remember that Federal records are records of the Revolution and records created since that time.)

STATE RECORDS:

1. Census - State and Territorial.
2. Militia and Pension.
3. Birth and Death records.
4. Tax Records: Real, Personal and Poll.
5. Land Lotteries, Land Grants, Homesteads.

TOWNSHIP OR TOWN RECORDS: Items vary according to the state. In Ohio I saw a list of men available and of the right age for Military duty from the late 1800's. Other states may have townships that function like a county or a city and have the equivalent records.

CITY RECORDS:

1. Birth and Death records.
2. Marriage records.
3. Cemetery records.
4. Tax records.
5. City directories (more currently, phone books).

HISTORICAL COLLECTIONS:

1. State Archives and Libraries.
2. County Historical Societies.
3. College Libraries.
4. Local Libraries.
5. Private Libraries (D.A.R., S.A.R., Railroad, etc.)

PUBLISHED RECORDS:
1. County Histories.
2. Town and City Histories.
3. Genealogies.
4. Genealogical and Historical Society Quarterlies.
5. Newspapers.

PRIVATE RECORDS:
1. Church records, Church Historical Libraries.
2. Funeral home records.
3. Cemetery records, Sextons Records, and transcripts of cemeteries made years ago.
4. School records, College or Grade.
5. Title and Abstract companies.
6. Private Land Co. such as the Holland Land Purchase in NY.

HOME SOURCES:
1. Bible records.
2. Photo albums.
3. Baby books.
4. Insurance policies.
5. Family letters, diaries, ledgers.

MISCELLANEOUS:
1. Lineage Societies.
2. Masonic Records.
3. Fraternal Records.

BOTTOM LINE: Analyze your problem and decide:
1. What information you really NEED!
2. What types of documents may provide that information!
3. Then analyze the locality or localities where that proof may be found.

From a program for the Oklahoma Genealogical Society, February 4, 1985, given by Mrs. Lois M. COPLE.

BACKWARD FOOTPRINTS - Lila Kobs Hubbard, Family Genealogist & Research Historian: Recall the story of the Tortoise & the Hare? Slow steady progress in genealogy is a must when trying to locate or trace the movement of immigrant ancestors. Genealogy is a science and should be approached from a scientific and/or historical like approach. Someone recently described genealogy as a huge jigsaw puzzle. This is true, gathering bits of information piece by piece seems unproductive until the pieces start to fit together. When a picture begins to emerge it is possible by carefully planned research to seek information to fill in the missing pieces. All avenues of research in the United States should be exhausted before a genealogist tries to trace the family line to its place of origin. This approach may seem like drudgery & it may seem boring even appear to be unrewarding! Who said it would be easy? No one, I know. There is an old saying, "A job worth doing is worth doing well." These suggestions are not to lighten your burden but more to direct & suggest advantageous routes for successful research. Valuable only if you keep very accurate records of your research. The search is on so start with you & your family.

Relatives may think they know nothing but some of them really do! Family stories, documents, member ship applications, old letters, etc. may give you a lot of small pieces to your family puzzle.

THINGS TO ASK ABOUT OR WRITE ABOUT:
1. Family records
2. Bible Records

3. Family Letters, Stories & Traditions
4. Employment & Societies Records
5. Wills, Deeds, Etc.
6. Certificates, Awards, Discharges, Etc.
7. Photographs
8. Books of Remembrance
9. Diaries, Printed or Manuscript Family Genealogies

If you find church information, or know the place of worship of your ancestor don't overlook the following types of church records:
1. Membership Records
2. Birth, Marriage & Death Records
3. Baptism Records
4. Confirmation Records
5. Communion Records
6. Society or Board Minutes
7. Church School Records
8. Church Cemetery Records
9. Church Archives State or National Levels

Contact the proper authorities in Hometown, U.S.A. for help or search   City, Town, Village Records:
1. Birth, Death, Marriage & Divorce Records
2. Tax Lists
3. School Records & Board Minutes
4. Town Histories & Historians
5. Newspaper Files (Obituary & News items)
6. Cemetery Records & Gravestones
7. Mortuary Records
8. Town Clerk's Minutes
9. Genealogical or Historical Societies
10. Libraries - many have genealogical information on the local level & may have hometown newspapers on microfilm.
11. Military Records, Statues, plaques, etc.

Your next move is to research County Records (Remember that old County boundaries change! Get a good atlas.)
1. County Census Records
2. Court Records
3. Wills, Administration & Guardianships
4. Marriage Licenses/ Bonds & Divorce Records
5. Birth & Death Records
6. Land Records
7. Deeds
8. Tax Records
9. School Records & Board Minutes
10. Naturalization Records
11. Orphans Court Records
12. Old Folks or Veterans Homes
13. Hospital & Mental Institutions Records
14. Military Records
15. County Histories with Biographies & Genealogy
16. County Genealogical & Historical Societies

The next step forward is to search state records. You may be re checking some of your already located information but do realize humans make mistakes & dates could have been entered incorrectly or even the minister in waiting months to record a number of things could have missed recording a marriage & did it later:

1. Birth & Death Records
2. Marriage & Divorce Records
3. Land Grants
4. Census Records
5. Tax Lists
6. Military Records. An Adj. General's Office provided the name, for a genealogist, of a GREAT UNCLE. The nameless male had existed in stories but his military records were only obtained because his name, company & regiment were sent from the State of Missouri.
7. Court Records
8. Hospital & Mental Institution Records
9. State Archives
10. State Genealogical & Historical Societies

The research now goes to national records & much can be done at your nearest branch of the National Archives or by mail, using the proper forms, with the NARS in Washington, DC:

1. Census Records
2. Military Records
3. Pension Records
4. Old Soldiers Homes Records
5. Bounty Land warrant Records
6. Records of Civilians During Wartime
7. Records of American Indians
8. Records of Black Americans
9. Records of Merchant Seamen
10. Records of Civilian Government Employees
11. Passenger Arrival Lists
12. Immigration Records
13. Passport Information
14. Naturalization Records
15. Land Records
16. Claims Records
17. Court Records
18. Records of the District of Columbia
19. Miscellaneous Records Including Social Security
20. Cartographic Records (Maps & Descriptions)
21. Organizational & Multi -Society Records

Your FOOTSTEPS BACKWARD may be difficult but if your research has been extensive, exacting & you are a 'lucky person' you will have the proper information to begin your FOREIGN RESEARCH. There are many fine genealogical societies in other countries that are willing to assist an American genealogist but PLEASE remember when writing to send International Response Certificates as a SASE is useless. Overseas postage costs about four times our normal postal rates.

GENEALOGY BY MAIL:
The most economical way to do your genealogy research is by correspondence. However, there are some basic rules of etiquette that you must.

Make sure your envelope is large enough to properly hold what you plan to send and be sure you have affixed sufficient postage - also be sure you neatly address it.

Always include a SASE (Self Addressed, Stamped Envelope) with your letters and make sure it is large enough to hold a reply and if you expect many pages of text to be returned to you, enclose a second stamp for your respondent to use, should it be necessary.

Be brief and to the point. In your contacts with officials, ask only one question in any letter and explain only the facts absolutely necessary to get your answer.

Label all pages, charts, envelopes, etc., with your name and address and date them all.

Be a "Giver" as well as a "Taker". Offer, and mean it, to exchange data.

Include payment, if you know the cost, of copying, etc., or make it clear you will reimburse for it promptly. Then do so, promptly.

Reread your letter before you mail it. If it is easily understood, mail it..

Acknowledge, always and promptly, any response you receive, whether or not that response has brought the desired results. You may wish to include another SASE with your acknowledgment, asking that your contact keep it in his files in case he should come across something for you later. Always reimburse postage for any reply.

You may wish to write your question on the upper half of a sheet of paper, leaving the lower half for the response. Anything you can do to make the action easier for your reader is advisable. If you suspect your contact may want to keep your letter for his files, include a carbon copy with the original.

Include a note to the effect that "If you have no information for me, won't you please drop my SASE in the mail. That way I'll know you did receive and consider my request."

For special favors, where payment is not expected to compensate for value received, send a personalized, localized or hand-made gift.

GENEALOGY RECORDS:
Federal and state census records, vital statistics, and records kept by a variety of churches and other organizations are just the beginning of the many storehouses for family historians. The swiftest and most comprehensive research begins at one of the seven NATIONAL ARCHIVES located across the United States. Among other collections, these archives house census collections, region-specific naturalization documents, and passenger lists.

More accessible than a branch of the NATIONAL ARCHIVES and potentially as useful, the thousands of MORMON FAMILY HISTORY CENTERS around the world deliver access to an indexed database of 360 million names. They also provide indexed census records from the United States and other countries that the main branch in Salt Lake City will ship for a nominal fee (see "Searching by Phone").

FEDERAL CENSUS RECORDS - are likely to produce the most accurate and fruitful beginnings for your search. Available at the National Archives and through the Mormon Family History Centers, these records range from the years 1790 to 1920, with a 72-year privacy act protecting the more recent data.

To view the document, you have to determine first off who would have been considered the official head of the household in a given year. Names convert to codes through a system referred to as "soundexing"; the access code then leads directly to the page of the census as it was copied that census year. Listed underneath the family name are the address as well as the ages, countries (and sometimes cities) of origins and birth, and even occupations. Such complete documentation can link parents and children through generations of migrations and expanding family trees.

ARRIVAL RECORDS - New York State began to officially document immigrants in 1855, when ships were docking at Castle Garden, a fort located near Ellis Island, in New York Harbor. Beginning in 1890, as an added means of tracking the thousands of people arriving in this country each year, the federal government became involved in processing immigrants. By 1892, two years after the opening of a federal processing facility in New York, U.S. agents on Ellis Island were routinely asking immigrants for specific places of origin, including cities and sometimes counties or provinces. These arrival records now reside in part at the National Archives and will soon be made available at the Ellis Island research center, which is slated to open by the year 2000.

NATURALIZATION RECORDS - When a law passed by Congress in 1906 turned over naturalization responsibilities to federal courts, the information inscribed on the documents significantly increased. Parents' names and specific cities and regions of origin - even photographs - numbered among the data commonly collected by 1920. Records of naturalization ceremonies performed in a circuit court reside in either the county or state office in the city where the court was convened.

SOCIAL SECURITY - These records may be useful for finding a deceased family member who applied for a Social Security number after 1930. The records, which often contain incomplete or inaccurate data, can be accessed on-line at an interactive site: ssdi2/ancestry.com/ssdi.

PASSENGER LISTS - To aid government researchers interested in knowing where their citizens migrated, Dr. Ira Glazier of the Balsch Institute for Ethnic Studies at Temple University, in Philadelphia, indexed the records of passengers who arrived at U.S. ports from Germany, Italy, and Ireland before government agencies installed documentation systems after the turn of the century.

The passenger list is one of the most important documents for genealogists - it's the link between the Old World and the New." Contained on the microfilmed originals are records indicating names and, at times, cities of origin, the ages of the passengers, and the exact date the embarked and arrived.

The records contain errors, mostly the result of confusion, including the infamous anglicizing and straightforward misspelling of names. Many records, federal census documents included, may have missed your family entirely Keep searching, however, trying alternate spelling and later census years, for example, and something just might turn up that surprises you.

CLOSER TO HOME:
Write letters to city, county, and state offices to locate vital records, including birth, death, and marriage certificates dating primarily from the turn of the century.

You may also discover land deeds and land records, both of which were often kept at a courthouse near the family's first residence. The local judicial authority, such as a county courthouse, also frequently houses naturalization records that were not processed before a federal circuit court. Many church dioceses retain baptism and other records that may hold clues, provided that you know the religion your ancestors practiced and the church where they worshiped.

Many of these sources, however, will not have the resources to assist in genealogical research, and tapping into these wells of information will require more patience and persistence than searching through the National Archives. The best chance of finding what you're looking for is to send a letter to the location, such as a courthouse or church. Indicate the name, dates, and where the person lived, as the more information provided, the better the likelihood of getting a reply.

When the county courthouse reports "records missing", write to the State Archives. With changes in county clerks, they are not always informed when records have been moved, usually as space limits their capacity for storage.

SEARCHING BY PHONE:
Perform the bulk of your initial research in a NATIONAL ARCHIVE, as this will curb the expenses in time and money required by the other avenues.

Possibly the most comprehensive source of genealogical information contained by a nongovernmental agency, the MORMON FAMILY HISTORY CENTERS provide easy access to remote documents. More than 2,800 centers are located around the world, and close to 3,000 visitors per day pour into the center in Salt Lake City. Call (800) 346-6044 for locations and more details.

For sources of family history in other countries, contact the general consulate representing your ancestors' country of origin.

LIVING RELATIVES - To locate a missing relative who is presumed living, requesting a search through the Salvation Army's Missing Person's Bureau may yield results. You'll need to provide the name and a description of the individual; the fee is 425, and the success rate is 31 percent. Call (800) 315-7699.

A VETERAN'S ADMINISTRATION HOSPITAL where a relative might have received treatment can also put you in contact with a living relation. If the person's status remains on file, the VA will forward a letter from you, allowing the relative to respond directly if he or she wishes to do so. These records are confidential and confined to the hospital where the patient was treated.

USING VITAL RECORDS:
Birth certificates and death certificates and other vital records contain valuable information, but they are sometimes expensive to obtain. Before you decide not to order them, keep in mind that they sometimes contain additional information that corroborates or conflicts with your present information, such as surname spellings or different dates.

Each state maintains vital records and decides where to keep them. Death certificates may be in the possession of the county but the state may also have a copy. Sometimes counties transfer their records elsewhere, possibly to the state archives. Therefore you have to know where to look for the records. Ancestry's Redbook as well as Everton's Handybook for Genealogists list every state and where to find records as well as when the county was formed and the years for which records are available. You may also find that information on the Web if you do some searching for the state's web page.

A start at the county in which the event took place should be your first step. A call or a letter to the proper office will usually tell you whether they have the type of record you are looking for and the cost to copy it for you. If they don't have it, they may be able to tell you where to obtain it. Cost could vary depending on whether you need a certified copy or a non-certified copy. Generally, for your research, a non-certified copy will suffice but for legal matters, you may need a certified copy. They both contain the same information.

Keep in mind, that a great deal of records were lost during the Civil War due to fire. The Superintendent of Documents, Government Printing Office, Washington, DC 20402 has an inexpensive and helpful booklet "Where to Write for Vital Records" . When you request your records, be sure to provide complete information. Give the full name, and any other names that the record might be under. If you are not sure of the date, give the closest approximation you can provide - or a range of years.

Delayed birth certificates are common if the person was born prior to the date of keeping records. They were sometimes obtained by the individual so they could obtain other forms of identification such as a passport or to obtain Social Security. Sometimes recent birth records may not be available to you unless you can prove a relationship to the deceased person.

Some states will not provide a birth record at all unless you prove the relationship. If it is your parent, a copy of your own birth record will help. Consider using census records to prove your relationship - or a death certificate if you have one - or an obit. The reasons for these rules, which vary from state to state, is that birth certificates can be used to obtain a new identity by obtaining driver's licenses, passports, etc.

Keep in mind when obtaining death certificates, they are only as good as the person's knowledge who gives the information. A child or a sibling would probably be more aware of the facts than a neighbor or a friend who may not know all the facts.

Marriage licenses are sometimes the only proof of a marriage - but keep in mind, the marriage may or may not have taken place. Sometimes you can find a church record to confirm that the marriage occurred.

More and more records are being transcribed, published in books and/or placed on the web but remember, in transcribing them - they are subject to errors on the part of the transcriber.

TO DOWNLOAD FREE CHARTS AND FORMS GO TO: http://www.ancestrycorner.com/

ROOTSWEB'S GUIDE TO TRACING FAMILY TREES. For an index and links that will help "jump-start" pursuit of your ancestors in 2000, see: http://www.rootsweb.com/~rwguide/

THIS AND THAT GENEALOGY TIPS ON VALLEY FORGE

AN INFORMATIVE VIEW OF MILITARY SERVICE AT VALLEY FORGE:
Although you may not have HARDWICK in your line... the below should be interesting for its content regarding military service at Valley Forge during the Revolution. George Hardwick is not mine either but I haven't come across any military file from the National Archives that gave me so much information of general interest. Following is the transcript of pension file for Pvt. George Hardwick (#S.8674) who served from Lawrence Co., KY. Apparently George was born Aug 31, 1759 in Amherst Co., VA and while a resident of Bedford Co., VA he enlisted Apr 1777.

"On the 13th day of Mar 1834, personally appeared before the undersigned a Justice of the Peace for said county now sitting, George Hardwick, resident in the county of Lawrence and state of Kentucky, aged seventy-five years, who being first duly sworn according to law, doth on his oath make the following declaration in order to obtain the benefit of an act of Congress dated Jun 7, 1832, that he entered the service of the United States under the following named officers and served as herein stated. To wit, under Col. Lynch and Captain George Lambert in Apr 1777 in Bedford Co., Virginia. The object was to join the northern Army. Lambert was a recruiting officer. He had recruited in Amherst Co., Virginia, he and Harman King and William Parish enlisted in state troops of Virginia for two years at the place and time before set forth (Apr 1777), he was immediately after the company filed (?) marched to Amherst Co., Virginia, from there to Albermarle to the barracks, from this place he was marched to the north to join the army under Washington. Before the Virginia troops reached the Potomac they all united, there was some difficulty about crossing the river. At length they all got over safe and went over into the State of Maryland and crossed a river some distance in that state, the name of which he has forgotten. After some time he was marched into the State of Pennsylvania near Lancaster and crossed the Susquehannah River in that state and the Schoolkile also, or rather went down it and in June he was marched into the city of Philadelphia. The British were about this time on their way to take Philadelphia. The most of the regular army were then in New Jersey that joins Pennsylvania, thence many regiments of Militia daily arriving. He was not quartered right in the city but was quartered in the suburb of the city. He remained but a short time. He was then marched over into the state of New Jersey and joined the army from New Jersey. The which army crossed a large river and in July or August he thinks the British marched toward Philadelphia. In the same month the two armies had a desperate battle ensued in which the Americans were defeated. He was in the battle of Germantown in the same year in which place the American forces were also defeated. The British were now in possession of Philadelphia and kept it that year. The American army marched off the battle ground and left the British in the possession of Germantown and no more battles ensued that year between Washington and the British Troops. During that year he staid in winter quarters at Valley Forge where his Captain Lambert was tried for stealing a hat and was ? and he left the army. This will be found to be the fact by reference to his case. This applicant was permitted to come home to Virginia to see his parents. He did so and came home with Captain Lambert. Many came home on paroles to see their friends and families. He has forgotten the month he got back but believes it was in Mar 1778. He remained at home he thinks about 4 or perhaps 5 weeks when he returned to the service. Those belonging to Virginia in upper counties in Campbell, Prince Edward and Bedford Co. that were out on parole were ordered to join Capt. Nathaniel Rice, an officer belonging to the Virginia establishment. He went into the service under him at Prince Edward Courthouse, Virginia. From there he was marched directly to old Jamestown on the River and marched for the North to headquarters. He marched through Maryland into Pennsylvania though by the way of Wilmington in Delaware or Pennsylvania, he forgets which. He then marched to Philadelphia the American army having made them give that place up. He came up with the main army after incessant marching under General Washington. This was but two days before the battle of Monmouth in which he was in. This battle was faught sometime in the summer of 1778. In July he thinks, but the length of time being so long, he cannot remember positively everything or one tenth that occurred for he was young and soldiers knew nothing but the order of their officers. From this place he was marched back to Philadelphia where he remained until October 1778 when he was marched with many of the Virginia troops back to that state. He marched directly to Prince Edward where the troops arrived early in the winter. The troops brought along with them some British prisoners and there being so also at Prince Edward Courthouse where there was a barracks kept. He guarded the prisoners in the barracks at Prince Edward Courthouse until his time expired. The spring following he thinks in April or May 1779, he was discharged from the service of the state for two years service and his discharge was signed by Nathan Rice at Prince Edward Courthouse 2 yrs.

In the Spring 1780, in March, a call was made for men to engage to go to Kentucky which at that time was a part of Virginia. He engaged as a volunteer under Capt. Charles Gwatkins (?). His name was always pronounced Watkins but he spelled his name Gwatkins. The company consisted of thirty-three men. It was in Bedford the company started from. Gwatkins lived in that county also in March 1780 as ? he marched across the blue ridge and through the western part of Virginia, crossed New River and marched on to Powels? Valley. There was in this valley but a few settlers and they were chiefly all ?. He states there was no settlement from Cumberland Gap to Boonsboro on the Kentucky River, a distance between one and two hundred miles and that an entire wilderness. On the way the company would sometimes keep ? old track, but generally keep off of it for fear of the Indians. He at length arrived at Boonsboro in the month of April 1780 about the 20th. The buckeye and sugar trees were the only timber? Col. Boone was in the first ? and Col. Dick Callaway also. There was not more than thirty? men in the first ? and the company of Gwatkins who was a son-in-law of Col. Dick Callaway, was raised for the express purpose of protecting Boonsboro.

The Company divided into scouting parties and while the settlers were at work making corn? the powder had got scarce and he was sent up to three? forks of Kentucky River at a salt? cave about 2 miles up the north fork and on the north side of the Kentucky River but three went, to wit Elaunders Callaway a brothers son of Col. Callaway and Benjamin Dunaway. This was in the month of July 1780. We arrived at the afso place and worked hard and made enough powder to do the fort. The powder was carried down in a canoe down the Kentucky river during this time? No Indians molested us from making powder. In Sep 1780 we got back to the fort and continued to scout until the leaves were all fallen. The Indians did not annoy or attack the fort or kill any of the settlers that winter 1780 but in Oct past he went with Boone to the Blue Licks at the lower to make salt forts? and the Indians broke us up and took several and all the kettles. He returned to Boonsboro by himself through the woods and this winter he stayed there and as he has before stated, no interference took place with fort by the Indians either to the fort or the settlement around. He remained guarding the fort and on constant duty until his time of service expired in March 1781. He received his discharge from Qwatkins at Boonsboro. He knew during his service in the fort many officers and persons that he will not mention a few of them. Col Callaway, Col Ben Logan were all the officers in commission that were in the fort. Sometime there were many private individuals who sometimes acted as officers but who were not commissioned as he understood. John Holder, Nicholas Anderson, John Smith, Michael Stoner, Flanders Calaway, Simon Kenton, Whitson George, John George and Squire Boone. Many others that he could not mention as a great many persons moved to Kentucky in the year 1780. A man by the name of Hoy? he during this last years service after he got into the district of Kentucky, marched only in Kentucky. The circumstances of his service are as above detailed. He served with no Continental Regiments or companies during his service.

In the month of May 1781 he went back to Virginia to Bedford Co., Virginia. He in August 1781 substituted for three months for David Wade (Wadetown?) under Capt. Jacob Moon?. Col. Blueford? was William Williams the place of ? was at new Sondon? in Campbell once in Bedford. And from this place he marched as hard as he could to York. His company marched directly for the American army. The militia was flocking in every day. On the 12th of Sep he joined the American line under Washington and the French Officer where he remained during the whole siege and until Lord Cornwualles (sic) surrendered. He witnessed the surrender. He was not in the storm of Pigeon Hole ? which took place a few days before the surrender but was in all the balance of the conflict during the time the siege lasted. After the surrender he was marched with some prisoners to Albermarle Barracks and there deposited them and on Nov 19th day he received his discharge for his three months of substitution for David Wade. That discharge he gave to Mr. Wade on his return to Bedford. He knew many continental officers and regiments. He knew Gen. Lafayette, Gen. Sloling?, Gen. Cadwalenden?, Gen. Smallwood, Col. Ben Williams, Gen. Locke?, Gen. Mullenburg?, Col. Blueford and many others that he has seen. The ? between an officer and soldier was such as not to leave very expressive recollection about them. There was no intimacy between a soldier and an officer. He has no documentary evidence in his favor. His discharge was destroyed in Clark Co., Kentucky on ? and every paper he had were destroyed by fire. Which fact are well known to the Hon. Henry Daniel, the former representative to Congress and by Amos Davis the present. ? he thinks knowing the fact from having heard so ever since he was a boy, and many others. He hereby relinquishes every claim whatever to a pension and annuity except the present and declares his name is not on the pension role of the agency of any state. Sworn to and subscribed the day and year aforesaid.

Where and in what year were you born? Ans. In Amherst Co., Virginia on the 31st of Aug 1759.

229

Have you any record of your age and if so where is it? Ans. He had which was taken from his fathers record in his Bible which was burnt in his home in Clark, Kentucky.

How were you called into service? Were you drafted? Did you volunteer or were you a substitute and if a substitute, for whom? Ans. By enlistment for two years the first time. I volunteered for 1 year the second time and a substitute for David Wade the third.

State the names of some of the regular officers who were with the troops where you served such continental and militia regiments as you recollect and the ? circumstances of your service? Ans. When the army in Philadelphia, Pennsylvania, Maryland, Delaware and New Jersey, he saw very many regular officers to wit Gen. Heath, Gen. Sterling(?), Col. Lee, Gen. Lee, Gen. Greene, Gen. Lawson, Col. Morgan, Gen. Mercer(?), Gen. Williams, Maj. Anderson, Capt. John H. Allen, and many brigadiers? Besides there was Col. Cateron?, Maj. Callow?, Col. McBride, Col. Dasfield, Col. Bradford, Col. Stansbury, Col. Johnson, Col. Henry T. Clary, Capt. John Garfe?, Col. Clayton, Capt. Jesse Kincaid, Col. Buford, Col. Mays, Col. Paxton, Col. Moore, Col. Dawson, Capt. Rice, Col. Brown, Col. Smith, Maj. James, Capt. John T. Dean, Capt. Robert T. Dollyhom, Col. Pikring?, Col. Chiles?, all belonging to the militia regiments. Some lived in Pennsylvania, some in New Jersey, some in Virginia, some in Maryland and Connecticut as he was told. When he Kentucky he knew Gen. Clark, Col. Boone, Col. Frig? and ? were killed in the battle of the blue licks. He was in that battle also. The circumstances of his service are these. In 1777 he enlisted in Bedford Co., Virginia for two years. He was marched to the north. He was in Philadelphia before and after it was taken by the British, he was in the Battle of Germantown, Monmouth and also at Brandywine under Gen. Wayne and he wintered one winter at the Valley Forge where the American army wintered. He was in the service 2 years the first time and was discharged at Prince Edward Courthouse in Virginia. He volunteered and went to Kentucky to the relief of Boonsborough in 1780 and served there one year and came home to Virginia and substituted three months time for David Wade and was at the siege of York when Cornwallis was taken. He was discharged at Albermarle Barracks and then came to Bedford.

War Dept. Pension Office - The evidence in support of your claim under Act of June 7, 1832 has been examined and the papers are herewith returned.

George was allowed pension on his application Mar 13, 1834.

CONTINENTAL ARMY AT VALLEY FORGE:
An archaeological study has shed more light on the daily life of the foot soldier who formed the bulk of the Continental Army wintering at Valley Forge.

Most are familiar with the story of how the poorly clad soldiers suffered through the cruel winter of 1777-1778 huddled in wooden huts, while snow lay 6" on the ground. The park at Valley Forge, Pennsylvania through exhibits and reconstructions, shows how the Continental Army came in as a ragtag group of unorganized farmers and shop owners and left as a well-trained fighting force.

Valley Forge has lots of records about what the officers had at dinner, their parties, and what George Washington was doing, but virtually no record of what the man in the army had to live on.

A new study, in a wooded, grassy area in the center of the park, used relatively non-invasive techniques, along with some excavation, to locate the billets of soldiers. The information gleaned has helped archaeologists and historians determine the internal structure of the army units.

When the army arrived at Valley Forge, outside of Philadelphia on December 19, 1777, there were about 12,000 soldiers, plus thousands more wives, children and camp followers. It was the third largest English-speaking settlement in the country. In the winter, numbers fell because of death from typhus, typhoid, dysentery and pneumonia, from desertions, or leave granted to those who lived nearby. During the spring of 1778, the ranks swelled again to about 18,000 when Valley Forge became a staging area for the summer campaign. It was not a randomly-built encampment, but one structured in a series of about 16 brigades. The area of archaeological investigation was a 150 x 600 ft. area occupied by Conway's Brigade. There were about 700 people there and they quartered them at least 10 people to a hut. Officers lived slightly apart. It is estimated that there were about 80 or 90 of those huts, but only six were found. Some huts were 7 ft x 10 ft and others were 20 ft x 10 ft. Still others were 16 ft. x 18 ft.

The artifacts found were extremely unspectacular. Ceramics were mostly fragments of common locally produced bowls known as redware. In 2 of 4 garbage pits uncovered there were animal bones and one fish spine. At the time, the shad came up the Schuylkill River nearby to spawn. Folklore has it that the British down river in Philadelphia tried to build a fish dam to keep the fish from coming upriver to feed the soldiers at Valley Forge.

Researchers did find that all their food remains were boiled or burned until they were tiny fragments, so they were getting every last bit out of everything they got. They had a pretty hard winter there.

In one hut they found a 6" cannon ball in the base of a fireplace. Presumably they were using that to retain heat so when the fire ran low the heat absorbed by the cannonball was radiated back into the hut.

With plenty of time on their hands until mid-June when the dirt roads finally dried out for the summer campaign, the soldiers spent their time making musket balls. A lot of little blobs of lead were found. Also found was about 40 buttons or fragments, but only two with any decoration. Most buttons were made of pewter, a cheap metal that deteriorates quickly in the ground.

The Continental Army couldn't afford anything better than the absolute minimum of necessities as evidenced by the plain, simple, ungarish, low level of material wealth that they possessed there.

SOCIETY OF DESCENDANTS OF WASHINGTON'S ARMY AT VALLEY FORGE:
Direct descendants over 18 years of age of a soldier serving in the U. S. Continental Army at Valley Forge under Gen. George Washington during 1777-1778 are eligible to join the Society of the Descendants of Washington's Army at Valley Forge, PO Box 915, Valley Forge, PA 19482-0915.

THIS AND THAT GENEALOGY TIPS FROM VARIOUS STATES

ALABAMA:

NATIVE AMERICAN TRIBES - If you have a genealogical or historical interest in the Indian tribes indigenous to Alabama -- Cherokee, Choctaw, Chickasaw, and Creek Nations, visit the Ethnic Groups - Native American page of ALGenWeb, part of the USGenWeb Project. Webmaster David W. Morgan, dmorgon@efn.org, has done an excellent job of compiling links to information about these tribes as well as to some general resources for Native American research: http://www.rootsweb.com/~algenweb/nativeam.html

FRANKLIN:

Have you located ancestors living in the state of Franklin in the 1784-1788 time period? This territory, belonging to North Carolina, was known as the State of Franklin for four years. Approval for statehood was denied by Congress in 1788, and in 1789, the colony ceded the territory to USA. From these lands the state of Tennessee was formed.

ILLINOIS:

The Illinois State Archives, Springfield, IL 62756 will respond to requests for genealogy help. Write to them for their brochure on details. They do not require a SASE and charge only $1.00 per record if they find your record. Two requests will be researched at a time in a specific record, i.e. census, military records, etc.

Request their brochure on Illinois Regional Archives Repository System (IRAD). Many Illinois records have been deposited in 6 IRAD depositories throughout Illinois and they accept requests for help by mail. Holdings vary from depository to depository but you may find Assessor's Books, Circuit Court Records, Collector's Books, Deed Records, Election Records, Land Sale Records, Occupational Registers, Probate Records, School Records, Occupational Registers, Probate Records, School Records and Wills. You may request from the Illinois State Archives a list of the holdings of five counties at a time.

The Illinois State Archives has acquired 102 rolls of film index to War of 1812 pension application files found in the National Archives. Each frame of the film shows the face of an envelope which gives the name of the veteran, name of his widow if any, service data, pension application and certificate numbers and/or a bounty land warrant application number if any. Copies of the relevant documents in the envelope may be obtained by writing to the National Archives. The Illinois State Archives will search the index and send a photocopy of the envelope if found. Send requests to Illinois State Archives, Springfield, IL 62756.

Illinois State Archives has indexed names of men who served in the Illinois units during Indian Wars, Civil War and Spanish American War.

KENTUCKY:

During and after the Revolution thousands of settlers poured over the Appalachians filling the region which was to become Tennessee and Kentucky, the firs states to be added to the original thirteen. Kentucky, created in 1792, was taken from land claimed by Virginia and is therefore a state-land state. East of the Tennessee River land was surveyed using the metes and bounds system. Entry into Blue Grass Kentucky was via the Ohio River on the north and by Daniel Boone's Wilderness Road from the Cumberland Gap on the east. Following the 1774 defeat of the Shawnees in Lord Dunsmore's War only the Cherokees presented an obstacle. Many early settlers were revolutionary veterans following the enticements of land speculators such as Richard Henderson and his Transylvania Company. Many Kentuckians were veterans of the War of 1812. Kentucky grants are normally categorized as: Virginia Grants (1782-1892 which include some for French and Indian War service; Old Kentucky Grants (1793-1856); Governor's Grants (1816-1873) for land east of the Tennessee River; Grants south of the Green River (1797-1866 for Virginia Revolutionary veterans and squatters; Grants West of the Tennessee River (1822-1858) which were given after Indian cessions; Tellico Grants (1805-1853) of Cherokee land in the eastern regions; Grants South of Walker's Line (1825-1923) which were located in Tennessee, and; County Court orders (1836-1948) which sold unowned land within county boundaries. Original records are in the Kentucky Land Office and the Kentucky Historical Society in

Frankfort. The standard reference is Willard R. Jillson, The Kentucky Land Grants, two volumes, which contain abstracts of over 150,000 grants. Land records should be used in conjunction with the Kentucky Tax Rolls created at county-level between 1780-1870. They have surprisingly few gaps and make excellent census substitutes. They are available on microfilm.

STATE MILITIA AND CIVIL WAR:
All records regarding the Kentucky State Militia from the Civil War era are with the Kentucky Military History Museum. Kentucky created a militia in 1860 (the former one being disbanded in 1840). In 1861, the entire state militia was supposed to muster at Camp Boone for drilling, however, the outbreak of the Civil War put an end to that, and muster rolls were, therefore, not turned in that year. Muster rolls do exist for 1862, 1863 and 1865; those from 1864 were lost or burned. Later, the county clerks only had to turn in numbers and not names. As far as these muster rolls are concerned, they are "merely" alphabetical listings of names by county and such. No other details accept generalizations about the men being of good character, etc. In only a few instances were any of these state militia groups actually "called out" by the governor; for these more detailed records may exist (they were "in the field" from 30 to 60 days.) None of these are on microfilm. Although many of these men weren't activated, the commanders still corresponded with the state leadership etc. If you want to look at these records, call (502) 564-5823 and make your request. There were some pictures at the museum that were taken at Camp Boone from the Civil War era of some units, commanders, etc.

If you receive a reply from a Kentucky county courthouse saying that the records you are seeking are "missing" try writing to the Kentucky Archives in Frankfort. While some records are missing, many have been moved to the Archives because the local courthouses do not have the space or the facilities for the records. Many records have been microfilmed.

With changes in County Clerks, the present clerk may not be aware that those records have been moved to Frankfort. Write: Kentucky Dept. of Library and Archives, 300 Coffee Tree Rd., PO Box 537, Frankfort, KY 40602 when courthouses are unable to locate the records you needs. (California Archives have similar situations as probably do other states).

MISSOURI:
The earliest settlement was along the Missouri river, following Lewis and Clark. Many of the earliest settlers were Southerners, principally from TN and KY, to such an extent that it was called "Little Dixie". The role of rivers as major transportation routes was significant. Later migration into Missouri was a mix of Northerners and Southerners. A population density map of the "colored presence" from the 1850 census is revealing in that it is much higher along the Missouri River than the rest of the state, which of course had profound implications on the pre-war slavery issue and the Civil War itself, and reflected the migration routes over time.

Another interesting factor with respect to the Ozarks is that people tended to seek out places like "back home" . Hence, the Ozarks attracted people who originated from the Appalachians - VA, NC, TN, KY. But it also attracted folks from the upper eastern Midwest - OH, IN, IL, who themselves had earlier come from Appalachia. In this migration route, the National Road played a big part. This was in a sense the first federal "Interstate". After winding its way through the mountains of PA, it ran a virtually arrow-straight course through OH, IN and IL, almost, but not quite to St. Louis.

A & P RAILROAD LAND - January 11, 1873 Rockport Indiana Journal Weekly - "The Atlantic and Pacific Railroad Company offers 1,200,000 acres of land in central and southwest Missouri at from $3. to $12. per acre on 7 years time with free transportation from St. Louis to all purchasers. Climate, soil, timber, mineral wealth, schools, churches and law abiding society invite emigrants from all points to this land of fruits and flowers".

STATE ARCHIVES will perform record searches free of charge and you can send your request by e-mail. It must be a specific request, only one at a time, and takes 2-4 weeks for a reply. Go here for instructions and the e-mail address: http://mosl.sos.state.mo.us/rec-man/archweb/emailpol.html

These URLs's describe the archives holdings:
RESOURCES FOR FAMILY & COMMUNITY HISTORY -
http://mosl.sos.state.mo.us/rec-man/archweb/history.html

MISSOURI BIRTH AND DEATH RECORDS 1883-1893 - http://mosl.sos.state.mo.us/rec-man/mobdrecs.html

MISSOURI STATE ARCHIVES MAIN PAGE - http://mosl.sos.state.mo.us/rec-man/arch.html

NEW YORK:
 LOCAL HISTORIANS - State law provides for a local historian in each town, city, village and county in the state.
For the address of one in your area of interest, send SASE to State Historian, State Education Bldg., Albany, NY
12207.

VIRGINIA:
The first permanent English settlement in North America was established on the shores of Virginia. Twelve years later,
in 1619, Jamestown was the meeting place of the first representative assembly in the New World. At about the same
time, the colony's destiny as a settlement for the families, rather than a military outpost, was shaped when the Virginia
Company of London sent several shipments of mail-order brides in return for payment in tobacco for the women's
passage.

This settlement was not the first in America though.   An early British colony was established at Roanoke Island,
presently part of North Carolina, in 1584 by Sir Walter Raleigh. This colony of over 100 people mysteriously
disappeared by 1591, leaving behind only the word "Croatoan" (the name of a nearby island) carved on a tree.
Of the 17th century colonies on the Atlantic coast of North America, England founded all but two, the first being
Jamestown and the second settlement was at Plymouth in 1620 and that colony was absorbed by Massachusetts in
1691.

In May 1607, during the reign of James I of England, three ships arrived along a marshy peninsula 30 miles inland from
Chesapeake Bay. The men who went ashore the next day founded the first permanent English settlement in America,
named Jamestown, for the English king. The tiny colony established by the Virginia Co. of London, almost failed
during its first years. The new governor, Lord De la Warr (Delaware) arrived with supplies in 1610, just as the colony
was being deserted. The pioneers fared better after 1612 when tobacco cultivation was introduced. At the time of
founding of Jamestown in 1607, the largest group of Native Americans in the area were the Powhaten Confederacy.
These were the Woodland Indians, led by Chief Powhaten, and the European colonists learned about tobacco
cultivation from them.

Virginia was named for the Virgin Queen, Elizabeth I of England. As the first of the 13 original colonies, Virginia
played a dominant role in the leadership of the country. For centuries, the issue of equal rights presented a major
challenge to the state. Virginia, after all, had been the primary site for the development of black slavery in the
Americas. In 1672, the king of England chartered the Royal African Co. to bring the shiploads of slaves into trading
centers like Jamestown, Hampton and Yorktown.

Most of the original white population of Virginia stems from two immigrant groups. In the Tidewater section, nearly
all the early settlers were English colonists. The other group consisted of Germans and Scots-Irish.

The British colonies on the western shores of the Atlantic were founded and developed in a variety of circumstances
during the seventeenth and eighteenth centuries: as a result their legal status and administrative arrangements followed
no common pattern. Control by the authorities in London was seldom close and in some colonies, at some periods,
almost nonexistent. Local government was generally conducted by officials of the colonies themselves, and the records
thereof are preserved, if they survive, in the appropriate state archive, where any inquiry should first be pursued.

The responsible authorities in London were the Secretaries of State and the Board of Trade. Of the two Secretaries, it was the Secretary of State for the Southern Department who was primarily, if not exclusively, charged with the oversight of colonial administrations, except for the period between 1768 and 1782, when a third Secretary of State, the Colonial or American Secretary, was appointed. For much executive action, advice and routine administration, however, the Secretaries were dependent on the Lords of Trade and Plantations, commonly known as the Board of Trade. The Board was founded in 1696 to succeed a variety of bodies with similar titles and overlapping jurisdictions which had existed at various periods since 1660. Its functions were originally purely advisory, but came in time to include much of the administration of the colonies, and to its offices at Plantations House were addressed many of the papers now in the Public Record Office.

ORIGIN OF THE NAMES OF THE STATES:

ALABAMA - was named in 1817, from its principal river. The origin of the word is doubtful. One authority states that De Soto's last battle was in 1541 at Alibamo, on the Yazoo River, where there was a strong fortress of a tribe called sometimes the Alibamos, and sometimes the Alabamas. Le Clerc, who resided with the Creek Indians for 20 years, says that the Alibamos came to Yazoo from the north part of Mexico, and that after the battle with De Soto, they removed to the river which now bears their name.

ALASKA - is from the Indian word Alakshak, meaning large country.

ARIZONA - is supposed to be from the Aztec word, "Arizuma," meaning rocky country.

ARKANSAS - took its name in 1819 from its principal river and the river from the tribe of Indians once living near its mouth. Schoolcraft thinks the names come from a species of acacia growing there and of which the Indians made bows, which led to the apellation of "arc or bow Indians."

CALIFORNIA - takes its name from a Spanish romance, in which was described "the great island of California, where a great abundance of gold and precious stones are found." The officers of Cortez, fancying the word, gave it to the Pacific Coast state in 1535.

CAROLINA (North and South) - was so called in 1654 by the French, in honor of Charles IX. of France, some say Charles I. of England. There is good reason for questioning the accuracy of this derivation.

COLORADO - is another state named for its chief river. Colorado is a Spanish word, meaning "ruddy" or "colored."

CONNECTICUT - was so called from the Indian name of its principal river, spelled Quinneh-tukyut meaning "land on a long tidal river."

DELAWARE - was so called in 1703, from Delaware Bay, on which it lies, and which received its name from Lord de la Warr, who died in this bay.

FLORIDA - was so called by Juan Ponce de Leon in 1512, because it was discovered on Easter Sunday, in Spanish Pascua Florida.

GEORGIA - was so called in 1732, in honor of George II.

HAWAII - was named originally by Capt. James Cook in 1778, the Sandwich Islands. It became The Republic of Hawaii Jul 4, 1894.

IDAHO - is the Indian word for "gem of the mountains."

ILLINOIS - was so called in 1809, from its principal river. The word is said by Gallatin to signify "superior men."

INDIANA - was so called in 1802 from the American Indians.

IOWA - took its name in 1838 from the tribe of Indians who lived within its borders. The word is said to be a contraction of the word Ah-hee-oo-ba, meaning "seepers."

KANSAS - takes its name from its great river, which in turn received its appellation from the tribe of Indians along its banks. The name is said to come from "Cayas," which was given the region by De Soto.

KENTUCKY - was so called in 1782, from the principal river. Several meanings are given to the word, the correct one probably being "at the head of a river."

LOUISIANA - was so called by La Salle in 1682, in honor of King Louis XIV of France.

MAINE - was so called as early as 1622, from the description in the charter calling it the "Mayne land" meaning the main or chief portion of the territory.

MARYLAND - was so called in honor of Henrietta Maria, queen of Charles I, in his patent to Lord Baltimore, June 30, 1632.

MASSACHUSETTS - derived its name from a tribe of Indians in the neighborhood of Boston. The word is a compound of "massa" meaning great, and wadchuash," meaning hills or mountains.

MICHIGAN - was so called in 1865, from the lake on its borders. The meaning of the word is undecided. It is believed to be derived from the Chippewa word "Mitcha" and the Algonquin word "gan," the two meaning "great lake."

MINNESOTA - takes the name of its chief stream, which is from the Indian word Mini-sotah, meaning "slightly turbid water."

MISSISSIPPI - was named in 1790, from the great stream on its eastern border. Mr. Gallatin says the word is from two Indian words, "missi," meaning all, and "sippi," meaning river - the two meaning "all." or "the whole river." because many streams unite in making it.

MISSOURI - was so called in 1821, from its principal river, from the Sioux word meaning "muddy water."

MONTANA - took its name from the Rocky Mountains which traverse the state.

NEBRASKA - is also named after its principal river. The meaning of the word is in doubt, one authority saying it is composed from the Indian words "nee," meaning river, and "braska," meaning shallow. Another authority says the Platte river in the Kaw dialect is Ne-blas-ka, signifying overspreading flats with shallow water.

NEVADA - is named for its mountain chain, which resembles the Sierra Nevadas of Granada, and was named after them.

NEW HAMPSHIRE - was the name given to the territory conveyed by the Plymouth company to Capt. John Mason by patent Nov. 7, 1739, with reference to the patentee, who was governor of Portsmouth, in Hampshire, England.

NEW JERSEY - (originally called New Sweden) was so named in 1644, in compliment to Sir George Carteret one of its original proprietors, who had defended the island of Jersey against the long parliament during the civil war of England.

NEW MEXICO - takes its name from the Aztec word, "Mexitll," the name of the war god of the people.

NEW YORK - (originally called New Netherlands) was so called in reference to the duke of York and Albany, to whom this territory was granted in 1664.

OHIO - was so called in 1802, from its southern boundary. The word is 0-he-zuh, meaning "something great."

OKLAHOMA - is from the Indian word meaning a beautiful land.

OREGON - was the name first applied to the Columbia River, and then to the territory. It is supposed to be a Sioux word, meaning a "great flowing river."

PENNSYLVANIA - was so called in 1681, after William Penn, the founder of Philadelphia "Penn Sylva," "Penn's wood."

RHODE ISLAND - was so called in 1644, from the Dutch Roode Eylandt, signifying "red island," a name given it by the early Dutch explorers.

TENNESSEE - was so called in 1796, from its principal river. The word Tennessee is said to signify a curved spoon or a bend in the river.

TEXAS - so called by the Spaniards in 1690, who in that year drove out a colony of French who had established themselves at Matagorda and made their first permanent settlement. The word is of doubtful origin. It is said to be derived from the Spanish word "tigas," signifying covered houses, and also to be derived from the Indian word "tachies," meaning friends. Texas was also called Teyas in early days.

The DAKOTAS - took their name from the tribe of Indians which had its former habitat in the vast region embracing Montana, the Dakotas, and Minnesota. The word was originally spelled Dahkotah, meaning "leagued."

UTAH - also adopted the name of the tribe of Indians formerly living in the region. The name was variously spelled Uta, Utah, Ute or Youta.

VERMONT - was so called by the inhabitants in their declaration of independence Jan. 16, 1777, from the French vert, green, and mont, mountain.

VIRGINIA - was so called in 1584, after Elizabeth, the virgin queen of England.

WASHINGTON - was named in honor of the first president of the U.S.

WEST VIRGINIA - When Virginia ceded from the Union in 1861, western counties objected and 50 united to form "The Restored Government of Virginia" and petitioned Congress for re-admittance to the Union. It was admitted into the Union in 1863 after Union victories in the area cleared out the Confederates.

WISCONSIN - was so named in 1836, from the river of the same name, when a territorial government was formed. The word is said to mean "westward flowing."

WYOMING - bears an Indian name the word being a corruption of Maughwauwame, meaning "large plains."

FINDING ANY CITY OR COUNTY IN ANY STATE IN THE U.S.:
To find the location of any city and/or county within any state, go to the following and choose the state you want. From there you can select Cities and Towns or Counties to find out where the location is:
http://www.com/hpi/us50/index.html

Here's a URL that will help you with information on how to obtain vital record information from every state:
http://vitalrec.com/index.html#USMap

THIS AND THAT GENEALOGY TIPS ON WARS AND MILITARY INFORMATION

Remnants of records exist for every war, but there is little uniformity of content or style in the records. The Revolutionary War Pension Applications at times, may include copies of the family Bible, listing marriage records and births of the children, place of enlistment, unit of service and places of residence following the war.

When the U. S. declared war against Great Britain in 1812, Congress authorized the President to increase the size of the regular military establishment, to accept and organize volunteers, to raise units of Rangers and Sea Fencibles, and to create a Flotilla Service. Many of the War of 1812 volunteer units were mustered into service for short periods of time. Consequently, many persons served more than one enlistment in the same or different units. Search the Index to Compiled Service Records of Volunteer Soldiers Who Served During the War of 1812.

Military Bounty Land Warrants were certificates issued to eligible veterans giving them rights to free land in the public domain. Officers and soldiers serving for 5 years (unless discharged sooner), or their heirs, would be entitled to 160 acres of land from the public domain. Six million acres of land were reserved for this purpose in the Territories of Michigan, Illinois, Louisiana (present day Arkansas) and later Missouri. The warrants could not be transferred or assigned to another person, except by inheritance. These are four indexes; Alphabetical Index of Missouri Patentees, Alphabetical Index of Arkansas Patentees, Partial Index of Illinois Patentees (for those whose surnames begin with letters "C" and "D", Index of Patentees Under the Act of 1842.

In the decades after the War of 1812, volunteer units often served during Indian hostilities. Various legislative acts reimbursed the states and territories for the service of volunteer units, and the men who served, or their heirs, received bounty land and sometimes pensions.

Compiled military service records of volunteer soldiers serving in the various Indian campaigns generally do not contain personal papers for officers or enlisted men.

Records for soldiers who served during the last 75 years are restricted to immediate family members. Most of these federal records are housed at the National Personnel Records Center, 9700 Page Blvd, St. Louis, MO 63132.

On July 12, 1973, fire broke out at the National Personnel Records Centers in St. Louis, destroying millions of military records and damaging millions more. Eighty percent of the army records for 1912-59, sixty percent of the air force records for 1947-63 and one percent or less of Army records for personnel discharged since 1 January 1973 were destroyed. Other military records were housed at the Federal Archives and Records Center in Atlanta, and were not destroyed. As a partial substitute for the lost records, the Atlanta Branch of the National Archives has the WWI Draft Card application cards. They are set up by state and selective service region. It is necessary for you to have the full name of the individual, city or county where registered, birth date and place and name of wife or nearest relative. For Chicago, a home or street address is required. Write to: National Archives, 1557 St. Joseph Ave., East Point, GA 30344.

Some Civil War records obtained from the National Archives contain little genealogical information. A researcher then applied to the state Archives in which the soldier served and received documents with much additional information.

MILITARY RANK:
Private; Private 2nd Class (ordnance), Matross (artillery) and Rifleman (Rifle Battalion or Regiment).

Private 1st Class: Ordnance only

Corporal

Sergeant

First Sergeant (Senior Sgt in the company)

Some staff positions were filled by Sergeant Major, Quartermaster Sergeant, Hospital Steward.

Two confusing terms commonly encountered are line and staff. Line troops, commissioned and enlisted, were those actually on the firing line during the Revolution the term "line" was frequently used to refer to Army National Troops were the Continental Line, etc. Staff positions are usually found beginning with a regiment. An organization as large as a regiment is too big for the commander to take care of all the details. These commander's would have a group of assistants, called his staff, who would take care of matters of supply, administration, etc. in the commander's name.

Another area of possible confusion is the difference between enlist and muster-in, and discharge and muster-out. When a soldier joined a state regiment he was enlisted. when his regiment was taken into Federal service, he was mustered-in. If at any time he left service while his regiment was on active duty, he was discharged. If he was still with the regiment when it was released from Federal service, he was mustered out.

SUTLER: A man who followed a regiment to sell necessary items to the soldiers. This was changed when Sutlers became official on 19 March 1862. They were replaced by the Post Exchange after the Civil War.

ZOUAVE: A special type of infantry copied from French North African regiments. Zouaves were noted for their precision drill, fast marching pace and gaudy uniforms (usually with baggy pants).

SAPPERS and PIONEERS: Specialized forms of Engineer troops.

RIFLEMEN: Until the Mexican War our Infantry was armed with the smooth bore musket, with selected men armed with a rifle and in special companies. After 1846 all infantry had a rifle, but some regiments kept the title Rifle Regiment as a mark of distinction.

BREVET: An officer who distinguished himself would be awarded a Brevet promotion. A Captain could be Brevet Major or Lt.Col while serving as a Captain. He would outrank all other Captains without Brevet, thus giving him an edge on future promotions.

ASSOCIATORS: Volunteers who had sworn to protect their homes by any means.

RANGERS: Scouts who guarded the frontier and were usually formed from the militia who were the "home guard", along with the "State Line," these were similar to the National Guard.

VETERAN'S PENSIONS:
Regarding granting pensions to certain enlisted men, soldiers, and officers who served in the Civil War and the War with Mexico. The Act: be it enacted by the Senate and House of Representatives of the United States of America in Congress assembled: That any person who served ninety days or more in the military or naval service of the United States during the late civil war, or sixty days in the war with Mexico, and has been honorably discharged therefrom, and who has reached the age of sixty-two years or over, shall, upon making proof of such facts according to such rules and regulations as the Secretary of the Interior may provide, be placed upon the pension roll, and be entitled to receive a pension as follows: In case such person has reached the age of sixty-two years, twelve dollars a month; seventy years, fifteen dollars a month; seventy-five years or over, twenty dollars per month; and such pension shall commence from the date of the filing of the application in the Bureau of Pensions after the passage and approval of this Act: provided, that pensioner who are sixty-two years of age or over, and who are now receiving pensions under existing laws, or whose claims are pending in the Bureau of Pensions may, by application to the Commissioner of Pensions, in such form as he may prescribe, receive the benefits of this Act; and nothing herein contained shall prevent any pensioner or person entitled to a pension from prosecuting his claim and receiving a pension under any other general or special act:

provided, that no person shall receive a pension under any other law at the same time or for the same period that he is receiving a pension under the provisions of this Act; provided further, that no person who is now receiving or shall hereafter receive a greater pension under any other general or special law than he would be entitled, to receive under the provisions herein shall be pensionable under this act.

Sec. 2 That rank in the service shall not be considered in applications filed hereunder.

Sec. 3 That no pension attorney, claim agent, or other person shall be entitled to receive any compensation for services rendered in presenting any claim to the Bureau of Pensions, or securing any pension under this Act.

APPROVED: February 6, 1907.

Pension records can provide a wealth of information about your ancestors. Pension files for Civil War veterans are often full of details about the veteran and sometimes contain information about his wife and other family members.

There are two places to check for military records for your ancestor - the National Archives and Records Administration (NARA) and the state archives of the state in which your ancestor lived. NARA is the repository for copies of all sorts of U.S. military records microfilmed and indexed. They have two types of Civil War records - military service and pension files. The National Archives in Washington, D.C. at http://www.nara.gov/ has an easy on-line option for ordering forms to request a search in older military and pension records. These forms are free and you can order several at time. They are: Form 80 -- Military Service and Pension Records prior to World War I. Or you can write to National Archives and Records Administration, 7th and Pennsylvania Avenue N.W., Washington, DC 20408.

Military service records contain information about dates of service, rank, details of assignment locations and battles, and other information. There is usually not much family information.

Pension records though, often contain much more family information. They often include information about his spouse and family. In order to apply for a pension, the veteran had to provide some proof of his service. In many cases, this was usually a sworn affidavit by the veteran and other soldiers who served with him and sometimes affidavits of neighbors or other family relatives. Sometimes the wife received the pension after the veteran's death or children would apply.

State archives files could be available for the State Militia. Pension applications filed by veterans at the state level are at the state archives and may hold entirely different information than found at NARA. Information may vary from state to state.

Recently a person I know encountered a problem with information furnished him from a Revolutionary War veteran's pension file. Briefly the problem concerned 3 soldiers, all first cousins, all having the same name, and from the same New York county. Their individual services were completely confused. Before the advent of photocopy machines, the National Archives responded to inquiries with extremely concise synopsis of each file's content in letter form. This person had at hand a 1937 letter that provided important details not confirmed by the copies of the pension file that had been received. Several letters to the Archives concerning the problem did not receive satisfactory answers to his questions. A visit to the Laguna Niguel branch of the Archives and a review of the microfilmed copy of the pension file resulted in the discovery of forty documents not remitted when he made his initial request. When he further checked their procedures, he found that they only remit a maximum of 20 documents and this file contained sixty! A quick review of other files he was familiar with resulted in the same ratio of remitted documents.

When requesting a pension or other record, it is strongly suggested that you offer to pay for the entire file! It's well worth the cost! If the National Archives returns the form that no records were found, try the state level next - or better yet, try both.

WAR GRAVE MARKER INFORMATION:
An article in the Elizabethton Star (Elizabethton, TN) related to a story about a man who had traced one of his ancestors back to the Revolutionary War. The man lived in Georgia, but found his ancestor in an unmarked grave in

Kentucky. Since there was no marker for the grave, he petitioned the Veteran's Administration for a plaque. The Veterans Administration checked their policy and it was determined that any Veteran of any war fought by the US did/does qualify for a bronze plaque. The problem was that they had never had a request for a veteran that "old". They did wade through the paperwork and since the veteran's war record was documented, they did comply with the request. A lovely bronze plaque was delivered (by a representative from the Federal Govt) to the door of the descendant. The dedicated descendant decided that it was worth another trip to Kentucky to see that his ancestor should have the memorial plaque. He built a cement stand, mounted the plaque, and loaded it in the back of a pickup truck. Thanks to a dedicated man, his ancestor now has an identify after nearly two hundred years! This may give some of you some ideas.

DATES OF ARMED CONFLICTS:

Conflict	Date	Location
French-Spanish -	1565-1567 -	Florida
English-French -	1613-1629 -	Canada
Anglo-French -	1629 -	St. Lawrence River
Pequot War -	1636-1637 -	New England
Pequot War -	1640-1645 -	New Netherlands
Iroquois -	1642-1653 -	New England, Acadia
Battle of the Severn -	1652	Maryland
Anglo-Dutch -	Jul 1653 -	New Netherlands
Bacon's Rebellion -	1675-1676 -	Virginia
King Philip's -	1675-1676 -	New England
Dayves-Pate Uprising -	03 Sep 1676 -	Calvert Co., MD
War in the North -	1676-1678 -	Maine
Culpepper's Rebellion -	1677-1680 -	Carolinas
Leisler's Rebellion -	1688-1691 -	New England
Revolution in Maryland -	1689 -	Maryland
Glorious Revolution -	1689 -	New England
King William's War -	1689-1697 -	Canada
Queen Anne's War -	1702-1713 -	New England
Tuscarora -	1711-1712 -	Virginia
Jenkin's Ear War -	1739-1742 -	Florida
King George's War -	1744-1748 -	GA & VA
Louisbourg -	1745 -	New England
Fort Necessity -	1754 -	Pennsylvania
Anglo-French -	1755-58 -	Canada
French and Indian -	1754-1763 -	New England, Virginia
Seige of Quebec -	1759 -	Canada
American Revolution -	1775-1783 -	North America
Wyoming Valley -	1782-1787 -	Pennsylvania
Shay's Rebellion -	12/1786-1/1787 -	Massachusetts
Whiskey Insurrection -	1794 -	Pennsylvania
Northwestern Indian War -	1790-1795 -	Ohio
War with France (Naval) -	1798-1800	Atlantic Ocean
War with Tripoli (Naval) -	1801-1805 -	N Coast of Africa
Burr's Insurrection -	1806-1807 -	Southern Mississippi Valley
Chesapeake (Naval) -	1807 -	Virginia
Northwestern Indian -	1811 -	Indiana
Florida Seminole Indian -	1812 -	Florida (GA Vols)
War of 1812 -	1812-1815 -	North America
Peoria Indian -	1813 -	Illinois
Creek Indian -	1813-1814 -	Southern US
Lafitte's Pirates -	1814 -	Local

Barbary Pirates -	1815 -	N Coast of Africa
Indian Wars -	1817-1858	
Seminole Indian -	1817-1818 -	Florida and Georgia
Arickaree Indians -	1823 -	Missouri River, Dakota Territory
Fever River Indian -	1827 -	Illinois
Winnabago Indian -	1827 -	Wisconsin
Sac and Fox Indian -	1831 -	Illinois
Black Hawk Indian -	1832 -	Illinois, Wisconsin
Toledo -	1835-1836 -	Ohio, Michigan
Texan -	1835-1836 -	Texas
Indian Stream -	1835-1836 -	New Hampshire
Florida Seminole Indian -	1835-1842 -	Florida, Georgia, Alabama
Heatherly Disturbance -	1836 -	Missouri
Creek Indian -	1836-1837 -	Florida, Georgia, Alabama
Sabine/Southwest Indian -	1836-1837 -	Louisiana
Cherokee -	1836-1838 -	
Osage Indian -	1837 -	Missouri
Mormon -	1839 -	Missouri
Aroostook Indian -	1839 -	Maine
Dorr's Rebellion -	1842 -	Rhode Island
Morman -	1844 -	Illinois
Mexican War -	1846-1848 -	Mexico
Cayuse Indian -	1846-1848 -	Oregon
TX and NM Indian -	1849-1855 -	Texas, New Mexico
California Indian -	1851-1852 -	California
Utah Indian -	1850-1853 -	
Rouge River Indian -	1851,53,56 -	Oregon
Oregon Indian -	1854 -	Oregon
Nicaraguan -	1854	
Kansas Troubles -	1854-1859 -	Kansas
Yakima Indian -	1855 -	Washington
Klamath & Salmon River Indian -	1855 -	Oregon, Idaho
Florida Indian -	1855-1858 -	Florida
John Brown's Raid -	1859 -	Virginia
American Civil War -	1861-1865 -	America, Atlantic and Pacific Oceans, Gulf of Mexico
Cheyenne Indian -	1861-1864 -	Local
Sioux Indian -	1862-1864 -	Minnesota
Indian Campaign -	1865-1868 -	Oregon, Idaho, California
Fenian Invasion of Canada -	1866 -	New England, Canada
Indian Campaign -	1867-1869 -	Indiana Territory, Kansas, Colorado
Modac Indian -	1872-1873 -	Oregon
Apaches -	1873 -	Arizona
Indian Campaign -	1874-1875 -	Kansas, New Mexico, Texas, Colorado, Indian Terr.
Cheyenne and Sioux -	1876-1877 -	Dakota Territory
Nez Perce -	1877 -	Idaho
Bannock -	1878 -	Washington, Idaho, Wyoming
Cheyenne -	1878-1879 -	Dakota Territory, Montana
White River (Ute Indian) -	1879 -	Utah, Colorado
Spanish American -	1898-1899 -	Cuba
Philippine Insurrection -	1899-1902 -	Phillipines
World War I -	1917-1918	
World War II -	1941-1945	

Korean Action -	1950-1953
Vietnam Action -	1961-1973

APPROXIMATE AGES OF ANCESTORS FIGHTING IN WARS IN USA - 1st column indicates "if born between ages", 2nd column names the war, and 3rd column indicates dates of the war

1600-1644 -	Dutch Indian War -	1655-1664
1626-1656 -	Bacon's Rebellion -	1676
1639-1743 -	Inter-Colonial Wars -	1689-1763
1713-1743 -	Pontiac's Rebellion -	1763-1766
1720-1750 -	Boston Massacre -	1770
1715-1770 -	American Revolution -	1775-1783
1740-1791 -	Indian Wars -	1790-1811
1756-1802 -	War of 1812 -	1812-1815
1762-1812 -	Black Hawk War -	1832
1780-1820 -	Texas War (Alamo) -	1836
1796-1828 -	Mexican War -	1846-1848
1806-1849 -	Civil War -	1861-1865
1849-1880 -	Spanish-American War -	1898
1870-1900 -	World War I -	1914-1918
1900-1930 -	World War II -	1939-1945
1910-1935 -	Korean War -	1950-1953
1915-1957 -	Vietnam War -	1956-1975

DECORATIONS AND MEDALS:
Generally speaking, ribbons and decorations are listed on the DD214 Report of Separation or Discharge from Active Duty. However, there are times when they are not listed such as the award actually being issued AFTER discharge of the individual. Upon the end of WWII, sometimes they were in such a hurry to process these veterans out of the service that not all of the awards they were entitled to were entered on their separation papers. The National Personnel Records Center, 9700 Page Blvd., St. Louis, MO 63132 is the place to write for copies of personnel records. For the WWII Veteran, you need to use Form 180 to request the records. The website to request this form is: http://www.nara.gov. Your local American Legion or VA office should also be able to provide this form to you. To obtain loved ones lost medals who served in the Army, you can write to:
Army Commander,
U. S. Army Reserve Personnel
ATTN: DARP-PAS-EAW
9700 Page Blvd.
St. Louis, MO 63132-5100

DRAFT REGISTRATION:
Twenty-four million men who were born between 13 Sep 1873 and 12 Sep 1900 (between 18 and 45) registered for the draft. Draft registration records are available for a fee of $5 by sending a "World War I Registration Card Request form to:
National Archives Southeast Region
1557 Saint Joseph Avenue
East Point, Georgia 30344
To find an individual's draft card, you must know his name and residence at the time of registration. The records are arranged by state, county, and surname (alphabetically within each draft board). Most counties had only one board; large cities had more. Finding your ancestor's street address in a city directory will help you determine the board number if he lived in a large city. To find board numbers for Chicago, New York, and 35 other major cities, see "United States of America Maps of World War I Draft Registration Boards" (FHL film 1,498,803). A typical card has the man's name and signature, home address, age, birth date, citizenship state, occupation, employer's name and

address, race, dependents or nearest relative, and physical description. For registrants born between 6 Jun 1886 and 28 Aug 1897 (45 percent of total), the cards also give city or town, state, and nation of birth, previous military service; and marital status.

BARBARY PIRATES:
The Barbary States were once greatly feared as the home of the Barbary pirates who attacked the ships of other nations in Mediterranean waters from about 1550 to 1816. The pirates, protected by the rulers of the Barbary States, demanded money and gifts from other countries in return for safe passage in the Mediterranean. The pirates seized English, French, Spanish, and American ships, kept the cargoes, and sold the passengers and crews as slaves. The U.S. paid large sums of money to the Barbary States from 1795 to 1801, despite protests of Thomas Jefferson and others. After Jefferson became President, a war was fought with Tripoli (1801-1805).

MILITARY RECORDS:
For those seeking information about a deceased family member who served in World War I or later, contact the National Personnel Records Center, 9700 Page Boulevard, St. Louis, MO 63132.

If you are the next of kin, you can request a copy of the service member's personnel records. Although a fire at this repository in 1973 destroyed many records, some have been reconstructed and others found that supplement the lost ones.

All of the services have outstanding home pages: The URLs are:

U.S. Air Force — http://www.af.mil/

Here you will find excellent tips on finding military personnel: http://www.au.af.mil/au/afhra/seeking.htm

U.S. Army -- http://www.army.mil/

U.S. Coast Guard -- http://www.dot.gov/dotinfo/uscg/

U.S. Navy (includes Marine Corps pages): http://www.navy.mil/

Vietnam Veterans Home Page: http://www.vietvet.org/index.htm

Don't neglect local sources either. These include:

-- Adjutant General's Office in the individual's state of residence for those who served in World War II, Korea or Vietnam.

-- Newspapers published in the city or county where the individual is presumed to have lived prior to entry into service.

-- Local posts of the American Legion, Veterans of Foreign Wars, American Veterans of World War II for information on local men and women who survived.

The National Archives, 8th and Pennsylvania Avenue, N.W., Washington, D.C. 20408, has some other military-related records that may be of interest to family historians. They include:

-- Application for Headstones (1879-1903). Arranged on cards, alphabetically by soldier's surname.

-- Applications for headstones of Confederate veterans (1879-1964). Most applications are arranged by place of burial and then by cemetery. Soldiers buried in foreign countries are arranged alphabetically by name.

-- Card Records of WWI era Soldiers Who Died Overseas (1917-1922). These are arranged alphabetically by name of soldier or name of cemetery. These records are mainly grave registrations of American buried in European chapels. Records for American soldiers who were buried in Russia are also included.

-- List of Soldiers Missing in Action (1923-1960). This includes the name of the missing soldier, units in which served, date of disappearance, and is arranged chronologically.

-- The Cemetery Service, National Cemetery System, Veterans Administration, 810 Vermont Avenue N.W., Washington, D.C. 20422. Its records, from 1861 to the present, identify almost all soldiers buried in national cemeteries and other cemeteries under federal jurisdiction. These records are arranged alphabetically on cards by name of soldier.

You may find additional family information in the records of your ancestor's siblings, uncles or other family members. It pays to be thorough in your research for military records -- they are valuable documents of your family's history.

If you're doing Military Research, check out the book, U.S. Military Records, by James C. Neagles, published by Ancestry. Gathered in this volume is source information for the National Archives and its adjuncts; historical institutions and archives of the armed forces; the Department of Veterans Affairs (Veterans Administration); state archives; libraries and historical organizations; and such patriotic organizations as the Daughters of the American Revolution. Extensive bibliographic listings of published sources for the United States in general and published sources for each state are also included.

WWII SERIAL NUMBERS:
There is a book "HOW TO LOCATE ANYONE WHO IS OR HAS BEEN IN THE MILITARY" by Lt. Col. Richard S. Johnson. P2 states:

"Beginning in 1940 each entrance and examining station in the US was allocated certain sets of service numbers for enlisted Army personnel. At times not all numbers were used because of an overestimate of needs in that area.

The US was divided into six Service areas which were later changed to Army areas. A set of numbers was allocated to each entrance station identified with that Army area. For example First Army 11,000,000 through 12,999,999 and 31,000,000 through 32,999,999 and 51,000,000 through 51,999,999; Second Army 13,000,000 through 15,999,999 and 52,000,000 through 52,999,999 also 33 and 35 million numbers; Third Army 14 million through 34 million and 53 million; Fourth Army 13 million through 38 million and 54 million; Fifth Army 16 million through 17 million and 36 million through 37 million and 55 million; Sixth Army 19 million through 39 million and 56 million.

Numbers in the 10 million and 50 million were assigned to members who entered the service outside the Continental US. Numbers in the 20,000,000 through 20,999,999 were assigned to members of the National Guard on active duty (1940-1946). Numbers 21 million through 29 million were assigned to members of the National Guard ((1946-1969).

Numbers in the 30 million series were assigned to those men who were inducted (drafted) during WWII (1940-1946). 42 through 46 million were assigned to members inducted between 1943-1946. Numbers in the 50 million series were assigned to those who were inducted in the Korean and Vietnam wars. (1948-1966).

LOCATING AIR FORCE RETIREES OR ACTIVE DUTY MEMBERS:
The Air Force may not release home or overseas duty addresses, but will forward a personal letter. Seal your letter in a stamped envelope, enter your return address (including retired grade) and send your letter and addressee's name, grade and Social Security number or service number in another envelope to AFPC/MSIMDL, 550 C Street West Suite 50, Randolph AFB, TX 78150-4752. (If addressee's SSN/SN is not available, the locator needs the most recent Air Force base assignments/dates, etc., to help research an address.) For a reply about the status of your letter, provide a stamped self-addressed envelope. Locator service free to retirees and their immediate families is limited to one address per request. The Air Force does not provide reunion locator service.

For those wanting to check out their ancestors in ILLINOIS for the Civil War, you can search through Dogpile (or any other search engine you use) and insert "civil war il" and you should come up with a lot of sources. Here are some URLs to search in Illinois and in all other states too.

http://www.outfitters.com/illinois/history/civil/

http://www.sos.state.il.us/depts/archives/datcivil.html

http://www.rootsweb.com/~ilcivilw/county/coles.htm

http://www.sos.state.il.us/depts/archives/datcivil.html#reghistory

http://www.civilwardata.com/pers_dir.html

http://www.sos.state.il.us/cgi-bin/civilwar

http://www.usgennet.org/~alhnilus/

THIS AND THAT GENEALOGY TIPS ON WESTWARD TRAVEL

WESTWARD TRAVEL:
Excerpt from notes of Morris Birkbeck concerning his journey to America in 1817, as quoted in PENN PICTURES OF EARLY WESTERN PENNSYLVANIA, edited by John Harpster, Univ. of Pittsburgh Press 1938 - (telling of travelers he met as he crossed Pennsylvania).

"The family are seen before, behind or within the vehicle according to the road of weather, or perhaps the spirits of the party. The New Englanders, they say, may be known by the cheerful air of the women advancing in front of the wagon; the Jersey people by their being fixed steadily within it; whilst the Pennsylvanians creep lingering behind, as though regretting the homes they have left...often the back of the poor pilgrims bears all his effects, and his wife follows, barefooted, bending under the hopes of the family".

"Go west young man" said John Babstone Lane Soule in the "Terre Haute Express" (an Indiana newspaper). And so they did, along the trails, byships, and later, by rail. Information about life on the long journey west and early settlement can provide a fascinating background for your family history and wonderful clues for further tracing your ancestors.

Where do you go for this information if you aren't lucky enough to have diaries, letters, or other biographical information outlining your ancestors' travels? Sources are becoming more and more abundant. Printed sources can provide valuable details and many of these publications are appearing online. Here is an excerpt from "Nebraska: the Land and the People: Volume 1," available online to Ancestry.com subscribers at:
http://www.ancestry.com/ancestry/search/3266.htm

"The hardships endured by the pioneer settlers of the Territory were at no time more severe than in the winter of 1856-57, during which there was an almost constant succession of heavy snow storms, accompanied by bitter cold. This weather set in December 1 and lasted until spring. Many wild and domestic animals perished and many settlers also lost their lives. In Richardson County, in the first December storm, twenty head of cattle were walled in a valley by the snow and most of them perished. Their owner, in February, found a few survivors that had maintained existence by feeding on the branches of trees. In Dodge County the sun was not seen for two months, and ravines thirty feet deep were filled with snow. A man was lost in the storm and his body not recovered until April, when the snow had melted. In Burt County snow fell for six days and nights without stopping, and the settlers would have starved had it not been for the game that they caught in the snowdrifts. In Cuming County the creeks and rivers were buried by the snow. Settlers traveled on foot to the Missouri River to obtain supplies and hauled them home on hand sleds. The deer, elk and antelope sought shelter in the timber along the streams, and one settler killed over seventy with an axe. In such weather, man had a certain advantage over hoofed animals, as the crust of snow would bear a man, but the animals, with their greater weight and small feet, broke through and were helpless. In Otoe County the deer ran through the streets of Nebraska City, pursued by hungry wolves. On the Oregon Trail, between Fort Kearny and Fort Laramie, the snow lay two feet deep from October to May, and the drifts filled the valleys. In no winter since has the snow been so deep, so badly drifted, or remained so long on the ground."

A great place to locate other sources like this is NUCMC (National Union Catalog of Manuscript Collections) available online at the Library of Congress' Web site at: http://lcweb.loc.gov/coll/nucmc/nucmc.html

A search with "oregon trail" as the subject turned up 87 hits with several diaries, letters, and other first hand accounts of the trip west on the Oregon Trail. "Colorado" and "pioneers" turned up 24 hits, also diaries, memoirs, and more.

The web is also a great source of background information. Trail sites with maps, diaries, pictures, and biographies are becoming very popular. Here are a few to start. If you don't find what you are looking for here, try using your favorite search engine. You'll be amazed at the wealth of information that it will turn up!

GO WEST:

Sources are becoming more and more available outlining the travels of our ancestors. Many publications are now appearing online. A search for Oregon Trail turned up almost 100 hits and had several diaries, letters and first-hand accounts of the trip West on the Oregon Trail. Some sites you may not want to overlook are:

http://www.over-land.com/index.html - The Overland Trail

http://members.aol.com/gedsearch/migrate.htm - American Migrations Web Site

http://www.ancestry.com/ancestry/testurllinks/search.asp - Juliana's Links. In the category Search, select "Miscellaneous" and then "Westward Movement".

http://calcite.rocky.edu/octa/octahome.htm - The Oregon-California Trails Association.

http://raven.cc.ukans.edu/heritage/research/sft/ - The Interactive Santa Fe Trail Homepages

http://www.southwind.net/ict/wht/wht-07s.html - The Chisholm Trail

http://www.ancestry.com/ancestry/Freeimages.asp?ImageID=299 - Westward Migration in the U. S. 1775-1860

The Northern Great Plains, 1880-1920 - http://memory.loc.gov/ammem/award97/ndfahtml/ngphome.html

Pioneering in the Upper Midwest, 1820-1910 - American Memory Project, LOC: http://memory.loc.gov/ammem/umhtml/umhome.html

End of the Oregon Trail Interpretive Center: http://www.teleport.com:80/~eotic/index.html

Oregon Trail: http://www.isu.edu/~trinmich/Allabout.html

Emigrant Summit Trail (to California): http://www.r5.pswfs.gov/heritage/010.htm

Opening of the California Trail: http://www.tahoenet.com/tdhs/tpstephn.html

MormonTrail.net: http://www.mormontrail.net/

History of the Mormon Trail: http://lserver.aea14.k12.ia.us/SWP/cdavis/MTOP.HOMEP

Iowa Mormon Trails: http://www.lisco.com/iowamormontr/

Santa Fe Trail, The Interactive Santa Fe Trail (SFT) Homepage: http://raven.cc.ukans.edu/heritage/research/sft/

Chisholm Trail: http://www.southwind.net/ict/wht/wht-07s.html

RAILROAD:

"The reality of a transcontinental railroad resulted in several changes in Mormon emigration policy. In the late '60's, missionaries often recommended to their converts that they remain in their homes until the completion of the railroad, thus avoiding much of the hardship, sickness and death that had marked the trail of the covered wagon. By so doing they would also be able to accumulate more money to bring with them to the new community, or to assure the passage of the entire family. And in Utah, men who would otherwise be called to leave their homes to guide the incoming Saints to Zion, could stay at home to carry on their own work. With this in mind, the missionaries were frequently given the responsibility of placing families in mid-west or eastern communities where they could find homes and employment."

The above excerpt is from "Our Pioneer Heritage, Volume 8," available online to Ancestry.com subscribers at: http://www.ancestry.com/ancestry/search/3239.htm

RRHistorical: http://rrhistorical.com

Railroad Maps from the Library of Congress: http://memory.loc.gov/ammem/gmdhtml/rrhtml/rrhome.html

Golden Spike National Historic Site: http://www.media.utah.edu/medsol/UCME/g/GOLDENSPIKE.html

Railroads in Kansas: http://history.cc.ukans.edu/heritage/research/rr/railroads.html

MAPS:
Westward Migration in U.S. 1775-1860: http://www.ancestry.com/ancestry/FreeImages.asp?ImageID=299

Exploration and Settlement Before 1675: http://www.ancestry.com/ancestry/FreeImages.asp?ImageID=641

Exploration and Settlement 1675-1800: http://www.ancestry.com/ancestry/FreeImages.asp?ImageID=643

Exploration and Settlement 1800-1820: http://www.ancestry.com/ancestry/FreeImages.asp?ImageID=644

Exploration and Settlement 1820-1835: http://www.ancestry.com/ancestry/FreeImages.asp?ImageID=645

Exploration and Settlement 1835-1850: http://www.ancestry.com/ancestry/FreeImages.asp?ImageID=647

Exploration and Settlement 1850-1890: http://www.ancestry.com/ancestry/FreeImages.asp?ImageID=648

SOURCES IN PRINT:
"U.S. Migration Patterns" by Wendy L. Elliott (Bountiful, UT: American Genealogical Lending Library, 1987)

"The Transportation Frontier: Trans-Mississippi West, 1865-1890" by Oscar Osburn Winther (Holt, Rinehart, and Winston, 1964

"Blazing a Wagon Trail to Oregon : A Weekly Chronicle of the Great Migration of 1843" by Lloyd W. Coffman (Echo Books, 1993

Thanks for the above to Juliana Smith, Editor, Ancestry Daily News - Joel White, Associate Editor and the Daily News. To subscribe to this newsletter, visit: http://www.ancestry.com/whatsnew.htm - and type your Email address in the box provided, or send your Email address to: support@ancestry-inc.com

Ancestry - http://www.ancestry.com - Search Ancestry's World Tree - the largest, free database of family files available on the Internet! Add your family tree today: http://www.ancestry.com/worldtree/tree.htm